Research and Composition

Research and Composition

LUMEN LEARNING AND JOSHUA DICKINSON

Published by SUNY OER Services

Milne Library

State University of New York at Geneseo

Geneseo, NY 14454

Distributed by State University of New York Press

Cover Image "Fall Kaleidoscope III" by Anne Worner, CC By SA, available from https://flic.kr/p/qfy1We

ISBN: 978-1-64176-063-8

Contents

What is Argument?

Reflective Learning

Thesis Statements

Causal Arguments

Definition

Rhetorical Analysis

The Research Project

Research Proposal

What Is Research?

Evaluating Sources

Integrating Sources

Citing Sources

Annotated Bibliographies

Structure & Outlining

Revising & Editing

Final Drafts

About This Book

Research and Composition is heavily adapted from the Lumen Learning English Composition 2 book on the SUNY OER list of texts. The original version of this book was released under a CC-BY license and is copyright by Lumen Learning.

It was then developed by Joshua Dickinson, Associate Professor of English at Jefferson Community College in Watertown, NY. The changes to this book listed are released under a CC-BY-SA license and are copyright by Joshua Dickinson of Jefferson Community College in Watertown, NY.

Note that titles of essays or articles in MLA normally appear in quotes. However, the software used to create the books does not allow for the use of quotes within title.

List of Changes

- Added Instructor Resources in private view: FAQs for Online Composition Courses, Sample Learning Contract, Sample ENG 101 Grading Rubric, and Are Online English Courses Right for You?
- Added section entitled Playing the Game: Critical Reading and Writing.
- Added the Determining Audience and Purpose section, moving two Lumen resources into it: Audience, and Discussion: Establishing Intended Audience (the latter in private view).
- Added Prewriting section with my lectures. Also moved Prewriting Strategies lecture material and (in private view) Assessment: 3 Research Topic Ideas.
- In Thesis Statements, added lecture Thesis Hints.
- Created What is Argument? section.
- In Visual Arguments, added Hanna Rosin, "Why Kids Sext" link.
- Added Causal Arguments section lectures Avoid Relativism (Because I Think So); Cause/Effect Tie in With Most Readings; Argue Without Filtering Through the Self; What is Academic Writing by L. Lennie Irvin; Sample Causal Argument; Ta-Nehisi Coates, "The First American President"; and Robert Kubey, Mihaly Csikszentmihalyi, "Television Addiction is no Mere Metaphor"; and Plato, *The Symposium*.
- Added Definition chapter.
- In Rhetorical Analysis, added Troubleshoot Your Reading; Sample Rhetorical Analysis Essay; Jonathan Swift, "A Modest Proposal"; Mark Twain, "Two Ways of Seeing a River"; and James Gleick, What Defines a Meme?
- Added The Research Project section, moving in several resources from the original text and then adding my lectures: Essay 4: Persuasion; Audiences Know the Topic Well. . . Alter Their Actions; Avoid Oversimplifying in Essays; Diotima's Ladder Video: Check Out the Forms; and Charles Pierce, "Greetings From Idiot America."
- In Research Proposal, added Persuasive Writing Differs Markedly From Previous Assignments.
- In Evaluating Sources, added Anatomy of a Journal Article and Library Research as Problem-Solving.
- In Integrating Sources, added Introduction of Borrowed Material; A Typical Body Paragraph Pattern; Transition Placemats; The Paragraph Body: Supporting Your Ideas; Signal Phrases; Integration Tips in Preparation for Peer Editing or Editing; and Proper Source Use in Paragraphs.
- In Citing Sources, added Academic Integrity Tutorial, MLA Checklist, Paragraph Settings Use No Extra Vertical Spaces, Avoid Word Templates for Citations, and Works Cited Entries: What to Include.
- In Annotated Bibliographies, added Annotated Bibliographies lecture, as well as Annotated Bibliography Assignment.
- In Structure & Outlining, added Synthesizing and Supporting Refutals, Logical Fallacies, Logical Fallacies Handlist, Academic Writing Review, and How Does "The Witch Sketch" Work Logically?
- In Revising & Editing, added Revision Strategies, Peer Editing, "Breaking Up is Hard to Do," and Page One in an Essay Abounds in Pitfalls for Errors.
- In Final Drafts, added Sample Definition Essay (MLA Style).

You are free to use, modify or adapt any of this material providing the terms of the Creative Commons licenses are adhered to.

PLAYING THE GAME: CRITICAL READING AND WRITING

Connecting Reading & Writing The Voice You Hear Response

Too often, reading is viewed as a passive act where the information is poured into static readers' minds. To succeed at the college level, a reworking of the way one reads may be necessary. Read the following passage from reading researcher Katherine McCormick and jot down your interpretation of its meaning:

Tony slowly got up from the mat, planning his escape. He hesitated a moment and thought. Things were not going well. What bothered him the most was being held, especially since the charge against him had been weak. He considered his present situation. The lock that held him was strong but he thought he could break it . . . . He was being ridden unmercifully . . . . He felt that he was ready to make his move.

From the two possible interpretations here, it seems clear that 1) readers use their previous experiences to make meaning out of a text, and 2) context influences meaning. After all, if we knew we were reading a short story on wrestling, our understanding of the passage would differ. Reading needs to be recognized as an active process. **Read the following poem by Thomas Lux and answer all of the questions below in complete sentences. The questions appear after the poem.**

The Voice You Hear When You Read Silently

is not silent, it is a speaking-out-loud voice in your head;

it is *spoken*, a voice is *saying* it as you read.

It's the writer's words, of course, in a literary sense his or her "voice"

but the sound of that voice is the sound of *your* voice.

Not the sound your friends know or the sound of a tape played back

but your voice

caught in the dark cathedral of your skull, your voice heard by an internal

ear informed by internal abstracts

and what you know by feeling, having felt.

It is your voice saying, for example, the word "barn" that the writer wrote

but the "barn" you say is a barn you know or knew.

The voice in your head, speaking as you read, never says anything

neutrally—some people hated the barn they knew,

some people love the barn they know

so you hear the word loaded and a sensory constellation is lit:

horse-gnawed stalls, hayloft, black heat tape wrapping a water pipe, a slippery spilled *chirr* of oats from a split sack,

the bony, filthy haunches of cows . . .

And "barn" is only a noun—no verb or subject has entered into the sentence yet!

The voice you hear when you read to yourself is the clearest voice: you speak its speaking to you.

1. When you hear the word *barn*, what barn or barns from your own life do you first see? What feelings and associations do you have with this word? How do you think the barn in your head is different from the barns in your classmates' heads?
2. When you hear the word *cathedral*, what images and associations from your own life come into your head? Once again, how might your classmates' internal images and associations with the word *cathedral* differ from yours?
3. Now reread the poem and consider the lines "Not the sound your friends know or the sound of a tape played back / but your voice / caught in the dark cathedral of your skull." What do you think Lux means by the metaphor "dark cathedral of your skull"? What seems important about his choice of the word *cathedral* (rather than, say, *house* or *cave* or *gymnasium* or *mansion*)? How does *skull* work (rather than *mind* or *brain* or *head*)? Freewriting for several minutes, create your interpretation of "dark cathedral of the skull."
4. Finally, reflect for a moment about your thinking processes in trying to interpret "cathedral of the skull." Did you go back and reread the poem, looking for how this line fits other lines of the poem? Did you explore further your own ideas about cathedrals and skull? See if you can catch yourself in the act of interacting with the text—or actively constructing meaning.

Relating Text with Citations

If you do *not* name the author in your text, you include the name in parentheses.

If you do name the author in you text, you *do* not include the name in parentheses.

One researcher concludes that "women impose a distinctive construction on moral problems, seeing moral dilemmas in terms of conflicting responsibilities" (Gilligan 105).

One researcher, Carol Gilligan, concludes that "women impose a distinctive construction on moral problems, seeing moral dilemmas in terms of conflicting responsibilities" (105).

CC licensed content, Original

Use Present Tense When Discussing Texts

Employ present tense when discussing the essays. When analyzing writing moves, Friedman *makes* one. . . *made* changes the tone and focus a bit. We use present tense even when discussing history.

This is not to say that one cannot use past tense. The consistent tense we use in academic writing, however, is present tense.

CC licensed content, Original

Not Taking Sides is Like That Beetlejuice Waiting Room Scene. . .

It is important that we recognize the benefits and limitations of methodology. Likely, you know your major discipline's approaches well. There are ways of being recognized or not. For instance, in *Jeopardy* contests, one has to phrase the answer in the form of a question. In discussion postings, many instructors require the post subject to be in sentence form. In *Fast Times at Ridgemont High*, Jeff Spicoli, the surfer, doesn't recognize his little brother: "Curtis, you know I don't hear you unless you knock. . ." (Heckerling). In science, hypotheses have to be provable. In academic writing, thesis claims must be both provable and arguable.

I'm reminded of the notion of Purgatory, an invention of Dante in his *La Divina Commedia* (*Divine Comedy*). This gets played up famously in *Beetlejuice* and its waiting room scene:

- https://youtu.be/ei-2xTsyL8w

What's interesting is that this echoes Dante, who puts people who failed to distinguish themselves into Hell. For Dante's Italians, not choosing was worse than choosing an opposite side to one's preferred side. Strangely enough, we are often more knowledgeable of our opponents—more tolerant of them, even—than of those who never choose. He even puts the neutral angels into Hell. In that era (1300 Florence), he even put living people into Hell, claiming that these people were so bad that demons inhabited their bodies and they were already in hell.

So these ideas can receive dogmatic answers. They get recognized or not, but over time they accrete meaning, slow down, and become concrete. (No *Dogma* references necessary. . .)

What I find interesting is that we're often struggling with the miniscule rules of MLA style in the same way.

> As with science, though, we can essentialize this a bit: We are always already entering ongoing conversations. We do have to be for or against something. Likely ways of being against something are going to lead to tone issues and assumptions about audience agreement.

As the *Beetlejuice* move states, "Take a number!" and "It's showtime!" (Burton).

Transitions

The word transition literally means movement from one piece of information to another. In writing, transition means moving from one sentence to another or one paragraph to another smoothly without abrupt shifts in logic or subject. To accomplish this smooth movement of thoughts, a writer will sometimes use certain words or phrases that act as bridges to carry readers into a new sentence or paragraph. Without these transitional elements, an essay can read like a list, or at best a group of loosely connected statements. Transitional elements prepare readers for each new idea and relate each new statement to the preceding ones.

Transitions can be

- Single words, phrases, clauses, or even whole sentences
- Repetitions of key words, ideas, or phrases
- Using pronouns such as this, these, and them
- Combining short sentences into compound and complex ones

Examples of Transitions

Use the list below as a guide only. Be creative and use words, phrases, clauses and even whole sentences to bridge the gaps between ideas. Don't use the same transitional device over and over. Vary the devices to avoid monotony and redundancy.

Transitions that Signal Chronological Order

First, second, third . . . next, then, after, before, during, meanwhile, at first, when, as soon as

Transitions that Signal Spatial Order

Nearby, near to, beside, over, far from, next to, under, around, through, in front of, behind, surrounding, alongside, away from, on top of, around, toward, at

Transitions that Signal Adding a Point Order (Random Order)

In addition, moreover, furthermore, too, finally, lastly

Transitions that Signal Contrast

However, nevertheless, on the other hand, on the contrary, even though, despite, in spite of

Transitions that Signal General Example

Sometimes, on certain occasions, often, many times, frequently, in some cases, in a few instances (Always follow general examples with specific ones.)

Transitions that Signal Specific Example

To illustrate, for example, for instance, as an illustration, in particular, especially in fact

Transitions that Signal Order of Importance

More important, most important, of least importance, of less importance, most of all, best of all, of greatest significance, least of all, even better, foremost, especially

Transitions that Signal Clarification of Point

That is, in other words, in effect, put simply, stated briefly

Transitions that Signal Summing up or Restating Central Point

In sum, to sum up, in summary, to conclude, as you can see, in short, in conclusion

Transitions that Signal Stages in a Process

First, second, third . . ., initially, at the outset, to begin with, first of all, up to now, so far, thus far, next after, finally, last of all

Transitions that Signal Cause/Effect Relationship

As a result, consequently, because, in consequence

Transitions that Signal Attitude

Fortunately, unfortunately, naturally, in a sense, luckily

Transitions that Signal Reference

The former, the latter, the following

CC licensed content, Original

Analyze This

You now learned about some of the many different forms an argument can take. It doesn't have to be presented in a traditional essay with a thesis and topic sentences for your paragraphs. Arguments can come in many forms, even stories.

In the following video (http://owl.excelsior.edu/argument-and-critical-thinking/argumentative-purposes/argumentative-purposes-analyze-this/) that you'd click on once linked to the OWL Excelsior "Analyze This" page, watch as a student analyzes a narrative argument, pointing to the key elements of narrative and demonstrating how a story can make for a very persuasive argument.

To read the full essay reviewed in the video, click **here (http://www.rd.com/advice/excuses-excuses-an-excerpt-from-teacher-man/)**.

With Analysis, Focus Upon Functions or Effects

At the college level, putting in the right-sounding quotes in the right-looking spots of a body paragraph is insufficient. Writers are expected to use the quotes as excuses to argue their points. Close reading is a crucial skill which helps the writer make sense of how something makes sense. Literature courses largely aim to enhance or bring about readers' abilities to handle complex, indirect texts that demand multiple responses.

Close reading is an analytical activity where the writer picks parts of larger whole and discusses how they function. This can be done while annotating or deciding what to say about an annotated chunk of text. Because your audience often knows the text and has ideas about how it works, it is up to you to do more than simply point out the existence of an important line, phrase, or word. Within the line, the critic must move from pointing out an idea to arguing how it functions. What effect is created by that phrase? How does this word affect readers? These questions get proved after careful setup and cited quotation work.

Once you have dissected a speech, description, or dialogue, remember that you have committed a fairly aggressive, destructive act. You yanked a part from the whole. Remember to use the late portions of paragraphs to put the pieces back together. ("Pick up your toys when you are done with them!")

What You Might Look For

Focus on an author's use of complexity by discussing the effects of any of the following:

word choice (diction) word order (syntax)

connotation denotation

irony (dramatic, situational, verbal) symbolism

mood tone

paradox (seeming contradiction) how words fit/bring about character

rhetorical appeals (logos, ethos, pathos) logical patterns (valid or not)

Rhetorical modes (description, narration, definition, process, illustration, comparison/contrast, classification/division, cause/effect, argument)Basically, looking for moves of any sort is a good starting point with analysis

- Analyze This. **Authored by**: OWL Excelsior Writing Lab; Josh Dickinson for all material after 2nd link. **Provided by**: Excelsior College; SUNY Jefferson. **Located at**: http://owl.excelsior.edu/argument-and-critical-thinking/argumentative-purposes/ argumentative-purposes-analyze-this/ (http://owl.excelsior.edu/argument-and-critical-thinking/argumentative-purposes/ argumentative-purposes-analyze-this/). **Project**: ENG 101. **License**: *CC BY-SA: Attribution-ShareAlike (https://creativecommons.org/licenses/by-sa/4.0/)*

Binary Patterns: A Western Obsession

This or that? Me or you? I or thou? Subject or object?

Along with these basic either/or questions, Western thought is built on other key binaries.

A binary is an either/or choice like the zeroes and ones making up DVDs or other digital codes. While some things lend themselves to "this or that" choices, we know that the world is often much more complicated. The answer "Pepsi or Coke?" might define a person privately, but whether you like one or the other may not carry much public meaning. Ironically, it did carry meaning in the 80s during the Cola Wars.

These either/or choices often have strange histories. For instance, the tragedy/comedy binary informs genres on television and in literature. It is based on a thinker, Aristotle, who was not even approving of literature. Dig into the history of tragedy and comedy and you will find some strangeness. For instance, tragedy was supposed by Aristotle to feature someone making a choice which leads inevitably to their downfall, which we witness and feel *catharsis*, a sense of purging out of both ends. . .! Weird enough for you? It makes a certain amount of sense, just as listening to a blues song makes us feel happy, but it's what we'd call *contingent*: based on a quirky, particular set of happenings that did not have to occur. So binaries are contingent. (Call this the non-tragic theory of approaching binaries.) And comedy was supposed to involve a mating and joining offstage in early Greek comedies—which were held at the festival of the god Dionysus, at which, originally, his devotees called Maenads were said to mate with willing victims on mountainsides, after which they would rend apart the sacrificial victim. And this is what informs our genres—and has done so for 2,500 years. So I'd add necessary vs. contingent as a binary that can be useful.

For more on the strangeness of binaries, you might do a search for *humor theory* or look at the history of academia (gowns, gavels, graduations. . .). Or if you're talking good or evil, one might look at how evil always comes back (Sauron, Voldemort). Weirdly enough, this even contributes to a type of cannibalism whereby an enemy's body is eaten so that his soul can be erased—for a time—from the eternal battlefield. As the cliche goes, "The truth is stranger than fiction." In fields like literary analysis, there is no "capital-T Truth." That idea of there being one would go back to Plato and his theory of Forms.

So these issues have histories of which we should become aware. As a critical reader, it is important for you to take note of binaries and gauge their effects. Though they may exclude other choices, it is the case that humans notice contrasts and oppositions.

Binaries are crutches, tools. They can work but can put blinders on what we notice. Early in stages of the writing or critical thinking processes, they can be useful.

> Which side of a binary does the author notice or value more?
>
> Which views are portrayed as negative?
>
> What is undervalued or missing from a given text?

In a writing course, then, you might create a persuasive essay that argues one side against another. We contribute to these ongoing debates most thoughtfully if we realize that they arguments will continue, however well we write about them! Just don't fall into the trap of thinking that the world is either/or, comforting as that notion may be.

- Binary Patterns: A Western Obsession. **Authored by**: Joshua Dickinson. **Provided by**: Jefferson Community College. **Located at**: http://www.sunyjefferson.edu (http://www.sunyjefferson.edu). **Project**: ENG 101. **License**: *CC BY-SA: Attribution-ShareAlike (https://creativecommons.org/licenses/by-sa/4.0/)*

Michael Shermer, The Pattern Behind Self-Deception

> How do we know what we know?
>
> What heuristics (method of checking) can we use on ourselves?
>
> Why is believing in something strongly *not* a good measure of believability in a writer?

The following TED Talk is by Michael Shermer, a skeptic and author who presents ideas about critical thinking in ways that continue to fascinate me. Watch for the ways he includes examples and definitions, moving between particular and general.

What does it mean to be a skeptic? How does Shermer's definition of critical thinking differ from what you might have thought before watching the video?

* https://www.ted.com/talks/michael_shermer_the_pattern_behind_self_deception

Michael Shermer, Why People Believe Weird Things

This video offers a humorous look and insightful at our patterns of thinking. Apply it to yourself, as well as to media patterns and the news flow coming out of political organizations.

You may laugh at the video's examples, but we actually used to listen to records (The Beatles, Black Sabbath, Judas Priest, Frank Zappa, for instance) for these hidden messages or peer into the images of ice cubes in drink ads (or the camel in the cigarette ad) for symbols. And you thought that this all started with Dan Brown's books!

- https://www.ted.com/talks/michael_shermer_on_believing_strange_things

VISUAL ARGUMENTS

Photos and Illustrations

Photos are used in professional documents as tools for communicating a message that a writer feels can be strengthened through the use of proper imagery. Photographs can do many things to enhance a message, some examples can be seen here:

Illustration Checklist

Planning

- What kinds of illustrations are your audience familiar with?
- Do you have information that could be more easily or quickly communicated to your audience visually or in a combination of words and graphics?
- Do you have definitions that could be displayed visually in whole or in part?
- Do you have any processes or procedures that could be depicted in a flowchart?
- Do you have information on trends or relationships that could be displayed in tables and graphics?
- Do you have masses of statistics that could be summarized in tables?
- Do you need to depict objects? If so, what do you need to display about the objects? Do you need to focus attention on specific aspects of the objects? Do you require the realism of photographs?
- What are the design conventions of your illustrations?
- Are there suitable illustrations you could borrow or adapt? Or will you need to create them yourself?

Revising

- Are you illustrations suited to your purpose and audience?
- Do your illustrations communicate information ethically?
- Are your illustrations effectively located and easy to find?
- Are your illustrations numbered and labeled?
- Do your verbal and visual elements reinforce each other?
- Are your illustrations genuinely informative instead of simply decorative?
- When necessary, have you helped your readers to interpret your illustrations with commentary or annotations?
- Have you acknowledged the sources for borrowed or adapted tables and figures?

How To Perform an Action

Pictures are an effective tool for giving visual representation of how to do something. They can can stand alone or work in conjunction with the given text, and they can enhance a message if used properly.

If you are using pictures in conjunction with text: As in a set of instructions, the imagery increases understanding of the task, in addition to decreasing confusion that may arise from text that stands alone. When using a picture to help portray how to perform a task, it is your responsibility to make sure the picture matches up with the text. You must explain the picture using text, and vice versa, explain the text using a picture. Also, the viewer will accomplish the task more often when the picture looks how it would if they were watching the task, not necessarily if they were experiencing it.

An example would be: if your task was doing a cartwheel, you wouldn't want the pictures at an angle where the person is looking through the eyes of the one doing the cartwheel. You would want the pictures to be from someone watching the event, so that the viewer isn't confused by what they can't see (such as where their feet are when they're looking at their hands). It's the simple things that make or break a document when using pictures. Think and re-think the pictures you are using and how someone seeing them for the first time will react to them.

How a Finished Product Should Look

When textual information does not capture the essence of what you're trying to describe, try putting an actual photo of what you're trying to describe in the document. This type of picture enables you to come as close to reality as possible. Make sure your pictures are in color and of high quality. Black and white photos tend to blur easily on paper and lack the detail needed to fully understand a photo. Images cut down on excessive use of describing words. "A picture is worth a thousand words" relates to this situation.

Be sure to use the text wrap abilities of most word processors. A well placed picture with clean text wrapping can make an otherwise overwhelming block of text seem reasonably approachable. Looking at 25 pages of block, justified alignment, plain black text is one of the most boring ways to see a report. A picture can liven up a report, make it more memorable, and help clarify the report all in one motion.

Map Out an Object, Place, or Process

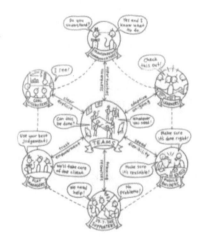

An example of these types of pictures can be found in an automotive manual or a science textbook. This can be anything from a picture of a machine to an example of how photosynthesis works. Arrows and labels can be used in order to show where everything is and how the process takes place. The picture should include a big enough background so that the reader can locate the area in relation to things around it. Photographs can also play a major role in connecting with the audience. They are useful in multi-cultural situations when a shared written language may not exist. Pictures can speak louder than words, and usually portray the message quicker. It is very important to keep the first initial reaction in mind when choosing the image you will place within your document. Be sure to avoid photos that may have several meanings, or the true meaning may be unclear. In order to avoid this type of situation, put yourself in the audience that you are writing for and try to be unbiased when you view the image. Better yet, test the image on someone who does not know much about your photo's topic and ask them what message the photo sends to them. Clarity is essential in conveying your message.

Do not rely too heavily on pictures though. Pictures and text should be used simultaneously in order to give the audience the most accurate direction. Pictures can make a great break in words, but are not always as useful to get a point across as words are.

Software Can Tremendously Increase Photograph Effectiveness

There are a great deal of photo editing programs for computers that can be utilized to bring out the right angle, zoom, view, and color of a photo. Some of the most popular photo editing software includes Photoshop, Corel, and Image Smart. Many computers now come with basic image editing software, which allows one to adjust color, brightness, crop, and other basic edits.

Cropping is an essential key feature that allows you to enlarge the area of the photo you want the reader to see, while omitting the background and obsolete area of the background. Cropping is equivalent to looking at an image under a microscope where you can focus on the areas you want the readers to see the clearest. However, this can decrease image quality and make the image hard to see. When possible, it is best to use images that need little to no editing.

When using imagery make sure it is of high image resolution (300 dpi for print, 72 dpi for screen) and the proper format to be inserting into your document. Typically, sticking with images from original sources, such as a camera or other .jpg or .tif file are best.

If you find your photograph is not using the right coloring, computer programs such as Photoshop, Corel, etc. will allow you to adjust the color balance and light in many different variations. This is an important feature, especially when the photograph was not professionally taken or lacks the appropriate lighting for the setting. Be careful not to over or under expose the photography.

Labeling is also another feature you can do in a computer program. You can insert boxes with text and arrows into a photograph in order to label key details. Labeling your photographs keeps the information you are trying to convey to the reader clear.

These computer programs may take some time to become familiar with how they work. It might be necessary to take a course or tutorial on how to use them to their full advantages, but it's worth it for all the features these programs have. There are some free tutorials available on the internet or through the actual program.

Using Graphics From the Artists, Internet, and Other Misc. Sources

Graphics can be found for just about any topic relatively easily if you know how to search for them and cite the artist properly. Like any written material, pictures are also property of the original artist in many cases. It is important to use good ethics and cite artists when necessary. The internet and your computer's clip art file have countless pictures and graphics as well. Knowing how to use these techniques and tools will make finding and using images easier.

Citing Images

In order to use or manipulate an image or graphic not your own, from either the Internet or any other source, you must obtain permission from whoever created or has rights to that image. Usually some type of arrangement between you and this person or organization will have to be negotiated. This could be anything from paying for the rights to use the image, or citing the image in the way that is expressed by the owner. Sometimes graphics will be considered public domain. Studying the copyright information of an image is one way to determine whether or not it is public domain. Images belonging to a government agency or even to your employer would typically be considered public domain. Even so, these images should still be cited. A quick guide to citing images from books and internet can be found at, [[1] (http://www.libraries.uc.edu/libraries/daap/resources/visualresources/how_to/cite_image.html)]

Finding Images on the Internet

If you are looking for a high resolution image from the internet, you can select in the Google header bar that you want it only to search for "large images, or extra large images". If you are not finding what you are looking for, there are many stock photography sites out there that allow you to have the image, royalty free for very little of your own money. Some sites to consider would be: Stock.XCHNG (this is a free site, with some restrictions), Stock Xpert, Corbis, Getty, or others, just type in stock photography in the search bar.

Clip Art/Illustrations

Graphics can portray ideas more easily than a picture. They give a different type of quality than text in the document. However, when presenting the ideas to well-educated and technologically savvy professionals, clip art may not present the information efficiently. Illustrations that have a low image resolution can take away from the details you are trying to portray to your audience.If this is the case then photos may be a better choice because they are more clear and may get you point across better.Illustrations are a great way to convey information easily and effectively to an audience of all ages. However, when using illustrations be sure that there is relevance from the illustration to the topic you're discussing. Illustrations can serve as tangents if they have no relevance to the topic being discussed. Illustrations must be chosen to highlight the topic you are discussing and not to distract readers from it.

Headline text

Headline text is used to introduce or even explain graphics. It is expected that you label all of your graphics in one way or another so that when you reference them in you document the reader knows which graphic you are talking about. Headline text can be as simple as a title for a graph or as complex as a short paragraph below a photo explaining the origin and context of the image. Your images and text may seem to go together logically without headlines to you, but your readers will not have your same familiarity.

CC licensed content, Shared previously

- Photos and Illustrations. **Provided by**: WikiBooks. **Located at**: http://en.wikibooks.org/wiki/ Professional_and_Technical_Writing/Design/Illustrations (http://en.wikibooks.org/wiki/Professional_and_Technical_Writing/ Design/Illustrations). **Project**: Professional and Technical Writing. **License**: *CC BY-SA: Attribution-ShareAlike (https://creativecommons.org/licenses/by-sa/4.0/)*

Video: Visualizing Data

Below you'll see a link to a TED Talk by David McCandless titled "The Beauty of Data Visualization." TED is a wonderful resource for intelligent, entertaining talks by experts on all kinds of subjects. You can probably find a video relevant to your own research project, if you look: http://www.ted.com/

Please watch this 18-minute video, and when finished, respond to this question:

> McCandless thinks that information design is really important because "we're all visualizers now; we're all demanding a visual aspect to our information." If we assume it's true, then how has this changed our educational system? Are there particularly good examples of how teachers and schools have responded? Extreme deficits?

Responses should be 1-2 paragraphs long, and reference your own experience with visual learning, either from your personal education or what you've witnessed from a friend or family member's experience.

- https://youtu.be/yYUOnvqm01l

Visual Elements: Play, Use, and Design

So far you have examined how primarily written arguments work rhetorically. But visuals (symbols, paintings, photographs, advertisements, cartoons, etc.) also work rhetorically, and their meaning changes from context to context. Here's an example:

> Imagine two straight lines intersecting each other at right angles. One line runs from north to south. The other from east to west. Now think about the meanings that this sign evokes.

+

What came to mind as you pondered this sign? Crossroads? A first aid sign? The Swiss flag? Your little brother making a cross sign with his forefingers that signals "step away from the hallowed ground that is my bedroom"?

> Now think of a circle around those lines so that the ends of the lines hit, or cross over, the circumference of the circle. What is the image's purpose now?

⊕

What did you come up with? The Celtic cross? A surveyor's target? A pizza cut into really generous sizes?

Did you know that this symbol is also the symbol for our planet Earth? And it's the symbol for the Norse god, Odin. Furthermore, a quick web search will also tell you that John Dalton, a British chemist who lead the way in atomic theory and died in 1844, used this exact same symbol to indicate the element sulfur.[17]

Recently, however, the symbol became the subject of a fiery political controversy. Former Alaska governor (and former vice-presidential candidate) Sarah Palin's marketing team placed several of these symbols—the lines crossed over the circumference of the circle in this case—on a map of the United States. The symbols indicated where the Republican Party had to concentrate their campaign because these two seemingly innocuous lines encompassed by a circle evoked, in this context, the symbol for crosshairs—which itself invokes a myriad of meanings that range from "focus" to "target."

However, after the shooting of Congresswoman Gabrielle Giffords in Arizona in January 2011, the symbol, and the image it was mapped onto, sparked a vehement nationwide debate about its connotative meaning. Clearly, the image's rhetorical effectiveness had transformed into something that some considered offensive. Palin's team withdrew the image from her website.[18]

How we understand symbols rhetorically, and indeed all images, depends on how the symbols work with the words they accompany, and on how we understand and read the image's context, or the social "landscape" within which the image is situated. As you have learned from earlier chapters, much of this contextual knowledge in persuasive situations is tacit, or unspoken.

Like writing, how we use images has real implications in the world. So when we examine visuals in rhetorical circumstances, we need to uncover this tacit knowledge. Even a seemingly innocuous symbol, like the one above, can denote a huge variety of meanings, and these meanings can become culturally loaded. The same is true for more complex images—something we will examine at length below.

In this chapter, then, we will explore how context—as well as purpose, audience, and design—render symbols and images rhetorically effective. The political anecdote above may seem shocking but, nevertheless, it indicates how persuasively potent visuals are, especially when they enhance the meaning of a text's words or vice versa. Our goal for this chapter, then, is to come to terms with the basics of visual analysis, which can encompass the analysis of words working with images or the analysis of images alone. When you compose your own arguments, you can put to use what you discover in this chapter when you select or consider creating visuals to accompany your own work.

Visual Analysis

Let's start with by reviewing what we mean by analysis. Imagine that your old car has broken down and your Uncle Bob has announced that he will fix it for you. The next day, you go to Uncle Bob's garage and find the engine of your car in pieces all over the driveway; you are further greeted with a vision of your hapless uncle greasily jabbing at the radiator with a screwdriver. Uncle Bob (whom you may never speak to again) has broken the car engine down into its component parts to try and figure out how your poor old car works and what is wrong with it.

Happy days are ahead, however. Despite the shock and horror that the scene above inspires, there is a method to Uncle Bob's madness. Amid the wreckage, he finds out how your car works and what is wrong with it so he can fix it and put it back together.

Analyzing, then, entails breaking down a text or an image into component parts (like your engine). And while analyzing doesn't entail *fixing* per se, it does allow you to figure out how a text or image works to convey the message it is trying to communicate. What constitutes the component parts of an image? How might we analyze a visual? What should we be looking for? To a certain extent we can analyze visuals in the same way we analyze written language; we break down a written text into component parts to figure out just *what* the creator's agenda might be and what effect the text might have on its readers.

When we analyze visuals we do take into account the same sorts of things we do when we analyze written texts, with some added features. We thus analyze visuals in terms of the following concepts—concepts that count for our component parts. Some of them you may recognize.

Genre

Genres that use visuals tell us a lot about what we can and can't do with them. Coming to terms with genre is rather like learning a new dance—certain moves, or conventions, are expected that dictate what kind of dance you have to learn. If you're asked to moonwalk, for instance, you know you have to glide backwards across the floor like Michael Jackson. It's sort of the same with visuals and texts; certain moves, or conventions, are expected that dictate what the genre allows and doesn't allow.

Below is a wonderful old bumper sticker from the 1960s 19. A bumper sticker, as we will discover, is a genre that involves specific conventions.

Bumper stickers today look quite a bit different, but the amount of space that a sticker's creator has to work with hasn't really changed. Bumper stickers demand that their creators come up with short phrases that are contextually understandable and accompanied by images that are easily readable—a photograph of an oil painting trying to squeeze itself on a bumper sticker would just be incomprehensible. In short, bumper stickers are an argument in a rush!

A bumper sticker calls for an analysis of images *and* words working together to create an argument. As for their rhetorical content, bumper stickers can demand that we vote a certain way, pay attention to a problem, act as part of a solution, or even recognize the affiliations of the driver of the car the sticker is stuck to. But their very success, given that their content is minimal, depends wholly on our understanding of the words and the symbols that accompany them in context.

Context/The Big Picture

Thinking about context is crucial when we are analyzing visuals, as it is with analyzing writing. We need to understand the political, social, economic, or historical situations from which the visual emerges. Moreover, we have to remember that the meaning of images change as time passes. For instance, what do we have to understand about the context from which the Kennedy sticker emerged in order to grasp its meaning? Furthermore, how has its meaning changed in the past 50 years?

First, to read the bumper sticker at face value, we have to know that a man named Kennedy is running for president. But president of what? Maybe that's obvious, but then again, how many know who the Australian prime minister was 50 years ago, or, for that matter, the leading official in China? Of course, we should know that the face on the bumper sticker belongs to John F. Kennedy, a US Democrat, who ran against the Republican nominee Richard Nixon, and who won the US presidential election in 1960. (We hope you know that anyway.)

Now think how someone seeing this bumper sticker, and the image of Kennedy on it, today would react differently than someone in 1960 would have. Since his election, JFK's status has transformed from American president into an icon of American history. We remember his historic debate with Nixon, the first televised presidential debate. (One wonders how much of a role this event played in his election given that the TV [a visual medium] turned a political underdog into a celebrity.20) We also remember Kennedy for his part in the Cuban missile crisis, his integral role in the Civil Rights Movement and, tragically, we remember his assassination in 1963. In other words, after the passage of 50 years, we might read the face on the bumper sticker quite differently than we did in 1960.

While we examine this "text" from 50 years ago, it reminds us that the images we are surrounded by now change in meaning all the time. For instance, we are all familiar with the Apple logo. The image itself, on its own terms, is simply a silhouette of an apple with a bite taken out of it. But, the visual does not now evoke the nourishment of a Granny Smith or a Golden Delicious. Instead, the logo is globally recognized as an icon of computer technology.

Purpose

Words and images can work together to present a point of view. But, in terms of visuals, that point of view often relies on what isn't explicit—what, as we noted above, is tacit.

The words on the sticker say quite simply "Kennedy For President." We know now that this simple statement reveals that John F. Kennedy ran for president in 1960. But what was its rhetorical value back then? What did the bumper sticker want us to *do* with its message? After all, taken literally, it doesn't really tell us to *do* anything.

For now, let's cheat and jump the gun and guess that the bumper sticker's argument in 1960 was "Vote to Elect John F Kennedy for United States President."

Okay. So knowing what we know from history, we can accept that the sticker is urging us to vote for Kennedy. It's trying to persuade us to do something. And the reason we know what we know about it is because we know how to read its genre and we comprehend its social, political, and historical context. But in order to be persuaded by its purpose, we need to know *why* voting for JFK is a good thing. We need to understand that its underlying message, "Vote for JFK," is that to vote for JFK is a good thing for the future of the United States.

So, to be persuaded by the bumper sticker, we must agree with the reasons why voting for JFK is a good thing. But the bumper sticker doesn't give us any. Instead, it relies on what we are supposed to know about why we should vote for Kennedy. (JFK campaigned on a platform of liberal reform as well as increased spending for the military and space travel technology.21); Moreover, we should be aware of the evidence for why we should vote that way.22 Consequently, if we voted for JFK, we accepted the above claim, reasons, and evidence driving the bumper sticker's purpose without being told any of it by the bumper sticker. The claim, reasons and evidence are all tacit.

What about the image itself? How does that further the bumper sticker's purpose? We see that the image of JFK's smiling face is projected on top of the words "Kennedy for President." The image is not placed off to the side; it is right in the middle of the bumper sticker. So for this bumper sticker to be visually persuasive, we need to agree that JFK, here represented by his smiling face, located right in the middle of the bumper sticker, on a backdrop of red, white, and blue, signifies a person we can trust to run the country.

Nowadays, JFK's face on the bumper sticker—or in any other genre for that matter —might underscore a different purpose. It might encompass nostalgia for an era gone by or it might be used as a resemblance argument, in order to compare President Kennedy with President Obama for example.23

Overall then, when we see a visual used for rhetorical purposes, we must first determine the argument (claim, reasons, evidence) from which the visual is situated and then try to grasp why the visual is being used to further its purpose.

Audience and Medium

In their book *Picturing Texts*, Lester Faigley et al24 claim that, when determining the audience for a visual, we must "think about how an author might expect the audience to receive the work" (104). Medium, then, dominates an audience's reception of an image. (So does **modality**. See below.) For instance, Faigley states that readers will most likely accept a photograph in a newspaper as news—unless of course one thinks that pictures in the tabloids of alien babies impersonating Elvis constitute news. Alien babies aside, readers of the news would expect that the picture on the front page of the *New York Times*, for instance, is a "faithful representation of something that actually happened" (105). An audience for a political cartoon in the newspaper, on the other hand, would know that the pictures they see in cartoons are not faithful representations of the news but opinions about current events and their participants, caricatured by a cartoonist. The expectations of the audience in terms of medium, then, determine much about how the visual is received.

As for our bumper sticker then, we might argue that the image of JFK speeding down the highway on the bumper of a spiffy new Ford Falcon would be persuasive to those who put their faith in the efficacy of bumper stickers, as well as the image of the man on the bumper sticker. Moreover, given that the Falcon is speeding by, we might assume that the bumper sticker would mostly appeal to those folks who are already thinking of voting for JFK—otherwise there's a chance that the Falcon's driver would be the recipient of some 1960s-style road rage.

Today, the audience for our bumper sticker has changed considerably. We might find it in a library collection. Indeed, Kansas University has a considerable collection of bumper stickers.25 Or we might find it collecting bids on eBay. Once again, the audience for this example of images and words working together rhetorically depends largely on its contextual landscape.

Design

Design actually involves several factors.

Arrangement

Designers are trained to emphasize certain features of a visual text. And they are also trained to compose images that are balanced and harmonized. Faigley et al suggest that we look at a text that uses images (with or without words) and think about where our eyes are drawn first (34).26 Moreover, in Western cultures, we are trained to read from left to right and top to bottom—a pattern that often has an impact on what text or image is accentuated in a visual arrangement.

Other arrangements that Faigley et al discuss are **closed and open forms** (105).27 A closed-form image means that, like our bumper sticker, everything we need to know about the image is enclosed within its frame. An open form, on the other hand, suggests that the visual's narrative continues outside the frame of the visual. Many sports ads employ open-frame visuals that suggest the dynamic of physical movement.

Another method of arrangement that is well known to designers is the **rule of thirds**. Here's an example of that rule in action28:

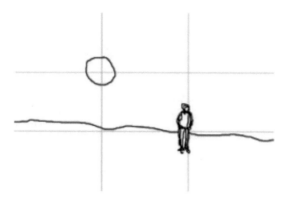

Note how the illustration above has been cordoned off into 9 sections. The drawings of the sun and the person, as well as the horizon, coincide with those lines. The rule of thirds dictates that this compositional method allows for an interesting and dynamic arrangement as opposed to one that is static. Now, unfortunately, our bumper sticker above doesn't really obey that rule. Nevertheless, our eye is still drawn to the image of JFK's head. Many modern bumper stickers do, however, obey the rule of thirds. Next time you see a bumper sticker on a parked car, check if the artist has paid attention to this rule. Or, seek out some landscape photography. The rule of thirds is the golden rule in landscape art and photography and is more or less a comprehensive way to analyze arrangement in design circles because of its focus on where one's eye is drawn.

Rhetorically speaking, what is accentuated in a visual is the most important thing to remember about arrangement. As far as professional design is concerned, it is never haphazard. Even a great photo, which might be seem to be the result of serendipity, can be cropped to highlight what a newspaper editor, for instance, wants highlighted.

Texts and Image in Play

Is the visual supported by words? *How* do the words support the visual? What is gained by the words and what would be lost if they weren't in accompaniment? What if we were to remove the words "Kennedy for President" from our bumper sticker? Would the sticker have the same rhetorical effect?

Moreover, when examining visual rhetoric, we should pinpoint how font emphasizes language. How does font render things more or less important, for instance? Is the font playful, like Comic Sans MS, or formal, like Arial? Is the font blocked, large, or small? What difference does the font make to the overall meaning of the visual? Imagine that our JFK bumper sticker was composed with a swirly- curly font. It probably wouldn't send the desired message. Why not, do you think?

Alternately, think about the default font in Microsoft Word. What does it look like and why? What happens to the font if it is bolded or enlarged? Does it maintain a sense of continuity with the rest of the text? If you scroll through the different fonts available to you on your computer, which do you think are most appropriate for essay writing, website design, or the poster you may have to compose?

Lastly, even the use of **white (or negative) space** in relation to text deserves attention in terms of arrangement. The mismanagement of the relation of space to text and/or visual can result in visual overload! For instance, in an essay, double spacing is often advised because it is easier on the reader's eye. In other words, the blank spaces between the lines of text render reading more manageable than would dense bricks of text. Similarly, one might arrange text and image against the blank space to create a balanced arrangement of both.

While in some situations the arrangement of text and visual (or white space) might not seem rhetorical (in an essay, for example), one could make the argument that cluttering one's work is not especially rhetorically effective. After all, if you are trying to persuade your instructor to give you an 'A', making your essay effortlessly readable seems like a good place to start.

Visual Figures

Faigley et al also ask us to consider the use of figures in a visual argument (32). Figurative language is highly rhetorical, as are figurative images. For instance, visual metaphors abound in visual rhetoric, especially advertising (32). A visual metaphor is at play when you encounter an image that signifies something other than its literal meaning. For instance, think of your favorite cereal: which cartoon character on the cereal box makes you salivate in anticipation of breakfast time? Next time, when you see a cartoon gnome and your tummy start to rumble in anticipation of chocolate-covered rice puffs, you'll know that the design folks down at ACME cereals have done their job. Let's hope, however, that you don't want to chow down on the nearest short fat fellow in a red cap that comes your way.

Visual rhetoric also relies on synecdoche, a trope in which a *part* of something represents the *whole*. In England, for instance, a crown is used to represent the British monarchy. The image of JFK's face on the bumper sticker, then, might suggest his competency to *head up* the country.

Color

Colors are loaded with rhetorical meaning, both in terms of the values and emotions associated with them and their contextual background. Gunther Kress and Theo Van Leeuwen29 show how the use of color is as contextually bound as writing and images themselves. For instance, they write, "red is for danger, green for hope. In most parts of Europe, black is for mourning, though in northern parts of Portugal, and perhaps elsewhere in Europe as well, brides wear black gowns for their wedding day. In China, and other parts of East Asia, white is the color of mourning; in most of Europe it is the color of purity, worn by the bride at her wedding. Contrasts like these shake our confidence in the security of meaning of colour and colour terms" (343).

So what colors have seemingly unshakeable meaning in the US? How about red, white, and blue? Red and blue are two out of the three primary colors. They evoke a sense of sturdiness. After all, they are the base colors from which others are formed.

The combined colors of the American flag have come to signal patriotism and American values. But even American values, reflected in the appearance of the red, white, and blue, change in different contexts. To prompt further thought, Faigley shows us that the flag has been used to lend different meaning to a variety of magazine covers—from *American Vogue* (fashion) to *Fortune* magazine (money) (91). An image of the red, white and blue on the cover lends a particularly American flavor to each magazine. And this can change the theme of each magazine? For instance, with what would you acquaint a picture of the American flag on the cover of *Bon Appétit* or *Rolling Stone*? Hot dogs and Bruce Springsteen perhaps?

What then does the red, white, and blue lend our bumper sticker? A distinctly patriotic flavor, for sure. Politically patriotic. And that can mean different things for different people. Thus, given that meanings change in a variety of contexts, we can see that the meaning of color can actually be more fluid than we might have originally thought.

Alternately, if our JFK sticker colors were anything other than red, white, and blue, we might read it very differently; indeed, it might seem extremely odd to us.

Modality

Kress and Van Leeuwen ask us to consider the modality in which an image is composed. Very simply, this means, how "real" does the image look? And what does this "realness" contribute to its persuasiveness? They write, "visuals can represent people, places, and things as though they are real, as though they actually exist in this way . . . or as though they do not" (161).30 As noted above in the "Audience and Medium" section, photographs are thus considered a more naturalistic representation of the world than clip art, for instance. We expect photographs to give us a representation of reality. Thus, when a photograph is manipulated to signify something fantastic, like a unicorn or a dinosaur, we marvel at its ability to construct something that looks "real." And when a visual shifts from one modality to another, it takes on additional meaning.

For instance, how might we read a cartoon version of JFK compared to the photograph that we see on our bumper sticker? Would the cartoon render the bumper sticker less formal? Less significant perhaps? Would a cartoon, given its associative meanings, somehow lessen the authenticity of the sticker's purpose? Or the authority of its subject?

Perspective/Point of View

Imagine standing beneath a wind turbine. Intimidating? Impressive Overwhelming? Now envision that you are flying over it in airplane. That very enormous thing seems rather insignificant now—a wind turbine in Toyland.

Now imagine the same proportions depicted in a photograph. One might get the same sense of power if the photo was taken from the bottom of the turbine, the lens pointed heavenward. Then again, an aerial photograph might offer us a different perspective. If the landscape presents us with an endless array of turbines stretching into the distance, we might get a sense that they are infinite—as infinite as wind energy.

Our Kennedy sticker offers neither of the above-described senses of perspective. Coming face to face with Kennedy, we neither feel overwhelmed nor superior. In fact, it's as if Kennedy's gaze is meeting ours at our own level. The artist is still using his powers of perspective; it's just that our gaze meets Kennedy's face to face. Consequently, Kennedy is portrayed as friendly and approachable.

Differently, a photo that artist Shepherd Fairey manipulated into the now iconic "Hope" poster from a 2006 Associated Press photograph of our current president (and got into all sorts of copyright infringement trouble for), makes subtle use of perspective: the visual positions the viewer slightly beneath Obama's gaze. As a result of Fairey's use of perspective, and as Joshuah Bearman puts it, Obama is portrayed with "the distant, upward gaze of a visionary leader."31

Social distance

Kress and Van Leeuwen include **social distance** in the components of design. Social distance accounts for the "psychology of people's use of space" (Van Leeuwen and Jewitt, 29).32 In short, a visual artist can exploit social distance to create a certain psychological effect between a person in an image and the image's audience.

To illustrate, imagine a photograph of a handsome man, head and shoulders only, smiling straight at you with warm eyes. He advertises chocolate, cigars, expensive cologne. A beautiful woman tosses her hair, smiling seductively at the camera. She looks straight at you. "Look at me," both seem to say, "buy this product; we invite you." Likewise, Kennedy smiles into the camera. "Vote for me," he encourages. "I'm a nice guy." Depicting head and shoulders only, we are given a sense of what Van Leeuwen and Carey Jewitt call "Close Personal Distance."33 The result is one of intimacy.

Alternately, a visual of several people, or a crowd, would suggest far less intimacy.

Mood and Lighting

Have you ever put a flashlight under your chin and lit your face from underneath? Maybe we aren't all budding scary movie makers, but jump out of the closet on a dark night with all the lights turned off and the flashlight propped under your chin and you're sure to give at least the cat a fright. What you have experimented with is mood and lighting. In short, the lighting as described eerily captures facial features that aren't usually accentuated. It can be quite offputting. Thus the position of the light has created a creepy face; it's created a visual **mood**. And, the mood combines with other elements of the visual to create an effect, which of course is rhetorical.

The next time you watch a movie, note how the filmmaker has played with lighting to create a mood. In the illustration below, we can see how *Film Noir*, for instance, capitalizes on techniques of mood and lighting to create an uncanny effect.34

Finally

In this chapter, we have introduced the basics of rhetoric and visual analysis. During the course of your semester, and throughout your academic career, you might be asked to use visuals in support of your own writing. For instance, you may be asked to construct a web page, a poster, or a pamphlet.

You may also be asked to represent data with graphs and charts. Lisa Ede offers a selection of visuals (as well as a description of their purpose) that you might need to include in some of your academic compositions. These do not include pictures, but arrange text visually to convey information specifically:

1. A **table** arranges text visually, in columns for example, to compare information.
2. A **pie chart** arranges text within a circle to show relationships of quantity, for instance.
3. A **bar graph** is typically used to show changes in data over a period of time.
4. A **map** calls attention to "spatial relationships and locations."35

Whatever the type of visual you use, whether it is a pie chart or a photograph, it is vital that you interrogate the *genre*, *purpose*, *audience* and *design conventions* suitable to the context within which you are working. Understanding these components will help you select the appropriate visual that works rhetorically in this context. In other words, and as an illustration, if you are working in the sciences and compiling visual data in a line graph, you need to be aware of all of the above in order to meet the expectations of your professor and your academic community. In short, even the most seemingly innocuous choices are rhetorical given the expectations of your audience. The components of the analysis listed above, then, offer a set of guidelines to think about when we are composing with visuals.

To Do

1. Can you think of any bumper stickers you have seen lately that capitalize on your external knowledge of an issue? What do you have to know for instance to be able to read and understand a peace sign on a bumper sticker? Or a picture of a cell phone with the words "Hang Up and Drive" next to it? What cultural, unspoken or tacit knowledge do these symbols demand that you have?

2. Go to your favorite search engine and type in the words "political cartoons." Choose a website and browse through the cartoons. You might notice that some of them you will laugh at, some of them you will grimace at, and for some of them, you may stop and think, "huh?" Pick a cartoon that makes you go "Huh?" In other words, pick a cartoon for which you don't get the punch line. Research the political context to which the cartoon refers. After your research, think about the tacit knowledge the cartoon taps into. Now how do you react? Why?

3. Can you think of how audiences have changed with regards to a particular image—like the Apple image? A further illustration might help: my students and I looked at an ad for a particular brand of jeans recently, and they told me that "no one wore those jeans anymore" and that they "were for old people." I was shocked and amazed (and emptied my closet of those jeans). Recently, the brand has been targeting a teen demographic, which leads me to marvel at the company's rhetorical astuteness—as well as to wonder exactly what jeans one should be wearing nowadays.

4. Find an image using your favorite search engine. Analyze it in terms of the elements of design listed above. How does a corroboration of these elements work in favor of the image's overall effect?

---

17 "John Dalton." *The Chemical Heritage Foundation*. 2010. Web. 20 Mar. 2012.

18 Warmowski, Jon. "Following Gifford's Shooting, Sarah Palin's Crosshairs Website Quickly Scrubbed From Internet." *The Huffington Post*. 8 Jan. 2011. Web. 4 Mar. 2012.

19 http://commons.wikimedia.org/wiki/File:1960_Kennedy_for_President_Campaign_Bumper_Sticker.gif

20 Webly, Kayla. "How the Nixon-Kennedy Debate Changed the World." *Time.com*. 23 Sept. 2010. Web. 12. Jul. 2012.

21 "Campaign of 1960." *Jfklibrary.org* John F. Kennedy: Presidential Library and Museum. Web. 30 Mar. 2012.

22 In terms of Space travel, the Soviet Union beat the US to the space punch, by sending Sputnik into orbit in 1957. This caused the U.S government great embarrassment given the implications of the Cold War. Evidence of the Sputnik launch fueled reasons why the US should send an American into space.

23 CBS News recently ran an article doing just that. Knoller, Mark. "JFK and Obama, their Similarities and Differences." *Cbsnews.com*. CBS NEWS. 20 Jan. 2011. Web. 20 Mar. 2012.

24 Faigley, Lester, Diana George, Anna Palchik and Cynthia Selfe. *Picturing Texts*. London: Norton, 2004. Print.

25 KU The University of Kansas. "Researcher Works to Preserve Bumper Stickers, A Kansas Invention." Youtube. Web. 30 Mar. 2012.

26 Faigley, Lester, Diana George, Anna Palchik and Cynthia Selfe. Picturing Texts. London: Norton, 2004. Print.

27 Faigley, Lester, Diana George, Anna Palchik and Cynthia Selfe. Picturing Texts. London: Norton, 2004. Print.

28 http://commons.wikimedia.org/wiki/File:Rule_of_thirds.jpg (http://commons.wikimedia.org/wiki/File:Rule_of_thirds.jpg)

29 Kress, Gunther, and Theo Van Leeuwen: "Colour as a Semiotic Mode: Notes for a Grammar or Colour." *Visual Communication* 1.3 (2002): 343-68.

30 Kress, Gunther and Theo Van Leeuwen. *Reading Images*. London: Routledge, 1996. Print.

31 Bearman, Joshuah. "Behind Obama's Iconic Hope Poster." *The Huffington Post*. 11 Nov. 2008. Web. 17 Jul. 2012.

32 Van Leeuwen, Theo and Carey Jewitt. *The Handbook of Visual Analysis*. Thousand Oaks: Sage, 2003. Print.

33 Van Leeuwen, Theo and Carey Jewitt. *The Handbook of Visual Analysis*. Thousand Oaks: Sage, 2003. Print.

34 http://commons.wikimedia.org/wiki/File:BigComboTrailer.jpg (http://commons.wikimedia.org/wiki/File:BigComboTrailer.jpg)

35 Ede, Lisa. The Academic Writer. 2nd ed. New York: Bedford, 2011. Print.

Torie Rose DeGhett, The War Photo No One Would Publish

Torie Rose DeGhett, "The War Photo No One Would Publish" and David Frum, "Photographs as Weapons of War in the Middle East" are two essays focusing on visual arguments. We will discuss both early in the course.

Here are their URLs:

DeGhett: https://www.theatlantic.com/international/archive/2014/08/the-war-photo-no-one-would-publish/375762/

Frum: https://www.theatlantic.com/international/archive/2014/08/photographs-as-weapons-of-war-in-the-middle-east/375492/

Hanna Rosin, Why Kids Sext

Read Hanna Rosin's November 2014 cover article for *The Atlantic* entitled "Why Kids Sext." Access it either through the permalink below or by accessing either your library databases or www.theatlantic.com

Be sure to get the full-color document with the images.

http://jccweb.sunyjefferson.edu:2055/login.aspx?direct=true&db=a9h&AN=98736514&site=ehost-live

DETERMINING AUDIENCE AND PURPOSE

Audience

What this handout is about

This handout will help you understand and write for the appropriate audience when you write an academic essay.

Audience matters

When you're in the process of writing a paper, it's easy to forget that you are actually writing to someone. Whether you've thought about it consciously or not, you always write to an audience: sometimes your audience is a very generalized group of readers, sometimes you know the individuals who compose the audience, and sometimes you write for yourself. Keeping your audience in mind while you write can help you make good decisions about what material to include, how to organize your ideas, and how best to support your argument.

To illustrate the impact of audience, imagine you're writing a letter to your grandmother to tell her about your first month of college. What details and stories might you include? What might you leave out? Now imagine that you're writing on the same topic but your audience is your best friend. Unless you have an extremely cool grandma to whom you're very close, it's likely that your two letters would look quite different in terms of content, structure, and even tone.

Isn't my instructor my audience?

Yes, your instructor or TA is probably the actual audience for your paper. Your instructors read and grade your essays, and you want to keep their needs and perspectives in mind when you write. However, when you write an essay with only your instructor in mind, you might not say as much as you should or say it as clearly as you should, because you assume that the person grading it knows more than you do and will fill in the gaps. This leaves it up to the instructor to decide what you are really saying, and she might decide differently than you expect. For example, she might decide that those gaps show that you don't know and understand the material. Remember that time when you said to yourself, "I don't have to explain communism; my instructor knows more about that than I do" and got back a paper that said something like "Shows no understanding of communism"? That's an example of what can go awry when you think of your instructor as your only audience.

Thinking about your audience differently can improve your writing, especially in terms of how clearly you express your argument. The clearer your points are, the more likely you are to have a strong essay. Your instructor will say, "He really understands communism—he's able to explain it simply and clearly!" By treating your instructor as an intelligent but uninformed audience, you end up addressing her more effectively.

How do I identify my audience and what they want from me?

Before you even begin the process of writing, take some time to consider who your audience is and what they want from you. Use the following questions to help you identify your audience and what you can do to address their wants and needs.

- Who is your audience?
- Might you have more than one audience? If so, how many audiences do you have? List them.
- Does your assignment itself give any clues about your audience? What does your audience need? What do they want? What do they value?
- What is most important to them?
- What are they least likely to care about?
- What kind of organization would best help your audience understand and appreciate your arguments?

- What do you have to say (or what are you doing in your research) that might surprise your audience?
- What do you want your audience to think, learn, or assume about you? What impression do you want your writing or your research to convey?

How much should I explain?

This is the hard part. As we said earlier, you want to show your instructor that you know the material. But different assignments call for varying degrees of information. Different fields also have different expectations. For more about what each field tends to expect from an essay, see the Writing Center handouts (http://writingcenter.unc.edu/handouts/) on writing in specific fields of study. The best place to start figuring out how much you should say about each part of your paper is in a careful reading of the assignment. We give you some tips for reading assignments and figuring them out in our handout on how to read an assignment (http://writingcenter.unc.edu/handouts/understanding-assignments/). The assignment may specify an audience for your paper; sometimes the instructor will ask you to imagine that you are writing to your congressperson, for a professional journal, to a group of specialists in a particular field, or for a group of your peers. If the assignment doesn't specify an audience, you may find it most useful to imagine your classmates reading the paper, rather than your instructor.

Now, knowing your imaginary audience, what other clues can you get from the assignment? If the assignment asks you to summarize something that you have read, then your reader wants you to include more examples from the text than if the assignment asks you to interpret the passage. Most assignments in college focus on argument rather than the repetition of learned information, so your reader probably doesn't want a lengthy, detailed, point-by-point summary of your reading (book reports in some classes and argument reconstructions in philosophy classes are big exceptions to this rule). If your assignment asks you to interpret or analyze the text (or an event or idea), then you want to make sure that your explanation of the material is focused and not so detailed that you end up spending more time on examples than on your analysis. If you are not sure about the difference between explaining something and analyzing it, see our handouts on reading the assignment (http://writingcenter.unc.edu/handouts/understanding-assignments/) and argument (http://writingcenter.unc.edu/handouts/argument/).

Once you have a draft, try your level of explanation out on a friend, a classmate, or a Writing Center tutor. Get the person to read your rough draft, and then ask her to talk to you about what she did and didn't understand. (Now is not the time to talk about proofreading stuff, so make sure she ignores those issues for the time being). You will likely get one of the following responses or a combination of them:

- If your listener/reader has **tons of questions** about what you are saying, then you probably need to explain more. Let's say you are writing a paper on piranhas, and your reader says, "What's a piranha? Why do I need to know about them? How would I identify one?" Those are vital questions that you clearly need to answer in your paper. You need more detail and elaboration.
- If your reader seems **confused**, you probably need to explain more clearly. So if he says, "Are there piranhas in the lakes around here?" you may not need to give more examples, but rather focus on making sure your examples and points are clear.
- If your reader **looks bored and can repeat back to you more details than she needs to know** to get your point, you probably explained too much. Excessive detail can also be confusing, because it can bog the reader down and keep her from focusing on your main points. You want your reader to say, "So it seems like your paper is saying that piranhas are misunderstood creatures that are essential to South American ecosystems," not, "Uh... piranhas are important?" or, "Well, I know you said piranhas don't usually attack people, and they're usually around 10 inches long, and some people keep them in aquariums as pets, and dolphins are one of their predators, and...a bunch of other stuff, I guess?"

Sometimes it's not the amount of explanation that matters, but the word choice and tone you adopt. Your word choice and tone need to match your audience's expectations. For example, imagine you are researching piranhas; you find an article in *National Geographic* and another one in an academic journal for scientists. How would you expect the two articles to sound?

National Geographic is written for a popular audience; you might expect it to have sentences like "The piranha generally lives in shallow rivers and streams in South America." The scientific journal, on the other hand, might use much more technical language, because it's written for an audience of specialists. A sentence like "*Serrasalmus piraya* lives in fresh and brackish intercoastal and proto-arboreal sub-tropical regions between the 45th and 38th parallels" might not be out of place in the journal.

Generally, you want your reader to know enough material to understand the points you are making. It's like the old forest/ trees metaphor. If you give the reader nothing but trees, she won't see the forest (your thesis, the reason for your paper). If you give her a big forest and no trees, she won't know how you got to the forest (she might say, "Your point is fine, but you haven't proven it to me"). You want the reader to say, "Nice forest, and those trees really help me to see it." Our handout on paragraph development (http://writingcenter.unc.edu/handouts/paragraphs/)can help you find a good balance of examples and explanation.

Reading your own drafts

Writers tend to read over their own papers pretty quickly, with the knowledge of what they are trying to argue already in their minds. Reading in this way can cause you to skip over gaps in your written argument because the gap-filler is in your head. A problem occurs when your reader falls into these gaps. Your reader wants you to make the necessary connections from one thought or sentence to the next. When you don't, the reader can become confused or frustrated. Think about when you read something and you struggle to find the most important points or what the writer is trying to say. Isn't that annoying? Doesn't it make you want to quit reading and surf the web or call a friend?

Putting yourself in the reader's position

Instead of reading your draft as if you wrote it and know what you meant, try reading it as if you have no previous knowledge of the material. Have you explained enough? Are the connections clear? This can be hard to do at first. Consider using one of the following strategies:

- Take a break from your work—go work out, take a nap, take a day off. This is why the Writing Center and your instructors encourage you to start writing more than a day before the paper is due. If you write the paper the night before it's due, you make it almost impossible to read the paper with a fresh eye.
- Try outlining after writing—after you have a draft, look at each paragraph separately. Write down the main point for each paragraph on a separate sheet of paper, in the order you have put them. Then look at your "outline"—does it reflect what you meant to say, in a logical order? Are some paragraphs hard to reduce to one point? Why? This technique will help you find places where you may have confused your reader by straying from your original plan for the paper.
- Read the paper aloud—we do this all the time at the Writing Center, and once you get used to it, you'll see that it helps you slow down and really consider how your reader experiences your text. It will also help you catch a lot of sentence-level errors, such as misspellings and missing words, which can make it difficult for your reader to focus on your argument.

These techniques can help you read your paper in the same way your reader will and make revisions that help your reader understand your argument. Then, when your instructor finally reads your finished draft, he or she won't have to fill in any gaps. The more work you do, the less work your audience will have to do—and the more likely it is that your instructor will follow and understand your argument.

CC licensed content, Shared previously

Discussion: Establishing Intended Audience

Material in this web article, "Determining Audience/Readership" (http://www.studygs.net/writing/audience.htm) from Study Guides and Strategies, will prove helpful in completing this assignment, as will other readings in this module.

In the discussion below, identify at least 3 potential groups of people who would be concerned about the topic you've chosen. For each of the three, tell us a bit about who they are, and what motivations they have. (It's always helpful to include a reminder about what your topic/thesis is, too).

For instance, in my Cheezlts argument, there are a variety of potential groups affected. One is consumers, who care about getting good values, low costs, and high quality products. They want to be sure the money they spend is worthwhile. Another group is retail outlets. They, too, are motivated by money, and making sure they keep the customer coming back to purchase the products they offer. A third potential group are health-food advocates, who would see snack foods like Cheezlts as a bad alternative to other options because of their fat and salt contents.

End your post by telling us which of the potential audience groups you're going to focus your own essay on, and why. What can you do to target your supporting claims to address the concerns of this particular group?

Your post should be at least 150-200 words. It doesn't have to be grammatically perfect, but should use standard English (no text-speak, please) and normal capitalization rules.

You will also need to return to this Discussion to reply to at least two of your classmates' posts. Content could include, but is not limited to, any of the following: Comment on the audience groups they've identified. If you can think of others, suggest who they would be and what their motivations are. Try to put yourself in the place of the group your colleague has chosen, and advance potential counter-arguments a person in that group would make.

Responses are weighed as heavily as your initial posting, and should be roughly as long (150-200 words) when combined. Responses should indicate you've read your classmate's post carefully. Include specific details from the post you're responding to in your reply.

CC licensed content, Shared previously

With Analysis, Focus Upon Functions or Effects

At the college level, putting in the right-sounding quotes in the right-looking spots of a body paragraph is insufficient. Writers are expected to use the quotes as excuses to argue their points. Close reading is a crucial skill which helps the writer make sense of how something makes sense. Humanities courses largely aim to enhance or bring about readers' abilities to handle complex, indirect texts that demand multiple responses.

Close reading is an analytical activity where the writer picks parts of larger whole and discusses how they function. This can be done while annotating or deciding what to say about an annotated chunk of text. Because your audience often knows the text and has ideas about how it works, it is up to you to do more than simply point out the existence of an important line, phrase, or word. Within the line, the critic must move from pointing out an idea to arguing how it functions. What effect is created by that phrase? How does this word affect readers? These questions get proved after careful setup and cited quotation work.

Once you have dissected a speech, description, or dialogue, remember that you have committed a fairly aggressive, destructive act. You yanked a part from the whole. Remember to use the late portions of paragraphs to put the pieces back together. ("Pick up your toys when you are done with them!")

What You Might Look for in a Text

Focus on an author's use of complexity by discussing the effects of any of the following:

word choice (diction) word order (syntax)

connotation denotation

irony (dramatic, situational, verbal) symbolism

mood tone

paradox (seeming contradiction) how words fit/bring about character

rhetorical appeals (logos, ethos, pathos) logical patterns (valid or not)

Rhetorical modes (description, narration, definition, process, illustration, comparison/contrast, classification/division, cause/effect, argument)

> Basically, looking for moves of any sort is a good starting point with analysis.

Analysis is the Breaking Down of a Whole into its Parts

Part-to-whole relationships and breaking those down into their functions is what we do when we analyze. We argue about how the parts function.

For practice, look at the following image. It is Edward Hicks's *The Cornell Farm/*. The image has a fascinating composition, so watch the way one's eyes are directed from area to area in the painting. Are there any symbols? Signs? (Do you know the difference between a sign and a symbol (https://en.wikipedia.org/wiki/Sign_%28semiotics%29)?)

When we write, we analyze most of the time. Whether we are reading a student post or model essay, we look over each text and think about how we are looking. It's a composition, so some of the vocabulary we use in its analysis is shared with other humanities courses like art appreciation or music appreciation.

Consider how the whole is broken down. If its artful, then there's a guiding of one's eyes as well as a frustration of easy expectations. See what you see and share that! Again, italicize the artworks' titles.

Edward Hicks, *The Cornell Farm* (1848).

Clearly, we can argue the parts and how they function. Analysis is all about functions in the structure and effects upon the viewer/reader. It's worth remembering that the act is destructive (*lysis* meaning just that), sort of like taking apart a watch and seeing if it will function without this or that gear. And, no, don't use the creationist blind watchmaker argument here just because I mentioned watches. Their idea that something as sophisticated as an eye could not have evolved is easily-enough refuted (http://darwiniana.org/eyes.htm).

CC licensed content, Original

- Analysis is the Breaking Down of a Whole into its Parts; Painting is from . **Authored by**: Joshua Dickinson. **Provided by**: Jefferson Community College. **Located at**: (). **Project**: ENG 101. **License**: *CC BY-SA: Attribution-ShareAlike (https://creativecommons.org/licenses/by-sa/4.0/)*

With Death, Ethical Issues Abound

"Dulce Et Decorum Est"

We have been reading about bioethical issues a lot recently and I thought of this old (and out-of-copyright) poem from high school that ties in.

This is Wilfred Owen's WWI poem "Dulce Et Decorum Est" ("It is sweet and fitting to die for one's country.) Owen died mere months (weeks?) after writing this and near the end of WWI's fighting.

Bent double, like old beggars under sacks,

Knock-kneed, coughing like hags, we cursed through sludge,

Till on the haunting flares we turned our backs,

And towards our distant rest began to trudge.

Men marched asleep. Many had lost their boots,

But limped on, blood-shod. All went lame; all blind;

Drunk with fatigue; deaf even to the hoots

Of gas-shells dropping softly behind.

Gas! GAS! Quick, boys!—An ecstasy of fumbling

Fitting the clumsy helmets just in time,

But someone still was yelling out and stumbling

And flound'ring like a man in fire or lime.—

Dim through the misty panes and thick green light,

As under a green sea, I saw him drowning.

In all my dreams before my helpless sight,

He plunges at me, guttering, choking, drowning.

If in some smothering dreams, you too could pace

Behind the wagon that we flung him in,

And watch the white eyes writhing in his face,

His hanging face, like a devil's sick of sin;

If you could hear, at every jolt, the blood

Come gargling from the froth-corrupted lungs,

Obscene as cancer, bitter as the cud

Of vile, incurable sores on innocent tongues,—

My friend, you would not tell with such high zest

To children ardent for some desperate glory,

The old Lie: *Dulce et decorum est*

Pro patria mori.

Notes: Latin phrase is from the Roman poet Horace: "It is sweet and fitting to die for one's country."

Source: *Poems* (Viking Press)

I suppose it's easier to throw this at people than to field papers on some of the more bias-prone of topics like ritual castration, assisted suicide, and the like.

How might this relate to our readings from the text?

Public domain content

- With Death, Ethical Issues Abound . **Authored by**: Joshua Dickinson, Wilfred Owen. **Provided by**: Jefferson Community College. **Located at**: http://www.sunyjefferson.edu (http://www.sunyjefferson.edu). **License**: *CC BY-SA: Attribution-ShareAlike (https://creativecommons.org/licenses/by-sa/4.0/)*

Heather Pringle, Beyond the Palace Walls

This 2014 *Archaeology* article by Heather Pringle (http://jccweb.sunyjefferson.edu:2055/login.aspx?direct=true&db=a9h&AN=95378097&site=ehost-live) is fascinating both for its content and for how we can read it to infer audience and purpose. Access it either through the JCC Library Databases or through this permalink. If you lack our library access, use your institution's library databases. (I used *Academic Search Complete* to locate this piece.)

The essay has images which are important to see, so try and access the PDF version.

http://jccweb.sunyjefferson.edu:2055/login.aspx?direct=true&db=a9h&AN=95378097&site=ehost-live

PREWRITING

Prewriting Strategies

The term "pre-writing" conjures up a lot of strange activities and practices. You've probably tried many different prewriting strategies in the past, and may have a good idea of what works for you and what doesn't. Keep in mind, that the KIND of writing project you're working on can impact how effective a particular technique is to use in a given situation.

Some resources for additional prewriting activities are listed here.

FREEWRITING

Setting a goal for a short amount of time (5 minutes or 10 minutes are good options), just write anything that comes to mind related to your topic. The goal is to not worry about what comes out of your pen, if handwriting, or keyboard, if typing. Instead, just free your mind to associate as it wishes. It's amazingly productive for rich ideas, and it's nice not to have to worry about spelling and grammar.

Additional information: About.com's "How to FreeWrite" (http://fictionwriting.about.com/od/writingexercises/ss/freewritecx.htm)

LIST-MAKING

If you're a list-maker by nature, there's no reason not to harness that for academic writing purposes. Jot notes about major ideas related to the subject you're working with. This also works well with a time limit, like 10 minutes. Bonus points—after you've had time to reflect on your list, you can rearrange it in hierarchical order, and create a basic outline quite simply.

Additional Information: Higher Awareness's "List Making – Journaling Tool" (http://www.higherawareness.com/journal-writing/list-making.html)

CLUSTERING

Also known as "mapping," this is a more visual form of brainstorming. It asks you to come up with topic ideas, and draw lines to connect ideas and figure out sub-categories and related ideas. You can end up with a quite extensive "bubble cloud" as a result. This also works well within a time limit, like 10 minutes.

Additional Information: Edudemic's 5 Innovative Mind-Mapping Tools for Education (http://edudemic.com/2012/03/mind-mapping/)

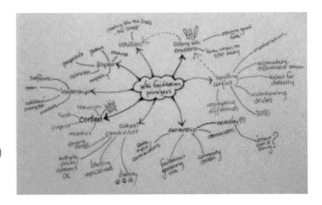

QUESTIONING

The way to find answers is to ask questions—seems simple enough. This applies to early-stage writing processes, just like everything else. When you have a topic in mind, asking and answering questions about it is a good way to figure out directions your writing might take.

Additional Information: Paradigm's The Journalists' Questions (7 pages) (http://www.powa.org/index.php/invent/journalists-questions)

Other prewriting strategies exist. Do you have a favorite method?

CC licensed content, Shared previously

- Composition II. **Authored by**: Alexis McMillan-Clifton. **Provided by**: Tacoma Community College. **Located at**: http://www.tacomacc.edu (http://www.tacomacc.edu). **Project**: Kaleidoscope Open Course Initiative. **License**: *CC BY: Attribution (https://creativecommons.org/licenses/by/4.0/)*
- Image of list. **Authored by**: sunshinecity. **Located at**: https://flic.kr/p/2v76ZB (https://flic.kr/p/2v76ZB). **License**: *CC BY: Attribution (https://creativecommons.org/licenses/by/4.0/)*
- Image of clustering. **Authored by**: Robyn Jay. **Located at**: https://flic.kr/p/9dZCyh (https://flic.kr/p/9dZCyh). **License**: *CC BY-SA: Attribution-ShareAlike (https://creativecommons.org/licenses/by-sa/4.0/)*

Public domain content

- Image of timer. **Authored by**: Pascal. **Located at**: https://flic.kr/p/6opKb8 (https://flic.kr/p/6opKb8). **License**: *Public Domain: No Known Copyright (https://creativecommons.org/about/pdm)*
- Image of questions. **Provided by**: Office for Emergency Management War Production Board. **Located at**: http://commons.wikimedia.org/wiki/File:Where,_When,_Who,_What,_Why,_How%5E_-_NARA_-_534144.jpg (http://commons.wikimedia.org/wiki/File:Where,_When,_Who,_What,_Why,_How%5E_-_NARA_-_534144.jpg). **License**: *Public Domain: No Known Copyright (https://creativecommons.org/about/pdm)*

Academic Voice

Assuming that your audience is a teacher of some sort, your main purpose is to demonstrate your ability to articulate knowledge and experience. When writing a research paper and other academic writing (what is called academic discourse) you'll want to use what is called **the academic voice**, which is meant to sound objective, authoritative, and reasonable. While a research paper will be based on your opinion on a topic, it will be an opinion based on evidence (from your research) and one that has been argued in a rational manner in your paper.

You use the academic voice because your opinion is based on thinking; in your paper you're revealing your thought process to your reader. Because you'll be appealing to reason, you want to use the voice of one intellectual talking to another intellectual.

If the subject matter for your academic writing isn't personal, as in the case of a formal research paper, you would take on a more detached, objective tone. While you may indeed feel strongly about what you're writing about, you should maintain a professional tone, rather than a friendly or intimate one.

However, it's important to note that even the most formal academic voice does not need to include convoluted sentence structure or abstract, stilted language, as some believe. As with all writing, you should strive to write with clarity and an active voice that avoids jargon. All readers appreciate a vigorous, lively voice.

Instead of:

The utilization of teams as a way of optimizing our capacity to meet and prioritize our goals will impact the productivity of the company.

Write:

Teams will execute the goals and enhance the company's output.

Of course, the decision about whether you use a specialized vocabulary depends entirely on who your audience is and the purpose of the paper.

REMEMBER: Some academic writing will require a more personal tone, such as when you are writing a formal narrative essay or perhaps an **ethnography** (study of a culture) essay. In general, the academic voice is a formal one, but there will be variations based on the situation.

Tips on Academic Voice

When using the academic voice you won't usually use first personal pronouns.

Instead of:

I think anyone who becomes a parent should have to take a parenting class.

Write:

Parenting classes should be mandatory for any biological or adoptive parents.

NOTE: There are exceptions for certain types of writing assignments.

Avoid using second person pronouns.

Instead of:

When you read "Letter from a Birmingham Jail," you will realize that King was writing to people besides the ministers who criticized him.

Write:

Upon reading "Letter from a Birmingham Jail," readers will note that King was addressing a wider audience than the clergy who condemned his actions.

Avoid contractions in more formal writing.

Instead of:

It shouldn't be difficult to record what we feel, but many of us just can't get our feelings down on paper.

Write:

It should not be difficult to record feelings, but many people are unable to do so.

Avoid informal language.

Instead of:

It's obvious that she's a feminist because she makes a big deal about women who were into the suffrage movement.

Write:

Because of her focus on the suffragists, one can assume she is a feminist.

Abbreviations for common terms should not be used in academic writing

Instead of:

Smith was declared the official winner at the P.O. last Mon. on Jan. 6th.

Write:

Smith was declared the official winner at the post office last Monday, on January 6.

CC licensed content, Shared previously

- Tips on Academic Voice. **Authored by**: OWL Excelsior Writing Lab. **Provided by**: Excelsior College. **Located at**: http://owl.excelsior.edu/writing-process/finding-your-voice/finding-your-voice-tips-on-academic-voice/ (http://owl.excelsior.edu/writing-process/finding-your-voice/finding-your-voice-tips-on-academic-voice/). **Project**: ENG 101. **License**: *CC BY: Attribution (https://creativecommons.org/licenses/by/4.0/)*

Finding Your Voice

In writing, just as in life, you're selective when choosing words and the tone of voice you use in various situations. When writing a thank-you to Great-Aunt Millie for the socks she sent you for your birthday, you probably use a polite, respectful voice. When you are having a fight with your partner or are gossiping with a friend, both your vocabulary and tone will be quite different. Likewise, you'll use a more formal voice in a research paper compared to a personal essay, an email, or a journal entry.

Deciding what kind of voice to use in writing depends entirely on who will be reading what you write and what your purpose is in writing. Are you writing about the first time you ever drove a car? Explaining your theory about why yoga is such a popular exercise regimen and spiritual practice? Putting forth your informed opinion of why hybrid cars are problematic for the environment despite their increased gas mileage?

What creates voice is simply the words you choose and the way you use them. What kind of voice you use in a paper depends on the assignment and the audience, as well as the effect you want to create. By making conscious choices about the words you use to communicate to your reader, you establish a voice.

When is it Okay to use I in Academic Essays?

There's no set answer as to whether one can use *I* in essays, always check with the professor.

In our essay, while it's fine to use it in a limited usage—without filtering everything through the self—the audience is often best engaged by moving toward a use of *readers*. The latter gives us a recognition that, yes, there is in fact an audience out there. Everyone has a limited point of view, so it can be a problem having too many sentences starting with *I*. Even so, I work with many students who share their relevant experiences. If we are writing an essay about war's impacts and the soldier-student has been deployed six times from Ft. Drum, they are subject experts with credibility. Blended with other voices, their views can be *credibly powerful*.

CC licensed content, Original

Assessment: 3 Research Topic Ideas

In the group discussions recently you've been chatting about initial topic ideas. You've probably gotten a better idea of what you'd actually like to pursue, and perhaps even had new ideas in the meantime.

For this assignment, I'd like you to narrow your options down to 3. For **each** of these 3 potential research topics, draft a paragraph of exploration including the following:

- what the topic is, and why it appeals to you
- questions you have about the topic you didn't already know the answers to
- an overview of some initial quick research you've done on the topic (Google & Wikipedia are fine for our purposes here), including at least one new discovery for you about the issue
- what you'd hope to be able to prove to your reader about this issue in a research essay about it

This is an informal assignment, though matters of proofreading and grammar are always helpful to check over before submitting.

These 3 topics can come straight from your list of 5 that you submitted to the weekly discussion, OR you can come up with 3 new ideas, or any combination of the two.

If you know **for sure** what topic you'd like to pursue for your essay, I'd still like to see three different potential sub-topics explored here. For instance, if you know you want to write about scuba diving, divide that into three directions you might then take: how scuba diving affects tourism, how scuba divers help or hurt natural underwater environments, what safety training scuba divers should have to complete for certification.

A sample paragraph: I'd like to consider writing my essay about Cheezits, because I'm always snacking on them while I work on my online classwork. I didn't really know who made them or how popular a snack food they were, beyond the fact that they are readily available in grocery stores. A Google search led me to the brand's website, where I learned they were made by Sunshine, and had a variety called "Scrabble Junior" that I'd never seen before, with letters printed on each cracker. In an essay about Cheezits, I'd like to be able to prove to myself and my readers that these are a better cheese-flavored snack than other options available right now.

WHAT IS ARGUMENT?

View The Argument Clinic, by Monty Python's Flying Circus

We often take tones toward annotation, reading and writing. I thought I'd add a funny bit of text: Monty Python's sketch "The Argument Clinic (https://www.youtube.com/watch?v=kQFKtl6gn9Y)." Check out this hilarious bit of coverage. These were guys who had been educated at the best English universities, so they often dealt with the same stuff we happen to be taking on.

If you like this, I recommend the following follow-ups:

"Confuse-a-Cat"

"The Witch Sketch"

"Novel Writing" (google it with Thomas Hardy and you'll find it)

"The Cheese Shop Sketch"

"The Village Idiot Sketch"

In each, you'll notice that heavy-duty logic or philosophy ideas are being sent up in ways relevant to our reading and writing.

"No, they're not!"

Pro and Con Practice

Using pro and con lists is a helpful prewriting technique, since any topic worth arguing has many sides. Writers need to capitalize on their side's strengths, proving that they are valid. Conversely, writers need to turn the other side's arguments against it. This is called refuting the opposition. In an even tone, the writer shows how the other side's arguments are invalid to some extent. Still, don't go too far. . . none of us likes being told that our ideas are useless. Listing the points of argument can help (it's sort of like picking teams in phys ed class). Through listing, careful writers find that each side is more complicated than they had thought.

Directions: Follow the alphabetized directions. Do all parts of the assignment. Imagine that you have been asked to write an objective essay for a prominent journal.

1. Pick one of the statements in the topic bank, and decide which side you take on the statement.
2. Then, create a list of 8-10 strong points *for* your side. Label it according to the issue. For example: "My side: against separate male/female military units"
3. Label the opposition's side, too. For example: "The opposition's side: for separate male/female military units."
4. After you have set up your side, create a list of 8-10 arguments made by the opposition. This means you'll think of the best points for each side. You may find that many of the points directly oppose arguments made by the other side.

Remember to narrow and focus the topic as necessary

Topic Bank (stick to these topics, and "make a withdrawal"):

1) Students should/should not work throughout the school year.

2) Televised instant replays should/should not be used to call plays in football and other sports.

3) Off-road recreational vehicles should/should not be banned from our national parks.

4) Persons over 14 charged with crimes should/should not be tried as adults.

5) Controversial names or symbols of athletic teams ("Redskins" the Confederate flag, the tomahawk chop) should/should not be changed or displayed.

6) During peacetime, students should/should not serve in a youth corps for two years following high school.

7) The math requirement at JCC should/should not be changed.

Here's an example: "Homeschooled athletes should be allowed to play on the public school teams of the district in which they live."

My side: Against including homeschooled students on public school teams	Opposition's side: In favor of including these homeschooled athletes on public school teams.

What ideas might you delete? Could you brainstorm 8-10 reasons for and against the claim? How do those pros tend to line up with their respective cons?

- Are there a couple of ideas that might work better if they were merged into one?
- If you had to write about the topic, how would you order or emphasize these points?
- What sort of thesis could you "spin out" of your points? (Remember the summarizing function of the thesis statement.)

CC licensed content, Original

- Pro and Con Practice. **Authored by**: Joshua Dickinson. **Provided by**: Jefferson Community College. **Located at**: http://www.sunyjefferson.edu (http://www.sunyjefferson.edu). **Project**: ENG 101. **License**: *CC BY-SA: Attribution-ShareAlike (https://creativecommons.org/licenses/by-sa/4.0/)*

Here are Some Dos and Don'ts Graders Think Through

What we want and what we get are often wildly variant. Adults all know this. Even so, I can be surprised by some combinations of elements sometimes. That's why I like to troubleshoot papers with you beforehand!

Problem: Paragraphs lacking topic sentences. These work in fiction, but not in explicit writing like ours. Even if it is not first, the topic sentence ought to be connected in obvious ways to your claim. We often defer to sources here or have paragraphs which only exist in the paper because of a source. It should be that the supporting role fits what you do, not vice versa.

One source for the first or last third (or any third) of a paper is a problem. We often see such overuse of one source: Great source? Great! Not great, however, if that source is the only voice in the paper or if, when it is used, the writer never questions it. Think of how ventriloquists' dummies only exist to parrot the words of someone else:

"Me and the office ventriloquist dummy" by TJ Ryan is licensed under CC BY 2.0

Statistics which get plagiarized, unused, treated as impressive, or passed off as if they are unbiased are likely to backfire, turning a possibly-good move into a definitely-bad move. I'm not phased by statistics–particularly if the writer fails to quote properly, doesn't look at the fact that the sample size was seventeen people paid by the company, or if the "citizens' group" spouting them turns out to be a hate group with a nice-sounding name or if that source actually ripped them off from a second source. As Mark Twain stated aptly, there are "lies, damned lies, and statistics."

Long quotes? They are often areas where summaries would work better, be shorter, and might actually receive interpretation. Filler long quotes nearly never get interpreted. Look at it as I do: the more a quote drones on, the more expectation it sets up that I would get something for it–some interpretation, anything! (I mean, people get free vacations in our country for sitting through two-day seminars . . . they obviously got something from the long setup.) We only quote if it's well-worded, the strongly-held opinion of a thinker, or a thought at variance with the widely-held opinion in that field of study. Otherwise, summarize or paraphrase.

Examples can often be scarce, appearing only by page six. By then, it's too late for readers. Don't overuse or under use examples. According to the Goldilocks Principle, there has to be a "just right" zone for source use, detail, even sentence and word length.

Lastly, the new game is to play with formatting. I know the trick of putting the punctuation in 16-point font to puff the piece. I have seen papers go from 10 to 3 pages because of ridiculous formatting tricks. That time is best spent writing, in my opinion. Some people have plagiarized by throwing in a source's bibliography and citations, figuring I wouldn't check or couldn't see that move. That's another bad one, since plagiarism requires that we look at intent and it takes intent to do something like that.

I hope that helps!

REFLECTIVE LEARNING

Reflection

Sometimes the process of figuring out who you are as writers requires reflection, a "looking back" to determine what you were thinking and how your thinking changed over time, relative to key experiences. Mature learners set goals, and achieve them by charting a course of action and making adjustments along the way when they encounter obstacles. They also build on strengths and seek reinforcement when weaknesses surface. What makes them *mature*? They're not afraid to make mistakes (own them even), and they know that struggle can be a rewarding part of the process. By equal measure, mature learners celebrate their strengths and use them strategically. By adopting a reflective position, they can pinpoint areas that work well and areas that require further help—and all of this without losing sight of their goals.

You have come to this course with your own writing goals. Now is a good time to think back on your writing practices with reflective writing, also called metacognitive writing. Reflective writing helps you think through and develop your intentions as writers. Leveraging reflective writing also creates learning habits that extend to any discipline of learning. It's a set of procedures that helps you step back from the work you have done and ask a series of questions: Is this really what I wanted to do? Is this really what I wanted to say? Is this the best way to communicate my intentions? Reflective writing helps you authenticate your intentions and start identifying places where you either hit the target or miss the mark. You may find, also, that when you communicate your struggles, you can ask others for help! Reflective writing helps you trace and articulate the patterns you have developed, and it fosters independence from relying too heavily on an instructor to tell you what you are doing.

Throughout this course, you have been working toward an authentic voice in your writing. Your reflection on writing should be equally authentic or honest when you look at your purposes for writing and the strategies you have been leveraging all the while.

Reflective Learning

Reflective thinking is a powerful learning tool. As we have seen throughout this course, proficient readers are reflective readers, constantly stepping back from the learning process to think about their reading. They understand that just as they need to activate prior knowledge at the beginning of a learning task and monitor their progress as they learn, they also need to make time during learning as well as at the end of learning to think about their learning process, to recognize what they have accomplished, how they have accomplished it, and set goals for future learning. This process of "thinking about thinking" is called metacognition. When we think about our thinking—articulating what we now know and how we came to know it—we close the loop in the learning process.

How do we engage in reflection? Educator Peter Pappas modified Bloom's Taxonomy of Learning to focus on reflection:

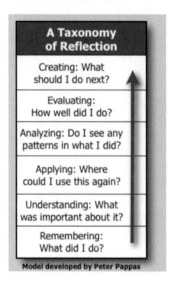

This "taxonomy of reflection" provides a structure for metacognition. Educator Silvia Rosenthal Tolisano has modified Pappas's taxonomy into a pyramid and expanded upon his reflection questions:

Use Pappas's and Tolisano's taxonomies of reflection to help you reflect on your learning, growth and development as a reader, writer, and thinker in this course.

CC licensed content, Shared previously

- Composition II. **Authored by**: Elisabeth Ellington, Ph.D.. **Provided by**: Chadron State College. **Located at**: http://www.csc.edu/ (http://www.csc.edu/). **Project**: Kaleidoscope Open Course Initiative. **License**: *CC BY: Attribution (https://creativecommons.org/licenses/by/4.0/)*
- Image of Taxonomy. **Authored by**: Peter Pappas. **Located at**: http://www.peterpappas.com/images/2011/08/taxonomy-of-reflection.png (http://www.peterpappas.com/images/2011/08/taxonomy-of-reflection.png). **Project**: Copy/Paste. **License**: *CC BY-NC: Attribution-NonCommercial (https://creativecommons.org/licenses/by-nc/4.0/)*
- Image of pyramid. **Authored by**: Silvia Rosenthal Tolisano. **Located at**: http://langwitches.org/blog/2011/06/20/reflectu00adreflectingu00adreflection/ (http://langwitches.org/blog/2011/06/20/reflectu00adreflectingu00adreflection/). **License**: *CC BY-NC-SA: Attribution-NonCommercial-ShareAlike (https://creativecommons.org/licenses/by-nc-sa/4.0/)*

Assessment: Personal Reflection

The previous page in this module, Reflective Learning (https://courses.lumenlearning.com/englishcomp2kscopexmaster/chapter/reflective-learning/), suggests two alternate ways of viewing our own progression in comprehension and skill development. The last line in the document presents a task:

"Use Pappas's and Tolisano's taxonomies of reflection to help you reflect on your learning, growth and
development as a reader, writer, and thinker in this course."

Consider questions like these as you work: Do you feel that one or both of these models speaks to your progress in this course? Where would you have placed yourself on either scale at the beginning of the quarter? Here, at the end of the quarter? How might you use this same process to create writing in future courses or in your personal/professional life?

This reflection should consist of 2-3 paragraphs of developed, edited prose. Make clear reference to one or both of the taxonomies in your reflection.

Want to see a sample of what this submission might look like? View 2 student samples available here (https://docs.google.com/document/d/1aaNDu0nEMcuywp69y5hndjH6C4NfQ50-rc6UDS7Eglc/edit?usp=sharing) (Google Doc link).

THESIS STATEMENTS

Thesis Hints

Function of the Thesis

As a writer, everything you do sends a message to readers. Your thesis should be the best sentence in your paper. Everything else should be related to the thesis. If it isn't, then it doesn't belong there. Here's an interesting definition: "The thesis is a provable opinion about which others may disagree." A well-worded thesis sets out what you will prove and offers a glimpse at your logic. It may show the other side, too, if that's what your task calls for.

What most Writers Fail to Do

Most people write essays where the body paragraphs don't match up with what they say they'll do in the paper. They have not reworded the working thesis that got them through the prewriting and drafting stages. Refine the thesis as you get a clearer idea of what you'll be able to prove. Make sure that the thesis reflects what the paper actually does.

Another weak point occurs when writers string together several questions in their introduction–and then hit readers with their thesis. They haven't answered the questions fully, and they are probably copying the questioning tactic from something they saw on television or read in a newspaper. Academic writing is a more formal situation, so "dress up" your style and the amount of previewing you will do. If you structure the introduction properly, the thesis will appear later in the introduction after it has been set up.

Preview what you will do in the paper. It's always necessary. However, it can be as easy as listing your major paragraph topics. I'll expect you to improve the introduction beyond these basic expectations. Preview at the start, though–and review with care at the end. If you don't, we won't care or remember.

Definition of Thesis

A thesis is a provable opinion about which reasonable people may disagree. You're familiar with writing these. It is helpful to remember a few things about good thesis statements:

A thesis is an **opinion** , not a fact. It's not useful to write a five-page paper with the thesis: "I really, strongly, vehemently believe that the Civil War was most likely fought between 1861 and 1865." Prove something about which people disagree.

Using my famous "Goldilocks principle," decide whether your thesis is appropriate to the scale of the assignment. Is it too large, too specific, or "just right" for your task? The answer depends on your audience, purpose, and assignment information, so read it!

Tone

Keep the tone confident. It's a thesis statement, not a thesis question. You are the person answering questions, not just asking them (so don't overuse rhetorical, unanswered questions). Avoid using "I" as well. For example, if I say, "Alice, close the door," my statement assumes "I want you to close the door, Alice." I didn't need to say "I" to communicate here, right? The same usually goes with academic writing. Avoid "I" or "you." (There's nothing like me getting a paper with the writer carelessly mentioning "When *you* are pregnant. . .")

Where it Goes

Placement ? Put the thesis near/at the end of the paragraph. Lead up to it with careful setup.

Finally, expect that you'll rework the thesis as you go along. You might create a working thesis out of a question, turning it into an answer as you prewrite. Sharpen it as you proceed!

Editing Checklist

To help your editing and drafting, here are some questions you can ask/answer about the thesis:

- Is the thesis limited enough for a short paper? How so?
- Have you included enough strong points to prove your thesis?
- What is the pattern your essay follows? List argument's sides and rhetorical modes (i.e., definition, narration, compare and contrast, etc.).
- Do you do enough to prove a number of points that support your thesis? (Remember that proving a point to doubting readers takes more time than you might expect.)
- Where could you include additional information to make the argument more persuasive?
- Did you refute at least one major opposing argument? Which one?
- Describe two of the tones you adopted at different places in the essay, and tell why they are appropriate.
- List your restated thesis that you put in the conclusion paragraph. (If you didn't put one in, then write one here, copy it in your notes, and put it into the paper.)

CC licensed content, Original

Formulating a Thesis

You need a good thesis statement for your essay but are having trouble getting started. You may have heard that your thesis needs to be specific and arguable, but still wonder what this really means.

Let's look at some examples. Imagine you're writing about John Hughes's film *Sixteen Candles (http://en.wikipedia.org/wiki/ Sixteen_Candles)* (1984).

You take a first pass at writing a thesis:

> *Sixteen Candles* is a romantic comedy about high school cliques.

Is this a strong thesis statement? Not yet, but it's a good start. You've focused on a topic–high school cliques–which is a smart move because you've settled on one of many possible angles. But the claim is weak because it's not yet arguable. Intelligent people would generally agree with this statement—so there's no real "news" for your reader. You want your thesis to say something surprising and debatable. If your thesis doesn't go beyond summarizing your source, it's descriptive and not yet argumentative.

The key words in the thesis statement are "romantic comedy" and "high school cliques." One way to sharpen the claim is to *start asking questions*.

For example, how does the film represent high school cliques in a surprising or complex way? How does the film reinforce stereotypes about high school groups and how does it undermine them? Or why does the film challenge our expectations about romantic comedies by focusing on high school cliques? If you can answer one of those questions (or others of your own), you'll have a strong thesis.

Tip : Asking "how" or "why" questions will help you refine your thesis, making it more arguable and interesting to your readers.

Take 2. You revise the thesis. Is it strong now?

Sixteen Candles is a romantic comedy criticizing the divisiveness created by high school cliques.

You're getting closer. You're starting to take a stance by arguing that the film identifies "divisiveness" as a problem and *criticizes* it, but your readers will want to know how this plays out and why it's important. Right now, the thesis still sounds bland – not risky enough to be genuinely contentious.

Tip: Keep raising questions that test your ideas. And ask yourself the "so what" question. Why is your thesis interesting or important?

Take 3. Let's try again. How about this version?

> Although the film *Sixteen Candles* appears to reinforce stereotypes about high school cliques, it undermines them in important ways, questioning its viewers' assumptions about what's normal.

Bingo! This thesis statement is pretty strong. It challenges an obvious interpretation of the movie (that is just reinforces stereotypes), offering a new and more complex reading in its place. We also have a sense of why this argument is important. The film's larger goal, we learn, is to question what we think we understand about normalcy.

What's a Strong Thesis?

As we've just seen, a strong thesis statement crystallizes your paper's argument and, most importantly, it's *arguable*.

A GOOD SIGN...

This means two things. It goes beyond merely summarizing or describing to stake out an interpretation or position that's not obvious, and others could challenge for good reasons. It's also arguable in the literal sense that it can be *argued*, or supported through a thoughtful analysis of your sources. If your argument lacks evidence, readers will think your thesis statement is an opinion or belief as opposed to an argument.

Exercises for Drafting an Arguable Thesis

A good thesis will be *focused* on your object of study (as opposed to making a big claim about the world) and will introduce the *key words* guiding your analysis.

To get started, you might experiment with some of these "mad libs." They're thinking exercises that will help propel you toward an arguable thesis.

By examining _____ [topic/approach], we can see _____[thesis—the claim that's surprising], which is important because _____.[1]

Example:

"By examining *Sixteen Candles* through the lens of Georg Simmel's writings on fashion, we can see that the protagonist's interest in fashion as an expression of her conflicted desire to be seen as both unique and accepted by the group. This is important because the film offers its viewers a glimpse into the ambivalent yearnings of middle class youth in the 1980s.

Although readers might assume _____ [the commonplace idea you're challenging], I argue that _____ [your surprising claim].

Example:

Although viewers might assume the romantic comedy *Sixteen Candles* is merely entertaining, I believe its message is political. The film uses the romance between Samantha, a middle class sophomore, and Jake, an affluent senior, to reinforce the fantasy that anyone can become wealthy and successful with enough cunning and persistence.

Still Having Trouble? Let's Back Up...

It helps to understand why readers value the arguable thesis. What larger purpose does it serve? Your readers will bring a set of expectations to your essay. The better you can anticipate the expectations of your readers, the better you'll be able to persuade them to entertain seeing things your way.

Academic readers (and readers more generally) read to learn something new. They want to see the writer challenge commonplaces—either everyday assumptions about your object of study or truisms in the scholarly literature. In other words, academic readers want to be surprised so that their thinking shifts or at least becomes more complex by the time they finish reading your essay. Good essays problematize what we think we know and offer an alternative explanation in its place. They leave their reader with a fresh perspective on a problem.

We all bring important past experiences and beliefs to our interpretations of texts, objects, and problems. You can harness these observational powers to engage critically with what you are studying. The key is to be alert to what strikes you as strange, problematic, paradoxical, or puzzling about your object of study. If you can articulate this and a claim in response, you're well on your way to formulating an arguable thesis in your introduction.

How do I set up a "problem" and an arguable thesis in response?

All good writing has a purpose or motive for existing. Your thesis is your surprising response to this problem or motive. This is why it seldom makes sense to start a writing project by articulating the thesis. The first step is to articulate the question or problem your paper addresses.

Here are some possible ways to introduce a conceptual problem in your paper's introduction.

1. Challenge a commonplace interpretation (or your own first impressions).

How are readers likely to interpret this source or issue? What might intelligent readers think at first glance? (Or, if you've been given secondary sources or have been asked to conduct research to locate secondary sources, what do other writers or scholars assume is true or important about your primary source or issue?)

What does this commonplace interpretation leave out, overlook, or under-emphasize?

2. Help your reader see the complexity of your topic.

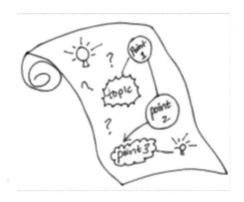

Identify and describe for your reader a paradox, puzzle, or contradiction in your primary source(s).

What larger questions does this paradox or contradiction raise for you and your readers?

3. If your assignment asks you to do research, piggyback off another scholar's research.

Summarize for your reader another scholar's argument about your topic, primary source, or case study and tell your reader why this claim is interesting.

Now explain how you will extend this scholar's argument to explore an issue or case study that the scholar doesn't address fully.

4. If your assignment asks you to do research, identify a gap in another scholar's or a group of scholars' research.

Summarize for your reader another scholar's argument about your topic, primary source, or case study and tell your reader why this claim is interesting. Or, summarize how scholars in the field tend to approach your topic.

Next, explain what important aspect this scholarly representation misses or distorts. Introduce your particular approach to your topic and its value

5. If your assignment asks you to do research, bring in a new lens for investigating your case study or problem.

Summarize for your reader how a scholar or group of scholars has approached your topic.

Introduce a theoretical source (possibly from another discipline) and explain how it helps you address this issue from a new and productive angle.

 Tip: your introductory paragraph will probably look like this:

Testing Your Thesis

You can test your thesis statement's arguability by asking the following questions:

 Does my thesis only or mostly summarize my source?

If so, try some of the exercises above to articulate your paper's conceptual problem or question.

Is my thesis arguable —can it be supported by evidence in my source, and is it surprising and contentious?

If not, return to your sources and practice the exercises above.

Is my thesis about my primary source or case study, or is it about the world?

If it's about the world, revise it so that it focuses on your primary source or case study. Remember you need solid evidence to support your thesis.

"Formulating a Thesis" was written by Andrea Scott, Princeton University

Acknowledgements

I'd like to thank my current and former colleagues in the Princeton Writing Program for helping me think through and test ways of teaching the arguable thesis. Special thanks go to Kerry Walk, Amanda Irwin Wilkins, Judy Swan, and Keith Shaw. A shout-out to Mark Gaipa as well, whose cartoons on teaching source use remain a program favorite.

[1] Adapted from Erik Simpson's "Five Ways of Looking at a Thesis" athttp://www.math.grinnell.edu/~simpsone/Teaching/fiveways.html (http://www.math.grinnell.edu/~simpsone/Teaching/fiveways.html)

5 Ways of Looking at a Thesis

1. A thesis says something a little strange.

Consider the following examples:

> A: By telling the story of Westley and Buttercup's triumph over evil, *The Princess Bride* affirms the power of true love.

> B: Although the main plot of *The Princess Bride* rests on the natural power of true love, an examination of the way that fighting sticks—baseball bats, tree branches, and swords—link the frame story to the romance plot suggests that the grandson is being trained in true love, that love is not natural but socialized.

I would argue that both of these statements are perfectly correct, but they are not both strange. Only the second one says something, well, weird. Weird is good. Sentence A encourages the paper to produce precisely the evidence that *The Princess Bride* presents explicitly; sentence B ensures that the paper will talk about something new.

Romeo and Juliet concerns the dangers of family pride, *Frankenstein* the dangers of taking science too far. Yup. How can you make those things unusual? Good papers go out on a limb. They avoid ugly falls by reinforcing the limb with carefully chosen evidence and rigorous argumentation.

2. A thesis creates an argument that builds from one point to the next, giving the paper a direction that your reader can follow as the paper develops.

This point often separates the best theses from the pack. A good thesis can prevent the two weakest ways of organizing a critical paper: the pile of information and the plot summary with comments. A paper that presents a pile of information will frequently introduce new paragraphs with transitions that simply indicate the addition of more stuff. ("Another character who exhibits these traits is X," for instance.) Consider these examples:

> A: The Rules and Jane Austen's Northanger Abbey both tell women how to act.

> B: By looking at The Rules, a modern conduct book for women, we can see how Jane Austen's Northanger Abbey is itself like a conduct book, questioning the rules for social success in her society and offering a new model.

Example A would almost inevitably lead to a paper organized as a pile of information. A plot summary with comments follows the chronological development of a text while picking out the same element of every segment; a transition in such a paper might read, "In the next scene, the color blue also figures prominently." Both of these approaches constitute too much of a good thing. Papers must compile evidence, of course, and following the chronology of a text can sometimes help a reader keep track of a paper's argument. The best papers, however, will develop according to a more complex logic articulated in a strong thesis. Example B above would lead a paper to organize its evidence according to the paper's own logic.

3. A thesis fits comfortably into the Magic Thesis Sentence (MTS).

The MTS: By looking at _____, we can see _____, which most readers don't see; it is important to look at this aspect of the text because _____.

Try it out with the examples from the first point:

A: By telling the story of Westley and Buttercup's triumph over evil, The Princess Bride affirms the power of true love.

B: Although the main plot of The Princess Bride rests on the natural power of true love, an examination of the way that fighting sticks—baseball bats, tree branches, and swords—link the frame story to the romance plot suggests that the grandson is being trained in true love, that love is not natural but socialized.

Notice that the MTS adds a new dimension to point number one above. The first part of the MTS asks you to find something strange ("which most readers don't see"), and the second part asks you to think about the importance of the strangeness. Thesis A would not work at all in the MTS; one could not reasonably state that "most readers [or viewers] don't see" that film's affirmation of true love, and the statement does not even attempt to explain the importance of its claim. Thesis B, on the other hand, gives us a way to complete the MTS, as in "By looking at the way fighting sticks link the plot and frame of *The Princess Bride*, we can see the way the grandson is trained in true love, which most people don't see; it is important to look at this aspect of the text because unlike the rest of the film, the fighting sticks suggest that love is not natural but socialized." One does not need to write out the MTS in such a neat one-sentence form, of course, but thinking through the structure of the MTS can help refine thesis ideas.

4. A thesis says something about the text(s) you discuss *exclusively*.

If your thesis could describe many works equally well, it needs to be more specific. Let's return to our examples from above.

> A: By telling the story of Westley and Buttercup's triumph over evil, *The Princess Bride* affirms the power of true love.

> B: Although the main plot of *The Princess Bride* rests on the natural power of true love, an examination of the way that fighting sticks—baseball bats, tree branches, and swords—link the frame story to the romance plot suggests that the grandson is being trained in true love, that love is not natural but socialized.

Try substituting other works:

> A: By telling the story of Darcy and Elizabeth's triumph over evil, *Pride and Prejudice* affirms the power of true love.

Sure, that makes sense. Bad sign.

> B: Although the main plot of *Pride and Prejudice* rests on the natural power of true love, an examination of the way that fighting sticks—baseball bats, tree branches, and swords—link the frame story to the romance plot suggests that the grandson is being trained in true love, that it is not natural but socialized.

Um, nope. Even if you have never read *Pride and Prejudice*, you can probably guess that such a precise thesis could hardly apply to other works. Good sign.

5. A thesis makes a lot of information irrelevant.

If your thesis is specific enough, it will make a point that focuses on only a small part of the text you are analyzing. You can and should ultimately apply that point to the work as a whole, but a thesis will call attention to specific parts of it. Let's look at those examples again. (This is the last time, I promise.)

> A: By telling the story of Westley and Buttercup's triumph over evil, *The Princess Bride* affirms the power of true love.

> B: Although the main plot of *The Princess Bride* rests on the natural power of true love, an examination of the way that fighting sticks—baseball bats, tree branches, and swords—link the frame story to the romance plot suggests that the grandson is being trained in true love, that love is not natural but socialized.

One way of spotting the problem with example A is to note that a simple plot summary would support its point. That is not of true example B, which tells the reader exactly what moments the paper will discuss and why.

If you find that your paper leads you to mark relevant passages on virtually every page of a long work, you need to find a thesis that helps you focus on a smaller portion of the text. As the MTS reminds us, the paper should still strive to show the reader something new about the text as a whole, but a specific area of concentration will help, not hinder, that effort.

Process: Writing a Thesis Statement

Thesis statements are easy to construct if you: 1. can condense your secondary sources—that you've read and understood—into a "main idea and argument" grid (explained below); and 2. answer a framework of organizational questions (also below). These two steps can help to ensure that your thesis simultaneously situates an idea within a particular "conversation" and specifies a unique perspective/makes a new argument/contribution to the conversation.

1. Condensing secondary sources:

> a. Include some brief information each of your secondary sources (books, journal articles, etc.) on a grid so that you can organize the authors' main ideas and perspectives in one space. For instance,

Author	Main Idea	Argument
Jones	Climate change policy	Climate change policy is at a standstill because the government is concerned about economic growth
Smith	Climate change policy	Climate change policy ought to be communicated as an ethical imperative because that will motivate the public to respond
Taylor	Climate change policy	Climate change policy needs to be communicated to the public by interdisciplinary teams of academics and politicians

> b. Once you've created an organizational table, you'll want to examine it for commonalities/linkages among the authors' ideas and arguments. In the example above, all authors have written about climate change policy, so now you know that you'll need to include something like this phrase, "climate change policy," in your thesis statement. Regarding the authors' arguments, Jones argues about how climate change policy is affected by the government's concern with economic growth; Smith argues that it needs to be communicated as an ethical imperative; and Taylor argues that it needs to be communicated by interdisciplinary teams.

> c. Given this information, the first half of your thesis – which explains the specific topic – needs to explain to the audience/reader that you are writing specifically about climate change policy. The second half of your thesis – which contextualizes the argument – needs to explain to the audience/reader your interpretation of these authors' arguments. For instance, you may choose to argue that:

>> i.climate change policy regarding the effect of government policies about economic growth is the greater imperative for accomplishing more effective climate change policies in the U.S.

>> ii.ethical imperatives are the motivating factor for encouraging the public to respond – causing academic institutions to work with government officials/decision-makers in responding to the public's opinion/support of climate change policy as an ethical concern

> d. The examples above are hypothetical; and only two of the many, creative possibilities for interpreting an *argument* out of a specific *topic*. Whereas an argument seeks to persuade an audience/reader about a way of interpreting others' information, a topic simply describes how to categorize/identify where the argument "fits" (i.e. which generalized group of people would be concerned with reading your writing)

e. Hint: oftentimes, the authors of academic journal articles conclude their arguments by suggesting potential research questions that they believe ought to be addressed in future scholarship. These suggestions can potentially provide some really excellent information about how to begin articulating a unique argument about a specific topic.

CC licensed content, Shared previously

Assessment: Topic and Working Thesis

Time to commit! By now you've explored several ideas, and probably ruled out a few easily. Now, though, I'm asking you to pick one particular topic to use for the final research essay project. You can change your mind later, if you'd like—but will have to get permission from me to do so.

For this assignment, I'd like you to do the following:

- Identify which particular topic you've decided on
- Describe a specific controversy that exists within this topic. Identify what the sides are (and there may be more than just 2 sides), and why each believes what it does.
- Define what side you agree with, and why.
- State the overall claim that you want your essay to prove beyond a shadow of a doubt. (This will be your working thesis, and it's welcome to change as you progress in later weeks. It's okay to start simple, for now, and build in more complexity later. I suggest looking at the Thesis statement websites in this module to get started).

A (Silly) Sample:

I have decided to focus on Cheezits for my research project. There are a number of serious controversies when the matter of cheese-flavored snack crackers is discussed, but I'd like to focus specifically on how they compare with their primary rival, Cheese Nips. Supporters of Cheese Nips believe their product to be superior because of the flavor, nutritional value, and cost; supporters of Cheezits use the same criteria to claim the better product. I personally find Cheezits to be preferable in every way, but primarily when it comes to taste. Cheese Nips taste oily to me, and leave a bad taste on my tongue, while the taste and texture of Cheezits is a perfect consistency.

Cheezits are a better food product than Cheese Nips.

Assessment: Reading Notebook Entry #2

Now that you've got an initial topic and viewpoint in mind, find ONE source that gives you helpful information about this topic. This source can come from anywhere, be any length, and can be the same source you consulted for the 3 Research Topic Ideas (https://courses.candelalearning.com/ englishcomp2kscopexmaster/chapter/assessment-3-research-topic-ideas/) task earlier, if you'd like.

Create an entry for your Reading Notebook that includes any or all of the following:

- questions you had while reading
- emotional reactions to the text
- key terms that seem important to you
- what you think the thesis or main idea of this source is
- what you think the intended audience for this source is
- how effective you think this source is
- anything else that comes to mind

This is an informal assignment. Your writing can be in complete sentences, or bullet points or fragments, as you see appropriate. Editing isn't vital for this work, though it should be proofread to the point that obvious typos or misspellings are addressed and corrected. Target word count is 150-300 words for this entry.

Please do include the web link URL to the source you've chosen. You do not have to cite it with MLA or APA citation, though you are welcome to if you want the practice.

Though it isn't mandatory that this reading notebook entry be about the same source you choose for the Source Evaluation Essay, you may find it very useful later on if it is.

CAUSAL ARGUMENTS

How to Write a Summary

Summarizing consists of two important skills:

1. identifying the important material in the text, and
2. restating the text in your own words.

Since writing a summary consists of omitting minor information, it will always be shorter than the original text.

How to Write a Summary

- A summary begins with an *introductory sentence* that states the text's title, author and main thesis or subject.
- A summary contains the main *thesis* (or main point of the text), restated in your own words.
- A summary is *written in your own words*. It contains few or no quotes.
- A summary is *always shorter than the original text*, often about 1/3 as long as the original. It is the ultimate "fat-free" writing. An article or paper may be summarized in a few sentences or a couple of paragraphs. A book may be summarized in an article or a short paper. A very large book may be summarized in a smaller book.
- A summary should *contain all the major points* of the original text, but should *ignore most of the fine details*, examples, illustrations or explanations.
- The backbone of any summary is formed by *critical information* (key names, dates, places, ideas, events, words and numbers). A summary must never rely on vague generalities.
- If you quote anything from the original text, even an unusual word or a catchy phrase, you need to put whatever you quote in quotation marks ("").
- A summary must contain only the ideas of the original text. *Do not insert* any of *your own opinions, interpretations, deductions or comments* into a summary.
- A summary, like any other writing, has to have a specific audience and purpose, and you must carefully write it to serve that audience and fulfill that specific purpose.

Research and Critical Reading

Introduction

Good researchers and writers examine their sources critically and actively. They do not just compile and summarize these research sources in their writing, but use them to create their own ideas, theories, and, ultimately, their own, new understanding of the topic they are researching. Such an approach means not taking the information and opinions that the sources contain at face value and for granted, but to investigate, test, and even doubt every claim, every example, every story, and every conclusion. It means not to sit back and let your sources control you, but to engage in active conversation with them and their authors. In order to be a good researcher and writer, one needs to be a critical and active reader.

This chapter is about the importance of critical and active reading. It is also about the connection between critical reading and active, strong writing. Much of the discussion you will find in this chapter in fundamental to research and writing, no matter what writing genre, medium, or academic discipline you read and write in. Every other approach to research writing, every other research method and assignment offered elsewhere in this book is, in some way, based upon the principles discussed in this chapter.

Reading is at the heart of the research process. No matter what kinds of research sources and, methods you use, you are always reading and interpreting text. Most of us are used to hearing the word "reading" in relation to secondary sources, such as books, journals, magazines, websites, and so on. But even if you are using other research methods and sources, such as interviewing someone or surveying a group of people, you are reading. You are reading their subjects" ideas and views on the topic you are investigating. Even if you are studying photographs, cultural artifacts, and other non-verbal research sources, you are reading them, too by trying to connect them to their cultural and social contexts and to understand their meaning. Principles of critical reading which we are about to discuss in this chapter apply to those research situations as well.

I like to think about reading and writing as not two separate activities but as two tightly connected parts of the same whole. That whole is the process of learning and making of new meaning. It may seem that reading and writing are complete opposite of one another. According to the popular view, when we read, we "consume" texts, and when we write, we "produce" texts. But this view of reading and writing is true only if you see reading as a passive process of taking in information from the text and not as an active and energetic process of making new meaning and new knowledge. Similarly, good writing does not come from nowhere but is usually based upon, or at least influenced by ideas, theories, and stories that come from reading. So, if, as a college student, you have ever wondered why your writing teachers have asked you to read books and articles and write responses to them, it is because writers who do not read and do not actively engage with their reading, have little to say to others.

We will begin this chapter with the definition of the term "critical reading." We will consider its main characteristics and briefly touch upon ways to become an active and critical reader. Next, we will discuss the importance of critical reading for research and how reading critically can help you become a better researcher and make the research process more enjoyable. Also in this chapter, a student-writer offers us an insight into his critical reading and writing processes. This chapter also shows how critical reading can and should be used for critical and strong writing. And, as all other chapters, this one offers you activities and projects designed to help you implement the advice presented here into practice.

What Kind of Reader Are You?

You read a lot, probably more that you think. You read school textbooks, lecture notes, your classmates' papers, and class websites. When school ends, you probably read some fiction, magazines. But you also read other texts. These may include CD liner notes, product reviews, grocery lists, maps, driving directions, road signs, and the list can go on and on. And you don't read all these texts in the same way. You read them with different purposes and using different reading strategies and techniques. The first step towards becoming a critical and active reader is examining your reading process and your reading preferences. Therefore, you are invited to complete the following exploration activity.

WRITING ACTIVITY: ANALYZING YOUR READING HABITS

List all the reading you have done in the last week. Include both "school" and "out-of school" reading. Try to list as many texts as you can think of, no matter how short and unimportant they might seem. Now, answer the following questions.

- What was your purpose in reading each of those texts? Did you read for information, to pass a test, for enjoyment, to decide on a product you wanted to buy, and so on? Or, did you read to figure out some complex problem that keeps you awake at night?
- You have probably come up with a list of different purposes. How did each of those purposes influence your reading strategies? Did you take notes or try to memorize what you read? How long did it take you to read different texts? Did you begin at the beginning and read till you reached the end, or did you browse some texts? Consider the time of day you were reading. Consider even whether some texts tired you out or whether you thought they were "boring." Why?
- What did you do with the results of your reading? Did you use them for some practical purpose, such as buying a new product or finding directions, or did you use them for a less practical purpose, such as understanding some topic better or learning something about yourself and others?

When you finish, share your results with the rest of the class and with your instructor.

Having answered the questions above, you have probably noticed that your reading strategies differed depending on the reading task you were facing and on what you planned to do with the results of the reading. If, for example, you read lecture notes in order to pass a test, chances are you "read for information," or "for the main" point, trying to remember as much material as possible and anticipating possible test questions. If, on the other hand, you read a good novel, you probably just focused on following the story. Finally, if you were reading something that you hoped would help you answer some personal question or solve some personal problem, it is likely that you kept comparing and contrasting the information that you read your own life and your own experiences.

You may have spent more time on some reading tasks than others. For example, when we are interested in one particular piece of information or fact from a text, we usually put that text aside once we have located the information we were looking for. In other cases, you may have been reading for hours on end taking careful notes and asking questions.

If you share the results of your investigation into your reading habits with your classmates, you may also notice that some of their reading habits and strategies were different from yours. Like writing strategies, approaches to reading may vary from person to person depending on our previous experiences with different topics and types of reading materials, expectations we have of different texts, and, of course, the purpose with which we are reading.

Life presents us with a variety of reading situations which demand different reading strategies and techniques. Sometimes, it is important to be as efficient as possible and read purely for information or "the main point." At other times, it is important to just "let go" and turn the pages following a good story, although this means not thinking about the story you are reading. At the heart of writing and research, however, lies the kind of reading known as critical reading. Critical examination of sources is what makes their use in research possible and what allows writers to create rhetorically effective and engaging texts.

Key Features of Critical Reading

Critical readers are able to interact with the texts they read through carefully listening, writing, conversation, and questioning. They do not sit back and wait for the meaning of a text to come to them, but work hard in order to create such meaning. Critical readers are not made overnight. Becoming a critical reader will take a lot of practice and patience. Depending on your current reading philosophy and experiences with reading, becoming a critical reader may require a significant change in your whole understanding of the reading process. The trade-off is worth it, however. By becoming a more critical and active reader, you will also become a better researcher and a better writer. Last but not least, you will enjoy reading and writing a whole lot more because you will become actively engaged in both.

One of my favorite passages describing the substance of critical and active reading comes from the introduction to their book *Ways of Reading* whose authors David Bartholomae and Anthony Petrosky write:

"

Reading involves a fair measure of push and shove. You make your mark on the book and it makes its mark on you. Reading is not simply a matter of hanging back and waiting for a piece, or its author, to tell you what the writing has to say. In fact, one of the difficult things about reading is that the pages before you will begin to speak only when the authors are silent and you begin to speak in their place, sometimes for them—doing their work, continuing their projects—and sometimes for yourself, following your own agenda (1).

Notice that Bartholomae and Petrosky describe reading process in pro-active terms. Meaning of every text is "made," not received. Readers need to "push and shove" in order to create their own, unique content of every text they read. It is up the you as a reader to make the pages in front of you "speak" by talking with and against the text, by questioning and expanding it.

Critical reading, then, is a two-way process. As reader, you are not a consumer of words, waiting patiently for ideas from the printed page or a web-site to fill your head and make you smarter. Instead, as a critical reader, you need to interact with what you read, asking questions of the author, testing every assertion, fact, or idea, and extending the text by adding your own understanding of the subject and your own personal experiences to your reading.

The following are key features of the critical approach to reading:

- No text, however well written and authoritative, contains its own, pre-determined meaning.
- Readers must work hard to create meaning from every text.
- Critical readers interact with the texts they read by questioning them, responding to them, and expanding them, usually in writing.
- To create meaning, critical readers use a variety of approaches, strategies, and techniques which include applying their personal experiences and existing knowledge to the reading process.
- Critical readers seek actively out other texts, related to the topic of their investigation.

The following section is an examination of these claims about critical reading in more detail.

Texts Present Ideas, Not Absolute Truths

In order to understand the mechanisms and intellectual challenges of critical reading, we need to examine some of our deepest and long-lasting assumptions about reading. Perhaps the two most significant challenges facing anyone who wants to become a more active and analytical reader is understanding that printed texts doe not contain inarguable truths and learning to questions and talk back to those texts. Students in my writing classes often tell me that the biggest challenge they face in trying to become critical readers is getting away from the idea that they have to believe everything they read on a printed page. Years of schooling have taught many of us to believe that published texts present inarguable, almost absolute truths. The printed page has authority because, before publishing his or her work, every writer goes through a lengthy process of approval, review, revision, fact-checking, and so on. Consequently, this theory goes, what gets published must be true. And if it is true, it must be taken at face value, not questioned, challenged, or extended in any way.

Perhaps, the ultimate authority among the readings materials encountered by college belongs to the textbook. As students, we all have had to read and almost memorize textbook chapters in order to pass an exam. We read textbooks "for information," summarizing their chapters, trying to find "the main points" and then reproducing these main points during exams. I have nothing against textbook as such, in fact, I am writing one right now. And it is certainly possible to read textbooks critically and actively. But, as I think about the challenges which many college students face trying to become active and critical readers, I come to the conclusion that the habit to read every text as if they were preparing for an exam on it, as if it was a source of unquestionable truth and knowledge prevents many from becoming active readers.

Treating texts as if they were sources of ultimate and unquestionable knowledge and truth represents the view of reading as consumption. According to this view, writers produce ideas and knowledge, and we, readers, consume them. Of course, sometimes we have to assume this stance and read for information or the "main point" of a text. But it is critical reading that allows us to create new ideas from what we read and to become independent and creative learners.

Critical reading is a collaboration between the reader and the writer. It offers readers the ability to be active participants in the construction of meaning of every text they read and to use that meaning for their own learning and self-fulfillment. Not even the best researched and written text is absolutely complete and finished. Granted, most fields of knowledge have texts which are called "definitive." Such texts usually represent our best current knowledge on their subjects. However, even the definitive works get revised over time and they are always open to questioning and different interpretations.

Reading is a Rhetorical Tool

To understand how the claim that every reader makes his or her meaning from texts works, it is necessary to examine what is know as the rhetorical theory of reading. The work that best describes and justifies the rhetorical reading theory is Douglas Brent"s 1992 book Reading as Rhetorical Invention: Knowledge, Persuasion, and the Teaching of Research-Based Writing. I like to apply Brent"s ideas to my discussions of critical reading because I think that they do a good job demystifying critical reading"s main claims. Brent"s theory of reading is a rhetorical device puts significant substance behind the somewhat abstract ideas of active and critical reading, explaining how the mechanisms of active interaction between readers and texts actually work.

Briefly explained, Brent treats reading not only as a vehicle for transmitting information and knowledge, but also as a means of persuasion. In fact, according to Brent, knowledge equals persuasion because, in his words, "Knowledge is not simply what one has been told. Knowledge is what one believes, what one accepts as being at least provisionally true." (xi). This short passage contains two assertions which are key to the understanding of mechanisms of critical reading. Firstly, notice that simply reading "for the main point" will not necessarily make you "believe" what you read. Surely, such reading can fill our heads with information, but will that information become our knowledge in a true sense, will we be persuaded by it, or will we simply memorize it to pass the test and forget it as soon as we pass it? Of course not! All of us can probably recall many instances in which we read a lot to pass a test only to forget, with relief, what we read as soon as we left the classroom where that test was held. The purpose of reading and research, then, is not to get as much as information out of a text as possible but to change and update one"s system of beliefs on a given subject (Brent 55-57).

Brent further states. "The way we believe or disbelieve certain texts clearly varies from one individual to the next. If you present a text that is remotely controversial to a group of people, some will be convinced by it and some not, and those who are convinced will be convinced in different degrees. The task of a rhetoric of reading is to explain systematically how these differences arise— how people are persuaded differently by texts" (18).

Critical and active readers not only accept the possibility that the same texts will have different meanings for different people, but welcome this possibility as an inherent and indispensable feature of strong, engaged, and enjoyable reading process. To answer his own questions about what factors contribute to different readers" different interpretations of the same texts, Brent offers us the following principles that I have summarized from his book:

- Readers are guided by personal beliefs, assumptions, and pre-existing knowledge when interpreting texts. You can read more on the role of the reader"s pre-existing knowledge in the construction of meaning later on in this chapter.
- Readers react differently to the logical proofs presented by the writers of texts.
- Readers react differently to emotional and ethical proofs presented by writers. For example, an emotional story told by a writer may resonate with one person more than with another because the first person lived through a similar experience and the second one did not, and so on.

The idea behind the rhetorical theory of reading is that when we read, we not only take in ideas, information, and facts, but instead we "update our view of the world." You cannot force someone to update their worldview, and therefore, the purpose of writing is persuasion and the purpose of reading is being persuaded. Persuasion is possible only when the reader is actively engaged with the text and understands that much more than simple retrieval of information is at stake when reading.

One of the primary factors that influence our decision to accept or not to accept an argument is what Douglas Brent calls our "repertoire of experience, much of [which] is gained through prior interaction with texts" (56). What this means is that when we read a new text, we do not begin with a clean slate, an empty mind. However unfamiliar the topic of this new reading may seem to us, we approach it with a large baggage of previous knowledge, experiences, points of view, and so on. When an argument "comes in" into our minds from a text, this text, by itself, cannot change our view on the subject. Our prior opinions and knowledge about the topic of the text we are reading will necessarily "filter out" what is incompatible with those views (Brent 56-57). This, of course, does not mean that, as readers, we should persist in keeping our old ideas about everything and actively resist learning new things. Rather, it suggests that the reading process is an interaction between the ideas in the text in front of us and our own ideas and pre-conceptions about the subject of our reading. We do not always consciously measure what we read according to our existing systems of knowledge and beliefs, but we measure it nevertheless. Reading, according to Brent, is judgment, and, like in life where we do not always consciously examine and analyze the reasons for which we make various decisions, evaluating a text often happens automatically or subconsciously (59).

Applied to research writing, Brent''s theory or reading means the following:

- The purpose of research is not simply to retrieve data, but to participate in a conversation about it. Simple summaries of sources is not research, and writers should be aiming for active interpretation of sources instead
- There is no such thing as an unbiased source. Writers make claims for personal reasons that critical readers need to learn to understand and evaluate.
- Feelings can be a source of shareable good reason for belief. Readers and writers need to use, judiciously, ethical and pathetic proofs in interpreting texts and in creating their own.
- Research is recursive. Critical readers and researchers never stop asking questions about their topic and never consider their research finished.

Active Readers Look for Connections Between Texts

Earlier on, I mentioned that one of the traits of active readers is their willingness to seek out other texts and people who may be able to help them in their research and learning. I find that for many beginning researchers and writers, the inability to seek out such connections often turns into a roadblock on their research route. Here is what I am talking about.

Recently, I asked my writing students to investigate some problem on campus and to propose a solution to it. I asked them to use both primary (interviews, surveys, etc.) and secondary (library, Internet, etc.) research. Conducting secondary research allows a writer to connect a local problem he or she is investigating and a local solution he or she is proposing with a national and even global context, and to see whether the local situation is typical or a-typical.

One group of students decided to investigate the issue of racial and ethnic diversity on our campus. The lack of diversity is a "hot" issue on our campus, and recently an institutional task force was created to investigate possible ways of making our university more diverse.

The students had no trouble designing research questions and finding people to interview and survey. Their subjects included students and faculty as well as the university vice-president who was changed with overseeing the work of the diversity task force. Overall, these authors have little trouble conducting and interpreting primary research that led them to conclude that, indeed, our campus is not diverse enough and that most students would like to see the situation change.

The next step these writers took was to look at the websites of some other schools similar in size and nature to ours, to see how our university compared on the issue of campus diversity with others. They were able to find some statistics on the numbers of minorities at other colleges and universities that allowed them to create a certain backdrop for their primary research that they had conducted earlier.

But good writing goes beyond the local situation. Good writing tries to connect the local and the national and the global. It tries to look beyond the surface of the problem, beyond simply comparing numbers and other statistics. It seeks to understand the roots of a problem and propose a solution based on a local and well as a global situation and research. The primary and secondary research conducted by these students was not allowing them to make that step from analyzing local data to understanding their problem in context. They needed some other type of research sources.

At that point, however, those writers hit an obstacle. How and where, they reasoned, would we find other secondary sources, such as books, journals, and websites, about the lack of diversity on our campus? The answer to that question was that, at this stage in their research and writing, they did not need to look for more sources about our local problem with the lack of diversity. They needed to look at diversity and ways to increase it as a national and global issue. They needed to generalize the problem and, instead of looking at a local example, to consider its implications for the issue they were studying overall. Such research would not only have allowed these writers to examine the problem as a whole but also to see how it was being solved in other places. This, in turn, might have helped them to propose a local solution.

Critical readers and researchers understand that it is not enough to look at the research question locally or narrowly. After conducting research and understanding their problem locally, or as it applies specifically to them, active researchers contextualize their investigation by seeking out texts and other sources which would allow them to see the big picture.

Sometimes, it is hard to understand how external texts which do not seem to talk directly about you can help you research and write about questions, problems, and issues in your own life. In her 2004 essay, "Developing 'Interesting Thoughts': Reading for Research," writing teacher my former colleague Janette Martin tells a story of a student who was writing a paper about what it is like to be a collegiate athlete. The emerging theme in that paper was that of discipline and sacrifice required of student athletes. Simultaneously, that student was reading a chapter from the book by the French philosopher Michel Foucault called Discipline and Punish. Foucault"s work is a study of the western penitentiary system, which, of course cannot be directly compared to experiences of a student athlete. At the same time, one of the leading themes in Foucault"s work is discipline. Martin states that the student was able to see some connection between Foucault and her own life and use the reading for her research and writing (6). In addition to showing how related texts can be used to explore various aspects of the writer"s own life, this example highlights the need to read texts critically and interpret them creatively. Such reading and research goes beyond simply comparing of facts and numbers and towards relating ideas and concepts with one another.

From Reading to Writing

Reading and writing are the two essential tools of learning. Critical reading is not a process of passive consumption, but one of interaction and engagement between the reader and the text. Therefore, when reading critically and actively, it is important not only to take in the words on the page, but also to interpret and to reflect upon what you read through writing and discussing it with others.

Critical Readers Understand the Difference Between Reacting and Responding to A Text

As stated earlier in this chapter, actively responding to difficult texts, posing questions, and analyzing ideas presented in them is the key to successful reading. The goal of an active reader is to engage in a conversation with the text he or she is reading. In order to fulfill this goal, it is important to understand the difference between reacting to the text and responding to it.

Reacting to a text is often done on an emotional, rather than on an intellectual level. It is quick and shallow. For example, if we encounter a text that advances arguments with which we strongly disagree, it is natural to dismiss those ideas out of hand as not wrong and not worthy of our attention. Doing so would be reacting to the text based only on emotions and on our pre-set opinions about its arguments. It is easy to see that reacting in this way does not take the reader any closer to understanding the text. A wall of disagreement that existed between the reader and the text before the reading continues to exist after the reading.

Responding to a text, on the other hand, requires a careful study of the ideas presented and arguments advanced in it. Critical readers who possess this skill are not willing to simply reject or accept the arguments presented in the text after the first reading right away. To continue with our example from the preceding paragraph, a reader who responds to a controversial text rather than reacting to it might apply several of the following strategies before forming and expressing an opinion about that text.

Read the text several times, taking notes, asking questions, and underlining key places.

- Study why the author of the text advances ideas, arguments, and convictions, so different from the reader's own. For example, is the text's author advancing an agenda of some social, political, religious, or economic group of which he or she is a member?
- Study the purpose and the intended audience of the text.
- Study the history of the argument presented in the text as much as possible. For example, modern texts on highly controversial issues such as the death penalty, abortion, or euthanasia often use past events, court cases, and other evidence to advance their claims. Knowing the history of the problem will help you to construct meaning of a difficult text.
- Study the social, political, and intellectual context in which the text was written. Good writers use social conditions to advance controversial ideas. Compare the context in which the text was written to the one in which it is read. For example, have social conditions changed, thus invalidating the argument or making it stronger?
- Consider the author's (and your own) previous knowledge of the issue at the center of the text and your experiences with it. How might such knowledge or experience have influenced your reception of the argument?

Taking all these steps will help you to move away from simply reacting to a text and towards constructing informed and critical response to it.

To better understand the key differences between reacting and responding and between binary and nuanced reading, consider the table below.

Reacting to Texts	Responding to Texts
• Works on an emotional level rather than an intellectual level • Prevents readers from studying purposes, intended audiences, and contexts of texts they are working with • Fails to establish dialog between the reader and the text by locking the reader in his or her pre-existing opinion about the argument	• Works on an intellectual and emotional level by asking the readers to use all three rhetorical appeals in reading and writing about the text • Allows for careful study of the text's rhetorical aspects • Establishes dialog among the reader, text, and other readers by allowing all sides to reconsider existing positions and opinions
Binary Reading	Nuanced Reading
• Provides only "agree or disagree" answers • Does not allow for an understanding of complex arguments • Prevents the reader from a true rhetorical engagement with the text	• Allows for a deep and detailed understanding of complex texts • Takes into account "gray areas" of complex arguments • Establishes rhetorical engagement between the reader and the text

Critical Readers Resist Oversimplified Binary Responses

Critical readers learn to avoid simple "agree-disagree" responses to complex texts. Such way of thinking and arguing is often called "binary" because is allows only two answers to every statement and every questions. But the world of ideas is complex and, a much more nuanced approach is needed when dealing with complex arguments.

When you are asked to "critique" a text, which readers are often asked to do, it does not mean that you have to "criticize" it and reject its argument out of hand. What you are being asked to do instead is to carefully evaluate and analyze the text"s ideas, to understand how and why they are constructed and presented, and only then develop a response to that text. Not every text asks for an outright agreement or disagreement. Sometimes, we as readers are not in a position to either simply support an argument or reject it. What we can do in such cases, though, is to learn more about the text"s arguments by carefully considering all of their aspects and to construct a nuanced, sophisticated response to them. After you have done all that, it will still be possible to disagree with the arguments presented in the reading, but your opinion about the text will be much more informed and nuanced than if you have taken the binary approach from the start.

Two Sample Student Responses

To illustrate the principles laid out in this section, consider the following two reading responses. Both texts respond to a very well known piece, "A Letter from Birmingham Jail," by Martin Luther King, Jr. In the letter, King responds to criticism from other clergymen who had called his methods of civil rights struggle "unwise and untimely." Both student writers were given the same response prompt:

> "After reading King's piece several times and with a pen or pencil in hand, consider what shapes King"s letter. Specifically, what rhetorical strategies is he using to achieve a persuasive effect on his readers? In making your decisions, consider such factors as background information that he gives, ways in which he addresses his immediate audience, and others. Remember that your goal is to explore King"s text, thus enabling you to understand his rhetorical strategies better."

Student "A"

Martin Luther King Jr's "Letter from Birmingham Jail" is a very powerful text. At the time when minorities in America were silenced and persecuted, King had the courage to lead his people in the struggle for equality. After being jailed in Birmingham, Alabama, King wrote a letter to his "fellow clergymen" describing his struggle for civil rights. In the letter, King recounts a brief history of that struggle and rejects the accusation that it is "unwise and untimely." Overall, I think that King's letter is a very rhetorically effective text, one that greatly helped Americans to understand the civil rights movement.

Student "B"

King begins his "Letter from Birmingham Jail" by addressing it to his "fellow clergymen." Thus, he immediately sets the tone of inclusion rather than exclusion. By using the word "fellow" in the address, I think he is trying to do two things. First of all, he presents himself as a colleague and a spiritual brother of his audience. That, in effect, says "you can trust me," "I am one of your kind." Secondly, by addressing his readers in that way, King suggests that everyone, even those Americans who are not directly involved in the struggle for civil rights, should be concerned with it. Hence the word "fellow." King's opening almost invokes the phrase "My fellow Americans" or "My fellow citizens" used so often by American Presidents when they address the nation.

King then proceeds to give a brief background of his actions as a civil rights leader. As I read this part of the letter, I was wondering whether his readers would really have not known what he had accomplished as a civil rights leader. Then I realized that perhaps he gives all that background information as a rhetorical move. His immediate goal is to keep reminding his readers about his activities. His ultimate goal is to show to his audience that his actions were non-violent but peaceful. In reading this passage by King, I remembered once again that it is important not to assume that your audience knows anything about the subject of the writing. I will try to use this strategy more in my own papers.

In the middle of the letter, King states: "The purpose of our direct-action program is to create a situation so crisis-packed that it will inevitably open the door to negotiation." This sentence looks like a thesis statement and I wonder why he did not place it towards the beginning of the text, to get his point across right away. After thinking about this for a few minutes and rereading several pages from our class textbook, I think he leaves his "thesis" till later in his piece because he is facing a notso-friendly (if not hostile) audience. Delaying the thesis and laying out some background information and evidence first helps a writer to prepare his or her audience for the coming argument. That is another strategy I should probably use more often in my own writing, depending on the audience I am facing.

Reflecting on the Responses

To be sure, much more can be said about King''s letter than either of these writers have said. However, these two responses allow us to see two dramatically different approaches to reading. After studying both responses, consider the questions below.

- Which response fulfills the goals set in the prompt better and why?
- Which responses shows a deeper understanding of the texts by the reader and why?
- Which writer does a better job at avoiding binary thinking and creating a sophisticated reading of King''s text and why?
- Which writer is more likely to use the results of the reading in his or her own writing in the future and why?
- Which writer leaves room for response to his text by others and why?

Critical Readers Do not Read Alone and in Silence

One of the key principles of critical reading is that active readers do not read silently and by themselves. By this I mean that they take notes and write about what they read. They also discuss the texts they are working with, with others and compare their own interpretations of those texts with the interpretations constructed by their colleagues.

As a college student, you are probably used to taking notes of what you read. When I was in college, my favorite way of preparing for a test was reading a chapter or two from my textbook, then closing the book, then trying to summarize what I have read on a piece of paper. I tried to get the main points of the chapters down and the explanations and proofs that the textbooks" authors used. Sometimes, I wrote a summary of every chapter in the textbook and then studied for the test from those summaries rather than from the textbook itself. I am sure you have favorite methods of note taking and studying from your notes, too.

But now it strikes me that what I did with those notes was not critical reading. I simply summarized my textbooks in a more concise, manageable form and then tried to memorize those summaries before the test. I did not take my reading of the textbooks any further than what was already on their pages. Reading for information and trying to extract the main points, I did not talk back to the texts, did not question them, and did not try to extend the knowledge which they offered in any way. I also did not try to connect my reading with my personal experiences or pre-existing knowledge in any way. I also read in silence, without exchanging ideas with other readers of the same texts. Of course, my reading strategies and techniques were dictated by my goal, which was to pass the test.

Critical reading has other goals, one of which is entering an on-going intellectual exchange. Therefore it demands different reading strategies, approaches, and techniques. One of these new approaches is not reading in silence and alone. Instead, critical readers read with a pen or pencil in hand. They also discuss what they read with others.

Strategies for Connecting Reading and Writing

If you want to become a critical reader, you need to get into a habit of writing as you read. You also need to understand that complex texts cannot be read just once. Instead, they require multiple readings, the first of which may be a more general one during which you get acquainted with the ideas presented in the text, its structure and style. During the second and any subsequent readings, however, you will need to write, and write a lot. The following are some critical reading and writing techniques which active readers employ as they work to create meanings from texts they read.

Underline Interesting and Important Places in the Text

Underline words, sentences, and passages that stand out, for whatever reason. Underline the key arguments that you believe the author of the text is making as well as any evidence, examples, and stories that seem interesting or important. Don"t be afraid to "get it wrong." There is no right or wrong here. The places in the text that you underline may be the same or different from those noticed by your classmates, and this difference of interpretation is the essence of critical reading.

Take Notes

Take notes on the margins. If you do not want to write on your book or journal, attach post-it notes with your comments to the text. Do not be afraid to write too much. This is the stage of the reading process during which you are actively making meaning. Writing about what you read is the best way to make sense of it, especially, if the text is difficult.

Do not be afraid to write too much. This is the stage of the reading process during which you are actively making meaning. Writing about what you read will help you not only to remember the argument which the author of the text is trying to advance (less important for critical reading), but to create your own interpretations of the text you are reading (more important).

Here are some things you can do in your comments

- Ask questions.
- Agree or disagree with the author.
- Question the evidence presented in the text
- Offer counter-evidence
- Offer additional evidence, examples, stories, and so on that support the author''s argument
- Mention other texts which advance the same or similar arguments
- Mention personal experiences that enhance your reading of the text

Write Exploratory Responses

Write extended responses to readings. Writing students are often asked to write one or two page exploratory responses to readings, but they are not always clear on the purpose of these responses and on how to approach writing them. By writing reading responses, you are continuing the important work of critical reading which you began when you underlined interesting passages and took notes on the margins. You are extending the meaning of the text by creating your own commentary to it and perhaps even branching off into creating your own argument inspired by your reading. Your teacher may give you a writing prompt, or ask you to come up with your own topic for a response. In either case, realize that reading responses are supposed to be exploratory, designed to help you delve deeper into the text you are reading than note-taking or underlining will allow.

When writing extended responses to the readings, it is important to keep one thing in mind, and that is their purpose. The purpose of these exploratory responses, which are often rather informal, is not to produce a complete argument, with an introduction, thesis, body, and conclusion. It is not to impress your classmates and your teacher with "big" words and complex sentences. On the contrary, it is to help you understand the text you are working with at a deeper level. The verb "explore" means to investigate something by looking at it more closely. Investigators get leads, some of which are fruitful and useful and some of which are dead-ends. As you investigate and create the meaning of the text you are working with, do not be afraid to take different directions with your reading response. In fact, it is important resist the urge to make conclusions or think that you have found out everything about your reading. When it comes to exploratory reading responses, lack of closure and presence of more leads at the end of the piece is usually a good thing. Of course, you should always check with your teacher for standards and format of reading responses.

Try the following guidelines to write a successful response to a reading:

Remember your goal—exploration. The purpose of writing a response is to construct the meaning of a difficult text. It is not to get the job done as quickly as possible and in as few words as possible.

As you write, "talk back to the text." Make comments, ask questions, and elaborate on complex thoughts. This part of the writing becomes much easier if, prior to writing your response, you had read the assignment with a pen in hand and marked important places in the reading.

If your teacher provides a response prompt, make sure you understand it. Then try to answer the questions in the prompt to the best of your ability. While you are doing that, do not be afraid of bringing in related texts, examples, or experiences. Active reading is about making connections, and your readers will appreciate your work because it will help them understand the text better.

While your primary goal is exploration and questioning, make sure that others can understand your response. While it is OK to be informal in your response, make every effort to write in a clear, error-free language.

Involve your audience in the discussion of the reading by asking questions, expressing opinions, and connecting to responses made by others.

Use Reading for Invention

Use reading and your responses to start your own formal writing projects. Reading is a powerful invention tool. While preparing to start a new writing project, go back to the readings you have completed and your responses to those readings in search for possible topics and ideas. Also look through responses your classmates gave to your ideas about the text. Another excellent way to start your own writing projects and to begin research for them is to look through the list of references and sources at the end of the reading that you are working with. They can provide excellent topic-generating and research leads.

Keep a Double-Entry Journal

Many writers like double-entry journals because they allow us to make that leap from summary of a source to interpretation and persuasion. To start a double-entry journal, divide a page into two columns. As you read, in the left column write down interesting and important words, sentences, quotations, and passages from the text. In the right column, right your reaction and responses to them. Be as formal or informal as you want. Record words, passages, and ideas from the text that you find useful for your paper, interesting, or, in any, way striking or unusual. Quote or summarize in full, accurately, and fairly. In the right-hand side column, ask the kinds of questions and provide the kinds of responses that will later enable you to create an original reading of the text you are working with and use that reading to create your own paper.

Don't Give Up

If the text you are reading seems too complicated or "boring," that might mean that you have not attacked it aggressively and critically enough. Complex texts are the ones worth pursuing and investigating because they present the most interesting ideas. Critical reading is a liberating practice because you do not have to worry about "getting it right." As long as you make an effort to engage with the text and as long as you are willing to work hard on creating a meaning out of what you read, the interpretation of the text you are working with will be valid.

IMPORTANT: So far, we have established that no pre-existing meaning is possible in written texts and that critical and active readers work hard to create such meaning. We have also established that interpretations differ from reader to reader and that there is no "right" or "wrong" during the critical reading process. So, you may ask, does this mean that any reading of a text that I create will be a valid and persuasive one? With the exception of the most outlandish and purposely-irrelevant readings that have nothing to do with the sources text, the answer is "yes." However, remember that reading and interpreting texts, as well as sharing your interpretations with others are rhetorical acts. First of all, in order to learn something from your critical reading experience, you, the reader, need to be persuaded by your own reading of the text. Secondly, for your reading to be accepted by others, they need to be persuaded by it, too. It does not mean, however, that in order to make your reading of a text persuasive, you simply have to find "proof" in the text for your point of view. Doing that would mean reverting to reading "for the main point," reading as consumption. Critical reading, on the other hand, requires a different approach. One of the components of this approach is the use of personal experiences, examples, stories, and knowledge for interpretive and persuasive purposes. This is the subject of the next section of this chapter.

One Critical Reader's Path to Creating a Meaning: A Case Study

Earlier on in this chapter, we discussed the importance of using your existing knowledge and prior experience to create new meaning out of unfamiliar and difficult texts. In this section, I'd like to offer you one student writer"s account of his meaningmaking process. Before I do that, however, it is important for me to tell you a little about the class and the kinds of reading and writing assignments that its members worked on.

All the writing projects offered to the members of the class were promoted by readings, and students were expected to actively develop their own ideas and provide their own readings of assigned texts in their essays. The main text for the class was the anthology *Ways of Reading* edited by David Bartholomae and Anthony Petrosky that contains challenging and complex texts. Like for most of his classmates, this approach to reading and writing was new to Alex who had told me earlier that he was used to reading "for information" or "for the main point."

In preparation for the first writing project, the class read Adrienne Rich's essay "When We Dead Awaken: Writing as Revision." In her essay, Rich offers a moving account of her journey to becoming a writer. She makes the case for constantly "revising" one"s life in the light of all new events and experiences. Rich blends voices and genres throughout the essay, using personal narrative, academic argument, and even poetry. As a result, Rich creates the kind of personal-public argument which, on the one hand, highlights her own life, and on the other, illustrates that her Rich's life is typical for her time and her environment and that her readers can also learn from her experiences.

To many beginning readers and writers, who are used to a neat separation of "personal" and "academic" argument, such a blend of genres and styles may seem odd. In fact, on of the challenges that many of the students in the class faced was understanding why Rich chooses to blend personal writing with academic and what rhetorical effects she achieves by doing so. To After writing informal responses to the essay and discussing it in class, the students were offered the following writing assignment:

> Although Rich tells a story of her own, she does so to provide an illustration of an even larger story—one about what it means to be a woman and a writer. Tell a story of your own about the ways you might be said to have been named or shaped or positioned by an established or powerful culture. Like Rich (and perhaps with similar hesitation), use your own experience as an illustration of both your own situation and the situation of people like you. You should imagine that the assignment is a way for you to use (and put to the test) some of Rich's terms, words like "re-vision," "renaming," and "structure." (Bartholomae and Petrosky 648).

Notice that this assignment does not ask students to simply analyze Rich's essay, to dissect its argument or "main points." Instead, writers are asked to work with their own experiences and events of their own lives in order to provide a reading of Rich which is affected and informed by the writers" own lives and own knowledge of life. This is critical reading in action when a reader creates his or her one's own meaning of a complex text by reflecting on the relationship between the content of that text and one"s own life.

In response to the assignment, one of the class members, Alex Clmino-Hurt, wrote a paper that re-examined and reevaluated his upbringing and how those factors have influenced his political and social views. In particular, Alex was trying to reconcile his own and his parents" anti-war views with the fact than a close relative of his was fighting in the war in Iraq as he worked on the paper. Alex used such terms as "revision" and "hesitation" to develop his piece.

Like most other writers in the class, initially Alex seemed a little puzzled, even confused by the requirement to read someone else"s text through the prism of his own life and his own experiences. However, as he drafted, revised, and discussed his writing with his classmates and his instructor, the new approach to reading and writing became clearer to him. After finishing the paper, Alex commented on his reading strategies and techniques and on what he learned about critical reading during the project:

On Previous Reading Habits and Techniques

Previously when working on any project whether it be for a History, English, or any other class that involved reading and research, there was a certain amount of minimalism. As a student I tried to balance the least amount of effort with the best grade. I distinctly remember that before, being taught to skim over writing and reading so that I found "main" points and highlighted them. The value of thoroughly reading a piece was not taught because all that was needed was a shallow interpretation of whatever information that was provided followed by a regurgitation. [Critical reading] provided a dramatic difference in perspective and helped me learn to not only dissect the meaning of a piece, but also to see why the writer is using certain techniques or how the reading applies to my life.

On Developing Critical Reading Strategies

When reading critically I found that the most important thing for me was to set aside a block of time in which I wouldn't have to hurry my reading or skip parts to "Get the gist of it". Developing an eye for...detail came in two ways. The first method is to read the text several times, and the second is to discuss it with my classmates and my teacher. It quickly became clear to me that the more I read a certain piece, the more I got from it as I became more comfortable with the prose and writing style. With respect to the second way, there is always something that you can miss and there is always a different perspective that can be brought to the table by either the teacher or a classmate.

On Reading Rich's Essay

In reading Adrienne Rich's essay, the problem for me wasn't necessarily relating to her work but instead just finding the right perspective from which to read it. I was raised in a very open family so being able to relate to others was learned early in my life. Once I was able to parallel my perspective to hers, it was just a matter of composing my own story. Mine was my liberalism in conservative environments—the fact that frustrates me sometimes. I felt that her struggle frustrated her, too. By using quotations from her work, I was able to show my own situation to my readers.

On Writing the Paper

The process that I went through to write an essay consisted of three stages. During the first stage, I wrote down every coherent idea I had for the essay as well as a few incoherent ones. This helped me create a lot of material to work with. While this initial material doesn"t always have direction it provides a foundation for writing. The second stage involved rereading Rich"s essay and deciding which parts of it might be relevant to my own story. Looking at my own life and at Rich"s work together helped me consolidate my paper. The third and final stage involved taking what is left and refining the style of the paper and taking care of the mechanics.

Advice for Critical Readers

The first key to being a critical and active reader is to find something in the piece that interests, bothers, encourages, or just confuses you. Use this to drive your analysis. Remember there is no such thing as a boring essay, only a boring reader.

- Reading something once is never enough so reading it quickly before class just won't cut it. Read it once to get your brain comfortable with the work, then read it again and actually try to understand what's going on in it. You can't read it too many times.
- Ask questions. It seems like a simple suggestion but if you never ask questions you'll never get any answers. So, while you"re reading, think of questions and just write them down on a piece of paper lest you forget them after about a line and a half of reading.

Conclusion

Reading and writing are rhetorical processes, and one does not exist without the other. The goal of a good writer is to engage his or her readers into a dialog presented in the piece of writing. Similarly, the goal of a critical and active reader is to participate in that dialog and to have something to say back to the writer and to others. Writing leads to reading and reading leads to writing. We write because we have something to say and we read because we are interested in ideas of others.

Reading what others have to say and responding to them help us make that all-important transition from simply having opinions about something to having ideas. Opinions are often over-simplified and fixed. They are not very useful because, if different people have different opinions that they are not willing to change or adjust, such people cannot work or think together. Ideas, on the other hand, are ever evolving, fluid, and flexible. Our ideas are informed and shaped by our interactions with others, both in person and through written texts. In a world where thought and action count, it is not enough to simply "agree to disagree." Reading and writing, used together, allow us to discuss complex and difficult issues with others, to persuade and be persuaded, and, most importantly, to act.

Reading and writing are inextricably connected, and I hope that this chapter has shown you ways to use reading to inform and enrich you writing and your learning in general. The key to becoming an active, critical, and interested reader is the development of varied and effective reading techniques and strategies. I'd like to close this chapter with the words from the writer Alex Cimino-Hurt: "Being able to read critically is important no matter what you plan on doing with your career or life because it allows you to understand the world around you."

Sources

Bartholomae, David and Anthony Petrosky, Eds. Introduction. *Ways of Reading*. 8th Ed. New York: Bedford/St. Martin's, 2008.

Brent, Douglas. 1992. *Reading as Rhetorical Invention*. NCTE, Urbana, Illinois. Cimino-Hurt, Alex. Personal Interview. 2003.

Martin, Janette. 2004. "Developing 'Interesting Thoughts:' Reading for Research." In *Research Writing Revisited: A Sourcebook for Teachers*, eds. Pavel Zemliansky and Wendy Bishop, Heinemann, Portsmouth, NH. (3-13).

Rich, Adrienne. 2002. "When We Dead Awaken: Writing as Re-vision." In *Ways of Reading*, 6th ed. Eds. Bartholomae, David and Anthony Petrosky. Bedford/St. Martin"s Boston, (627-645).

Avoid Relativism (Because I Think So)

So that we avoid the major problem of relativism, heed the following warnings:

- If you don't happen to resemble an author's audience, don't attack the audience that writer appealed to
- What I often see in essays based on model reading assignments is reactive rather than flexible reading. For instance, I often teach skeptic Michael Shermer's book *The Science of Good and Evil*. In online discussion posts, I'll see people react with "Well, he is sarcastic but people already agreeing with him would find that funny. I just find it offensive." Then the student writer proceeds to do that Samuel L. Jackson "Allow me to retort" move from *Pulp Fiction* (Tarantino), trying to match snarkiness with Shermer or to refute him. When they get really desperate, they go to the web and find attack sites. "Allow me to retort!" is not our purpose in most academic writing. Later in the course, though, we will cover refutals, which are appropriately-handled counterarguments.
- "It's true for me" doesn't work here. I see this happen a lot in definition or rhetorical analysis essays that often start courses. If the writing is rhetorical analysis, cut out one's views from this process . . . it is supposed to be about form, not content, so if you start getting too much into content, you're not doing a formal analysis. In fact, to the extent that you go off (or gush in support) at the writer, you're not doing your job of analyzing. And definitions—while they may not seem arguable—actually contain areas of genuine, ongoing disagreement that we would do well to recognize.
- Academic writing is public, not private. Don't overuse *I* or *you*. Filtering this through the self is a bad idea. As Charlton Heston says of the mystery food in the movie *Soylent Green* "It's people!" (Fleischer). Don't serve us yourself . . . your friend Willie Wonka says "But that is called cannibalism, my dear children, and is in fact frowned upon in most societies" (Burton). I'm having fun with this, but the idea remains: The chapter is the source, not the self. Subjectivism pushes discussion only through our limited selves.

I realize I am only going against the whole of American culture by stating this. . .

Cause/Effect Tie in With Most Readings

This is Complex Stuff!

You have a surprising amount of choice in arguing cause and effect. In creating causal chains, which are basically links between this and that, there's actually a dizzying variety of factors to consider. We can make errors easily, so consider the following binary, either/or choices.

Also remember that either/or is a logical fallacy; though these either/or choices below offer comforting structure as you think about your topic, do not be limited by them. For instance, below there's the short term vs. long term binary. Can't one argue middle term, intermediate causes or effect, too?

Think of the following types of causes and effects:

indirect vs. direct (in obviousness, the ease with which we can see something leading to something)
Example: Having polio in childhood may lead one to have a heart attack sixty years later. It may be one of many causes.

primary vs. secondary (in importance)
That childhood polio situation might be the one reason why a person has a heart attack. That's tough to prove, though! Still, with a heart attack (or a car accident), it's likely that there's a primary cause that can be assigned. That cause can be direct or indirect, right?

short term vs. long term (causes or effects) This can be really tricky. There are often both types of effects, but how are they connected? How can you isolate your cause as leading to a certain effect?

positive vs. negative
Too often, people only focus on the negatives. Even with a tough issue like suicide, it's at least possible that one could argue that some positive effects could spin out of a suicide. Though not obvious, these can be argued to exist. We need to get beyond the obvious as we structure this blend. It offers another chance at our topic.

If you're getting distracted by the language of causal chains, think of synonyms. "Causes" can be "influences," and "effects" might be switched to "consequences." Maybe switching the names will help. (Sounds like some discipline plan in high school, eh?)

Argue Without Filtering Through the Self

In academic writing, we argue without filtering everything through *I think* statements, just as we avoid *you* overuse. Not only are those pronouns prone to tone problems, but also they create logical dead-ends.

"It's true for me" is one such issue: relativism. In academic argumentation, this carries no weight. That's why we only even allow personal examples on a limited basis. But things do change over time, since most of the time *you* and *I* had been completely omitted in past decades.

Why bring up these points? Skeptical readers do nt want an argument to be filtered through "I really believe that _____" statements, even though we realize that the thesis is one's opinion. We dress up the thesis by avoiding *I*. We pretend an objectivity we know is an ideal but unachievable vantage. This is typical of academic writing. Call it a game, but by now we know why this can be an important game to know how to play well.

One opening into the writing of the claim might be to argue how the term is typically viewed. Again, this can be done only if the writer is careful with wording and avoids stereotyping.

Pitfalls for argument include passivity in setup or interpretation (realize that I'm more interested in your use of a source bit than in the bit itself), tone problems, pointing out of facts masquerading as argument—since this should be an argument to alter the meaning of the term to some clear extent, and lack of examples.

Also, if the writer chooses examples, do the show the extent to which the are typical or representative? Such use of illustration is important as we move between showing and telling, concrete and abstract.

Too much generalizing and you'll have a newspaper editorial or sermon. . . not what we are looking for! Do not write as if you are speaking. *Do* set up the sources you bring to our attention. Oh, and it also helps if the sources support what you think, such that the paragraphs are yours and not merely in the paper because they are 80% from them.

Definitional arguments are the plagiarized of the essays in the course. Knowing the traps in student tendencies, can you slip them?

Go back to the chapter material in the text about arguments of definition. There are good reminders there.

—Hope this helps!Eeeewwww! That post subject of *filtering* seems a bit graphic. I'm reminded of the notion that what we drink is dinosaur urine (http://www.techtimes.com/articles/56727/20150530/you-are-drinking-dinosaur-pee-everyday-heres-why.htm). . . check out why in the linked *Tech Times* article.

CC licensed content, Original

What is Academic Writing by L. Lennie Irvin

The Open Textbook Library has a PDF version of a book entitled *Writing Spaces: Readings on Writing* Vol. I. Its second essay is "What is Academic Writing," by L. Lennie Irvin. Access and read this (https://open.umn.edu/opentextbooks/BookDetail.aspx?bookId=45). (I would paste it in, but it would lose images and formatting.)

CC licensed content, Shared previously

- What is Academic Writing from the online text Writing Spaces: Readings on Writing Vol. I. **Authored by**: Charlie Lowe, Grand Valley State University Pavel Zemliansky, James Madison University. **Provided by**: Open Textbook Library. **Located at**: https://open.umn.edu/opentextbooks/BookDetail.aspx?bookId=45 (https://open.umn.edu/opentextbooks/BookDetail.aspx?bookId=45). **Project**: Center for Open Education. **License**: *CC BY-NC: Attribution-NonCommercial (https://creativecommons.org/licenses/by-nc/4.0/)*

Primary Source: Sustaining Our Commonwealth of Nature and Knowledge

Let's start with this phrase: "sustaining our commonwealth." By sustaining, I don't mean preserving inviolate; I mean using, without using up. Using with maintenance and replenishment is an important idea in economics. It's the very basis of the concept of income, because income is the maximum that you can consume today and still be able to produce and consume the same amount tomorrow – that is, maximum consumption without depleting capital in the broad sense of future productive capacity. By commonwealth, I mean the wealth that no one has made, or the wealth that practically everyone has made. So it's either nature – nobody made it, we all inherited it – or knowledge – everybody contributed to making it, but everyone's contribution is small in relation to the total and depends on the contributions of others. In managing the commonwealth of nature, our big problem is that we tend to treat the truly scarce as if it were non-scarce. The opposite problem arises with the commonwealth of knowledge, in which we tend to treat what is truly not scarce as if it were.

Clarifying Scarcity

There are two sets of important distinctions about goods, and they make four cross-classifications (see figure below). Goods can be either rival or non-rival, and they can be either excludable or non-excludable. My shirt, for example, is a rival good because if I'm wearing it, you can't wear it at the same time. The warmth of the sun is non-rival because I can enjoy the warmth of the sun, and everyone else can enjoy it at the same time. Rivalness is a physical property that precludes the simultaneous use of goods by more than one person. Goods are also excludable or non-excludable. That's not a physical concept, that's a legal concept, a question of property. For example, you could wear my shirt tomorrow if I let you, but that's up to me because it's my property. My shirt is both rival and excludable, and that's the case with most market goods. Meanwhile, the warmth of the sun is both non-rival and also non-excludable. We cannot buy and sell solar warmth; we cannot bottle it and charge for it. Goods that are rival and excludable are market goods. Goods that are non-rival and non-excludable are public goods. That leaves two other categories. Fish in the ocean are an example of goods that are rival and non-excludable. They are rival, because if I catch the fish, you can't catch it. But they are also non-excludable, because I can't stop you from fishing in the open seas. The management of goods that are rival and non-excludable gives rise to the famous tragedy of the commons – or the tragedy of open-access resources, as it's more accurately called. Now, the other problematic category consists of goods that are non-rival and excludable. If I use the Pythagorean Theorem, I don't prevent you from using it at the same time. Knowledge is non-rival, but it often is made excludable through intellectual property and patent rights. So those are two difficult categories that create problems. One is the tragedy of the commons, and the other we could call the tragedy of artificial scarcity.

The Commonwealth of Nature

Fish in the ocean are an example of the commonwealth of nature. I'll ague that natural goods and services that are rival and have so far remained non-excludable should be enclosed in the market in order to avoid unsustainable use. Excludability can take the form of individual property rights or social property rights – what needs to be avoided is open access. For dealing with the broad class of rival but, up to now, non-excludable goods, the so-called cap-auction-trade system is a market-based institution that merits consideration.

In addition to its practical value, the cap-auction-trade system also sheds light on a fundamental issue of economic theory: the logically separate issues of scale, distribution, and allocation. Neoclassical economics deals mainly with the question of allocation. Allocation is the apportionment of resources among competing uses: how many resources go to produce beans, how many to cars, how many to haircuts. Properly functioning markets allocate resources efficiently, more or less. Yet the concept of efficient allocation presupposes a given distribution. Distribution is the apportionment of goods and resources among different people: how many resources go to you, how many to somebody else. A good distribution is one that is fair or just – not efficient, but fair. The third issue is scale: the physical size of the economy relative to the ecosystem that sustains it. How many of us are there and how large are the associated matter-energy flows from producing all our stuff, relative to natural cycles and the maintenance of the biosphere. In neoclassical economics, the issue of scale is completely off the radar screen.

The cap-auction-trade system works like this. Some environmental assets, say fishing rights or the rights to emit sulfur dioxide, have been treated as non-excludable free goods. As economic growth increases the scale of the economy relative to that of the biosphere, it becomes recognized that these goods are in fact physically rival. The first step is to put a cap – a maximum – on the scale of use of that resource, at a level which is deemed to be environmentally sustainable. Setting that cap – deciding what it should be – is not a market decision, but a social and ecological decision. Then, the right to extract that resource or emit that waste, up to the cap, becomes a scarce asset. It was a free good. Now it has a price. We've created a new valuable asset, so the question is: Who owns it? This also has to be decided politically, outside the market. Ownership of this new asset should be auctioned to the highest bidder, with the proceeds entering the public treasury. Sometimes rights are simply given to the historical private users – a bad idea, I think, but frequently done under the misleading label of "grandfathering." The cap-auction-trade system is not, as often called, "free-market environmentalism." It is really socially constrained, market environmentalism. Someone must own the assets before they can be traded in the market, and that is an issue of distribution. Only after the scale question is answered, and then the distribution question, can we have market exchange to answer the question of allocation.

Another good policy for managing the commonwealth of nature is ecological tax reform. This means shifting the tax base away from income earned by labor and capital and onto the resource flow from nature. Taxing what we want less of, depletion and pollution, seems to be a better idea than taxing what we want more of, namely income. Unlike the cap-auction-trade system, ecological tax reform would exert only a very indirect and uncertain limit on the scale of the economy relative to the biosphere. Yet, it would go a long way toward improving allocation and distribution.

The Commonwealth of Knowledge

If you stand in front of the McKeldin Library at the University of Maryland, you'll see a quotation from Thomas Jefferson carved on one of the stones: "Knowledge is the common property of mankind." Well, I think Mr. Jefferson was right. Once knowledge exists, it is non-rival, which means it has a zero opportunity cost. As we know from studying price theory, price is supposed to measure opportunity cost, and if opportunity cost is zero, then price should be zero. Certainly, new knowledge, even though it should be allocated freely, does have a cost of production. Sometimes that cost of production is substantial, as with the space program's discovery that there's no life on Mars. On the other hand, a new insight could occur to you while you're lying in bed staring at the ceiling and cost absolutely nothing, as was the case with Renee Descartes' invention of analytic geometry. Many new discoveries are accidental. Others are motivated by the joy and excitement of research, independent of any material motivation. Yet the dominant view is that unless knowledge is kept scarce enough to have a significant price, nobody in the market will have an incentive to produce it. Patent monopolies and intellectual property rights are urged as the way to provide an extrinsic reward for knowledge production. Even within that restricted vision, keeping knowledge scarce still makes very little sense, because the main input to the production of new knowledge is existing knowledge. If you keep existing knowledge expensive, that's surely going to slow down the production of new knowledge.

In Summary

Managing the commonwealth of nature and knowledge presents us two rather opposite problems and solutions. I've argued that the commonwealth of nature should be enclosed as property, as much as possible as public property, and administered so as to capture scarcity rents for public revenue. Examples of natural commons include: mining, logging, grazing rights, the electromagnetic spectrum, the absorptive capacity of the atmosphere, and the orbital locations of satellites. The commonwealth of knowledge, on the other hand, should be freed from enclosure as property and treated as the non-rival good that it is. Abolishing all intellectual property rights tomorrow is draconian, but I do think we could grant patent monopolies for fewer "inventions" and for shorter time periods.

Does use by one person physically preclude use by others?

		Yes rival	No non-rival
Do laws prohibit access to these goods?	Yes excludable	**Market Goods** (e.g., automobiles and fishing reels) *Let the market allocate these goods.*	**Tragedy of Artificial Scarcity** (e.g., patented meds and knowledge in heads) *Reduce patent monopolies and intellectual property rights—share these goods.*
	No non-excludable	**Tragedy of the Commons** (e.g., old growth trees and fish in the seas) *Designate property rights and use cap-auction-trade to allocate these goods.*	**Public Goods** (e.g., national security and roads that are free) *Collect depletion and pollution taxes so that government can provide these goods.*
		Different types of goods and policies to achieve a sustainable, fair, and efficient economy.	

Primary Source: The Zombie as Barometer of Capitalist Anxiety

The modern incarnation of the zombie, as seen strewn across pop culture horror novels and films in ever-increasing numbers, is easily recognized and radically different from its historical roots; any member of our modern Western culture can spot the gray, often rotting flesh, the black eyes, the dishevelled appearance, the shuffling gait, the wretched moaning, and, of course, the bloody mouths flecked with fresh flesh and detritus. However, the zombie goes beyond cheap thrills; zombies, as well as other variations of horror monsters, represent a fear that pervades society as a whole, a collective nervousness of destruction at the hands of a seemingly invulnerable foe.

According to Peter Dendle, in his essay, "The Zombie as Barometer of Cultural Anxiety," the zombie has "...tapped into a deep-seated anxiety about society, government, individual protection, and our increasing disconnectedness from subsistence skills."[1] Dendle states that the prevalence of the zombie in pop culture correlates to society's fear that any sudden jolt of the status quo, undead or otherwise, would result in mass chaos, that people would be unable to protect themselves or to survive on their own. Yet one may take the thought of this collective anxiety a step further to discern one of the underlying causes and major contributions to the general nervousness of the public and the widespread appearances of zombies in films and literature: capitalism.

Past to Present

According to Dendle, "the zombie, a soul-less hulk mindlessly working at the bidding of another, thus records a residual communal memory of slavery: of living a life without dignity or meaning, of going through the motions."[1] Here we see the zombie's origins, as corpses reanimated by bourgeois landowners or factory foremen through some rites of magick for the sake of performing menial labour without demanding fair wages, hours, and treatment, never tiring or making mistakes.

This is one of the earliest iterations of the zombie, and the origin of the capitalist metaphor. The proto-capitalist economy of nineteenth century America was dependent on slave labour, and pro-slavery politicians of the time argued that the economy of the South would have collapsed entirely should slavery be outlawed. Here it is evident how a fear and disdain of capitalism would have been imprinted on the minds of the enslaved Africans and Haitians, from whose culture the zombie originated. They were slaves because slavery was profitable, vital to economy and thus not morally bankrupt to the slave owners, and an implicit resistance to this system would have been planted.

From here the zombie transformed from a worker drone to a bloodthirsty monster, personality vanished, flesh rotting off of bone, an insatiable hunger for long pig, and most importantly a horde—one capable of the annihilation of human society. Zombies went from a cheap work force to a full-blown apocalypse, and they had never been more popular as capitalism conquered the world.

The capitalist metaphor came to a head with George Romero's 1978 film Dawn of the Dead, in which the main characters attempt to escape the zombie apocalypse by finding sanctuary in a shopping mall. When the survivors find temporary safety, they return to their consumer roots and ransack the mall for products, and, after observing his comrades and the encroaching zombies, one character remarks, "They're us."[2]

Later, much more subtle hints at the metaphor of consumer capitalism occur in the Resident Evil cycle and many other films and books, where the zombie outbreak is, directly or otherwise, the result of illicit business practices of faceless corporations. This possibly stems from a mistrust of large conglomerates whose GDPs began to exceed entire nations'; Wal-Mart currently has more purchasing power than Saudi Arabia does.

In Max Brooks' World War Z, a critique of capitalism is offered in the form of Phalanx, a vaccine manufactured to prevent "rabies" and sold as a solution to the developing zombie crisis; Phalanx was pushed through the FDA by the government (and the corporations that control it) despite a lack of testing and evidence regarding the zombie virus, for the sake of keeping the populace calm while earning unprecedented profits at the expense of the victimized masses. According to Breckenridge Scott, the character responsible for Phalanx:

"It protected them from their fears. That's all I was selling. Hell, because of Phalanx, the biomed sector started to recover, which, in turn, jump-started the stock market, which then gave the impression of a recovery, which then restored consumer confidence to stimulate an actual recovery!"3

This passage shows how the bourgeois businessman Scott justified selling his snake oil to the masses, in that the mass production of Phalanx and its widespread sales led to an economic recovery, and the reader is presented with the conflicting viewpoints between economic recovery and the deaths of millions of misled humans. The reader is presented with the question of whether the economy should take precedent over the well-being of the people, and while the choice is obvious, it shows the reader that corporations will sacrifice lives for their bottom lines.

And so, as zombies enter the world of prime-time television dramas, so too does our anxiety grow.

Anxiety Disorder

The zombie as we know it today, by its very nature, is a mindless creature which was once a human being, a sentient individual with a name and free will, but has been warped to become a ravenous consumer without thought or emotion. It meanders through city streets, around small towns, and along highways with no thought or desire but to consume anything and everything it can—namely, human flesh.

If one listens to the cries of anti-capitalist dissenters, an eerie similarity between zombies and members of capitalist economies appears, at least in terms of behavior; the masses go out from their homes and flock to shopping centers and department stores, willingly giving away the fruits of their labour in exchange for luxury items, and often really don't know why.

A defining feature of the zombie is the loss of the individual's sentience once transformed into the undead, just as a loss of sentience occurs in the individual within a consumer capitalist culture, at the hands of mass marketing and advertising. On the subject of the loss of free will, author Chuck Palahniuk wittily writes:

"Experts in ancient Greek culture say that people back then didn't see their thoughts as belonging to them. When ancient Greeks had a thought, it occurred to them as a god or goddess giving an order... Now people hear a commercial for sour cream potato chips and rush out to buy, but now they call this free will. At least the ancient Greeks were being honest."4

Here Palahniuk's anti-capitalist sentiments can be translated to the parallel between zombies and consumers, as both experiences a loss of sentience, and of the individual. The zombie is a monster of majority, unlike its vampiric and lupine counterparts, as those in our society who are given to the consumer instinct are a majority and the few individuals who criticize capitalism from within it are persecuted and defamed in the way that zombies will swarm and attack an uninfected human. In addition, the zombie is a mechanism of annihilation; while vampires are a small minority living in the underground of a human world, feeding to survive, the zombie horde exists only for the purpose of consuming or converting all humans until the species is extinct and the paradigm shifts to a world inhabited only by zombies.

This is similar to the cries of the left wing, who accuse the right—the upholders of laissez-faire capitalism and unwavering nationalism—of demanding conformity of all to their belief systems and ways of living (if you don't like America, well you can just get out).

However, Dendle postulates that while zombie apocalypse films and novels capitalize on the anxiety of the masses, the underlying purpose of zombie culture is not to display the end of the world but to illustrate how the world may be profoundly changed for the better by means of the old world's destruction. Dendle states: "Post-apocalyptic zombie worlds are fantasies of liberation: the intrepid pioneers of a new world trek through the shattered remnants of the old, trudging through the shells of buildings and the husks of people."1

In World War Z, the sundering of the zeitgeist in the United States shatters the pre-existing capitalistic and highly individualized philosophy of the masses and opens up the populace, through their vulnerability, to survival only through communal life and cooperation. However, even Brooks' profound statements regarding cooperation are contradicted within his novel, in the example of socialist Cuba becoming a booming post-war capitalist force. One can infer from the critiques of both capitalism and communism that Brooks supports neither in his writing, adding another layer to the zombie-capitalist.

I believe that the impact of Brooks' novel regarding our economic anxiety can be summarized by this statement of a Japanese character late in the novel: "His generation wanted to rule the world, and mine was content to let the world, and by the world I mean [the United States], rule us. There has to be a better way, a middle path where we take responsibility..."2 This is a powerful line, as it transforms the novel from a simple metaphor for capitalism to a statement that the world must take a path between capitalism and communism in order to survive and prosper, and that this path is now available as the world has an opportunity to rebuild. This is the ultimate function of the zombie, beyond cheap thrills of a horror film and beyond a criticism of the right-wing and consumer capitalism; the zombie functions to clean the slate and enable the world to rebuild anew.

1. Dendle, Peter. "The Zombie as Barometer of Cultural Anxiety." 45-55. Print.
2. Brooks, Max. World War Z. Print.
3. Ramero, George A. Dawn of the Dead. Film.
4. Palahniuk, Chuck. Lullaby. Print.

Primary Source: Zombies vs. Animals? The Living Dead Wouldn't Stand a Chance

National Wildlife Federation naturalist David Mizejewski explains how nature would deal with a zombie outbreak: brutally, and without quarter.

With *The Walking Dead's* fourth season premiere and Halloween upon us, the living dead are back in full-force.

Zombies are scary. We humans are evolutionarily pre-programmed to abhor the dead bodies of our own species. It's a natural reaction, helping healthy individuals avoid fatal pathogens.

The thought of being eaten alive is a natural fear, and when it's your own species doing the eating, it's even more terrifying.

Relax. Next time you're lying in bed, unable to fall asleep thanks to the vague anxiety of half-rotten corpses munching on you in the dark, remember this: if there was ever a zombie uprising, wildlife (http://www.nwf.org/Wildlife.aspx) would kick its ass.

To enjoy zombie horror, you suspend disbelief and put aside some of science's rules. That said, If we assume zombies can't spread whatever is causing them to reanimate to other species, and that they are relatively slow moving—both true (*so far! — Ed.*) of Walking Dead zombies—there are more than enough wild animals (http://www.nwf.org/Wildlife/Wildlife-Library.aspx) out there to dispatch the undead.

That's because zombies are essentially walking carrion, and Mother Nature doesn't let *anything* go to waste.

Carrion is on the menu for a vast number of species, from tiny micro-organisms to the largest carnivores.

Here's just some of the North American wildlife that would make short work of a zombie horde.

BIRDS: WINGED ZOMBIE ANNIHILATORS

Many birds feed themselves by scavenging on dead things. The two vulture species native to North America, the turkey vulture (http://www.nwf.org/News-and-Magazines/National-Wildlife/Birds/Archives/2010/Turkey-Vulture-Sterling.aspx) and the black vulture, flock up to make short work of any corpses they find. Both vulture species are dwarfed by the massive California condor, whose wingspan can reach 10 feet and which relish carrion. A sluggish zombie wouldn't stand a change against one of these giants or a flock of vultures. California condors are endangered (http://blog.nwf.org/2010/10/california-condor-population-hits-100/), so a zombie apocalypse could really give a boost to their population by providing them with an abundance of food.

This video shows a juvenile California condor ripping the heart out of a dead carcass, surrounding by ravens picking up scraps. Ravens are not small birds—just look at the size of this baby condor in comparison.

- https://youtu.be/TuGpuxlb0dw

Ravens (http://www.nwf.org/News-and-Magazines/National-Wildlife/Birds/Archives/2010/Common-Raven-Sterling.aspx), crows, and magpies are expert scavengers as well, in addition to being bold and extremely intelligent. Many species of gulls (http://www.nwf.org/photocontest/ViewPhoto.aspx?imageid=409202), known for their brash behavior when it comes to scoring a meal, would also gladly feed off slow-moving zombies in coastal areas. These birds usually require other animals to break through or break down the tough skin and hide of their carrion meals. So they'd have to wait until the zombies decomposed a bit, or were dismembered by others animals, before they tucked in. But once started, nothing would stop them from devouring the undead with gusto.

Raven Symmetry by ingridtaylar

Despite being expert hunters, eagles are not above scavenging. Bald eagles (http://www.shopnwf.org/Adoption-Center/Adopt-a-Bald-Eagle/index.cat) make carrion a regular part of their diet, and with their huge talons, they're not afraid to dispatch animals that are near-death—or undead. The slightly larger golden eagle is no stranger to scavenging, either, and has also been documented attacking and killing animals as large as deer (http://bit.ly/1b9h9wf). A torpid zombie wouldn't pose much of a challenge.

Watch these bald eagles and crows strip a deer carcass down to nothing in 48 hours.

- https://youtu.be/fxceV0PuSaw

MAMMALS: ZOMBIE DISMEMBERMENT CREW

North America's large mammal predators would be more than a match for zombies. We have two bear species, brown (or grizzly (http://www.nwf.org/Wildlife/Wildlife-Library/Mammals/Grizzly-Bear.aspx)) and black bears (http://www.nwf.org/Wildlife/Wildlife-Library/Mammals/Black-Bear.aspx). Male brown bears can weigh in at 1,000 pounds. They are not afraid of humans. They can deliver a bite of 1200 pounds per square inch and have long, sharp claws designed to rip open logs and flip boulders in search of insects and other small critters to eat. They would easily tear apart rotting zombie flesh. Black bears are much smaller and typically run from humans, but even a black bear, when approached or cornered, would make short work of a zombie. Both bear species have an incredible sense of smell and both love to eat carrion, so even if zombies didn't approach them, the bears eventually would learn that these walking bags of flesh make good eating.

Like black bears, gray wolves (http://www.nwf.org/Wildlife/Wildlife-Library/Mammals/Gray-Wolf.aspx) are very shy of humans and typically run away at the first sight of us. Nor are they strangers to scavenging. They'd soon take advantage of the easy pickings presented by lumbering zombies. Coyotes are far less shy than wolves and can happily live alongside humans, including in the heart of our cities (http://www.nwf.org/News-and-Magazines/National-Wildlife/Animals/Archives/2010/City-Coyotes.aspx). These intelligent canids would quickly learn that they could take down zombies one by one, especially the eastern populations of coyote, which are larger and bolder (http://news.nationalgeographic.com/news/2011/11/

111107-hybrids-coyotes-wolf-virginia-dna-animals-science/) due to past interbreeding with wolves and domestic dogs.

Unlike bears, wolves and coyotes, mountain lions prefer fresh meat and don't typically feed on carrion, other than what they kill themselves. Like all cats, they hunt by stealth and are irresistibly attracted to signs of weakness in potential prey. Unlike most other North American predators, mountain lions can put humans on the menu. Any zombie shuffling through mountain lion territory (which can be surprisingly close (http://blog.nwf.org/2013/08/cyclist-has-amazing-encounter-with-a-mountain-lion-in-los-angeles/) to our cities) would trigger those feline predatory instincts, and would likely end up with one of these big cats sneak-attacking from behind and delivering a spine severing bite to the back of the neck.

Even bigger and more powerful than mountain lions are jaguars, which range through Mexico and are still sometimes found (http://blog.nwf.org/2013/01/arizona-mine-threatens-endangered-jaguar/) in the desert southwest of the United States. Jaguars also hunt by stealth, and have a special technique to quickly dispatch their prey: a skull crushing bite to the head, delivered with their huge canine teeth. A jaguar bite delivers 2,000 pounds of pressure per inch, the most powerful mammalian bite on the continent. That, combined with a killing technique perfect for dispatching zombies, makes the jaguar its natural predator.

Jaguar Woodland Park Zoo by symonty

Watch this video of a jaguar making short work of a caiman. A zombie wouldn't stand a chance against these big cats.

- https://youtu.be/DBNYwxDZ_pA

It's not just mammalian carnivores that would take apart zombies. On *The Walking Dead*, Rick's horse fell victim to a horde of zombies in season one, but I can only chalk that up to the fact that it was a domestic beast that didn't view humans (even undead ones) as a threat. Wild hoofed mammals would not be so passive as to let zombies to get close enough to swarm and overwhelm them.

In fact, hoofed mammals are more dangerous to humans than carnivores. Moose attack and kill more people (http://www.mnn.com/earth-matters/animals/photos/15-cute-animals-that-could-kill-you/moose) than bears do every year. They consider humans a threat, but as the largest living deer species, they are not afraid of human-sized creatures. If a zombie got too close, a moose (http://blog.nwf.org/2013/02/climate-crisis-deepens-for-americas-moose/) would stomp it into an immobile pile of gore without a second's hesitation.

This video shows moose fighting technique, which involves delivering powerful blows with their sharp hooves. https://youtu.be/gu_zMTQkM1s

And moose are nothing compared to bison. Bison (http://www.nwf.org/Wildlife/Wildlife-Library/Mammals/Bison.aspx) are a ton of muscle, horn, and hide. They do not tolerate being approached, and would effortlessly gore and trample as many zombies as dared approached them. Watch this video of what a bison can do to a car with a flick of its head, and think about what a zombified human body would look like on the receiving end of its wrath. https://youtu.be/ULBuLedK2Nw

Speaking of hoofed mammals ramming cars, this video of bull elk (http://www.nwf.org/News-and-Magazines/National-Wildlife/PhotoZone/Archives/2012/photo-of-the-week-10-15-12.aspx) will give you some perspective on the size of this large deer species and their aggression during the breeding season. Bull elk are armed with giant antlers with spear-like tips—perfect to impale and dismember a pack of zombies. https://youtu.be/tEv-hwjhEiE

Mountain goats (http://www.nwf.org/News-and-Magazines/National-Wildlife/Animals/Archives/1997/King-of-the-Mountain.aspx) would probably not encounter too many zombies, simply due to the inaccessibility of the steep mountain slopes they call home. Every so often, however, they do head down to more manageable terrain. Even though they are not large, they can be fierce and are armed with dagger-like horns, just as this unfortunate hiker learned (http://blogs.discovery.com/animal_oddities/2010/10/mountain-goat-kills-hiker.html).

REPTILES: SCALY ZOMBIE CLEAN-UP COMMITTEE

Most North American reptiles—small lizards, turtles and snakes—wouldn't pose much threat to zombies. Ironically, it would probably be venomous rattlesnakes (http://www.nwf.org/Wildlife/Wildlife-Library/Amphibians-Reptiles-and-Fish/ Rattlesnakes.aspx) that would be at most risk from zombie attack. When camouflage fails them, their survival tactic is to draw attention to themselves with a loud rattle, and then hold their ground, striking out at anything that approaches them. With no circulatory system or living tissue, snake venom wouldn't have any effect on zombies, and they'd easily be able to pick up the snake and eat it.

Western Diamondback Rattlesnake (Crotalus atrox) by rarvesen, on Flickr

That said, we do have a few reptiles particularly suited for zombie clean-up. Two crocodilian species call North America home: the American alligator and the American crocodile (http://www.nwf.org/News-and-Magazines/National-Wildlife/ Animals/Archives/2002/The-Crocodiles-Power-Play.aspx). American crocodiles are extremely endangered and found only in limited areas of Florida, but like California condors, they could benefit from an influx of slow-moving, half-rotten, staggering prey to their wetland habitat.

Alligators (http://www.nwf.org/Wildlife/Wildlife-Library/Amphibians-Reptiles-and-Fish/American-Alligator.aspx) are far more numerous and are found throughout Florida, west to Texas, and along the coastal plain wetlands as far north as the Carolinas. Once almost totally wiped out, alligators are now numerous due to protections under the Endangered Species Act (http://www.nwf.org/Wildlife/ Wildlife-Conservation/Endangered-Species-Act.aspx), and they sometimes even show up in people's backyards. 'Gators can grow to be 13 feet long and deliver an extremely powerful bite, with over 2,000 pounds of pressure per inch.

Alligator 1, by Bogeskov

Both species are stealth hunters, and can burst from the water at surprising speeds to pluck large prey from the shoreline. They are quite capable of tearing a human-sized meal into bite sized chunks of meat with their toothy, vice-like mouths. Soft zombie flesh would melt in their mouths like butter.

Any zombie that lumbered into fresh water ponds, lakes streams or swamps would likely fall prey to aquatic turtles too, who, with their beak-like jaws, would feast on zombie flesh. Painted turtles, river cooters and sliders of all sorts make carrion a part of their normal diet. To the undead, it would be a second "death by a thousand bites." The ubiquitous common snapping turtle specializes in carrion-eating. As the name suggests, it can tear off substantial chunks and swallow them whole. Snapping turtles are even used by police to find corpses underwater (http://www.strangezoo.com/content/item/141325.html) due to their relish for dead flesh.

Common snapping turtles are dwarfed by the alligator snapping turtle (http://blog.nwf.org/2011/03/martha-stewart-and-wildlife-adoption/), which is the world's largest freshwater turtle. They can weigh in at more than 200 pounds. Disguised to look like rotten leaves, resting in the murky depths which they live, they are the perfect foil for any zombie that ends up in the water. Check out the massive head on this one.

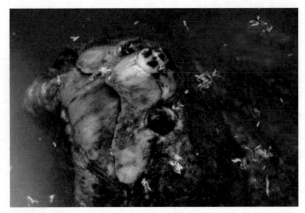

alligator snapping turtle by me and the sysop

DECOMPOSERS: MASTERS OF THE ZOMBIE BUFFET

Ultimately, it's not the North America's mega-fauna that pose the most threat to zombies. In nature, there are a whole host of tiny creatures whose main purpose is to feed upon and break down the flesh of the dead: the decomposers. Zombies, with their rotting flesh, are obviously not immune to these decomposers (what do you think causes the rotting effect?), many of which are too small to see with the bare eye. Bacteria, fungi, molds, Insects such as fly maggots or flesh-eating beetles, and other invertebrates, all make up nature's diminutive clean-up crew (http://www.nwf.org/How-to-Help/Garden-for-Wildlife/Gardening-Tips/How-to-Build-a-Worm-Compost-Bin.aspx). And it can obliterate a dead body in surprisingly little time. The clumsy undead wouldn't have the dexterity to pick off these decomposers, even if they could see or feel them. It would just be a matter of time. Stripped off all soft tissue, including brains, the zombies would be reduced to hollowed-out skeletons.

Not convinced? Check out this video of a rabbit being consumed down to the bone, by wildlife decomposers, in just a week.

- https://youtu.be/C6sFP_7Vezg

Here is a time-lapse video showing Dermestid flesh-eating beetles (http://newswatch.nationalgeographic.com/2013/01/17/flesh-eating-beetles-explained/) consuming the flesh off a series of birds for the Natural History Museum of London. These beetle are easy to raise in captivity and only feed on (un)dead flesh, so they pose no harm to the living. Survivors of a zombie apocalypse could raise these beetles by the millions, and drop them onto zombies to do their work. It might take a few weeks per zombie, but they'd get the job done.

- https://youtu.be/–AT2j3YCu8

Here are some maggots going to town on a carcass. Flies produce millions of grotesque larvae in no time at all. There would be no way for zombies to escape these flying insects—or avoid being engulfed utterly by writhing, insatiable maggots.

- https://youtu.be/dBOjBRaMfSM

ZOMBIES NO MATCH FOR WILDLIFE, WILDLIFE NO MATCH FOR HUMANS

There you have it. Even if zombies managed to feed on smaller, slow-moving animals, or mob and overtake a few individuals of the larger species, it's pretty clear that they're no match for much of North America's wildlife...at least not on a one-on-one basis. In reality, however, the battle between wildlife and *living* humans is not going so well for the wildlife.

Sadly, much of our continent's wildlife has disappeared, and many species continue to decline. Habitat loss, invasive species and climate change (http://www.nwf.org/What-We-Do.aspx) are just some of the human-induced challenges our wildlife are facing. You can get involved protecting wildlife with the National Wildlife Federation (http://www.nwf.org/How-To-Help.aspx) and help make sure that we have a future filled with these amazing species.

PUBLISHED 12:30 PM MON, OCT 14, 2013

ABOUT THE AUTHOR

David Mizejewski (http://www.nwf.org/david-mizejewski.aspx) is a naturalist and media personality with the National Wildlife Federation.

Sample Causal Argument

Now that you have had the chance to learn about writing a causal argument, it's time to see what one might look like. Linked, you'll see a sample causal argument essay (http://owl.excelsior.edu/argument-and-critical-thinking/argumentative-purposes/ argumentative-purposes-sample-causal-argument/) written following **MLA (http://owl.excelsior.edu/research-and-citations/ documenting/mla-style/)**formatting guidelines.

Public domain content

Causal Analysis Essay Assignment

Essay 1

Relating Supply Chains to Conflicts (750 points)

The Writing Situation

Thomas L. Friedman argues that countries participating in global supply chains become economically interdependent and are thus less likely to be involved in political conflicts. At the same time, he warns that terrorists are using similar supply chains to spread violence around the world. How can we mitigate terrorist supply chains? Write a four-page paper (not counting the works cited page) to an informed audience in which you assess how the tools that Friedman describes might be used effectively to combat global terrorism. As you focus your argument, consider these questions:

- How can we use collaboration to combat terrorism?
- Are economic incentives and growth a possible solution or part of the problem?
- Could other kinds of supply chains work against terrorism?

Include at least two sources from the JCC library databases. No websites will be considered; you must use library database articles.

To earn passing credit on the final copy, an on-time formal sentence outline is due in Discussion 1 by the due date listed in the schedule. After making significant improvements to the formal outline, you will submit only the final copy as a Word attachment within the Unit 1 Assignments folder. Times and Arial are the only accepted fonts.

Follow the steps outlined below:

1. If you haven't done this yet, **read** the assigned chapters from the textbook as well as mini-lectures on Bb related to this assignment.
2. Brainstorm an arguable point of view and working thesis claim. The thesis is an arguable opinion about which others may disagree; it is neither a fact nor question.
3. Identify at least **three major reasons** you will focus on in this essay. Write a provable, arguable thesis sentence and at least three topic sentences, each directly related to your thesis. The claim must be an arguable assertion, neither a question nor a statement of fact. Note that you shouldn't follow the "one paragraph per reason" approach; a five-paragraph essay this isn't! Your reasons may not use the wording of the bullets above! Think on one's own here.
4. **Research** your selected reasons, using books, JCC databases and web sources, getting at least 2-3 database sources producing diverse forms of evidence. Evaluate the sources. Follow acceptable source guidelines listed in your syllabus. The JCC Information Literacy Tutorial (http://sunyjefferson.libguides.com/informationliteracytutorial) is a good resource to refresh one's skills.
5. Using ides generated in freewriting exercise as well as researched from outside sources, write a **formal sentence outline** of the body ¶s (paragraphs) by integrating multiple source materials with your own commentary. Each reason should have a clear topic sentence and rich, specific and relevant details to make your writing vivid. Cite where needed. **Tie** your examples, stories, expert testimony, studies, statistical evidence (in other words, support) **to the thesis sentence**. The outline must include the working thesis and works cited page. The outline is required for a passing paper and must be a formal sentence outline; use no fragments, please!
6. **Document** any information from sources (whether paraphrased, summarized or quoted), using **parenthetical citations**. Use **signal phrases** to introduce outside data. **Interpret.**

7. Prepare a **Works Cited** page, using MLA format. Refer to current models at OWL at Purdue (https://owl.english.purdue.edu/owl/resource/747/01/).

8. Write introductory and concluding ¶s. Refer to the text as well as my lectures for writing effective introductions and satisfying conclusions.

9. **Revise** and **edit** your essay significantly. Final copies must reflect significant improvement from the outline.

Audience and Purpose

Your audience knows the essay and topic, so argue to establish the validity of your interpretations. Do not write an informative report. *Do* write an argumentative essay.

Tutoring

I am not a tutor. I am happy to look over your paper *if* you provide me with one or two areas to focus upon. JCC also offers tutoring services (http://sunyjefferson.edu/academics/academic-support-services/tutoring).

The proper MLA spacing appears below:

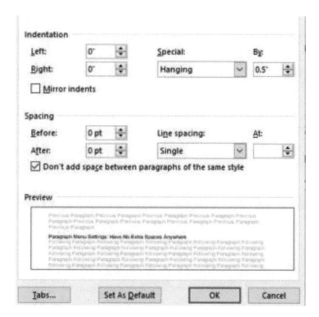

The following sites have useful models for formal sentence outlines. . . .just be sure you're following the *sentence outline* formatting.

- https://app.shoreline.edu/doldham/102/HTML/Sentence%20Outline.html
- https://youtu.be/7cFWkV3ZCCs
- www.llcc.edu/wp-content/uploads/2014/10/formal-outlining.pdf

Ta-Nehisi Coates, The First White President

Read this 2017 feature article from *The Atlantic*, "The First White President." We will focus upon its use of causal arguments in our discussions. Access it either through the permalink below or by accessing either your library databases or www.theatlantic.com

Be sure to access the document with the images.

http://jccweb.sunyjefferson.edu:2055/login.aspx?direct=true&db=a9h&AN=125092135&site=ehost-live

Robert Kubey, Mihaly Csikszentmihalyi, Television Addiction is no Mere Metaphor

What causes addiction? How is it defined? Read this 2004 feature article from *Scientific American*, "Television Addiction is no Mere Metaphor."

We will focus upon its use of persuasion in our discussions. Access it either through the permalink below or by accessing either your library databases or by doing a search online.

Be sure to access the document with the images.

http://jccweb.sunyjefferson.edu:2055/login.aspx?direct=true&db=a9h&AN=12545983&site=ehost-live

Plato, Symposium

by Plato

Translated by Benjamin Jowett

INTRODUCTION.

Of all the works of Plato the Symposium is the most perfect in form, and may be truly thought to contain more than any commentator has ever dreamed of; or, as Goethe said of one of his own writings, more than the author himself knew. For in philosophy as in prophecy glimpses of the future may often be conveyed in words which could hardly have been understood or interpreted at the time when they were uttered (compare Symp.)—which were wiser than the writer of them meant, and could not have been expressed by him if he had been interrogated about them. Yet Plato was not a mystic, nor in any degree affected by the Eastern influences which afterwards overspread the Alexandrian world. He was not an enthusiast or a sentimentalist, but one who aspired only to see reasoned truth, and whose thoughts are clearly explained in his language. There is no foreign element either of Egypt or of Asia to be found in his writings. And more than any other Platonic work the Symposium is Greek both in style and subject, having a beauty 'as of a statue,' while the companion Dialogue of the Phaedrus is marked by a sort of Gothic irregularity. More too than in any other of his Dialogues, Plato is emancipated from former philosophies. The genius of Greek art seems to triumph over the traditions of Pythagorean, Eleatic, or Megarian systems, and 'the old quarrel of poetry and philosophy' has at least a superficial reconcilement. (Rep.)

An unknown person who had heard of the discourses in praise of love spoken by Socrates and others at the banquet of Agathon is desirous of having an authentic account of them, which he thinks that he can obtain from Apollodorus, the same excitable, or rather 'mad' friend of Socrates, who is afterwards introduced in the Phaedo. He had imagined that the discourses were recent. There he is mistaken: but they are still fresh in the memory of his informant, who had just been repeating them to Glaucon, and is quite prepared to have another rehearsal of them in a walk from the Piraeus to Athens. Although he had not been present himself, he had heard them from the best authority. Aristodemus, who is described as having been in past times a humble but inseparable attendant of Socrates, had reported them to him (compare Xen. Mem.).

The narrative which he had heard was as follows:—

Aristodemus meeting Socrates in holiday attire, is invited by him to a banquet at the house of Agathon, who had been sacrificing in thanksgiving for his tragic victory on the day previous. But no sooner has he entered the house than he finds that he is alone; Socrates has stayed behind in a fit of abstraction, and does not appear until the banquet is half over. On his appearing he and the host jest a little; the question is then asked by Pausanias, one of the guests, 'What shall they do about drinking? as they had been all well drunk on the day before, and drinking on two successive days is such a bad thing.' This is confirmed by the authority of Eryximachus the physician, who further proposes that instead of listening to the flute-girl and her 'noise' they shall make speeches in honour of love, one after another, going from left to right in the order in which they are reclining at the table. All of them agree to this proposal, and Phaedrus, who is the 'father' of the idea, which he has previously communicated to Eryximachus, begins as follows:—

He descants first of all upon the antiquity of love, which is proved by the authority of the poets; secondly upon the benefits which love gives to man. The greatest of these is the sense of honour and dishonour. The lover is ashamed to be seen by the beloved doing or suffering any cowardly or mean act. And a state or army which was made up only of lovers and their loves would be invincible. For love will convert the veriest coward into an inspired hero.

And there have been true loves not only of men but of women also. Such was the love of Alcestis, who dared to die for her husband, and in recompense of her virtue was allowed to come again from the dead. But Orpheus, the miserable harper, who went down to Hades alive, that he might bring back his wife, was mocked with an apparition only, and the gods afterwards contrived his death as the punishment of his cowardliness. The love of Achilles, like that of Alcestis, was courageous and true; for he was willing to avenge his lover Patroclus, although he knew that his own death would immediately follow: and the gods, who honour the love of the beloved above that of the lover, rewarded him, and sent him to the islands of the blest.

Pausanias, who was sitting next, then takes up the tale:—He says that Phaedrus should have distinguished the heavenly love from the earthly, before he praised either. For there are two loves, as there are two Aphrodites—one the daughter of Uranus, who has no mother and is the elder and wiser goddess, and the other, the daughter of Zeus and Dione, who is popular and common. The first of the two loves has a noble purpose, and delights only in the intelligent nature of man, and is faithful to the end, and has no shadow of wantonness or lust. The second is the coarser kind of love, which is a love of the body rather than of the soul, and is of women and boys as well as of men. Now the actions of lovers vary, like every other sort of action, according to the manner of their performance. And in different countries there is a difference of opinion about male loves. Some, like the Boeotians, approve of them; others, like the Ionians, and most of the barbarians, disapprove of them; partly because they are aware of the political dangers which ensue from them, as may be seen in the instance of Harmodius and Aristogeiton. At Athens and Sparta there is an apparent contradiction about them. For at times they are encouraged, and then the lover is allowed to play all sorts of fantastic tricks; he may swear and forswear himself (and 'at lovers' perjuries they say Jove laughs'); he may be a servant, and lie on a mat at the door of his love, without any loss of character; but there are also times when elders look grave and guard their young relations, and personal remarks are made. The truth is that some of these loves are disgraceful and others honourable. The vulgar love of the body which takes wing and flies away when the bloom of youth is over, is disgraceful, and so is the interested love of power or wealth; but the love of the noble mind is lasting. The lover should be tested, and the beloved should not be too ready to yield. The rule in our country is that the beloved may do the same service to the lover in the way of virtue which the lover may do to him.

A voluntary service to be rendered for the sake of virtue and wisdom is permitted among us; and when these two customs—one the love of youth, the other the practice of virtue and philosophy—meet in one, then the lovers may lawfully unite. Nor is there any disgrace to a disinterested lover in being deceived: but the interested lover is doubly disgraced, for if he loses his love he loses his character; whereas the noble love of the other remains the same, although the object of his love is unworthy: for nothing can be nobler than love for the sake of virtue. This is that love of the heavenly goddess which is of great price to individuals and cities, making them work together for their improvement.

The turn of Aristophanes comes next; but he has the hiccough, and therefore proposes that Eryximachus the physician shall cure him or speak in his turn. Eryximachus is ready to do both, and after prescribing for the hiccough, speaks as follows:—

He agrees with Pausanias in maintaining that there are two kinds of love; but his art has led him to the further conclusion that the empire of this double love extends over all things, and is to be found in animals and plants as well as in man. In the human body also there are two loves; and the art of medicine shows which is the good and which is the bad love, and persuades the body to accept the good and reject the bad, and reconciles conflicting elements and makes them friends. Every art, gymnastic and husbandry as well as medicine, is the reconciliation of opposites; and this is what Heracleitus meant, when he spoke of a harmony of opposites: but in strictness he should rather have spoken of a harmony which succeeds opposites, for an agreement of disagreements there cannot be. Music too is concerned with the principles of love in their application to harmony and rhythm. In the abstract, all is simple, and we are not troubled with the twofold love; but when they are applied in education with their accompaniments of song and metre, then the discord begins. Then the old tale has to be repeated of fair Urania and the coarse Polyhymnia, who must be indulged sparingly, just as in my own art of medicine care must be taken that the taste of the epicure be gratified without inflicting upon him the attendant penalty of disease.

There is a similar harmony or disagreement in the course of the seasons and in the relations of moist and dry, hot and cold, hoar frost and blight; and diseases of all sorts spring from the excesses or disorders of the element of love. The knowledge of these elements of love and discord in the heavenly bodies is termed astronomy, in the relations of men towards gods and parents is called divination. For divination is the peacemaker of gods and men, and works by a knowledge of the tendencies of merely human loves to piety and impiety. Such is the power of love; and that love which is just and temperate has the greatest power, and is the source of all our happiness and friendship with the gods and with one another. I dare say that I have omitted to mention many things which you, Aristophanes, may supply, as I perceive that you are cured of the hiccough.

Aristophanes is the next speaker:—

He professes to open a new vein of discourse, in which he begins by treating of the origin of human nature. The sexes were originally three, men, women, and the union of the two; and they were made round—having four hands, four feet, two faces on a round neck, and the rest to correspond. Terrible was their strength and swiftness; and they were essaying to scale heaven and attack the gods. Doubt reigned in the celestial councils; the gods were divided between the desire of quelling the pride of man and the fear of losing the sacrifices. At last Zeus hit upon an expedient. Let us cut them in two, he said; then they will only have half their strength, and we shall have twice as many sacrifices. He spake, and split them as you might split an egg with an hair; and when this was done, he told Apollo to give their faces a twist and re-arrange their persons, taking out the wrinkles and tying the skin in a knot about the navel. The two halves went about looking for one another, and were ready to die of hunger in one another's arms. Then Zeus invented an adjustment of the sexes, which enabled them to marry and go their way to the business of life. Now the characters of men differ accordingly as they are derived from the original man or the original woman, or the original man-woman. Those who come from the man-woman are lascivious and adulterous; those who come from the woman form female attachments; those who are a section of the male follow the male and embrace him, and in him all their desires centre. The pair are inseparable and live together in pure and manly affection; yet they cannot tell what they want of one another. But if Hephaestus were to come to them with his instruments and propose that they should be melted into one and remain one here and hereafter, they would acknowledge that this was the very expression of their want. For love is the desire of the whole, and the pursuit of the whole is called love. There was a time when the two sexes were only one, but now God has halved them,—much as the Lacedaemonians have cut up the Arcadians,—and if they do not behave themselves he will divide them again, and they will hop about with half a nose and face in basso relievo. Wherefore let us exhort all men to piety, that we may obtain the goods of which love is the author, and be reconciled to God, and find our own true loves, which rarely happens in this world. And now I must beg you not to suppose that I am alluding to Pausanias and Agathon (compare Protag.), for my words refer to all mankind everywhere.

Some raillery ensues first between Aristophanes and Eryximachus, and then between Agathon, who fears a few select friends more than any number of spectators at the theatre, and Socrates, who is disposed to begin an argument. This is speedily repressed by Phaedrus, who reminds the disputants of their tribute to the god. Agathon's speech follows:—

He will speak of the god first and then of his gifts: He is the fairest and blessedest and best of the gods, and also the youngest, having had no existence in the old days of Iapetus and Cronos when the gods were at war. The things that were done then were done of necessity and not of love. For love is young and dwells in soft places,—not like Ate in Homer, walking on the skulls of men, but in their hearts and souls, which are soft enough. He is all flexibility and grace, and his habitation is among the flowers, and he cannot do or suffer wrong; for all men serve and obey him of their own free will, and where there is love there is obedience, and where obedience, there is justice; for none can be wronged of his own free will. And he is temperate as well as just, for he is the ruler of the desires, and if he rules them he must be temperate. Also he is courageous, for he is the conqueror of the lord of war. And he is wise too; for he is a poet, and the author of poesy in others. He created the animals; he is the inventor of the arts; all the gods are his subjects; he is the fairest and best himself, and the cause of what is fairest and best in others; he makes men to be of one mind at a banquet, filling them with affection and emptying them of disaffection; the pilot, helper, defender, saviour of men, in whose footsteps let every man follow, chanting a strain of love. Such is the discourse, half playful, half serious, which I dedicate to the god.

The turn of Socrates comes next. He begins by remarking satirically that he has not understood the terms of the original agreement, for he fancied that they meant to speak the true praises of love, but now he finds that they only say what is good of him, whether true or false. He begs to be absolved from speaking falsely, but he is willing to speak the truth, and proposes to begin by questioning Agathon. The result of his questions may be summed up as follows:—

Love is of something, and that which love desires is not that which love is or has; for no man desires that which he is or has. And love is of the beautiful, and therefore has not the beautiful. And the beautiful is the good, and therefore, in wanting and desiring the beautiful, love also wants and desires the good. Socrates professes to have asked the same questions and to have obtained the same answers from Diotima, a wise woman of Mantinea, who, like Agathon, had spoken first of love and then of his works. Socrates, like Agathon, had told her that Love is a mighty god and also fair, and she had shown him in return that Love was neither, but in a mean between fair and foul, good and evil, and not a god at all, but only a great demon or intermediate power (compare the speech of Eryximachus) who conveys to the gods the prayers of men, and to men the commands of the gods.

Socrates asks: Who are his father and mother? To this Diotima replies that he is the son of Plenty and Poverty, and partakes of the nature of both, and is full and starved by turns. Like his mother he is poor and squalid, lying on mats at doors (compare the speech of Pausanias); like his father he is bold and strong, and full of arts and resources. Further, he is in a mean between ignorance and knowledge:—in this he resembles the philosopher who is also in a mean between the wise and the ignorant. Such is the nature of Love, who is not to be confused with the beloved.

But Love desires the beautiful; and then arises the question, What does he desire of the beautiful? He desires, of course, the possession of the beautiful;—but what is given by that? For the beautiful let us substitute the good, and we have no difficulty in seeing the possession of the good to be happiness, and Love to be the desire of happiness, although the meaning of the word has been too often confined to one kind of love. And Love desires not only the good, but the everlasting possession of the good. Why then is there all this flutter and excitement about love? Because all men and women at a certain age are desirous of bringing to the birth. And love is not of beauty only, but of birth in beauty; this is the principle of immortality in a mortal creature. When beauty approaches, then the conceiving power is benign and diffuse; when foulness, she is averted and morose.

But why again does this extend not only to men but also to animals? Because they too have an instinct of immortality. Even in the same individual there is a perpetual succession as well of the parts of the material body as of the thoughts and desires of the mind; nay, even knowledge comes and goes. There is no sameness of existence, but the new mortality is always taking the place of the old. This is the reason why parents love their children—for the sake of immortality; and this is why men love the immortality of fame. For the creative soul creates not children, but conceptions of wisdom and virtue, such as poets and other creators have invented. And the noblest creations of all are those of legislators, in honour of whom temples have been raised. Who would not sooner have these children of the mind than the ordinary human ones? (Compare Bacon's Essays, 8:—'Certainly the best works and of greatest merit for the public have proceeded from the unmarried or childless men; which both in affection and means have married and endowed the public.')

I will now initiate you, she said, into the greater mysteries; for he who would proceed in due course should love first one fair form, and then many, and learn the connexion of them; and from beautiful bodies he should proceed to beautiful minds, and the beauty of laws and institutions, until he perceives that all beauty is of one kindred; and from institutions he should go on to the sciences, until at last the vision is revealed to him of a single science of universal beauty, and then he will behold the everlasting nature which is the cause of all, and will be near the end. In the contemplation of that supreme being of love he will be purified of earthly leaven, and will behold beauty, not with the bodily eye, but with the eye of the mind, and will bring forth true creations of virtue and wisdom, and be the friend of God and heir of immortality.

Such, Phaedrus, is the tale which I heard from the stranger of Mantinea, and which you may call the encomium of love, or what you please.

The company applaud the speech of Socrates, and Aristophanes is about to say something, when suddenly a band of revellers breaks into the court, and the voice of Alcibiades is heard asking for Agathon. He is led in drunk, and welcomed by Agathon, whom he has come to crown with a garland. He is placed on a couch at his side, but suddenly, on recognizing Socrates, he starts up, and a sort of conflict is carried on between them, which Agathon is requested to appease. Alcibiades then insists that they shall drink, and has a large wine-cooler filled, which he first empties himself, and then fills again and passes on to Socrates. He is informed of the nature of the entertainment; and is ready to join, if only in the character of a drunken and disappointed lover he may be allowed to sing the praises of Socrates:—

He begins by comparing Socrates first to the busts of Silenus, which have images of the gods inside them; and, secondly, to Marsyas the flute-player. For Socrates produces the same effect with the voice which Marsyas did with the flute. He is the great speaker and enchanter who ravishes the souls of men; the convincer of hearts too, as he has convinced Alcibiades, and made him ashamed of his mean and miserable life. Socrates at one time seemed about to fall in love with him; and he thought that he would thereby gain a wonderful opportunity of receiving lessons of wisdom. He narrates the failure of his design. He has suffered agonies from him, and is at his wit's end. He then proceeds to mention some other particulars of the life of Socrates; how they were at Potidaea together, where Socrates showed his superior powers of enduring cold and fatigue; how on one occasion he had stood for an entire day and night absorbed in reflection amid the wonder of the spectators; how on another occasion he had saved Alcibiades' life; how at the battle of Delium, after the defeat, he might be seen stalking about like a pelican, rolling his eyes as Aristophanes had described him in the Clouds. He is the most wonderful of human beings, and absolutely unlike anyone but a satyr. Like the satyr in his language too; for he uses the commonest words as the outward mask of the divinest truths.

When Alcibiades has done speaking, a dispute begins between him and Agathon and Socrates. Socrates piques Alcibiades by a pretended affection for Agathon. Presently a band of revellers appears, who introduce disorder into the feast; the sober part of the company, Eryximachus, Phaedrus, and others, withdraw; and Aristodemus, the follower of Socrates, sleeps during the whole of a long winter's night. When he wakes at cockcrow the revellers are nearly all asleep. Only Socrates, Aristophanes, and Agathon hold out; they are drinking from a large goblet, which they pass round, and Socrates is explaining to the two others, who are half-asleep, that the genius of tragedy is the same as that of comedy, and that the writer of tragedy ought to be a writer of comedy also. And first Aristophanes drops, and then, as the day is dawning, Agathon. Socrates, having laid them to rest, takes a bath and goes to his daily avocations until the evening. Aristodemus follows.

...

If it be true that there are more things in the Symposium of Plato than any commentator has dreamed of, it is also true that many things have been imagined which are not really to be found there. Some writings hardly admit of a more distinct interpretation than a musical composition; and every reader may form his own accompaniment of thought or feeling to the strain which he hears. The Symposium of Plato is a work of this character, and can with difficulty be rendered in any words but the writer's own. There are so many half-lights and cross-lights, so much of the colour of mythology, and of the manner of sophistry adhering—rhetoric and poetry, the playful and the serious, are so subtly intermingled in it, and vestiges of old philosophy so curiously blend with germs of future knowledge, that agreement among interpreters is not to be expected. The expression 'poema magis putandum quam comicorum poetarum,' which has been applied to all the writings of Plato, is especially applicable to the Symposium.

The power of love is represented in the Symposium as running through all nature and all being: at one end descending to animals and plants, and attaining to the highest vision of truth at the other. In an age when man was seeking for an expression of the world around him, the conception of love greatly affected him. One of the first distinctions of language and of mythology was that of gender; and at a later period the ancient physicist, anticipating modern science, saw, or thought that he saw, a sex in plants; there were elective affinities among the elements, marriages of earth and heaven. (Aesch. Frag. Dan.) Love became a mythic personage whom philosophy, borrowing from poetry, converted into an efficient cause of creation. The traces of the existence of love, as of number and figure, were everywhere discerned; and in the Pythagorean list of opposites male and female were ranged side by side with odd and even, finite and infinite.

But Plato seems also to be aware that there is a mystery of love in man as well as in nature, extending beyond the mere immediate relation of the sexes. He is conscious that the highest and noblest things in the world are not easily severed from the sensual desires, or may even be regarded as a spiritualized form of them. We may observe that Socrates himself is not represented as originally unimpassioned, but as one who has overcome his passions; the secret of his power over others partly lies in his passionate but self-controlled nature. In the Phaedrus and Symposium love is not merely the feeling usually so called, but the mystical contemplation of the beautiful and the good. The same passion which may wallow in the mire is capable of rising to the loftiest heights—of penetrating the inmost secret of philosophy. The highest love is the love not of a person, but of the highest and purest abstraction. This abstraction is the far-off heaven on which the eye of the mind is fixed in fond amazement. The unity of truth, the consistency of the warring elements of the world, the enthusiasm for knowledge when first beaming upon mankind, the relativity of ideas to the human mind, and of the human mind to ideas, the faith in the invisible, the adoration of the eternal nature, are all included, consciously or unconsciously, in Plato's doctrine of love.

The successive speeches in praise of love are characteristic of the speakers, and contribute in various degrees to the final result; they are all designed to prepare the way for Socrates, who gathers up the threads anew, and skims the highest points of each of them. But they are not to be regarded as the stages of an idea, rising above one another to a climax. They are fanciful, partly facetious performances, 'yet also having a certain measure of seriousness,' which the successive speakers dedicate to the god. All of them are rhetorical and poetical rather than dialectical, but glimpses of truth appear in them. When Eryximachus says that the principles of music are simple in themselves, but confused in their application, he touches lightly upon a difficulty which has troubled the moderns as well as the ancients in music, and may be extended to the other applied sciences. That confusion begins in the concrete, was the natural feeling of a mind dwelling in the world of ideas. When Pausanias remarks that personal attachments are inimical to despots. The experience of Greek history confirms the truth of his remark. When Aristophanes declares that love is the desire of the whole, he expresses a feeling not unlike that of the German philosopher, who says that 'philosophy is home sickness.' When Agathon says that no man 'can be wronged of his own free will,' he is alluding playfully to a serious problem of Greek philosophy (compare Arist. Nic. Ethics). So naturally does Plato mingle jest and earnest, truth and opinion in the same work.

The characters—of Phaedrus, who has been the cause of more philosophical discussions than any other man, with the exception of Simmias the Theban (Phaedrus); of Aristophanes, who disguises under comic imagery a serious purpose; of Agathon, who in later life is satirized by Aristophanes in the Thesmophoriazusae, for his effeminate manners and the feeble rhythms of his verse; of Alcibiades, who is the same strange contrast of great powers and great vices, which meets us in history—are drawn to the life; and we may suppose the less-known characters of Pausanias and Eryximachus to be also true to the traditional recollection of them (compare Phaedr., Protag.; and compare Sympos. with Phaedr.). We may also remark that Aristodemus is called 'the little' in Xenophon's Memorabilia (compare Symp.).

The speeches have been said to follow each other in pairs: Phaedrus and Pausanias being the ethical, Eryximachus and Aristophanes the physical speakers, while in Agathon and Socrates poetry and philosophy blend together. The speech of Phaedrus is also described as the mythological, that of Pausanias as the political, that of Eryximachus as the scientific, that of Aristophanes as the artistic (!), that of Socrates as the philosophical. But these and similar distinctions are not found in Plato;—they are the points of view of his critics, and seem to impede rather than to assist us in understanding him.

When the turn of Socrates comes round he cannot be allowed to disturb the arrangement made at first. With the leave of Phaedrus he asks a few questions, and then he throws his argument into the form of a speech (compare Gorg., Protag.). But his speech is really the narrative of a dialogue between himself and Diotima. And as at a banquet good manners would not allow him to win a victory either over his host or any of the guests, the superiority which he gains over Agathon is ingeniously represented as having been already gained over himself by her. The artifice has the further advantage of maintaining his accustomed profession of ignorance (compare Menex.). Even his knowledge of the mysteries of love, to which he lays claim here and elsewhere (Lys.), is given by Diotima.

The speeches are attested to us by the very best authority. The madman Apollodorus, who for three years past has made a daily study of the actions of Socrates—to whom the world is summed up in the words 'Great is Socrates'—he has heard them from another 'madman,' Aristodemus, who was the 'shadow' of Socrates in days of old, like him going about barefooted, and who had been present at the time. 'Would you desire better witness?' The extraordinary narrative of Alcibiades is ingeniously represented as admitted by Socrates, whose silence when he is invited to contradict gives consent to the narrator. We may observe, by the way, (1) how the very appearance of Aristodemus by himself is a sufficient indication to Agathon that Socrates has been left behind; also, (2) how the courtesy of Agathon anticipates the excuse which Socrates was to have made on Aristodemus' behalf for coming uninvited; (3) how the story of the fit or trance of Socrates is confirmed by the mention which Alcibiades makes of a similar fit of abstraction occurring when he was serving with the army at Potidaea; like (4) the drinking powers of Socrates and his love of the fair, which receive a similar attestation in the concluding scene; or the attachment of Aristodemus, who is not forgotten when Socrates takes his departure. (5) We may notice the manner in which Socrates himself regards the first five speeches, not as true, but as fanciful and exaggerated encomiums of the god Love; (6) the satirical character of them, shown especially in the appeals to mythology, in the reasons which are given by Zeus for reconstructing the frame of man, or by the Boeotians and Eleans for encouraging male loves; (7) the ruling passion of Socrates for dialectics, who will argue with Agathon instead of making a speech, and will only speak at all upon the condition that he is allowed to speak the truth. We may note also the touch of Socratic irony, (8) which admits of a wide application and reveals a deep insight into the world:—that in speaking of holy things and persons there is a general understanding that you should praise them, not that you should speak the truth about them—this is the sort of praise which Socrates is unable to give. Lastly, (9) we may remark that the banquet is a real banquet after all, at which love is the theme of discourse, and huge quantities of wine are drunk.

The discourse of Phaedrus is half-mythical, half-ethical; and he himself, true to the character which is given him in the Dialogue bearing his name, is half-sophist, half-enthusiast. He is the critic of poetry also, who compares Homer and Aeschylus in the insipid and irrational manner of the schools of the day, characteristically reasoning about the probability of matters which do not admit of reasoning. He starts from a noble text: 'That without the sense of honour and dishonour neither states nor individuals ever do any good or great work.' But he soon passes on to more common-place topics. The antiquity of love, the blessing of having a lover, the incentive which love offers to daring deeds, the examples of Alcestis and Achilles, are the chief themes of his discourse. The love of women is regarded by him as almost on an equality with that of men; and he makes the singular remark that the gods favour the return of love which is made by the beloved more than the original sentiment, because the lover is of a nobler and diviner nature.

There is something of a sophistical ring in the speech of Phaedrus, which recalls the first speech in imitation of Lysias, occurring in the Dialogue called the Phaedrus. This is still more marked in the speech of Pausanias which follows; and which is at once hyperlogical in form and also extremely confused and pedantic. Plato is attacking the logical feebleness of the sophists and rhetoricians, through their pupils, not forgetting by the way to satirize the monotonous and unmeaning rhythms which Prodicus and others were introducing into Attic prose (compare Protag.). Of course, he is 'playing both sides of the game,' as in the Gorgias and Phaedrus; but it is not necessary in order to understand him that we should discuss the fairness of his mode of proceeding. The love of Pausanias for Agathon has already been touched upon in the Protagoras, and is alluded to by Aristophanes. Hence he is naturally the upholder of male loves, which, like all the other affections or actions of men, he regards as varying according to the manner of their performance. Like the sophists and like Plato himself, though in a different sense, he begins his discussion by an appeal to mythology, and distinguishes between the elder and younger love. The value which he attributes to such loves as motives to virtue and philosophy is at variance with modern and Christian notions, but is in accordance with Hellenic sentiment. The opinion of Christendom has not altogether condemned passionate friendships between persons of the same sex, but has certainly not encouraged them, because though innocent in themselves in a few temperaments they are liable to degenerate into fearful evil. Pausanias is very earnest in the defence of such loves; and he speaks of them as generally approved among Hellenes and disapproved by barbarians. His speech is 'more words than matter,' and might have been composed by a pupil of Lysias or of Prodicus, although there is no hint given that Plato is specially referring to them. As Eryximachus says, 'he makes a fair beginning, but a lame ending.'

Plato transposes the two next speeches, as in the Republic he would transpose the virtues and the mathematical sciences. This is done partly to avoid monotony, partly for the sake of making Aristophanes 'the cause of wit in others,' and also in order to bring the comic and tragic poet into juxtaposition, as if by accident. A suitable 'expectation' of Aristophanes is raised by the ludicrous circumstance of his having the hiccough, which is appropriately cured by his substitute, the physician Eryximachus. To Eryximachus Love is the good physician; he sees everything as an intelligent physicist, and, like many professors of his art in modern times, attempts to reduce the moral to the physical; or recognises one law of love which pervades them both. There are loves and strifes of the body as well as of the mind. Like Hippocrates the Asclepiad, he is a disciple of Heracleitus, whose conception of the harmony of opposites he explains in a new way as the harmony after discord; to his common sense, as to that of many moderns as well as ancients, the identity of contradictories is an absurdity. His notion of love may be summed up as the harmony of man with himself in soul as well as body, and of all things in heaven and earth with one another.

Aristophanes is ready to laugh and make laugh before he opens his mouth, just as Socrates, true to his character, is ready to argue before he begins to speak. He expresses the very genius of the old comedy, its coarse and forcible imagery, and the licence of its language in speaking about the gods. He has no sophistical notions about love, which is brought back by him to its common-sense meaning of love between intelligent beings. His account of the origin of the sexes has the greatest (comic) probability and verisimilitude. Nothing in Aristophanes is more truly Aristophanic than the description of the human monster whirling round on four arms and four legs, eight in all, with incredible rapidity. Yet there is a mixture of earnestness in this jest; three serious principles seem to be insinuated:—first, that man cannot exist in isolation; he must be reunited if he is to be perfected: secondly, that love is the mediator and reconciler of poor, divided human nature: thirdly, that the loves of this world are an indistinct anticipation of an ideal union which is not yet realized.

The speech of Agathon is conceived in a higher strain, and receives the real, if half-ironical, approval of Socrates. It is the speech of the tragic poet and a sort of poem, like tragedy, moving among the gods of Olympus, and not among the elder or Orphic deities. In the idea of the antiquity of love he cannot agree; love is not of the olden time, but present and youthful ever. The speech may be compared with that speech of Socrates in the Phaedrus in which he describes himself as talking dithyrambs. It is at once a preparation for Socrates and a foil to him. The rhetoric of Agathon elevates the soul to 'sunlit heights,' but at the same time contrasts with the natural and necessary eloquence of Socrates. Agathon contributes the distinction between love and the works of love, and also hints incidentally that love is always of beauty, which Socrates afterwards raises into a principle. While the consciousness of discord is stronger in the comic poet Aristophanes, Agathon, the tragic poet, has a deeper sense of harmony and reconciliation, and speaks of Love as the creator and artist.

All the earlier speeches embody common opinions coloured with a tinge of philosophy. They furnish the material out of which Socrates proceeds to form his discourse, starting, as in other places, from mythology and the opinions of men. From Phaedrus he takes the thought that love is stronger than death; from Pausanias, that the true love is akin to intellect and political activity; from Eryximachus, that love is a universal phenomenon and the great power of nature; from Aristophanes, that love is the child of want, and is not merely the love of the congenial or of the whole, but (as he adds) of the good; from Agathon, that love is of beauty, not however of beauty only, but of birth in beauty. As it would be out of character for Socrates to make a lengthened harangue, the speech takes the form of a dialogue between Socrates and a mysterious woman of foreign extraction. She elicits the final truth from one who knows nothing, and who, speaking by the lips of another, and himself a despiser of rhetoric, is proved also to be the most consummate of rhetoricians (compare Menexenus).

The last of the six discourses begins with a short argument which overthrows not only Agathon but all the preceding speakers by the help of a distinction which has escaped them. Extravagant praises have been ascribed to Love as the author of every good; no sort of encomium was too high for him, whether deserved and true or not. But Socrates has no talent for speaking anything but the truth, and if he is to speak the truth of Love he must honestly confess that he is not a good at all: for love is of the good, and no man can desire that which he has. This piece of dialectics is ascribed to Diotima, who has already urged upon Socrates the argument which he urges against Agathon. That the distinction is a fallacy is obvious; it is almost acknowledged to be so by Socrates himself. For he who has beauty or good may desire more of them; and he who has beauty or good in himself may desire beauty and good in others. The fallacy seems to arise out of a confusion between the abstract ideas of good and beauty, which do not admit of degrees, and their partial realization in individuals.

But Diotima, the prophetess of Mantineia, whose sacred and superhuman character raises her above the ordinary proprieties of women, has taught Socrates far more than this about the art and mystery of love. She has taught him that love is another aspect of philosophy. The same want in the human soul which is satisfied in the vulgar by the procreation of children, may become the highest aspiration of intellectual desire. As the Christian might speak of hungering and thirsting after righteousness; or of divine loves under the figure of human (compare Eph. 'This is a great mystery, but I speak concerning Christ and the church'); as the mediaeval saint might speak of the 'fruitio Dei;' as Dante saw all things contained in his love of Beatrice, so Plato would have us absorb all other loves and desires in the love of knowledge. Here is the beginning of Neoplatonism, or rather, perhaps, a proof (of which there are many) that the so-called mysticism of the East was not strange to the Greek of the fifth century before Christ. The first tumult of the affections was not wholly subdued; there were longings of a creature moving about in worlds not realized, which no art could satisfy. To most men reason and passion appear to be antagonistic both in idea and fact. The union of the greatest comprehension of knowledge and the burning intensity of love is a contradiction in nature, which may have existed in a far-off primeval age in the mind of some Hebrew prophet or other Eastern sage, but has now become an imagination only. Yet this 'passion of the reason' is the theme of the Symposium of Plato. And as there is no impossibility in supposing that 'one king, or son of a king, may be a philosopher,' so also there is a probability that there may be some few—perhaps one or two in a whole generation—in whom the light of truth may not lack the warmth of desire. And if there be such natures, no one will be disposed to deny that 'from them flow most of the benefits of individuals and states;' and even from imperfect combinations of the two elements in teachers or statesmen great good may often arise.

Yet there is a higher region in which love is not only felt, but satisfied, in the perfect beauty of eternal knowledge, beginning with the beauty of earthly things, and at last reaching a beauty in which all existence is seen to be harmonious and one. The limited affection is enlarged, and enabled to behold the ideal of all things. And here the highest summit which is reached in the Symposium is seen also to be the highest summit which is attained in the Republic, but approached from another side; and there is 'a way upwards and downwards,' which is the same and not the same in both. The ideal beauty of the one is the ideal good of the other; regarded not with the eye of knowledge, but of faith and desire; and they are respectively the source of beauty and the source of good in all other things. And by the steps of a 'ladder reaching to heaven' we pass from images of visible beauty (Greek), and from the hypotheses of the Mathematical sciences, which are not yet based upon the idea of good, through the concrete to the abstract, and, by different paths arriving, behold the vision of the eternal (compare Symp. (Greek) Republic (Greek) also Phaedrus). Under one aspect 'the idea is love'; under another, 'truth.' In both the lover of wisdom is the 'spectator of all time and of all existence.' This is a 'mystery' in which Plato also obscurely intimates the union of the spiritual and fleshly, the interpenetration of the moral and intellectual faculties.

The divine image of beauty which resides within Socrates has been revealed; the Silenus, or outward man, has now to be exhibited. The description of Socrates follows immediately after the speech of Socrates; one is the complement of the other. At the height of divine inspiration, when the force of nature can no further go, by way of contrast to this extreme idealism, Alcibiades, accompanied by a troop of revellers and a flute-girl, staggers in, and being drunk is able to tell of things which he would have been ashamed to make known if he had been sober. The state of his affections towards Socrates, unintelligible to us and perverted as they appear, affords an illustration of the power ascribed to the loves of man in the speech of Pausanias. He does not suppose his feelings to be peculiar to himself: there are several other persons in the company who have been equally in love with Socrates, and like himself have been deceived by him. The singular part of this confession is the combination of the most degrading passion with the desire of virtue and improvement. Such an union is not wholly untrue to human nature, which is capable of combining good and evil in a degree beyond what we can easily conceive. In imaginative persons, especially, the God and beast in man seem to part asunder more than is natural in a well-regulated mind. The Platonic Socrates (for of the real Socrates this may be doubted: compare his public rebuke of Critias for his shameful love of Euthydemus in Xenophon, Memorabilia) does not regard the greatest evil of Greek life as a thing not to be spoken of; but it has a ridiculous element (Plato's Symp.), and is a subject for irony, no less than for moral reprobation (compare Plato's Symp.). It is also used as a figure of speech which no one interpreted literally (compare Xen. Symp.). Nor does Plato feel any repugnance, such as would be felt in modern times, at bringing his great master and hero into connexion with nameless crimes. He is contented with representing him as a saint, who has won 'the Olympian victory' over the temptations of human nature. The fault of taste, which to us is so glaring and which was recognized by the Greeks of a later age (Athenaeus), was not perceived by Plato himself. We are still more surprised to find that the philosopher is incited to take the first step in his upward progress (Symp.) by the beauty of young men and boys, which was alone capable of inspiring the modern feeling of romance in the Greek mind. The passion of love took the spurious form of an enthusiasm for the ideal of beauty—a worship as of some godlike image of an Apollo or Antinous. But the love of youth when not depraved was a love of virtue and modesty as well as of beauty, the one being the expression of the other; and in certain Greek states, especially at Sparta and Thebes, the honourable attachment of a youth to an elder man was a part of his education. The 'army of lovers and their beloved who would be invincible if they could be united by such a tie' (Symp.), is not a mere fiction of Plato's, but seems actually to have existed at Thebes in the days of Epaminondas and Pelopidas, if we may believe writers cited anonymously by Plutarch, Pelop. Vit. It is observable that Plato never in the least degree excuses the depraved love of the body (compare Charm.; Rep.; Laws; Symp.; and once more Xenophon, Mem.), nor is there any Greek writer of mark who condones or approves such connexions. But owing partly to the puzzling nature of the subject these friendships are spoken of by Plato in a manner different from that customary among ourselves. To most of them we should hesitate to ascribe, any more than to the attachment of Achilles and Patroclus in Homer, an immoral or licentious character. There were many, doubtless, to whom the love of the fair mind was the noblest form of friendship (Rep.), and who deemed the friendship of man with man to be higher than the love of woman, because altogether separated from the bodily appetites. The existence of such attachments may be reasonably attributed to the inferiority and seclusion of woman, and the want of a real family or social life and parental influence in Hellenic cities; and they were encouraged by the practice of gymnastic exercises, by the meetings of political clubs, and by the tie of military companionship. They were also an educational institution: a young person was specially entrusted by his parents to some elder friend who was expected by them to train their son in manly exercises and in virtue. It is not likely that a Greek parent committed him to a lover, any more than we should to a schoolmaster, in the expectation that he would be corrupted by him, but rather in the hope that his morals would be better cared for than was possible in a great household of slaves.

It is difficult to adduce the authority of Plato either for or against such practices or customs, because it is not always easy to determine whether he is speaking of 'the heavenly and philosophical love, or of the coarse Polyhymnia:' and he often refers to this (e.g. in the Symposium) half in jest, yet 'with a certain degree of seriousness.' We observe that they entered into one part of Greek literature, but not into another, and that the larger part is free from such associations. Indecency was an element of the ludicrous in the old Greek Comedy, as it has been in other ages and countries. But effeminate love was always condemned as well as ridiculed by the Comic poets; and in the New Comedy the allusions to such topics have disappeared. They seem to have been no longer tolerated by the greater refinement of the age. False sentiment is found in the Lyric and Elegiac poets; and in mythology 'the greatest of the Gods' (Rep.) is not exempt from evil imputations. But the morals of a nation are not to be judged of wholly by its literature. Hellas was not necessarily more corrupted in the days of the Persian and Peloponnesian wars, or of Plato and the Orators, than England in the time of Fielding and Smollett, or France in the nineteenth century. No one supposes certain French novels to be a representation of ordinary French life. And the greater part of Greek literature, beginning with Homer and including the tragedians, philosophers, and, with the exception of the Comic poets (whose business was to raise a laugh by whatever means), all the greater writers of Hellas who have been preserved to us, are free from the taint of indecency.

Some general considerations occur to our mind when we begin to reflect on this subject. (1) That good and evil are linked together in human nature, and have often existed side by side in the world and in man to an extent hardly credible. We cannot distinguish them, and are therefore unable to part them; as in the parable 'they grow together unto the harvest:' it is only a rule of external decency by which society can divide them. Nor should we be right in inferring from the prevalence of any one vice or corruption that a state or individual was demoralized in their whole character. Not only has the corruption of the best been sometimes thought to be the worst, but it may be remarked that this very excess of evil has been the stimulus to good (compare Plato, Laws, where he says that in the most corrupt cities individuals are to be found beyond all praise). (2) It may be observed that evils which admit of degrees can seldom be rightly estimated, because under the same name actions of the most different degrees of culpability may be included. No charge is more easily set going than the imputation of secret wickedness (which cannot be either proved or disproved and often cannot be defined) when directed against a person of whom the world, or a section of it, is predisposed to think evil. And it is quite possible that the malignity of Greek scandal, aroused by some personal jealousy or party enmity, may have converted the innocent friendship of a great man for a noble youth into a connexion of another kind. Such accusations were brought against several of the leading men of Hellas, e.g. Cimon, Alcibiades, Critias, Demosthenes, Epaminondas: several of the Roman emperors were assailed by similar weapons which have been used even in our own day against statesmen of the highest character. (3) While we know that in this matter there is a great gulf fixed between Greek and Christian Ethics, yet, if we would do justice to the Greeks, we must also acknowledge that there was a greater outspokenness among them than among ourselves about the things which nature hides, and that the more frequent mention of such topics is not to be taken as the measure of the prevalence of offences, or as a proof of the general corruption of society. It is likely that every religion in the world has used words or practised rites in one age, which have become distasteful or repugnant to another. We cannot, though for different reasons, trust the representations either of Comedy or Satire; and still less of Christian Apologists. (4) We observe that at Thebes and Lacedemon the attachment of an elder friend to a beloved youth was often deemed to be a part of his education; and was encouraged by his parents—it was only shameful if it degenerated into licentiousness. Such we may believe to have been the tie which united Asophychus and Cephisodorus with the great Epaminondas in whose companionship they fell (Plutarch, Amat.; Athenaeus on the authority of Theopompus). (5) A small matter: there appears to be a difference of custom among the Greeks and among ourselves, as between ourselves and continental nations at the present time, in modes of salutation. We must not suspect evil in the hearty kiss or embrace of a male friend 'returning from the army at Potidaea' any more than in a similar salutation when practised by members of the same family. But those who make these admissions, and who regard, not without pity, the victims of such illusions in our own day, whose life has been blasted by them, may be none the less resolved that the natural and healthy instincts of mankind shall alone be tolerated (Greek); and that the lesson of manliness which we have inherited from our fathers shall not degenerate into sentimentalism or effeminacy. The possibility of an honourable connexion of this kind seems to have died out with Greek civilization. Among the Romans, and also among barbarians, such as the Celts and Persians, there is no trace of such attachments existing in any noble or virtuous form.

(Compare Hoeck's Creta and the admirable and exhaustive article of Meier in Ersch and Grueber's Cyclopedia on this subject; Plutarch, Amatores; Athenaeus; Lysias contra Simonem; Aesch. c. Timarchum.)

The character of Alcibiades in the Symposium is hardly less remarkable than that of Socrates, and agrees with the picture given of him in the first of the two Dialogues which are called by his name, and also with the slight sketch of him in the Protagoras. He is the impersonation of lawlessness—'the lion's whelp, who ought not to be reared in the city,' yet not without a certain generosity which gained the hearts of men,—strangely fascinated by Socrates, and possessed of a genius which might have been either the destruction or salvation of Athens. The dramatic interest of the character is heightened by the recollection of his after history. He seems to have been present to the mind of Plato in the description of the democratic man of the Republic (compare also Alcibiades 1).

There is no criterion of the date of the Symposium, except that which is furnished by the allusion to the division of Arcadia after the destruction of Mantinea. This took place in the year B.C. 384, which is the forty-fourth year of Plato's life. The Symposium cannot therefore be regarded as a youthful work. As Mantinea was restored in the year 369, the composition of the Dialogue will probably fall between 384 and 369. Whether the recollection of the event is more likely to have been renewed at the destruction or restoration of the city, rather than at some intermediate period, is a consideration not worth raising.

The Symposium is connected with the Phaedrus both in style and subject; they are the only Dialogues of Plato in which the theme of love is discussed at length. In both of them philosophy is regarded as a sort of enthusiasm or madness; Socrates is himself 'a prophet new inspired' with Bacchanalian revelry, which, like his philosophy, he characteristically pretends to have derived not from himself but from others. The Phaedo also presents some points of comparison with the Symposium. For there, too, philosophy might be described as 'dying for love;' and there are not wanting many touches of humour and fancy, which remind us of the Symposium. But while the Phaedo and Phaedrus look backwards and forwards to past and future states of existence, in the Symposium there is no break between this world and another; and we rise from one to the other by a regular series of steps or stages, proceeding from the particulars of sense to the universal of reason, and from one universal to many, which are finally reunited in a single science (compare Rep.). At first immortality means only the succession of existences; even knowledge comes and goes. Then follows, in the language of the mysteries, a higher and a higher degree of initiation; at last we arrive at the perfect vision of beauty, not relative or changing, but eternal and absolute; not bounded by this world, or in or out of this world, but an aspect of the divine, extending over all things, and having no limit of space or time: this is the highest knowledge of which the human mind is capable. Plato does not go on to ask whether the individual is absorbed in the sea of light and beauty or retains his personality. Enough for him to have attained the true beauty or good, without enquiring precisely into the relation in which human beings stood to it. That the soul has such a reach of thought, and is capable of partaking of the eternal nature, seems to imply that she too is eternal (compare Phaedrus). But Plato does not distinguish the eternal in man from the eternal in the world or in God. He is willing to rest in the contemplation of the idea, which to him is the cause of all things (Rep.), and has no strength to go further.

The Symposium of Xenophon, in which Socrates describes himself as a pander, and also discourses of the difference between sensual and sentimental love, likewise offers several interesting points of comparison. But the suspicion which hangs over other writings of Xenophon, and the numerous minute references to the Phaedrus and Symposium, as well as to some of the other writings of Plato, throw a doubt on the genuineness of the work. The Symposium of Xenophon, if written by him at all, would certainly show that he wrote against Plato, and was acquainted with his works. Of this hostility there is no trace in the Memorabilia. Such a rivalry is more characteristic of an imitator than of an original writer. The (so-called) Symposium of Xenophon may therefore have no more title to be regarded as genuine than the confessedly spurious Apology.

There are no means of determining the relative order in time of the Phaedrus, Symposium, Phaedo. The order which has been adopted in this translation rests on no other principle than the desire to bring together in a series the memorials of the life of Socrates.

()

SYMPOSIUM

PERSONS OF THE DIALOGUE: Apollodorus, who repeats to his companion the dialogue which he had heard from Aristodemus, and had already once narrated to Glaucon. Phaedrus, Pausanias, Eryximachus, Aristophanes, Agathon, Socrates, Alcibiades, A Troop of Revellers.

SCENE: The House of Agathon.

Concerning the things about which you ask to be informed I believe that I am not ill-prepared with an answer. For the day before yesterday I was coming from my own home at Phalerum to the city, and one of my acquaintance, who had caught a sight of me from behind, calling out playfully in the distance, said: Apollodorus, O thou Phalerian (Probably a play of words on (Greek), 'bald-headed.') man, halt! So I did as I was bid; and then he said, I was looking for you, Apollodorus, only just now, that I might ask you about the speeches in praise of love, which were delivered by Socrates, Alcibiades, and others, at Agathon's supper. Phoenix, the son of Philip, told another person who told me of them; his narrative was very indistinct, but he said that you knew, and I wish that you would give me an account of them. Who, if not you, should be the reporter of the words of your friend? And first tell me, he said, were you present at this meeting?

Your informant, Glaucon, I said, must have been very indistinct indeed, if you imagine that the occasion was recent; or that I could have been of the party.

Why, yes, he replied, I thought so.

Impossible: I said. Are you ignorant that for many years Agathon has not resided at Athens; and not three have elapsed since I became acquainted with Socrates, and have made it my daily business to know all that he says and does. There was a time when I was running about the world, fancying myself to be well employed, but I was really a most wretched being, no better than you are now. I thought that I ought to do anything rather than be a philosopher.

Well, he said, jesting apart, tell me when the meeting occurred.

In our boyhood, I replied, when Agathon won the prize with his first tragedy, on the day after that on which he and his chorus offered the sacrifice of victory.

Then it must have been a long while ago, he said; and who told you—did Socrates?

No indeed, I replied, but the same person who told Phoenix;—he was a little fellow, who never wore any shoes, Aristodemus, of the deme of Cydathenaeum. He had been at Agathon's feast; and I think that in those days there was no one who was a more devoted admirer of Socrates. Moreover, I have asked Socrates about the truth of some parts of his narrative, and he confirmed them. Then, said Glaucon, let us have the tale over again; is not the road to Athens just made for conversation? And so we walked, and talked of the discourses on love; and therefore, as I said at first, I am not ill-prepared to comply with your request, and will have another rehearsal of them if you like. For to speak or to hear others speak of philosophy always gives me the greatest pleasure, to say nothing of the profit. But when I hear another strain, especially that of you rich men and traders, such conversation displeases me; and I pity you who are my companions, because you think that you are doing something when in reality you are doing nothing. And I dare say that you pity me in return, whom you regard as an unhappy creature, and very probably you are right. But I certainly know of you what you only think of me—there is the difference.

COMPANION: I see, Apollodorus, that you are just the same—always speaking evil of yourself, and of others; and I do believe that you pity all mankind, with the exception of Socrates, yourself first of all, true in this to your old name, which, however deserved, I know not how you acquired, of Apollodorus the madman; for you are always raging against yourself and everybody but Socrates.

APOLLODORUS: Yes, friend, and the reason why I am said to be mad, and out of my wits, is just because I have these notions of myself and you; no other evidence is required.

COMPANION: No more of that, Apollodorus; but let me renew my request that you would repeat the conversation.

APOLLODORUS: Well, the tale of love was on this wise:—But perhaps I had better begin at the beginning, and endeavour to give you the exact words of Aristodemus:

He said that he met Socrates fresh from the bath and sandalled; and as the sight of the sandals was unusual, he asked him whither he was going that he had been converted into such a beau:—

To a banquet at Agathon's, he replied, whose invitation to his sacrifice of victory I refused yesterday, fearing a crowd, but promising that I would come to-day instead; and so I have put on my finery, because he is such a fine man. What say you to going with me unasked?

I will do as you bid me, I replied.

Follow then, he said, and let us demolish the proverb:—

'To the feasts of inferior men the good unbidden go;'

instead of which our proverb will run:—

'To the feasts of the good the good unbidden go;'

and this alteration may be supported by the authority of Homer himself, who not only demolishes but literally outrages the proverb. For, after picturing Agamemnon as the most valiant of men, he makes Menelaus, who is but a fainthearted warrior, come unbidden (Iliad) to the banquet of Agamemnon, who is feasting and offering sacrifices, not the better to the worse, but the worse to the better.

I rather fear, Socrates, said Aristodemus, lest this may still be my case; and that, like Menelaus in Homer, I shall be the inferior person, who

'To the feasts of the wise unbidden goes.'

But I shall say that I was bidden of you, and then you will have to make an excuse.

'Two going together,'

he replied, in Homeric fashion, one or other of them may invent an excuse by the way (Iliad).

This was the style of their conversation as they went along. Socrates dropped behind in a fit of abstraction, and desired Aristodemus, who was waiting, to go on before him. When he reached the house of Agathon he found the doors wide open, and a comical thing happened. A servant coming out met him, and led him at once into the banqueting-hall in which the guests were reclining, for the banquet was about to begin. Welcome, Aristodemus, said Agathon, as soon as he appeared—you are just in time to sup with us; if you come on any other matter put it off, and make one of us, as I was looking for you yesterday and meant to have asked you, if I could have found you. But what have you done with Socrates?

I turned round, but Socrates was nowhere to be seen; and I had to explain that he had been with me a moment before, and that I came by his invitation to the supper.

You were quite right in coming, said Agathon; but where is he himself?

He was behind me just now, as I entered, he said, and I cannot think what has become of him.

Go and look for him, boy, said Agathon, and bring him in; and do you, Aristodemus, meanwhile take the place by Eryximachus.

The servant then assisted him to wash, and he lay down, and presently another servant came in and reported that our friend Socrates had retired into the portico of the neighbouring house. 'There he is fixed,' said he, 'and when I call to him he will not stir.'

How strange, said Agathon; then you must call him again, and keep calling him.

Let him alone, said my informant; he has a way of stopping anywhere and losing himself without any reason. I believe that he will soon appear; do not therefore disturb him.

Well, if you think so, I will leave him, said Agathon. And then, turning to the servants, he added, 'Let us have supper without waiting for him. Serve up whatever you please, for there is no one to give you orders; hitherto I have never left you to yourselves. But on this occasion imagine that you are our hosts, and that I and the company are your guests; treat us well, and then we shall commend you.' After this, supper was served, but still no Socrates; and during the meal Agathon several times expressed a wish to send for him, but Aristodemus objected; and at last when the feast was about half over—for the fit, as usual, was not of long duration—Socrates entered. Agathon, who was reclining alone at the end of the table, begged that he would take the place next to him; that 'I may touch you,' he said, 'and have the benefit of that wise thought which came into your mind in the portico, and is now in your possession; for I am certain that you would not have come away until you had found what you sought.'

How I wish, said Socrates, taking his place as he was desired, that wisdom could be infused by touch, out of the fuller into the emptier man, as water runs through wool out of a fuller cup into an emptier one; if that were so, how greatly should I value the privilege of reclining at your side! For you would have filled me full with a stream of wisdom plenteous and fair; whereas my own is of a very mean and questionable sort, no better than a dream. But yours is bright and full of promise, and was manifested forth in all the splendour of youth the day before yesterday, in the presence of more than thirty thousand Hellenes.

You are mocking, Socrates, said Agathon, and ere long you and I will have to determine who bears off the palm of wisdom—of this Dionysus shall be the judge; but at present you are better occupied with supper.

Socrates took his place on the couch, and supped with the rest; and then libations were offered, and after a hymn had been sung to the god, and there had been the usual ceremonies, they were about to commence drinking, when Pausanias said, And now, my friends, how can we drink with least injury to ourselves? I can assure you that I feel severely the effect of yesterday's potations, and must have time to recover; and I suspect that most of you are in the same predicament, for you were of the party yesterday. Consider then: How can the drinking be made easiest?

I entirely agree, said Aristophanes, that we should, by all means, avoid hard drinking, for I was myself one of those who were yesterday drowned in drink.

I think that you are right, said Eryximachus, the son of Acumenus; but I should still like to hear one other person speak: Is Agathon able to drink hard?

I am not equal to it, said Agathon.

Then, said Eryximachus, the weak heads like myself, Aristodemus, Phaedrus, and others who never can drink, are fortunate in finding that the stronger ones are not in a drinking mood. (I do not include Socrates, who is able either to drink or to abstain, and will not mind, whichever we do.) Well, as of none of the company seem disposed to drink much, I may be forgiven for saying, as a physician, that drinking deep is a bad practice, which I never follow, if I can help, and certainly do not recommend to another, least of all to any one who still feels the effects of yesterday's carouse.

I always do what you advise, and especially what you prescribe as a physician, rejoined Phaedrus the Myrrhinusian, and the rest of the company, if they are wise, will do the same.

It was agreed that drinking was not to be the order of the day, but that they were all to drink only so much as they pleased.

Then, said Eryximachus, as you are all agreed that drinking is to be voluntary, and that there is to be no compulsion, I move, in the next place, that the flute-girl, who has just made her appearance, be told to go away and play to herself, or, if she likes, to the women who are within (compare Prot.). To-day let us have conversation instead; and, if you will allow me, I will tell you what sort of conversation. This proposal having been accepted, Eryximachus proceeded as follows:—

I will begin, he said, after the manner of Melanippe in Euripides,

'Not mine the word'

which I am about to speak, but that of Phaedrus. For often he says to me in an indignant tone:—'What a strange thing it is, Eryximachus, that, whereas other gods have poems and hymns made in their honour, the great and glorious god, Love, has no encomiast among all the poets who are so many. There are the worthy sophists too—the excellent Prodicus for example, who have descanted in prose on the virtues of Heracles and other heroes; and, what is still more extraordinary, I have met with a philosophical work in which the utility of salt has been made the theme of an eloquent discourse; and many other like things have had a like honour bestowed upon them. And only to think that there should have been an eager interest created about them, and yet that to this day no one has ever dared worthily to hymn Love's praises! So entirely has this great deity been neglected.' Now in this Phaedrus seems to me to be quite right, and therefore I want to offer him a contribution; also I think that at the present moment we who are here assembled cannot do better than honour the god Love. If you agree with me, there will be no lack of conversation; for I mean to propose that each of us in turn, going from left to right, shall make a speech in honour of Love. Let him give us the best which he can; and Phaedrus, because he is sitting first on the left hand, and because he is the father of the thought, shall begin.

No one will vote against you, Eryximachus, said Socrates. How can I oppose your motion, who profess to understand nothing but matters of love; nor, I presume, will Agathon and Pausanias; and there can be no doubt of Aristophanes, whose whole concern is with Dionysus and Aphrodite; nor will any one disagree of those whom I see around me. The proposal, as I am aware, may seem rather hard upon us whose place is last; but we shall be contented if we hear some good speeches first. Let Phaedrus begin the praise of Love, and good luck to him. All the company expressed their assent, and desired him to do as Socrates bade him.

Aristodemus did not recollect all that was said, nor do I recollect all that he related to me; but I will tell you what I thought most worthy of remembrance, and what the chief speakers said.

Phaedrus began by affirming that Love is a mighty god, and wonderful among gods and men, but especially wonderful in his birth. For he is the eldest of the gods, which is an honour to him; and a proof of his claim to this honour is, that of his parents there is no memorial; neither poet nor prose-writer has ever affirmed that he had any. As Hesiod says:—

'First Chaos came, and then broad-bosomed Earth, The everlasting seat of all that is, And Love.'

In other words, after Chaos, the Earth and Love, these two, came into being. Also Parmenides sings of Generation:

'First in the train of gods, he fashioned Love.'

And Acusilaus agrees with Hesiod. Thus numerous are the witnesses who acknowledge Love to be the eldest of the gods. And not only is he the eldest, he is also the source of the greatest benefits to us. For I know not any greater blessing to a young man who is beginning life than a virtuous lover, or to the lover than a beloved youth. For the principle which ought to be the guide of men who would nobly live—that principle, I say, neither kindred, nor honour, nor wealth, nor any other motive is able to implant so well as love. Of what am I speaking? Of the sense of honour and dishonour, without which neither states nor individuals ever do any good or great work. And I say that a lover who is detected in doing any dishonourable act, or submitting through cowardice when any dishonour is done to him by another, will be more pained at being detected by his beloved than at being seen by his father, or by his companions, or by any one else. The beloved too, when he is found in any disgraceful situation, has the same feeling about his lover. And if there were only some way of contriving that a state or an army should be made up of lovers and their loves (compare Rep.), they would be the very best governors of their own city, abstaining from all dishonour, and emulating one another in honour; and when fighting at each other's side, although a mere handful, they would overcome the world. For what lover would not choose rather to be seen by all mankind than by his beloved, either when abandoning his post or throwing away his arms? He would be ready to die a thousand deaths rather than endure this. Or who would desert his beloved or fail him in the hour of danger? The veriest coward would become an inspired hero, equal to the bravest, at such a time; Love would inspire him. That courage which, as Homer says, the god breathes into the souls of some heroes, Love of his own nature infuses into the lover.

Love will make men dare to die for their beloved—love alone; and women as well as men. Of this, Alcestis, the daughter of Pelias, is a monument to all Hellas; for she was willing to lay down her life on behalf of her husband, when no one else would, although he had a father and mother; but the tenderness of her love so far exceeded theirs, that she made them seem to be strangers in blood to their own son, and in name only related to him; and so noble did this action of hers appear to the gods, as well as to men, that among the many who have done virtuously she is one of the very few to whom, in admiration of her noble action, they have granted the privilege of returning alive to earth; such exceeding honour is paid by the gods to the devotion and virtue of love. But Orpheus, the son of Oeagrus, the harper, they sent empty away, and presented to him an apparition only of her whom he sought, but herself they would not give up, because he showed no spirit; he was only a harp-player, and did not dare like Alcestis to die for love, but was contriving how he might enter Hades alive; moreover, they afterwards caused him to suffer death at the hands of women, as the punishment of his cowardliness. Very different was the reward of the true love of Achilles towards his lover Patroclus—his lover and not his love (the notion that Patroclus was the beloved one is a foolish error into which Aeschylus has fallen, for Achilles was surely the fairer of the two, fairer also than all the other heroes; and, as Homer informs us, he was still beardless, and younger far). And greatly as the gods honour the virtue of love, still the return of love on the part of the beloved to the lover is more admired and valued and rewarded by them, for the lover is more divine; because he is inspired by God. Now Achilles was quite aware, for he had been told by his mother, that he might avoid death and return home, and live to a good old age, if he abstained from slaying Hector. Nevertheless he gave his life to revenge his friend, and dared to die, not only in his defence, but after he was dead. Wherefore the gods honoured him even above Alcestis, and sent him to the Islands of the Blest. These are my reasons for affirming that Love is the eldest and noblest and mightiest of the gods; and the chiefest author and giver of virtue in life, and of happiness after death.

This, or something like this, was the speech of Phaedrus; and some other speeches followed which Aristodemus did not remember; the next which he repeated was that of Pausanias. Phaedrus, he said, the argument has not been set before us, I think, quite in the right form;—we should not be called upon to praise Love in such an indiscriminate manner. If there were only one Love, then what you said would be well enough; but since there are more Loves than one,—should have begun by determining which of them was to be the theme of our praises. I will amend this defect; and first of all I will tell you which Love is deserving of praise, and then try to hymn the praiseworthy one in a manner worthy of him. For we all know that Love is inseparable from Aphrodite, and if there were only one Aphrodite there would be only one Love; but as there are two goddesses there must be two Loves. And am I not right in asserting that there are two goddesses? The elder one, having no mother, who is called the heavenly Aphrodite—she is the daughter of Uranus; the younger, who is the daughter of Zeus and Dione—her we call common; and the Love who is her fellow-worker is rightly named common, as the other love is called heavenly. All the gods ought to have praise given to them, but not without distinction of their natures; and therefore I must try to distinguish the characters of the two Loves. Now actions vary according to the manner of their performance. Take, for example, that which we are now doing, drinking, singing and talking—these actions are not in themselves either good or evil, but they turn out in this or that way according to the mode of performing them; and when well done they are good, and when wrongly done they are evil; and in like manner not every love, but only that which has a noble purpose, is noble and worthy of praise. The Love who is the offspring of the common Aphrodite is essentially common, and has no discrimination, being such as the meaner sort of men feel, and is apt to be of women as well as of youths, and is of the body rather than of the soul—the most foolish beings are the objects of this love which desires only to gain an end, but never thinks of accomplishing the end nobly, and therefore does good and evil quite indiscriminately. The goddess who is his mother is far younger than the other, and she was born of the union of the male and female, and partakes of both. But the offspring of the heavenly Aphrodite is derived from a mother in whose birth the female has no part,—she is from the male only; this is that love which is of youths, and the goddess being older, there is nothing of wantonness in her. Those who are inspired by this love turn to the male, and delight in him who is the more valiant and intelligent nature; any one may recognise the pure enthusiasts in the very character of their attachments. For they love not boys, but intelligent beings whose reason is beginning to be developed, much about the time at which their beards begin to grow. And in choosing young men to be their companions, they mean to be faithful to them, and pass their whole life in company with them, not to take them in their inexperience, and deceive them, and play the fool with them, or run away from one to another of them. But the love of young boys should be forbidden by law, because their future is uncertain; they may turn out good or bad, either in body or soul, and much noble enthusism may be thrown away upon them; in this matter the good are a law to themselves, and the coarser sort of lovers ought to be restrained by force; as we restrain or attempt to restrain them from fixing their affections on women of free birth. These are the persons who bring a reproach on love; and some have been led to deny the lawfulness of such attachments because they see the impropriety and evil of them; for surely nothing that is decorously and lawfully done can justly be censured. Now here and in Lacedaemon the rules about love are perplexing, but in most cities they are simple and easily intelligible; in Elis and Boeotia, and in countries having no gifts of eloquence, they are very straightforward; the law is simply in favour of these connexions, and no one, whether young or old, has anything to say to their discredit; the reason being, as I suppose, that they are men of few words in those parts, and therefore the lovers do not like the trouble of pleading their suit. In Ionia and other places, and generally in countries which are subject to the barbarians, the custom is held to be dishonourable; loves of youths share the evil repute in which philosophy and gymnastics are held, because they are inimical to tyranny; for the interests of rulers require that their subjects should be poor in spirit (compare Arist. Politics), and that there should be no strong bond of friendship or society among them, which love, above all other motives, is likely to inspire, as our Athenian tyrants learned by experience; for the love of Aristogeiton and the constancy of Harmodius had a strength which undid their power. And, therefore, the ill-repute into which these attachments have fallen is to be ascribed to the evil condition of those who make them to be ill-reputed; that is to say, to the self-seeking of the governors and the cowardice of the governed; on the other hand, the indiscriminate honour which is given to them in some countries is attributable to the laziness of those who hold this opinion of them. In our own country a far better principle prevails, but, as I was saying, the explanation of it is rather perplexing. For, observe that open loves are held to be more honourable than secret ones, and that the love of the noblest and highest, even if their persons are less beautiful than others, is especially honourable. Consider, too, how great is the encouragement which all the world gives to the lover; neither is he supposed to be doing anything dishonourable; but if he succeeds he is praised, and if he fail he is blamed. And in the pursuit of his love the custom of mankind allows him to do many strange things, which philosophy would bitterly censure if they were done from any motive of interest, or wish for office or power. He may pray, and entreat, and supplicate, and swear, and lie on a mat at the door, and endure a slavery worse than that of any slave—in any other case friends and enemies would be equally ready to prevent him, but now there is no friend who will be ashamed of him and admonish him, and no enemy will charge him with meanness or flattery; the actions of a lover have a grace which ennobles them; and custom has decided that they are highly commendable and that there no loss of character in them; and, what is strangest of all, he only may swear and forswear himself (so men say), and the gods will forgive his transgression, for there is no such thing as a lover's oath. Such is the entire liberty which gods and men have allowed the lover, according to the custom which prevails in our part of the world. From this point of view a man fairly argues that in Athens to love and to be loved is held to be a very honourable thing. But when parents forbid their sons to talk with their lovers, and place them under a tutor's care, who is appointed to see to these things, and their companions and equals cast in their teeth anything of the sort which they may observe, and their elders refuse to silence the reprovers and do not rebuke them—any one who reflects on all this will, on the contrary, think that we hold these practices to be most disgraceful. But, as I was saying at first, the truth as I imagine is, that whether such practices are honourable or whether they are dishonourable is not a simple question; they are honourable to him who follows them honourably, dishonourable to him who follows them dishonourably. There is dishonour in yielding to the evil, or in an evil manner; but there is honour in yielding to the good, or in an honourable manner. Evil is the vulgar lover who loves the body rather than the soul, inasmuch as he is not even stable, because he loves a thing which is in itself unstable, and therefore when the bloom of youth which he was desiring is over, he takes wing and flies away, in spite of all his words and promises; whereas the love of the noble disposition is life-long, for it becomes one with the everlasting. The custom of our country would have both of them proven well and truly, and would have us yield to the one sort of lover and avoid the other, and therefore encourages some to pursue, and others to fly; testing both the lover and beloved in contests and trials, until they show to which of the two classes they respectively belong. And this is the reason why, in the first place, a hasty attachment is held to be dishonourable, because time is the true test of this as of most other things; and secondly there is a dishonour in being overcome by the love of money, or of wealth, or of political power, whether a man is frightened into surrender by the loss of them, or, having experienced the benefits of money and political corruption, is unable to rise above the seductions of them. For none of these things are of a permanent or lasting nature; not to mention that no generous friendship ever sprang from them. There remains, then, only one way of honourable attachment which custom allows in the beloved, and this is the way of virtue; for as we admitted that any service which the lover does to him is not to be accounted flattery or a dishonour to himself, so the beloved has one way only of voluntary service which is not dishonourable, and this is virtuous service.

For we have a custom, and according to our custom any one who does service to another under the idea that he will be improved by him either in wisdom, or in some other particular of virtue—such a voluntary service, I say, is not to be regarded as a dishonour, and is not open to the charge of flattery. And these two customs, one the love of youth, and the other the practice of philosophy and virtue in general, ought to meet in one, and then the beloved may honourably indulge the lover. For when the lover and beloved come together, having each of them a law, and the lover thinks that he is right in doing any service which he can to his gracious loving one; and the other that he is right in showing any kindness which he can to him who is making him wise and good; the one capable of communicating wisdom and virtue, the other seeking to acquire them with a view to education and wisdom, when the two laws of love are fulfilled and meet in one—then, and then only, may the beloved yield with honour to the lover. Nor when love is of this disinterested sort is there any disgrace in being deceived, but in every other case there is equal disgrace in being or not being deceived. For he who is gracious to his lover under the impression that he is rich, and is disappointed of his gains because he turns out to be poor, is disgraced all the same: for he has done his best to show that he would give himself up to any one's 'uses base' for the sake of money; but this is not honourable. And on the same principle he who gives himself to a lover because he is a good man, and in the hope that he will be improved by his company, shows himself to be virtuous, even though the object of his affection turn out to be a villain, and to have no virtue; and if he is deceived he has committed a noble error. For he has proved that for his part he will do anything for anybody with a view to virtue and improvement, than which there can be nothing nobler. Thus noble in every case is the acceptance of another for the sake of virtue. This is that love which is the love of the heavenly godess, and is heavenly, and of great price to individuals and cities, making the lover and the beloved alike eager in the work of their own improvement. But all other loves are the offspring of the other, who is the common goddess. To you, Phaedrus, I offer this my contribution in praise of love, which is as good as I could make extempore.

Pausanias came to a pause—this is the balanced way in which I have been taught by the wise to speak; and Aristodemus said that the turn of Aristophanes was next, but either he had eaten too much, or from some other cause he had the hiccough, and was obliged to change turns with Eryximachus the physician, who was reclining on the couch below him. Eryximachus, he said, you ought either to stop my hiccough, or to speak in my turn until I have left off.

I will do both, said Eryximachus: I will speak in your turn, and do you speak in mine; and while I am speaking let me recommend you to hold your breath, and if after you have done so for some time the hiccough is no better, then gargle with a little water; and if it still continues, tickle your nose with something and sneeze; and if you sneeze once or twice, even the most violent hiccough is sure to go. I will do as you prescribe, said Aristophanes, and now get on.

Eryximachus spoke as follows: Seeing that Pausanias made a fair beginning, and but a lame ending, I must endeavour to supply his deficiency. I think that he has rightly distinguished two kinds of love. But my art further informs me that the double love is not merely an affection of the soul of man towards the fair, or towards anything, but is to be found in the bodies of all animals and in productions of the earth, and I may say in all that is; such is the conclusion which I seem to have gathered from my own art of medicine, whence I learn how great and wonderful and universal is the deity of love, whose empire extends over all things, divine as well as human. And from medicine I will begin that I may do honour to my art. There are in the human body these two kinds of love, which are confessedly different and unlike, and being unlike, they have loves and desires which are unlike; and the desire of the healthy is one, and the desire of the diseased is another; and as Pausanias was just now saying that to indulge good men is honourable, and bad men dishonourable:—so too in the body the good and healthy elements are to be indulged, and the bad elements and the elements of disease are not to be indulged, but discouraged. And this is what the physician has to do, and in this the art of medicine consists: for medicine may be regarded generally as the knowledge of the loves and desires of the body, and how to satisfy them or not; and the best physician is he who is able to separate fair love from foul, or to convert one into the other; and he who knows how to eradicate and how to implant love, whichever is required, and can reconcile the most hostile elements in the constitution and make them loving friends, is a skilful practitioner. Now the most hostile are the most opposite, such as hot and cold, bitter and sweet, moist and dry, and the like. And my ancestor, Asclepius, knowing how to implant friendship and accord in these elements, was the creator of our art, as our friends the poets here tell us, and I believe them; and not only medicine in every branch but the arts of gymnastic and husbandry are under his dominion. Any one who pays the least attention to the subject will also perceive that in music there is the same reconciliation of opposites; and I suppose that this must have been the meaning of Heracleitus, although his words are not accurate; for he says that The One is united by disunion, like the harmony of the bow and the lyre. Now there is an absurdity saying that harmony is discord or is composed of elements which are still in a state of discord. But what he probably meant was, that harmony is composed of differing notes of higher or lower pitch which disagreed once, but are now reconciled by the art of music; for if the higher and lower notes still disagreed, there could be no harmony,—clearly not. For harmony is a symphony, and symphony is an agreement; but an agreement of disagreements while they disagree there cannot be; you cannot harmonize that which disagrees. In like manner rhythm is compounded of elements short and long, once differing and now in accord; which accordance, as in the former instance, medicine, so in all these other cases, music implants, making love and unison to grow up among them; and thus music, too, is concerned with the principles of love in their application to harmony and rhythm. Again, in the essential nature of harmony and rhythm there is no difficulty in discerning love which has not yet become double. But when you want to use them in actual life, either in the composition of songs or in the correct performance of airs or metres composed already, which latter is called education, then the difficulty begins, and the good artist is needed. Then the old tale has to be repeated of fair and heavenly love—the love of Urania the fair and heavenly muse, and of the duty of accepting the temperate, and those who are as yet intemperate only that they may become temperate, and of preserving their love; and again, of the vulgar Polyhymnia, who must be used with circumspection that the pleasure be enjoyed, but may not generate licentiousness; just as in my own art it is a great matter so to regulate the desires of the epicure that he may gratify his tastes without the attendant evil of disease. Whence I infer that in music, in medicine, in all other things human as well as divine, both loves ought to be noted as far as may be, for they are both present.

The course of the seasons is also full of both these principles; and when, as I was saying, the elements of hot and cold, moist and dry, attain the harmonious love of one another and blend in temperance and harmony, they bring to men, animals, and plants health and plenty, and do them no harm; whereas the wanton love, getting the upper hand and affecting the seasons of the year, is very destructive and injurious, being the source of pestilence, and bringing many other kinds of diseases on animals and plants; for hoar-frost and hail and blight spring from the excesses and disorders of these elements of love, which to know in relation to the revolutions of the heavenly bodies and the seasons of the year is termed astronomy. Furthermore all sacrifices and the whole province of divination, which is the art of communion between gods and men—these, I say, are concerned only with the preservation of the good and the cure of the evil love. For all manner of impiety is likely to ensue if, instead of accepting and honouring and reverencing the harmonious love in all his actions, a man honours the other love, whether in his feelings towards gods or parents, towards the living or the dead. Wherefore the business of divination is to see to these loves and to heal them, and divination is the peacemaker of gods and men, working by a knowledge of the religious or irreligious tendencies which exist in human loves. Such is the great and mighty, or rather omnipotent force of love in general. And the love, more especially, which is concerned with the good, and which is perfected in company with temperance and justice, whether among gods or men, has the greatest power, and is the source of all our happiness and harmony, and makes us friends with the gods who are above us, and with one another. I dare say that I too have omitted several things which might be said in praise of Love, but this was not intentional, and you, Aristophanes, may now supply the omission or take some other line of commendation; for I perceive that you are rid of the hiccough.

Yes, said Aristophanes, who followed, the hiccough is gone; not, however, until I applied the sneezing; and I wonder whether the harmony of the body has a love of such noises and ticklings, for I no sooner applied the sneezing than I was cured.

Eryximachus said: Beware, friend Aristophanes, although you are going to speak, you are making fun of me; and I shall have to watch and see whether I cannot have a laugh at your expense, when you might speak in peace.

You are right, said Aristophanes, laughing. I will unsay my words; but do you please not to watch me, as I fear that in the speech which I am about to make, instead of others laughing with me, which is to the manner born of our muse and would be all the better, I shall only be laughed at by them.

Do you expect to shoot your bolt and escape, Aristophanes? Well, perhaps if you are very careful and bear in mind that you will be called to account, I may be induced to let you off.

Aristophanes professed to open another vein of discourse; he had a mind to praise Love in another way, unlike that either of Pausanias or Eryximachus. Mankind, he said, judging by their neglect of him, have never, as I think, at all understood the power of Love. For if they had understood him they would surely have built noble temples and altars, and offered solemn sacrifices in his honour; but this is not done, and most certainly ought to be done: since of all the gods he is the best friend of men, the helper and the healer of the ills which are the great impediment to the happiness of the race. I will try to describe his power to you, and you shall teach the rest of the world what I am teaching you. In the first place, let me treat of the nature of man and what has happened to it; for the original human nature was not like the present, but different. The sexes were not two as they are now, but originally three in number; there was man, woman, and the union of the two, having a name corresponding to this double nature, which had once a real existence, but is now lost, and the word 'Androgynous' is only preserved as a term of reproach. In the second place, the primeval man was round, his back and sides forming a circle; and he had four hands and four feet, one head with two faces, looking opposite ways, set on a round neck and precisely alike; also four ears, two privy members, and the remainder to correspond. He could walk upright as men now do, backwards or forwards as he pleased, and he could also roll over and over at a great pace, turning on his four hands and four feet, eight in all, like tumblers going over and over with their legs in the air; this was when he wanted to run fast. Now the sexes were three, and such as I have described them; because the sun, moon, and earth are three; and the man was originally the child of the sun, the woman of the earth, and the man-woman of the moon, which is made up of sun and earth, and they were all round and moved round and round like their parents. Terrible was their might and strength, and the thoughts of their hearts were great, and they made an attack upon the gods; of them is told the tale of Otys and Ephialtes who, as Homer says, dared to scale heaven, and would have laid hands upon the gods. Doubt reigned in the celestial councils. Should they kill them and annihilate the race with thunderbolts, as they had done the giants, then there would be an end of the sacrifices and worship which men offered to them; but, on the other hand, the gods could not suffer their insolence to be unrestrained. At last, after a good deal of reflection, Zeus discovered a way. He said: 'Methinks I have a plan which will humble their pride and improve their manners; men shall continue to exist, but I will cut them in two and then they will be diminished in strength and increased in numbers; this will have the advantage of making them more profitable to us. They shall walk upright on two legs, and if they continue insolent and will not be quiet, I will split them again and they shall hop about on a single leg.' He spoke and cut men in two, like a sorb-apple which is halved for pickling, or as you might divide an egg with a hair; and as he cut them one after another, he bade Apollo give the face and the half of the neck a turn in order that the man might contemplate the section of himself: he would thus learn a lesson of humility. Apollo was also bidden to heal their wounds and compose their forms. So he gave a turn to the face and pulled the skin from the sides all over that which in our language is called the belly, like the purses which draw in, and he made one mouth at the centre, which he fastened in a knot (the same which is called the navel); he also moulded the breast and took out most of the wrinkles, much as a shoemaker might smooth leather upon a last; he left a few, however, in the region of the belly and navel, as a memorial of the primeval state. After the division the two parts of man, each desiring his other half, came together, and throwing their arms about one another, entwined in mutual embraces, longing to grow into one, they were on the point of dying from hunger and self-neglect, because they did not like to do anything apart; and when one of the halves died and the other survived, the survivor sought another mate, man or woman as we call them,—being the sections of entire men or women,—and clung to that. They were being destroyed, when Zeus in pity of them invented a new plan: he turned the parts of generation round to the front, for this had not been always their position, and they sowed the seed no longer as hitherto like grasshoppers in the ground, but in one another; and after the transposition the male generated in the female in order that by the mutual embraces of man and woman they might breed, and the race might continue; or if man came to man they might be satisfied, and rest, and go their ways to the business of life: so ancient is the desire of one another which is implanted in us, reuniting our original nature, making one of two, and healing the state of man. Each of us when separated, having one side only, like a flat fish, is but the indenture of a man, and he is always looking for his other half. Men who are a section of that double nature which was once called Androgynous are lovers of women; adulterers are generally of this breed, and also adulterous women who lust after men: the women who are a section of the woman do not care for men, but have female attachments; the female companions are of this sort. But they who are a section of the male follow the male, and while they are young, being slices of the original man, they hang about men and embrace them, and they are themselves the best of boys and youths, because they have the most manly nature. Some indeed assert that they are shameless, but this is not true; for they do not act thus from any want of shame, but because they are valiant and manly, and have a manly countenance, and they embrace that which is like them. And these when they grow up become our statesmen, and these only, which is a great proof of the truth of what I am saying. When they reach manhood they are lovers of youth, and are not naturally inclined to marry or beget children,—if at all, they do so only in obedience to the law; but they are satisfied if they may be allowed to live with one another unwedded; and such a nature is prone to love and ready to return love, always embracing that which is akin to him. And when one of them meets with his other half, the actual half of himself, whether he be a lover of youth or a lover of another sort, the pair are lost in an amazement of love and friendship and intimacy, and one will not be out of the other's sight, as I may say, even for a moment: these are the people who pass their whole lives together; yet they could not explain what they desire of one another. For the intense yearning which each of them has towards the other does not appear to be the desire of lover's intercourse, but of something else which the soul of either evidently desires and cannot tell, and of which she has only a dark and doubtful presentiment. Suppose Hephaestus, with his instruments, to come to the pair who are lying side by side and to say to them, 'What do you people want of one another?' they would be unable to explain. And suppose further, that when he saw their perplexity he said: 'Do you desire to be wholly one; always day and night to be in one another's company? for if this is what you desire, I am ready to melt you into one and let you grow together, so that being two you shall become one, and while you live live a common life as if you were a single man, and after your death in the world below still be one departed soul instead of two—I ask whether this is what you lovingly desire, and whether you are satisfied to attain this?'—there is not a man of them who when he heard the proposal would deny or would not acknowledge that this meeting and melting into one another, this becoming one instead of two, was the very expression of his ancient need (compare Arist. Pol.). And the reason is that human nature was originally one and we were a whole, and the desire and pursuit of the whole is called love. There was a time, I say, when we were one, but now because of the wickedness of mankind God has dispersed us, as the Arcadians were dispersed into villages by the Lacedaemonians (compare Arist. Pol.). And if we are not obedient to the gods, there is a danger that we shall be split up again and go about in basso-relievo, like the profile figures having only half a nose which are sculptured on monuments, and that we shall be like tallies. Wherefore let us exhort all men to piety, that we may avoid evil, and obtain the good, of which Love is to us the lord and minister; and let no one oppose him—he is the enemy of the gods who opposes him. For if we are friends of the God and at peace with him we shall find our own true loves, which rarely happens in this world at present. I am serious, and therefore I must beg Eryximachus not to make fun or to find any allusion in what I am saying to Pausanias and Agathon, who, as I suspect, are both of the manly nature, and belong to the class which I have been describing. But my words have a wider application—they include men and women everywhere; and

I believe that if our loves were perfectly accomplished, and each one returning to his primeval nature had his original true love, then our race would be happy. And if this would be best of all, the best in the next degree and under present circumstances must be the nearest approach to such an union; and that will be the attainment of a congenial love. Wherefore, if we would praise him who has given to us the benefit, we must praise the god Love, who is our greatest benefactor, both leading us in this life back to our own nature, and giving us high hopes for the future, for he promises that if we are pious, he will restore us to our original state, and heal us and make us happy and blessed. This, Eryximachus, is my discourse of love, which, although different to yours, I must beg you to leave unassailed by the shafts of your ridicule, in order that each may have his turn; each, or rather either, for Agathon and Socrates are the only ones left.

Indeed, I am not going to attack you, said Eryximachus, for I thought your speech charming, and did I not know that Agathon and Socrates are masters in the art of love, I should be really afraid that they would have nothing to say, after the world of things which have been said already. But, for all that, I am not without hopes.

Socrates said: You played your part well, Eryximachus; but if you were as I am now, or rather as I shall be when Agathon has spoken, you would, indeed, be in a great strait.

You want to cast a spell over me, Socrates, said Agathon, in the hope that I may be disconcerted at the expectation raised among the audience that I shall speak well.

I should be strangely forgetful, Agathon replied Socrates, of the courage and magnanimity which you showed when your own compositions were about to be exhibited, and you came upon the stage with the actors and faced the vast theatre altogether undismayed, if I thought that your nerves could be fluttered at a small party of friends.

Do you think, Socrates, said Agathon, that my head is so full of the theatre as not to know how much more formidable to a man of sense a few good judges are than many fools?

Nay, replied Socrates, I should be very wrong in attributing to you, Agathon, that or any other want of refinement. And I am quite aware that if you happened to meet with any whom you thought wise, you would care for their opinion much more than for that of the many. But then we, having been a part of the foolish many in the theatre, cannot be regarded as the select wise; though I know that if you chanced to be in the presence, not of one of ourselves, but of some really wise man, you would be ashamed of disgracing yourself before him—would you not?

Yes, said Agathon.

But before the many you would not be ashamed, if you thought that you were doing something disgraceful in their presence?

Here Phaedrus interrupted them, saying: not answer him, my dear Agathon; for if he can only get a partner with whom he can talk, especially a good-looking one, he will no longer care about the completion of our plan. Now I love to hear him talk; but just at present I must not forget the encomium on Love which I ought to receive from him and from every one. When you and he have paid your tribute to the god, then you may talk.

Very good, Phaedrus, said Agathon; I see no reason why I should not proceed with my speech, as I shall have many other opportunities of conversing with Socrates. Let me say first how I ought to speak, and then speak:—

The previous speakers, instead of praising the god Love, or unfolding his nature, appear to have congratulated mankind on the benefits which he confers upon them. But I would rather praise the god first, and then speak of his gifts; this is always the right way of praising everything. May I say without impiety or offence, that of all the blessed gods he is the most blessed because he is the fairest and best? And he is the fairest: for, in the first place, he is the youngest, and of his youth he is himself the witness, fleeing out of the way of age, who is swift enough, swifter truly than most of us like:—Love hates him and will not come near him; but youth and love live and move together—like to like, as the proverb says. Many things were said by Phaedrus about Love in which I agree with him; but I cannot agree that he is older than Iapetus and Kronos:—not so; I maintain him to be the youngest of the gods, and youthful ever. The ancient doings among the gods of which Hesiod and Parmenides spoke, if the tradition of them be true, were done of Necessity and not of Love; had Love been in those days, there would have been no chaining or mutilation of the gods, or other violence, but peace and sweetness, as there is now in heaven, since the rule of Love began. Love is young and also tender; he ought to have a poet like Homer to describe his tenderness, as Homer says of Ate, that she is a goddess and tender:—

'Her feet are tender, for she sets her steps, Not on the ground but on the heads of men:'

herein is an excellent proof of her tenderness,—that she walks not upon the hard but upon the soft. Let us adduce a similar proof of the tenderness of Love; for he walks not upon the earth, nor yet upon the skulls of men, which are not so very soft, but in the hearts and souls of both gods and men, which are of all things the softest: in them he walks and dwells and makes his home. Not in every soul without exception, for where there is hardness he departs, where there is softness there he dwells; and nestling always with his feet and in all manner of ways in the softest of soft places, how can he be other than the softest of all things? Of a truth he is the tenderest as well as the youngest, and also he is of flexile form; for if he were hard and without flexure he could not enfold all things, or wind his way into and out of every soul of man undiscovered. And a proof of his flexibility and symmetry of form is his grace, which is universally admitted to be in an especial manner the attribute of Love; ungrace and love are always at war with one another. The fairness of his complexion is revealed by his habitation among the flowers; for he dwells not amid bloomless or fading beauties, whether of body or soul or aught else, but in the place of flowers and scents, there he sits and abides. Concerning the beauty of the god I have said enough; and yet there remains much more which I might say. Of his virtue I have now to speak: his greatest glory is that he can neither do nor suffer wrong to or from any god or any man; for he suffers not by force if he suffers; force comes not near him, neither when he acts does he act by force. For all men in all things serve him of their own free will, and where there is voluntary agreement, there, as the laws which are the lords of the city say, is justice. And not only is he just but exceedingly temperate, for Temperance is the acknowledged ruler of the pleasures and desires, and no pleasure ever masters Love; he is their master and they are his servants; and if he conquers them he must be temperate indeed. As to courage, even the God of War is no match for him; he is the captive and Love is the lord, for love, the love of Aphrodite, masters him, as the tale runs; and the master is stronger than the servant. And if he conquers the bravest of all others, he must be himself the bravest. Of his courage and justice and temperance I have spoken, but I have yet to speak of his wisdom; and according to the measure of my ability I must try to do my best. In the first place he is a poet (and here, like Eryximachus, I magnify my art), and he is also the source of poesy in others, which he could not be if he were not himself a poet. And at the touch of him every one becomes a poet, even though he had no music in him before (A fragment of the Sthenoaoea of Euripides.); this also is a proof that Love is a good poet and accomplished in all the fine arts; for no one can give to another that which he has not himself, or teach that of which he has no knowledge. Who will deny that the creation of the animals is his doing? Are they not all the works of his wisdom, born and begotten of him? And as to the artists, do we not know that he only of them whom love inspires has the light of fame?—he whom Love touches not walks in darkness. The arts of medicine and archery and divination were discovered by Apollo, under the guidance of love and desire; so that he too is a disciple of Love. Also the melody of the Muses, the metallurgy of Hephaestus, the weaving of Athene, the empire of Zeus over gods and men, are all due to Love, who was the inventor of them. And so Love set in order the empire of the gods—the love of beauty, as is evident, for with deformity Love has no concern. In the days of old, as I began by saying, dreadful deeds were done among the gods, for they were ruled by Necessity; but now since the birth of Love, and from the Love of the beautiful, has sprung every good in heaven and earth. Therefore, Phaedrus, I say of Love that he is the fairest and best in himself, and the cause of what is fairest and best in all other things. And there comes into my mind a line of poetry in which he is said to be the god who

'Gives peace on earth and calms the stormy deep, Who stills the winds and bids the sufferer sleep.'

This is he who empties men of disaffection and fills them with affection, who makes them to meet together at banquets such as these: in sacrifices, feasts, dances, he is our lord—who sends courtesy and sends away discourtesy, who gives kindness ever and never gives unkindness; the friend of the good, the wonder of the wise, the amazement of the gods; desired by those who have no part in him, and precious to those who have the better part in him; parent of delicacy, luxury, desire, fondness, softness, grace; regardful of the good, regardless of the evil: in every word, work, wish, fear—saviour, pilot, comrade, helper; glory of gods and men, leader best and brightest: in whose footsteps let every man follow, sweetly singing in his honour and joining in that sweet strain with which love charms the souls of gods and men. Such is the speech, Phaedrus, half-playful, yet having a certain measure of seriousness, which, according to my ability, I dedicate to the god.

When Agathon had done speaking, Aristodemus said that there was a general cheer; the young man was thought to have spoken in a manner worthy of himself, and of the god. And Socrates, looking at Eryximachus, said: Tell me, son of Acumenus, was there not reason in my fears? and was I not a true prophet when I said that Agathon would make a wonderful oration, and that I should be in a strait?

The part of the prophecy which concerns Agathon, replied Eryximachus, appears to me to be true; but not the other part—that you will be in a strait.

Why, my dear friend, said Socrates, must not I or any one be in a strait who has to speak after he has heard such a rich and varied discourse? I am especially struck with the beauty of the concluding words—who could listen to them without amazement? When I reflected on the immeasurable inferiority of my own powers, I was ready to run away for shame, if there had been a possibility of escape. For I was reminded of Gorgias, and at the end of his speech I fancied that Agathon was shaking at me the Gorginian or Gorgonian head of the great master of rhetoric, which was simply to turn me and my speech into stone, as Homer says (Odyssey), and strike me dumb. And then I perceived how foolish I had been in consenting to take my turn with you in praising love, and saying that I too was a master of the art, when I really had no conception how anything ought to be praised. For in my simplicity I imagined that the topics of praise should be true, and that this being presupposed, out of the true the speaker was to choose the best and set them forth in the best manner. And I felt quite proud, thinking that I knew the nature of true praise, and should speak well. Whereas I now see that the intention was to attribute to Love every species of greatness and glory, whether really belonging to him or not, without regard to truth or falsehood—that was no matter; for the original proposal seems to have been not that each of you should really praise Love, but only that you should appear to praise him. And so you attribute to Love every imaginable form of praise which can be gathered anywhere; and you say that 'he is all this,' and 'the cause of all that,' making him appear the fairest and best of all to those who know him not, for you cannot impose upon those who know him. And a noble and solemn hymn of praise have you rehearsed. But as I misunderstood the nature of the praise when I said that I would take my turn, I must beg to be absolved from the promise which I made in ignorance, and which (as Euripides would say (Eurip. Hyppolytus)) was a promise of the lips and not of the mind. Farewell then to such a strain: for I do not praise in that way; no, indeed, I cannot. But if you like to hear the truth about love, I am ready to speak in my own manner, though I will not make myself ridiculous by entering into any rivalry with you. Say then, Phaedrus, whether you would like to have the truth about love, spoken in any words and in any order which may happen to come into my mind at the time. Will that be agreeable to you?

Aristodemus said that Phaedrus and the company bid him speak in any manner which he thought best. Then, he added, let me have your permission first to ask Agathon a few more questions, in order that I may take his admissions as the premises of my discourse.

I grant the permission, said Phaedrus: put your questions. Socrates then proceeded as follows:—

In the magnificent oration which you have just uttered, I think that you were right, my dear Agathon, in proposing to speak of the nature of Love first and afterwards of his works—that is a way of beginning which I very much approve. And as you have spoken so eloquently of his nature, may I ask you further, Whether love is the love of something or of nothing? And here I must explain myself: I do not want you to say that love is the love of a father or the love of a mother—that would be ridiculous; but to answer as you would, if I asked is a father a father of something? to which you would find no difficulty in replying, of a son or daughter: and the answer would be right.

Very true, said Agathon.

And you would say the same of a mother?

He assented.

Yet let me ask you one more question in order to illustrate my meaning: Is not a brother to be regarded essentially as a brother of something?

Certainly, he replied.

That is, of a brother or sister?

Yes, he said.

And now, said Socrates, I will ask about Love:—Is Love of something or of nothing?

Of something, surely, he replied.

Keep in mind what this is, and tell me what I want to know—whether Love desires that of which love is.

Yes, surely.

And does he possess, or does he not possess, that which he loves and desires?

Probably not, I should say.

Nay, replied Socrates, I would have you consider whether 'necessarily' is not rather the word. The inference that he who desires something is in want of something, and that he who desires nothing is in want of nothing, is in my judgment, Agathon, absolutely and necessarily true. What do you think?

I agree with you, said Agathon.

Very good. Would he who is great, desire to be great, or he who is strong, desire to be strong?

That would be inconsistent with our previous admissions.

True. For he who is anything cannot want to be that which he is?

Very true.

And yet, added Socrates, if a man being strong desired to be strong, or being swift desired to be swift, or being healthy desired to be healthy, in that case he might be thought to desire something which he already has or is. I give the example in order that we may avoid misconception. For the possessors of these qualities, Agathon, must be supposed to have their respective advantages at the time, whether they choose or not; and who can desire that which he has? Therefore, when a person says, I am well and wish to be well, or I am rich and wish to be rich, and I desire simply to have what I have—to him we shall reply: 'You, my friend, having wealth and health and strength, want to have the continuance of them; for at this moment, whether you choose or no, you have them. And when you say, I desire that which I have and nothing else, is not your meaning that you want to have what you now have in the future?' He must agree with us—must he not?

He must, replied Agathon.

Then, said Socrates, he desires that what he has at present may be preserved to him in the future, which is equivalent to saying that he desires something which is non-existent to him, and which as yet he has not got:

Very true, he said.

Then he and every one who desires, desires that which he has not already, and which is future and not present, and which he has not, and is not, and of which he is in want;—these are the sort of things which love and desire seek?

Very true, he said.

Then now, said Socrates, let us recapitulate the argument. First, is not love of something, and of something too which is wanting to a man?

Yes, he replied.

Remember further what you said in your speech, or if you do not remember I will remind you: you said that the love of the beautiful set in order the empire of the gods, for that of deformed things there is no love—did you not say something of that kind?

Yes, said Agathon.

Yes, my friend, and the remark was a just one. And if this is true, Love is the love of beauty and not of deformity?

He assented.

And the admission has been already made that Love is of something which a man wants and has not?

True, he said.

Then Love wants and has not beauty?

Certainly, he replied.

And would you call that beautiful which wants and does not possess beauty?

Certainly not.

Then would you still say that love is beautiful?

Agathon replied: I fear that I did not understand what I was saying.

You made a very good speech, Agathon, replied Socrates; but there is yet one small question which I would fain ask:—Is not the good also the beautiful?

Yes.

Then in wanting the beautiful, love wants also the good?

I cannot refute you, Socrates, said Agathon:—Let us assume that what you say is true.

Say rather, beloved Agathon, that you cannot refute the truth; for Socrates is easily refuted.

And now, taking my leave of you, I would rehearse a tale of love which I heard from Diotima of Mantineia (compare 1 Alcibiades), a woman wise in this and in many other kinds of knowledge, who in the days of old, when the Athenians offered sacrifice before the coming of the plague, delayed the disease ten years. She was my instructress in the art of love, and I shall repeat to you what she said to me, beginning with the admissions made by Agathon, which are nearly if not quite the same which I made to the wise woman when she questioned me: I think that this will be the easiest way, and I shall take both parts myself as well as I can (compare Gorgias). As you, Agathon, suggested (supra), I must speak first of the being and nature of Love, and then of his works. First I said to her in nearly the same words which he used to me, that Love was a mighty god, and likewise fair; and she proved to me as I proved to him that, by my own showing, Love was neither fair nor good. 'What do you mean, Diotima,' I said, 'is love then evil and foul?' 'Hush,' she cried; 'must that be foul which is not fair?' 'Certainly,' I said. 'And is that which is not wise, ignorant? do you not see that there is a mean between wisdom and ignorance?' 'And what may that be?' I said. 'Right opinion,' she replied; 'which, as you know, being incapable of giving a reason, is not knowledge (for how can knowledge be devoid of reason? nor again, ignorance, for neither can ignorance attain the truth), but is clearly something which is a mean between ignorance and wisdom.' 'Quite true,' I replied. 'Do not then insist,' she said, 'that what is not fair is of necessity foul, or what is not good evil; or infer that because love is not fair and good he is therefore foul and evil; for he is in a mean between them.' 'Well,' I said, 'Love is surely admitted by all to be a great god.' 'By those who know or by those who do not know?' 'By all.' 'And how, Socrates,' she said with a smile, 'can Love be acknowledged to be a great god by those who say that he is not a god at all?' 'And who are they?' I said. 'You and I are two of them,' she replied. 'How can that be?' I said. 'It is quite intelligible,' she replied; 'for you yourself would acknowledge that the gods are happy and fair—of course you would—would you dare to say that any god was not?' 'Certainly not,' I replied. 'And you mean by the happy, those who are the possessors of things good or fair?' 'Yes.' 'And you admitted that Love, because he was in want, desires those good and fair things of which he is in want?' 'Yes, I did.' 'But how can he be a god who has no portion in what is either good or fair?' 'Impossible.' 'Then you see that you also deny the divinity of Love.'

'What then is Love?' I asked; 'Is he mortal?' 'No.' 'What then?' 'As in the former instance, he is neither mortal nor immortal, but in a mean between the two.' 'What is he, Diotima?' 'He is a great spirit (daimon), and like all spirits he is intermediate between the divine and the mortal.' 'And what,' I said, 'is his power?' 'He interprets,' she replied, 'between gods and men, conveying and taking across to the gods the prayers and sacrifices of men, and to men the commands and replies of the gods; he is the mediator who spans the chasm which divides them, and therefore in him all is bound together, and through him the arts of the prophet and the priest, their sacrifices and mysteries and charms, and all prophecy and incantation, find their way. For God mingles not with man; but through Love all the intercourse and converse of God with man, whether awake or asleep, is carried on. The wisdom which understands this is spiritual; all other wisdom, such as that of arts and handicrafts, is mean and vulgar. Now these spirits or intermediate powers are many and diverse, and one of them is Love.' 'And who,' I said, 'was his father, and who his mother?' 'The tale,' she said, 'will take time; nevertheless I will tell you. On the birthday of Aphrodite there was a feast of the gods, at which the god Poros or Plenty, who is the son of Metis or Discretion, was one of the guests. When the feast was over, Penia or Poverty, as the manner is on such occasions, came about the doors to beg. Now Plenty who was the worse for nectar (there was no wine in those days), went into the garden of Zeus and fell into a heavy sleep, and Poverty considering her own straitened circumstances, plotted to have a child by him, and accordingly she lay down at his side and conceived Love, who partly because he is naturally a lover of the beautiful, and because Aphrodite is herself beautiful, and also because he was born on her birthday, is her follower and attendant. And as his parentage is, so also are his fortunes. In the first place he is always poor, and anything but tender and fair, as the many imagine him; and he is rough and squalid, and has no shoes, nor a house to dwell in; on the bare earth exposed he lies under the open heaven, in the streets, or at the doors of houses, taking his rest; and like his mother he is always in distress. Like his father too, whom he also partly resembles, he is always plotting against the fair and good; he is bold, enterprising, strong, a mighty hunter, always weaving some intrigue or other, keen in the pursuit of wisdom, fertile in resources; a philosopher at all times, terrible as an enchanter, sorcerer, sophist. He is by nature neither mortal nor immortal, but alive and flourishing at one moment when he is in plenty, and dead at another moment, and again alive by reason of his father's nature. But that which is always flowing in is always flowing out, and so he is never in want and never in wealth; and, further, he is in a mean between ignorance and knowledge. The truth of the matter is this: No god is a philosopher or seeker after wisdom, for he is wise already; nor does any man who is wise seek after wisdom. Neither do the ignorant seek after wisdom. For herein is the evil of ignorance, that he who is neither good nor wise is nevertheless satisfied with himself: he has no desire for that of which he feels no want.' 'But who then, Diotima,' I said, 'are the lovers of wisdom, if they are neither the wise nor the foolish?' 'A child may answer that question,' she replied; 'they are those who are in a mean between the two; Love is one of them. For wisdom is a most beautiful thing, and Love is of the beautiful; and therefore Love is also a philosopher or lover of wisdom, and being a lover of wisdom is in a mean between the wise and the ignorant. And of this too his birth is the cause; for his father is wealthy and wise, and his mother poor and foolish. Such, my dear Socrates, is the nature of the spirit Love. The error in your conception of him was very natural, and as I imagine from what you say, has arisen out of a confusion of love and the beloved, which made you think that love was all beautiful. For the beloved is the truly beautiful, and delicate, and perfect, and blessed; but the principle of love is of another nature, and is such as I have described.'

I said, 'O thou stranger woman, thou sayest well; but, assuming Love to be such as you say, what is the use of him to men?' 'That, Socrates,' she replied, 'I will attempt to unfold: of his nature and birth I have already spoken; and you acknowledge that love is of the beautiful. But some one will say: Of the beautiful in what, Socrates and Diotima?—or rather let me put the question more clearly, and ask: When a man loves the beautiful, what does he desire?' I answered her 'That the beautiful may be his.' 'Still,' she said, 'the answer suggests a further question: What is given by the possession of beauty?' 'To what you have asked,' I replied, 'I have no answer ready.' 'Then,' she said, 'let me put the word "good" in the place of the beautiful, and repeat the question once more: If he who loves loves the good, what is it then that he loves?' 'The possession of the good,' I said. 'And what does he gain who possesses the good?' 'Happiness,' I replied; 'there is less difficulty in answering that question.' 'Yes,' she said, 'the happy are made happy by the acquisition of good things. Nor is there any need to ask why a man desires happiness; the answer is already final.' 'You are right.' I said. 'And is this wish and this desire common to all? and do all men always desire their own good, or only some men?—what say you?' 'All men,' I replied; 'the desire is common to all.' 'Why, then,' she rejoined, 'are not all men, Socrates, said to love, but only some of them? whereas you say that all men are always loving the same things.' 'I myself wonder,' I said, 'why this is.' 'There is nothing to wonder at,' she replied; 'the reason is that one part of love is separated off and receives the name of the whole, but the other parts have other names.' 'Give an illustration,' I said. She answered me as follows: 'There is poetry, which, as you know, is complex and manifold. All creation or passage of non-being into being is poetry or making, and the processes of all art are creative; and the masters of arts are all poets or makers.' 'Very true.' 'Still,' she said, 'you know that they are not called poets, but have other names; only that portion of the art which is separated off from the rest, and is concerned with music and metre, is termed poetry, and they who possess poetry in this sense of the word are called poets.' 'Very true,' I said. 'And the same holds of love. For you may say generally that all desire of good and happiness is only the great and subtle power of love; but they who are drawn towards him by any other path, whether the path of money-making or gymnastics or philosophy, are not called lovers—the name of the whole is appropriated to those whose affection takes one form only—they alone are said to love, or to be lovers.' 'I dare say,' I replied, 'that you are right.' 'Yes,' she added, 'and you hear people say that lovers are seeking for their other half; but I say that they are seeking neither for the half of themselves, nor for the whole, unless the half or the whole be also a good. And they will cut off their own hands and feet and cast them away, if they are evil; for they love not what is their own, unless perchance there be some one who calls what belongs to him the good, and what belongs to another the evil. For there is nothing which men love but the good. Is there anything?' 'Certainly, I should say, that there is nothing.' 'Then,' she said, 'the simple truth is, that men love the good.' 'Yes,' I said. 'To which must be added that they love the possession of the good?' 'Yes, that must be added.' 'And not only the possession, but the everlasting possession of the good?' 'That must be added too.' 'Then love,' she said, 'may be described generally as the love of the everlasting possession of the good?' 'That is most true.'

'Then if this be the nature of love, can you tell me further,' she said, 'what is the manner of the pursuit? what are they doing who show all this eagerness and heat which is called love? and what is the object which they have in view? Answer me.' 'Nay, Diotima,' I replied, 'if I had known, I should not have wondered at your wisdom, neither should I have come to learn from you about this very matter.' 'Well,' she said, 'I will teach you:—The object which they have in view is birth in beauty, whether of body or soul.' 'I do not understand you,' I said; 'the oracle requires an explanation.' 'I will make my meaning clearer,' she replied. 'I mean to say, that all men are bringing to the birth in their bodies and in their souls. There is a certain age at which human nature is desirous of procreation—procreation which must be in beauty and not in deformity; and this procreation is the union of man and woman, and is a divine thing; for conception and generation are an immortal principle in the mortal creature, and in the inharmonious they can never be. But the deformed is always inharmonious with the divine, and the beautiful harmonious. Beauty, then, is the destiny or goddess of parturition who presides at birth, and therefore, when approaching beauty, the conceiving power is propitious, and diffusive, and benign, and begets and bears fruit: at the sight of ugliness she frowns and contracts and has a sense of pain, and turns away, and shrivels up, and not without a pang refrains from conception. And this is the reason why, when the hour of conception arrives, and the teeming nature is full, there is such a flutter and ecstasy about beauty whose approach is the alleviation of the pain of travail. For love, Socrates, is not, as you imagine, the love of the beautiful only.' 'What then?' 'The love of generation and of birth in beauty.' 'Yes,' I said. 'Yes, indeed,' she replied. 'But why of generation?' 'Because to the mortal creature, generation is a sort of eternity and immortality,' she replied; 'and if, as has been already admitted, love is of the everlasting possession of the good, all men will necessarily desire immortality together with good: Wherefore love is of immortality.'

All this she taught me at various times when she spoke of love. And I remember her once saying to me, 'What is the cause, Socrates, of love, and the attendant desire? See you not how all animals, birds, as well as beasts, in their desire of procreation, are in agony when they take the infection of love, which begins with the desire of union; whereto is added the care of offspring, on whose behalf the weakest are ready to battle against the strongest even to the uttermost, and to die for them, and will let themselves be tormented with hunger or suffer anything in order to maintain their young. Man may be supposed to act thus from reason; but why should animals have these passionate feelings? Can you tell me why?' Again I replied that I did not know. She said to me: 'And do you expect ever to become a master in the art of love, if you do not know this?' 'But I have told you already, Diotima, that my ignorance is the reason why I come to you; for I am conscious that I want a teacher; tell me then the cause of this and of the other mysteries of love.' 'Marvel not,' she said, 'if you believe that love is of the immortal, as we have several times acknowledged; for here again, and on the same principle too, the mortal nature is seeking as far as is possible to be everlasting and immortal: and this is only to be attained by generation, because generation always leaves behind a new existence in the place of the old. Nay even in the life of the same individual there is succession and not absolute unity: a man is called the same, and yet in the short interval which elapses between youth and age, and in which every animal is said to have life and identity, he is undergoing a perpetual process of loss and reparation—hair, flesh, bones, blood, and the whole body are always changing. Which is true not only of the body, but also of the soul, whose habits, tempers, opinions, desires, pleasures, pains, fears, never remain the same in any one of us, but are always coming and going; and equally true of knowledge, and what is still more surprising to us mortals, not only do the sciences in general spring up and decay, so that in respect of them we are never the same; but each of them individually experiences a like change. For what is implied in the word "recollection," but the departure of knowledge, which is ever being forgotten, and is renewed and preserved by recollection, and appears to be the same although in reality new, according to that law of succession by which all mortal things are preserved, not absolutely the same, but by substitution, the old worn-out mortality leaving another new and similar existence behind—unlike the divine, which is always the same and not another? And in this way, Socrates, the mortal body, or mortal anything, partakes of immortality; but the immortal in another way. Marvel not then at the love which all men have of their offspring; for that universal love and interest is for the sake of immortality.'

I was astonished at her words, and said: 'Is this really true, O thou wise Diotima?' And she answered with all the authority of an accomplished sophist: 'Of that, Socrates, you may be assured;—think only of the ambition of men, and you will wonder at the senselessness of their ways, unless you consider how they are stirred by the love of an immortality of fame. They are ready to run all risks greater far than they would have run for their children, and to spend money and undergo any sort of toil, and even to die, for the sake of leaving behind them a name which shall be eternal. Do you imagine that Alcestis would have died to save Admetus, or Achilles to avenge Patroclus, or your own Codrus in order to preserve the kingdom for his sons, if they had not imagined that the memory of their virtues, which still survives among us, would be immortal? Nay,' she said, 'I am persuaded that all men do all things, and the better they are the more they do them, in hope of the glorious fame of immortal virtue; for they desire the immortal.

'Those who are pregnant in the body only, betake themselves to women and beget children—this is the character of their love; their offspring, as they hope, will preserve their memory and giving them the blessedness and immortality which they desire in the future. But souls which are pregnant—for there certainly are men who are more creative in their souls than in their bodies—conceive that which is proper for the soul to conceive or contain. And what are these conceptions?—wisdom and virtue in general. And such creators are poets and all artists who are deserving of the name inventor. But the greatest and fairest sort of wisdom by far is that which is concerned with the ordering of states and families, and which is called temperance and justice. And he who in youth has the seed of these implanted in him and is himself inspired, when he comes to maturity desires to beget and generate. He wanders about seeking beauty that he may beget offspring—for in deformity he will beget nothing—and naturally embraces the beautiful rather than the deformed body; above all when he finds a fair and noble and well-nurtured soul, he embraces the two in one person, and to such an one he is full of speech about virtue and the nature and pursuits of a good man; and he tries to educate him; and at the touch of the beautiful which is ever present to his memory, even when absent, he brings forth that which he had conceived long before, and in company with him tends that which he brings forth; and they are married by a far nearer tie and have a closer friendship than those who beget mortal children, for the children who are their common offspring are fairer and more immortal. Who, when he thinks of Homer and Hesiod and other great poets, would not rather have their children than ordinary human ones? Who would not emulate them in the creation of children such as theirs, which have preserved their memory and given them everlasting glory? Or who would not have such children as Lycurgus left behind him to be the saviours, not only of Lacedaemon, but of Hellas, as one may say? There is Solon, too, who is the revered father of Athenian laws; and many others there are in many other places, both among Hellenes and barbarians, who have given to the world many noble works, and have been the parents of virtue of every kind; and many temples have been raised in their honour for the sake of children such as theirs; which were never raised in honour of any one, for the sake of his mortal children.

'These are the lesser mysteries of love, into which even you, Socrates, may enter; to the greater and more hidden ones which are the crown of these, and to which, if you pursue them in a right spirit, they will lead, I know not whether you will be able to attain. But I will do my utmost to inform you, and do you follow if you can. For he who would proceed aright in this matter should begin in youth to visit beautiful forms; and first, if he be guided by his instructor aright, to love one such form only—out of that he should create fair thoughts; and soon he will of himself perceive that the beauty of one form is akin to the beauty of another; and then if beauty of form in general is his pursuit, how foolish would he be not to recognize that the beauty in every form is and the same! And when he perceives this he will abate his violent love of the one, which he will despise and deem a small thing, and will become a lover of all beautiful forms; in the next stage he will consider that the beauty of the mind is more honourable than the beauty of the outward form. So that if a virtuous soul have but a little comeliness, he will be content to love and tend him, and will search out and bring to the birth thoughts which may improve the young, until he is compelled to contemplate and see the beauty of institutions and laws, and to understand that the beauty of them all is of one family, and that personal beauty is a trifle; and after laws and institutions he will go on to the sciences, that he may see their beauty, being not like a servant in love with the beauty of one youth or man or institution, himself a slave mean and narrow-minded, but drawing towards and contemplating the vast sea of beauty, he will create many fair and noble thoughts and notions in boundless love of wisdom; until on that shore he grows and waxes strong, and at last the vision is revealed to him of a single science, which is the science of beauty everywhere. To this I will proceed; please to give me your very best attention:

'He who has been instructed thus far in the things of love, and who has learned to see the beautiful in due order and succession, when he comes toward the end will suddenly perceive a nature of wondrous beauty (and this, Socrates, is the final cause of all our former toils)—a nature which in the first place is everlasting, not growing and decaying, or waxing and waning; secondly, not fair in one point of view and foul in another, or at one time or in one relation or at one place fair, at another time or in another relation or at another place foul, as if fair to some and foul to others, or in the likeness of a face or hands or any other part of the bodily frame, or in any form of speech or knowledge, or existing in any other being, as for example, in an animal, or in heaven, or in earth, or in any other place; but beauty absolute, separate, simple, and everlasting, which without diminution and without increase, or any change, is imparted to the ever-growing and perishing beauties of all other things. He who from these ascending under the influence of true love, begins to perceive that beauty, is not far from the end. And the true order of going, or being led by another, to the things of love, is to begin from the beauties of earth and mount upwards for the sake of that other beauty, using these as steps only, and from one going on to two, and from two to all fair forms, and from fair forms to fair practices, and from fair practices to fair notions, until from fair notions he arrives at the notion of absolute beauty, and at last knows what the essence of beauty is. This, my dear Socrates,' said the stranger of Mantineia, 'is that life above all others which man should live, in the contemplation of beauty absolute; a beauty which if you once beheld, you would see not to be after the measure of gold, and garments, and fair boys and youths, whose presence now entrances you; and you and many a one would be content to live seeing them only and conversing with them without meat or drink, if that were possible—you only want to look at them and to be with them. But what if man had eyes to see the true beauty—the divine beauty, I mean, pure and clear and unalloyed, not clogged with the pollutions of mortality and all the colours and vanities of human life—thither looking, and holding converse with the true beauty simple and divine? Remember how in that communion only, beholding beauty with the eye of the mind, he will be enabled to bring forth, not images of beauty, but realities (for he has hold not of an image but of a reality), and bringing forth and nourishing true virtue to become the friend of God and be immortal, if mortal man may. Would that be an ignoble life?'

Such, Phaedrus—and I speak not only to you, but to all of you—were the words of Diotima; and I am persuaded of their truth. And being persuaded of them, I try to persuade others, that in the attainment of this end human nature will not easily find a helper better than love: And therefore, also, I say that every man ought to honour him as I myself honour him, and walk in his ways, and exhort others to do the same, and praise the power and spirit of love according to the measure of my ability now and ever.

The words which I have spoken, you, Phaedrus, may call an encomium of love, or anything else which you please.

When Socrates had done speaking, the company applauded, and Aristophanes was beginning to say something in answer to the allusion which Socrates had made to his own speech, when suddenly there was a great knocking at the door of the house, as of revellers, and the sound of a flute-girl was heard. Agathon told the attendants to go and see who were the intruders. 'If they are friends of ours,' he said, 'invite them in, but if not, say that the drinking is over.' A little while afterwards they heard the voice of Alcibiades resounding in the court; he was in a great state of intoxication, and kept roaring and shouting 'Where is Agathon? Lead me to Agathon,' and at length, supported by the flute-girl and some of his attendants, he found his way to them. 'Hail, friends,' he said, appearing at the door crowned with a massive garland of ivy and violets, his head flowing with ribands. 'Will you have a very drunken man as a companion of your revels? Or shall I crown Agathon, which was my intention in coming, and go away? For I was unable to come yesterday, and therefore I am here to-day, carrying on my head these ribands, that taking them from my own head, I may crown the head of this fairest and wisest of men, as I may be allowed to call him. Will you laugh at me because I am drunk? Yet I know very well that I am speaking the truth, although you may laugh. But first tell me; if I come in shall we have the understanding of which I spoke (supra Will you have a very drunken man? etc.)? Will you drink with me or not?'

The company were vociferous in begging that he would take his place among them, and Agathon specially invited him. Thereupon he was led in by the people who were with him; and as he was being led, intending to crown Agathon, he took the ribands from his own head and held them in front of his eyes; he was thus prevented from seeing Socrates, who made way for him, and Alcibiades took the vacant place between Agathon and Socrates, and in taking the place he embraced Agathon and crowned him. Take off his sandals, said Agathon, and let him make a third on the same couch.

By all means; but who makes the third partner in our revels? said Alcibiades, turning round and starting up as he caught sight of Socrates. By Heracles, he said, what is this? here is Socrates always lying in wait for me, and always, as his way is, coming out at all sorts of unsuspected places: and now, what have you to say for yourself, and why are you lying here, where I perceive that you have contrived to find a place, not by a joker or lover of jokes, like Aristophanes, but by the fairest of the company?

Socrates turned to Agathon and said: I must ask you to protect me, Agathon; for the passion of this man has grown quite a serious matter to me. Since I became his admirer I have never been allowed to speak to any other fair one, or so much as to look at them. If I do, he goes wild with envy and jealousy, and not only abuses me but can hardly keep his hands off me, and at this moment he may do me some harm. Please to see to this, and either reconcile me to him, or, if he attempts violence, protect me, as I am in bodily fear of his mad and passionate attempts.

There can never be reconciliation between you and me, said Alcibiades; but for the present I will defer your chastisement. And I must beg you, Agathon, to give me back some of the ribands that I may crown the marvellous head of this universal despot—I would not have him complain of me for crowning you, and neglecting him, who in conversation is the conqueror of all mankind; and this not only once, as you were the day before yesterday, but always. Whereupon, taking some of the ribands, he crowned Socrates, and again reclined.

Then he said: You seem, my friends, to be sober, which is a thing not to be endured; you must drink—for that was the agreement under which I was admitted—and I elect myself master of the feast until you are well drunk. Let us have a large goblet, Agathon, or rather, he said, addressing the attendant, bring me that wine-cooler. The wine-cooler which had caught his eye was a vessel holding more than two quarts—this he filled and emptied, and bade the attendant fill it again for Socrates. Observe, my friends, said Alcibiades, that this ingenious trick of mine will have no effect on Socrates, for he can drink any quantity of wine and not be at all nearer being drunk. Socrates drank the cup which the attendant filled for him.

Eryximachus said: What is this, Alcibiades? Are we to have neither conversation nor singing over our cups; but simply to drink as if we were thirsty?

Alcibiades replied: Hail, worthy son of a most wise and worthy sire!

The same to you, said Eryximachus; but what shall we do?

That I leave to you, said Alcibiades.

'The wise physician skilled our wounds to heal (from Pope's Homer, Il.)'

shall prescribe and we will obey. What do you want?

Well, said Eryximachus, before you appeared we had passed a resolution that each one of us in turn should make a speech in praise of love, and as good a one as he could: the turn was passed round from left to right; and as all of us have spoken, and you have not spoken but have well drunken, you ought to speak, and then impose upon Socrates any task which you please, and he on his right hand neighbour, and so on.

That is good, Eryximachus, said Alcibiades; and yet the comparison of a drunken man's speech with those of sober men is hardly fair; and I should like to know, sweet friend, whether you really believe what Socrates was just now saying; for I can assure you that the very reverse is the fact, and that if I praise any one but himself in his presence, whether God or man, he will hardly keep his hands off me.

For shame, said Socrates.

Hold your tongue, said Alcibiades, for by Poseidon, there is no one else whom I will praise when you are of the company.

Well then, said Eryximachus, if you like praise Socrates.

What do you think, Eryximachus? said Alcibiades: shall I attack him and inflict the punishment before you all?

What are you about? said Socrates; are you going to raise a laugh at my expense? Is that the meaning of your praise?

I am going to speak the truth, if you will permit me.

I not only permit, but exhort you to speak the truth.

Then I will begin at once, said Alcibiades, and if I say anything which is not true, you may interrupt me if you will, and say 'that is a lie,' though my intention is to speak the truth. But you must not wonder if I speak any how as things come into my mind; for the fluent and orderly enumeration of all your singularities is not a task which is easy to a man in my condition.

And now, my boys, I shall praise Socrates in a figure which will appear to him to be a caricature, and yet I speak, not to make fun of him, but only for the truth's sake. I say, that he is exactly like the busts of Silenus, which are set up in the statuaries' shops, holding pipes and flutes in their mouths; and they are made to open in the middle, and have images of gods inside them. I say also that he is like Marsyas the satyr. You yourself will not deny, Socrates, that your face is like that of a satyr. Aye, and there is a resemblance in other points too. For example, you are a bully, as I can prove by witnesses, if you will not confess. And are you not a flute-player? That you are, and a performer far more wonderful than Marsyas. He indeed with instruments used to charm the souls of men by the power of his breath, and the players of his music do so still: for the melodies of Olympus (compare Arist. Pol.) are derived from Marsyas who taught them, and these, whether they are played by a great master or by a miserable flute-girl, have a power which no others have; they alone possess the soul and reveal the wants of those who have need of gods and mysteries, because they are divine. But you produce the same effect with your words only, and do not require the flute: that is the difference between you and him. When we hear any other speaker, even a very good one, he produces absolutely no effect upon us, or not much, whereas the mere fragments of you and your words, even at second-hand, and however imperfectly repeated, amaze and possess the souls of every man, woman, and child who comes within hearing of them. And if I were not afraid that you would think me hopelessly drunk, I would have sworn as well as spoken to the influence which they have always had and still have over me. For my heart leaps within me more than that of any Corybantian reveller, and my eyes rain tears when I hear them. And I observe that many others are affected in the same manner. I have heard Pericles and other great orators, and I thought that they spoke well, but I never had any similar feeling; my soul was not stirred by them, nor was I angry at the thought of my own slavish state. But this Marsyas has often brought me to such a pass, that I have felt as if I could hardly endure the life which I am leading (this, Socrates, you will admit); and I am conscious that if I did not shut my ears against him, and fly as from the voice of the siren, my fate would be like that of others,—he would transfix me, and I should grow old sitting at his feet. For he makes me confess that I ought not to live as I do, neglecting the wants of my own soul, and busying myself with the concerns of the Athenians; therefore I hold my ears and tear myself away from him. And he is the only person who ever made me ashamed, which you might think not to be in my nature, and there is no one else who does the same. For I know that I cannot answer him or say that I ought not to do as he bids, but when I leave his presence the love of popularity gets the better of me. And therefore I run away and fly from him, and when I see him I am ashamed of what I have confessed to him. Many a time have I wished that he were dead, and yet I know that I should be much more sorry than glad, if he were to die: so that I am at my wit's end.

And this is what I and many others have suffered from the flute-playing of this satyr. Yet hear me once more while I show you how exact the image is, and how marvellous his power. For let me tell you; none of you know him; but I will reveal him to you; having begun, I must go on. See you how fond he is of the fair? He is always with them and is always being smitten by them, and then again he knows nothing and is ignorant of all things—such is the appearance which he puts on. Is he not like a Silenus in this? To be sure he is: his outer mask is the carved head of the Silenus; but, O my companions in drink, when he is opened, what temperance there is residing within! Know you that beauty and wealth and honour, at which the many wonder, are of no account with him, and are utterly despised by him: he regards not at all the persons who are gifted with them; mankind are nothing to him; all his life is spent in mocking and flouting at them. But when I opened him, and looked within at his serious purpose, I saw in him divine and golden images of such fascinating beauty that I was ready to do in a moment whatever Socrates commanded: they may have escaped the observation of others, but I saw them. Now I fancied that he was seriously enamoured of my beauty, and I thought that I should therefore have a grand opportunity of hearing him tell what he knew, for I had a wonderful opinion of the attractions of my youth. In the prosecution of this design, when I next went to him, I sent away the attendant who usually accompanied me (I will confess the whole truth, and beg you to listen; and if I speak falsely, do you, Socrates, expose the falsehood). Well, he and I were alone together, and I thought that when there was nobody with us, I should hear him speak the language which lovers use to their loves when they are by themselves, and I was delighted. Nothing of the sort; he conversed as usual, and spent the day with me and then went away. Afterwards I challenged him to the palaestra; and he wrestled and closed with me several times when there was no one present; I fancied that I might succeed in this manner. Not a bit; I made no way with him. Lastly, as I had failed hitherto, I thought that I must take stronger measures and attack him boldly, and, as I had begun, not give him up, but see how matters stood between him and me. So I invited him to sup with me, just as if he were a fair youth, and I a designing lover. He was not easily persuaded to come; he did, however, after a while accept the invitation, and when he came the first time, he wanted to go away at once as soon as supper was over, and I had not the face to detain him. The second time, still in pursuance of my design, after we had supped, I went on conversing far into the night, and when he wanted to go away, I pretended that the hour was late and that he had much better remain. So he lay down on the couch next to me, the same on which he had supped, and there was no one but ourselves sleeping in the apartment. All this may be told without shame to any one. But what follows I could hardly tell you if I were sober. Yet as the proverb says, 'In vino veritas,' whether with boys, or without them (In allusion to two proverbs.); and therefore I must speak. Nor, again, should I be justified in concealing the lofty actions of Socrates when I come to praise him. Moreover I have felt the serpent's sting; and he who has suffered, as they say, is willing to tell his fellow-sufferers only, as they alone will be likely to understand him, and will not be extreme in judging of the sayings or doings which have been wrung from his agony. For I have been bitten by a more than viper's tooth; I have known in my soul, or in my heart, or in some other part, that worst of pangs, more violent in ingenuous youth than any serpent's tooth, the pang of philosophy, which will make a man say or do anything. And you whom I see around me, Phaedrus and Agathon and Eryximachus and Pausanias and Aristodemus and Aristophanes, all of you, and I need not say Socrates himself, have had experience of the same madness and passion in your longing after wisdom. Therefore listen and excuse my doings then and my sayings now. But let the attendants and other profane and unmannered persons close up the doors of their ears.

When the lamp was put out and the servants had gone away, I thought that I must be plain with him and have no more ambiguity. So I gave him a shake, and I said: 'Socrates, are you asleep?' 'No,' he said. 'Do you know what I am meditating? 'What are you meditating?' he said. 'I think,' I replied, 'that of all the lovers whom I have ever had you are the only one who is worthy of me, and you appear to be too modest to speak. Now I feel that I should be a fool to refuse you this or any other favour, and therefore I come to lay at your feet all that I have and all that my friends have, in the hope that you will assist me in the way of virtue, which I desire above all things, and in which I believe that you can help me better than any one else. And I should certainly have more reason to be ashamed of what wise men would say if I were to refuse a favour to such as you, than of what the world, who are mostly fools, would say of me if I granted it.' To these words he replied in the ironical manner which is so characteristic of him:—'Alcibiades, my friend, you have indeed an elevated aim if what you say is true, and if there really is in me any power by which you may become better; truly you must see in me some rare beauty of a kind infinitely higher than any which I see in you. And therefore, if you mean to share with me and to exchange beauty for beauty, you will have greatly the advantage of me; you will gain true beauty in return for appearance—like Diomede, gold in exchange for brass. But look again, sweet friend, and see whether you are not deceived in me. The mind begins to grow critical when the bodily eye fails, and it will be a long time before you get old.' Hearing this, I said: 'I have told you my purpose, which is quite serious, and do you consider what you think best for you and me.' 'That is good,' he said; 'at some other time then we will consider and act as seems best about this and about other matters.' Whereupon, I fancied that he was smitten, and that the words which I had uttered like arrows had wounded him, and so without waiting to hear more I got up, and throwing my coat about him crept under his threadbare cloak, as the time of year was winter, and there I lay during the whole night having this wonderful monster in my arms. This again, Socrates, will not be denied by you. And yet, notwithstanding all, he was so superior to my solicitations, so contemptuous and derisive and disdainful of my beauty—which really, as I fancied, had some attractions—hear, O judges; for judges you shall be of the haughty virtue of Socrates—nothing more happened, but in the morning when I awoke (let all the gods and goddesses be my witnesses) I arose as from the couch of a father or an elder brother.

What do you suppose must have been my feelings, after this rejection, at the thought of my own dishonour? And yet I could not help wondering at his natural temperance and self-restraint and manliness. I never imagined that I could have met with a man such as he is in wisdom and endurance. And therefore I could not be angry with him or renounce his company, any more than I could hope to win him. For I well knew that if Ajax could not be wounded by steel, much less he by money; and my only chance of captivating him by my personal attractions had failed. So I was at my wit's end; no one was ever more hopelessly enslaved by another. All this happened before he and I went on the expedition to Potidaea; there we messed together, and I had the opportunity of observing his extraordinary power of sustaining fatigue. His endurance was simply marvellous when, being cut off from our supplies, we were compelled to go without food—on such occasions, which often happen in time of war, he was superior not only to me but to everybody; there was no one to be compared to him. Yet at a festival he was the only person who had any real powers of enjoyment; though not willing to drink, he could if compelled beat us all at that,—wonderful to relate! no human being had ever seen Socrates drunk; and his powers, if I am not mistaken, will be tested before long. His fortitude in enduring cold was also surprising. There was a severe frost, for the winter in that region is really tremendous, and everybody else either remained indoors, or if they went out had on an amazing quantity of clothes, and were well shod, and had their feet swathed in felt and fleeces: in the midst of this, Socrates with his bare feet on the ice and in his ordinary dress marched better than the other soldiers who had shoes, and they looked daggers at him because he seemed to despise them.

I have told you one tale, and now I must tell you another, which is worth hearing,

'Of the doings and sufferings of the enduring man'

while he was on the expedition. One morning he was thinking about something which he could not resolve; he would not give it up, but continued thinking from early dawn until noon—there he stood fixed in thought; and at noon attention was drawn to him, and the rumour ran through the wondering crowd that Socrates had been standing and thinking about something ever since the break of day. At last, in the evening after supper, some Ionians out of curiosity (I should explain that this was not in winter but in summer), brought out their mats and slept in the open air that they might watch him and see whether he would stand all night. There he stood until the following morning; and with the return of light he offered up a prayer to the sun, and went his way (compare supra). I will also tell, if you please—and indeed I am bound to tell—of his courage in battle; for who but he saved my life? Now this was the engagement in which I received the prize of valour: for I was wounded and he would not leave me, but he rescued me and my arms; and he ought to have received the prize of valour which the generals wanted to confer on me partly on account of my rank, and I told them so, (this, again, Socrates will not impeach or deny), but he was more eager than the generals that I and not he should have the prize. There was another occasion on which his behaviour was very remarkable—in the flight of the army after the battle of Delium, where he served among the heavy-armed,—I had a better opportunity of seeing him than at Potidaea, for I was myself on horseback, and therefore comparatively out of danger. He and Laches were retreating, for the troops were in flight, and I met them and told them not to be discouraged, and promised to remain with them; and there you might see him, Aristophanes, as you describe (Aristoph. Clouds), just as he is in the streets of Athens, stalking like a pelican, and rolling his eyes, calmly contemplating enemies as well as friends, and making very intelligible to anybody, even from a distance, that whoever attacked him would be likely to meet with a stout resistance; and in this way he and his companion escaped—for this is the sort of man who is never touched in war; those only are pursued who are running away headlong. I particularly observed how superior he was to Laches in presence of mind. Many are the marvels which I might narrate in praise of Socrates; most of his ways might perhaps be paralleled in another man, but his absolute unlikeness to any human being that is or ever has been is perfectly astonishing. You may imagine Brasidas and others to have been like Achilles; or you may imagine Nestor and Antenor to have been like Pericles; and the same may be said of other famous men, but of this strange being you will never be able to find any likeness, however remote, either among men who now are or who ever have been—other than that which I have already suggested of Silenus and the satyrs; and they represent in a figure not only himself, but his words. For, although I forgot to mention this to you before, his words are like the images of Silenus which open; they are ridiculous when you first hear them; he clothes himself in language that is like the skin of the wanton satyr—for his talk is of pack-asses and smiths and cobblers and curriers, and he is always repeating the same things in the same words (compare Gorg.), so that any ignorant or inexperienced person might feel disposed to laugh at him; but he who opens the bust and sees what is within will find that they are the only words which have a meaning in them, and also the most divine, abounding in fair images of virtue, and of the widest comprehension, or rather extending to the whole duty of a good and honourable man.

This, friends, is my praise of Socrates. I have added my blame of him for his ill-treatment of me; and he has ill-treated not only me, but Charmides the son of Glaucon, and Euthydemus the son of Diocles, and many others in the same way—beginning as their lover he has ended by making them pay their addresses to him. Wherefore I say to you, Agathon, 'Be not deceived by him; learn from me and take warning, and do not be a fool and learn by experience, as the proverb says.'

When Alcibiades had finished, there was a laugh at his outspokenness; for he seemed to be still in love with Socrates. You are sober, Alcibiades, said Socrates, or you would never have gone so far about to hide the purpose of your satyr's praises, for all this long story is only an ingenious circumlocution, of which the point comes in by the way at the end; you want to get up a quarrel between me and Agathon, and your notion is that I ought to love you and nobody else, and that you and you only ought to love Agathon. But the plot of this Satyric or Silenic drama has been detected, and you must not allow him, Agathon, to set us at variance.

I believe you are right, said Agathon, and I am disposed to think that his intention in placing himself between you and me was only to divide us; but he shall gain nothing by that move; for I will go and lie on the couch next to you.

Yes, yes, replied Socrates, by all means come here and lie on the couch below me.

Alas, said Alcibiades, how I am fooled by this man; he is determined to get the better of me at every turn. I do beseech you, allow Agathon to lie between us.

Certainly not, said Socrates, as you praised me, and I in turn ought to praise my neighbour on the right, he will be out of order in praising me again when he ought rather to be praised by me, and I must entreat you to consent to this, and not be jealous, for I have a great desire to praise the youth.

Hurrah! cried Agathon, I will rise instantly, that I may be praised by Socrates.

The usual way, said Alcibiades; where Socrates is, no one else has any chance with the fair; and now how readily has he invented a specious reason for attracting Agathon to himself.

Agathon arose in order that he might take his place on the couch by Socrates, when suddenly a band of revellers entered, and spoiled the order of the banquet. Some one who was going out having left the door open, they had found their way in, and made themselves at home; great confusion ensued, and every one was compelled to drink large quantities of wine. Aristodemus said that Eryximachus, Phaedrus, and others went away—he himself fell asleep, and as the nights were long took a good rest: he was awakened towards daybreak by a crowing of cocks, and when he awoke, the others were either asleep, or had gone away; there remained only Socrates, Aristophanes, and Agathon, who were drinking out of a large goblet which they passed round, and Socrates was discoursing to them. Aristodemus was only half awake, and he did not hear the beginning of the discourse; the chief thing which he remembered was Socrates compelling the other two to acknowledge that the genius of comedy was the same with that of tragedy, and that the true artist in tragedy was an artist in comedy also. To this they were constrained to assent, being drowsy, and not quite following the argument. And first of all Aristophanes dropped off, then, when the day was already dawning, Agathon. Socrates, having laid them to sleep, rose to depart; Aristodemus, as his manner was, following him. At the Lyceum he took a bath, and passed the day as usual. In the evening he retired to rest at his own home.

DEFINITION

Definition Arguments Walk-Through

The *Excelsior OWL* site has a useful walk-through for each of the rhetorical modes. Its coverage of definition (http://owl.excelsior.edu/rhetorical-styles/definition-essay/) is worth looking through as you narrow your argument.

Public domain content

- Definition Arguments. **Authored by**: OWL Excelsior Writing Lab. **Provided by**: Excelsior College. **Located at**: http://owl.excelsior.edu/rhetorical-styles/definition-essay/ (http://owl.excelsior.edu/rhetorical-styles/definition-essay/). **Project**: ENG 101. **License**: *CC BY-SA: Attribution-ShareAlike (https://creativecommons.org/licenses/by-sa/4.0/)*

Definition Structure

The definition argument focuses on clarifying a definition for a controversial term or concept. In other words, a definition argument is one that asserts we cannot make clear assertions or possess a clear understanding of an issue until we understand exactly what the terms mean.

> The danger is that writers only point out the existence of the ideas about the term rather than establishing exigency. Another common issue is that writers will only point out an issue's importance without actually arguing anything about the best (and thus arguable) meaning of that word/phrase.

Examples of this type of argument might look something like this: An argumentative essay calling for a re-examination of the birth control requirements in the Affordable Health Care Act with a focus on explaining what birth control is, what the options are, and how they work.

An argumentative essay calling for an end to the two-party system of government in the United States with a focus on defining what a two-party system really is and what the laws are related to it.

An argumentative essay arguing for the benefits of organic foods with a focus on defining what organic really means.

Structure

Access the *Excelsior OWL* site's page on "Definition Argument" (http://owl.excelsior.edu/argument-and-critical-thinking/ argumentative-purposes/argumentative-purposes-definition/) here and click to see another walk-through of how to structure this type of argument. (This differs from the previous mini-lecture's link.)

TIPS: When writing a definition argument, it's important to keep your essay focused. Choose an issue where there is a clear misunderstanding of a term or terms. Focus on those terms in relation to your claim.

If you're having trouble thinking of topics for a definition argument, read a little bit about what is going on in the world. Look for issues that come up related to misunderstandings over what certain terms mean.

Brainstorming Definition Thesis Claims

When Brainstorming Definition Theses, Try the Following Moves

Getting started properly on an argument like this can be daunting, so try breaking this down using any of the following tips:

- Take some examples that might be borderline and write about them. They can be argued about and fitted to the term you're arguing. In doing this, you might find that the term itself needs some fitting back, and that the example alters the term.
- Use both high and low culture for examples. If you clear sources with me, there's nothing to say you cannot use a website. Video games, songs, movies and television shows can be used, as can current news. If I were writing this, I'd be looking for examples so that the essay I produce would not be too vague.
- Abstraction translates as "writing away from." We have to remember to bring something back. What examples fit/ contradict/call into question the example?
- Since we cannot expect a dictionary to have that exact phrase, we would also look for synonyms like *situational ethics*. Playing the "Open, sesame!" game of searches, we have to figure out which terms will get the hits.
- To properly understand_____, one must _____. That's the basic pattern, right? You're not totally dismissing the readers but neither are you totally agreeing with them. They know the term and think that they have examples of it. You're showing them something about the term that they didn't realize.
- You can expand, contract, or show in which situations the term can be relevant. "While most people think *provisional ethics* means 'Whatever one decides is actually right', actually this is a childish and limited way of looking at Michael Shermer's term. Provisional ethics requires a scientific check of one's decisions, and is anything but the anything goes of relativism that most people think it is." That's a working claim that I could refine, but I'm saying that most people are wrong about something or think that they know the term when, actually, they don't.
- For now, the key is to figure out the extent to which you'll alter the definition and which examples work to support it.

Defining is a Process of Exposing and Arguing Boundaries

The words we read often break down in important fashion. De (*away, from*) and –fine are one of these. (*Definire*, in Latin, meant to limit or determine.) Definitions, then, have this feeling of ending things. We'll see, though, that they actually begin debate. Since only a part of a word's meaning is its dictionary definition—the vast complement being its many connotations, which you or I can be expected to bring—then we have a dynamic system. (*Dynam* means power in Greek.) We have to take seriously the idea that words matter and that they weave effects upon readers or listeners—even if the writer doesn't know the story of the word.

Watch for boundaries between what's left out and included. Definitions are all about borders. Like some nasty neighbors, tricky writers can try and get us to accept shifting borders. Let's keep an eye on what is involved (literally "spun into") the definitions in this unit and the rest of the course!

CC licensed content, Original

Sample Definition Argument

Now that you have had the chance to learn about writing a definition argument, it's time to see what one might look like. Linked, you'll see a sample definition argumentative essay (http://owl.excelsior.edu/argument-and-critical-thinking/argumentative-purposes/argumentative-purposes-sample-definition-argument/) written following **MLA (http://owl.excelsior.edu/research-and-citations/documenting/mla-style/)**formatting guidelines.

Public domain content

- Sample Definition Essay. **Authored by**: OWL Excelsior Writing Lab. **Provided by**: Excelsior College. **Located at**: http://owl.excelsior.edu/argument-and-critical-thinking/argumentative-purposes/argumentative-purposes-sample-definition-argument/ (http://owl.excelsior.edu/argument-and-critical-thinking/argumentative-purposes/argumentative-purposes-sample-definition-argument/). **Project**: ENG 101. **License**: *Public Domain: No Known Copyright (https://creativecommons.org/about/pdm)*

Assumptions Impact Definition Arguments

We Know About What Assumptions do. . . Watch the Following Willingham Video: "Learning Styles Don't Exist"

Since definition is about broadening, narrowing, or otherwise altering the circles of meaning we put around words and ideas, why not take on a cherished chestnut of parents, product developers and students: the notion of learning styles.

Watch the Following Willingham Video

I wanted to complicate our assumption that operates with those learning styles.
Check out Daniel Willingham's "Learning Styles Don't Exist" video (7 minutes) at:

- https://youtu.be/slv9rz2NTUk

He has some FAQs at:
http://www.danielwillingham.com/learning-styles-faq.html

Note that Willingham is making a particular distinction in his argument about these that gets right at our assumptions. Watch how he does that while metaphorically keeping us "in the room" and still watching.

Public domain content

- Assumptions Impact Definition Argume. **Authored by**: Joshua Dickinson. **Provided by**: YouTube. **Located at**: https://youtu.be/slv9rz2NTUk (https://youtu.be/slv9rz2NTUk). **License**: *CC BY-SA: Attribution-ShareAlike (https://creativecommons.org/licenses/by-sa/4.0/)*

For Whatever Reason, People Mess up Quoting Definitions

Some serious problems can occur if we're placing definitions in the wrong spots or failing to quote them properly. Here are some common (and, since we're doing definition, *common* here means 35% or higher incidence from semester to semester) errors:

- Used words matter, so we quote definitions.
- The titles of dictionaries get italicized, but those aren't what go in the citations. Actually, the cited word would go in the parenthetical citation and would begin its works cited entry.
- Do not use italics to set off quotes.
- Callouts like *common* above get italicized.

Mostly, I'm mentioning this because of the unquoted quotes issue. Remember, anytime you fail to quote you're indicating that the words are yours. . . which looks bad when that gaffe is done with the term the entire essay is built upon.

Near-Humans Freak Out Humans

If you're a gamer, you have likely heard of the uncanny valley. (Heck, it's even the name of a game.)

It's that near-humanness that can innately bother us. I think it's fascinating.

Here's a quick video on this.

- https://youtu.be/CNdAlPoh8a4

For more, check out *Blade Runner* in its entirety, or at least this little clip or some that follow:

- https://youtu.be/Umc9ezAyJv0

If we're in the mode of defining human, we can see the works of science fiction in a new light, since they are often about this, or about how technology affirms or denies our humanity.

And now you understand why I can never watch more than fifteen seconds of the PBS show *Sid the Science Kid*. . . !

Public domain content

Graeme Wood, What ISIS Really Wants

This March 2015 article by Graeme Wood from *The Atlantic* (http://jccweb.sunyjefferson.edu:2055/login.aspx?direct=true&db=a9h&AN=100848076&site=ehost-live)is a powerful argument of definition. Access it either through the permalink below or by accessing either your library databases or www.theatlantic.com

Be sure to get the full-color document with the images.

http://jccweb.sunyjefferson.edu:2055/login.aspx?direct=true&db=a9h&AN=100848076&site=ehost-live

Steven Pinker, The Moral Instinct

Read "The Moral Instinct," an article by Steven Pinker. I accessed it through the JCC Library databases and its *Literature Resource Center*, but I know it is also available as a PDF using a web search.

The New York Times Magazine. (Jan. 13, 2008): News: p32(L). From *Literature Resource Center*.

RHETORICAL ANALYSIS

Basic Questions for Rhetorical Analysis

What is the rhetorical situation?

- What occasion gives rise to the need or opportunity for persuasion?
- What is the historical occasion that would give rise to the composition of this text?

Who is the author/speaker?

- How does he or she establish ethos (personal credibility)?
- Does he/she come across as knowledgeable? fair?
- Does the speaker's reputation convey a certain authority?

What is his/her intention in speaking?

- To attack or defend?
- To exhort or dissuade from certain action?
- To praise or blame?
- To teach, to delight, or to persuade?

Who make up the audience?

- Who is the intended audience?
- What values does the audience hold that the author or speaker appeals to?
- Who have been or might be secondary audiences?
- If this is a work of fiction, what is the nature of the audience within the fiction?

What is the content of the message?

- Can you summarize the main idea?
- What are the principal lines of reasoning or kinds of arguments used?
- What topics of invention are employed?
- How does the author or speaker appeal to reason? to emotion?

What is the form in which it is conveyed?

- What is the structure of the communication; how is it arranged?
- What oral or literary genre is it following?
- What figures of speech (schemes and tropes) are used?
- What kind of style and tone is used and for what purpose?

How do form and content correspond?

- Does the form complement the content?

- What effect could the form have, and does this aid or hinder the author's intention?

Does the message/speech/text succeed in fulfilling the author's or speaker's intentions?

- For whom?
- Does the author/speaker effectively fit his/her message to the circumstances, times, and audience?
- Can you identify the responses of historical or contemporary audiences?

What does the nature of the communication reveal about the culture that produced it?

- What kinds of values or customs would the people have that would produce this?
- How do the allusions, historical references, or kinds of words used place this in a certain time and location?

CC licensed content, Shared previously

Troubleshoot Your Reading

Sometimes reading may seem difficult, you might have trouble getting started, or other challenges will surface. Here are some troubleshooting ideas.

Problem: "Sometimes I put my reading off or don't have time to do it, and then when I do have time, well, I'm out of time."

Suggestions: That's a problem, for sure. I always suggest to students that rather than trying to do a bunch of reading at once, they try to do a little bit every day. That makes it easier.

If you're stuck up against a deadline with no reading done, one suggestion is to do some good pre-reading. That should at least give you the idea of the main topic.

Another idea is to divide the total pages assigned by the number of available days, figuring out how many pages you'll need to read each day to finish the assignment. Sometimes approaching the text in smaller pieces like this can make it feel more doable. Also, once you figure out how long it takes you to read, say, five pages, you can predict how much time it will take to read a larger section.

Problem: "If I don't understand some part of the reading, I just skip over it and hope someone will explain it later in class."

Suggestions: Not understanding reading can be frustrating—and it can make it hard to succeed on your assignments. The best suggestion is to talk with your teacher. Let them know you don't understand the reading, and they should be able to help.

Another suggestion is to read sentence by sentence. Be sure you understand each word—if you don't, look them up. As you read, master each sentence before going on to the next one, and then, at the end of a paragraph, stop and summarize the entire paragraph, reflecting on what you just read.

Yet another idea: use the Web and do a search for the title of the reading followed by the word 'analysis.' Reading what other people have said about the text may help you get past your stuck points. If you're in a face-to-face classroom, asking a question in class will encourage discussion and will also help your fellow students, who may have the same confusions.

Problem: "I really don't like to read that much, so I read pretty fast and tend to stick with the obvious meanings. But then the teacher is always asking us to dig deeper and try to figure out what the author really meant. I get so frustrated with that!"

Suggestions: College-level writing tends to have multiple layers of significance. The easiest way to think about this is by separating the "obvious or surface meaning" from the "buried treasure meaning." This can actually be one of the most fun parts of a reading—you get to play detective. As you read, try to ask questions of the text: Why? Who? Where? For what reason? These questions will help you think more deeply about the text.

Problem: "Sometimes I jump to conclusions about what a text means and then later find out I wasn't understanding it completely."

Suggestions: This usually happens when we read too quickly and don't engage with the text. The best way to avoid this is to slow down and take time with the text, following all the guidelines for effective and critical reading.

Problem: "When a text suggests an idea I strongly disagree with, I can't seem to go any further."

Suggestions: Aristotle was known for saying, "It is the mark of an educated mind to be able to entertain a thought without accepting it." As a college student, you must be ready to explore and examine a wide range of ideas, whether you agree with them or not. In approaching texts with an open and willing mind, you leave yourself ready to engage with a wide world of ideas—many of which you may not have encountered before. This is what college is all about.

Problem: "I'm a slow reader. It takes me a long time to read material, and sometimes the amount of assigned reading panics me."

Suggestions: Two thoughts. One, the more you read, the easier it gets: like anything, reading improves with practice. And two, you'll probably find your reading is most effective if you try to do a little bit every day rather than several hours of reading all at one time. Plan ahead! Be aware of what you need to read and divide it up among the available days. Reading 100 pages in a week may seem overwhelming, but reading 15 pages a day will be easier. Be sure to read when you're fresh, too, rather than at day's end, when you're exhausted.

Problem: "Sometimes the teacher assigns content in an area I really know nothing about. I want to be an accountant. Why should I read philosophy or natural history, and how am I supposed to understand them?"

Suggestions: By reading a wide variety of texts, we don't just increase our knowledge base—we also make our minds work. This kind of "mental exercise" teaches the brain and prepares it to deal with all kinds of critical and innovative thinking. It also helps train us to different reading and writing tasks, even when they're not familiar to us.

Problem: "When I examine a text, I tend to automatically accept what it says. But the teacher is always encouraging us to ask questions and not make assumptions."

Suggestions: What you're doing is reading as a reader—reading for yourself and making your own assumptions. The teacher wants you to reach for the next level by reading critically. By engaging with the text and digging through it as if you're on an archaeological expedition, you'll discover even more about the text. This can be fun, and it also helps train your brain to explore texts with an analytic eye.

Problem: "I really hate reading. I've found I can skip the readings, read the Sparks Notes, and get by just fine."

Suggestions: First, if you aren't familiar with Sparks Notes, it's an online site that provides summary and analysis of many literary texts and other materials, and students often use this to either replace reading or to better understand materials. You may be able to get by, at least for a while, with reading Sparks Notes alone, for they do a decent basic job of summarizing content and talking about simple themes. But Sparks isn't good at reading texts deeply or considering deep analysis, which means a Sparks-only approach will result in your missing a lot of what the text includes.

You'll also be missing some great experiences. The more you read, the easier reading becomes. The more you read deeply and critically and the more comfortable you become with analyzing texts, the easier that process becomes. And as your textual skills become stronger, you'll find yourself more successful with all of your college studies, too. Reading remains a vital college (and life!) skill—the more you practice reading, the better you'll be at it. And honestly, reading can be fun, too– not to mention a great way to relax and an almost instant stress reducer.

CC licensed content, Shared previously

- Troubleshoot Your Reading, from The Word on College Reading and Writing. **Authored by**: Monique Babin, Clackamas Community College Carol Burnell, Clackamas Community College Susan Pesznecker, Portland State University. **Provided by**: Open Textbook Library. **Located at**: https://open.umn.edu/opentextbooks/BookDetail.aspx?bookId=471 (https://open.umn.edu/opentextbooks/BookDetail.aspx?bookId=471). **Project**: Center for Open Education. **License**: *CC BY-NC: Attribution-NonCommercial (https://creativecommons.org/licenses/by-nc/4.0/)*

Rogerian Argument

The Rogerian argument, inspired by the influential psychologist Carl Rogers, aims to find compromise on a controversial issue.

If you are using the Rogerian approach your introduction to the argument should accomplish three objectives:

Carl Rogers

1. **Introduce the author and work**
   Usually, you will introduce the author and work in the first sentence, as in this example:*In Dwight Okita's "In Response to Executive Order 9066," the narrator addresses an inevitable by-product of war – racism.*The first time you refer to the author, refer to him or her by his or her full name. After that, refer to the author by last name only. Never refer to an author by his or her first name only.
2. **Provide the audience a short but concise summary of the work to which you are responding**
   Remember, your audience has already read the work you are responding to.
   Therefore, you do not need to provide a lengthy summary. Focus on the main points of the work to which you are responding and use direct quotations sparingly. Direct quotations work best when they are powerful and compelling.
3. **State the main issue addressed in the work** Your thesis, or claim, will come after you summarize the two sides of the issue.

The Introduction

The following is an example of how the introduction of a Rogerian argument can be written. The topic is racial profiling.

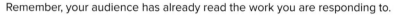

> In Dwight Okita's "In Response to Executive Order 9066," the narrator — a young Japanese-American — writes a letter to the government, who has ordered her family into a relocation camp after Pearl Harbor. In the letter, the narrator details the people in her life, from her father to her best friend at school. Since the narrator is of Japanese descent, her best friend accuses her of "trying to start a war" (18). The narrator is seemingly too naïve to realize the ignorance of this statement, and tells the government that she asked this friend to plant tomato seeds in her honor. Though Okita's poem deals specifically with World War II, the issue of race relations during wartime is still relevant. Recently, with the outbreaks of terrorism in the United States, Spain, and England, many are calling for racial profiling to stifle terrorism. The issue has sparked debate, with one side calling it racism and the other calling it common sense.

Once you have written your introduction, you must now show the two sides to the debate you are addressing. Though there are always more than two sides to a debate, Rogerian arguments put two in stark opposition to one another. Summarize each side, then provide a middle path. Your summary of the two sides will be your first two body paragraphs. Use quotations from outside sources to effectively illustrate the position of each side.

An outline for a Rogerian argument might look like this:

- Introduction
- Side A
- Side B
- Claim

- Conclusion

The Claim

Since the goal of Rogerian argument is to find a common ground between two opposing positions, you must identify the shared beliefs or assumptions of each side. In the example above, both sides of the racial profiling issue want the U.S. A solid Rogerian argument acknowledges the desires of each side, and tries to accommodate both. Again, using the racial profiling example above, both sides desire a safer society, perhaps a better solution would focus on more objective measures than race; an effective start would be to use more screening technology on public transportation. Once you have a claim that disarms the central dispute, you should support the claim with evidence, and quotations when appropriate.

Quoting Effectively

Remember, you should quote to illustrate a point you are making. You should not, however, quote to simply take up space. Make sure all quotations are compelling and intriguing: Consider the following example. In "The Danger of Political Correctness," author Richard Stein asserts that, "the desire to not offend has now become more important than protecting national security" (52). This statement sums up the beliefs of those in favor of profiling in public places.

The Conclusion

Your conclusion should:

- Bring the essay back to what is discussed in the introduction
- Tie up loose ends
- End on a thought-provoking note

The following is a sample conclusion:

> Though the debate over racial profiling is sure to continue, each side desires to make the United States a safer place. With that goal in mind, our society deserves better security measures than merely searching a person who appears a bit dark. We cannot waste time with such subjective matters, especially when we have technology that could more effectively locate potential terrorists. Sure, installing metal detectors and cameras on public transportation is costly, but feeling safe in public is priceless.

Sources

Taken from Michael Franco's PowerPoint Presentation Writing Essay 4: Rogerian Argument (http://www.occc.edu/mfranco/Writing_Essay_2.ppt)

CC licensed content, Shared previously

- Rogerian Argument. **Provided by**: Utah State University. **Located at**: http://ocw.usu.edu/English/introduction-to-writing-academic-prose/rogerian-argument.html (http://ocw.usu.edu/English/introduction-to-writing-academic-prose/rogerian-argument.html). **License**: *CC BY-NC-SA: Attribution-NonCommercial-ShareAlike (https://creativecommons.org/licenses/by-nc-sa/4.0/)*

- Image of Carl Rogers. **Authored by**: Didius. **Provided by**: Wikimedia. **Located at**: http://commons.wikimedia.org/wiki/File:Carl_Ransom_Rogers.jpg (http://commons.wikimedia.org/wiki/File:Carl_Ransom_Rogers.jpg). **License**: *CC BY: Attribution (https://creativecommons.org/licenses/by/4.0/)*

Sample Rhetorical Analysis Essay

Student essay is used with permission. It was originally submitted double-spaced with no extra spaces between the lines, featured proper MLA pagination, and 1/2″ paragraph indents. The writing assignment asks for an argument about how several rhetorical elements work together to create a functioning whole in a given chapter of Michael Shermer's 2004 book *The Science of Good and Evil: Why People Cheat, Gossip, Care, Share, and Follow the Golden Rule.*

Liana Monnat

English 101

Instructor: Joshua Dickinson

October 16, 2016

Michael Shermer Successfully Proves That Humans Can Be Good Without God

In his chapter entitled "Can We Be Good Without God?" Michael Shermer's objective is to prove that one does not need to be religious to be capable of moral behavior. Shermer has, in his previous four chapters, taken care to establish ethos by demonstrating that he is an open-minded and intelligent fellow. Judging by his use of vocabulary, he assumes his readers are also intelligent people, with whom he attempts to develop a connection through his intermittent use of humor. Shermer has already proved that his arguments are well-supported by large quantities of evidence, which lets his audience know that what he is saying is inherently trustworthy. Taking all of this into consideration and having carefully analyzed this chapter, the reader is compelled by logic to agree with Shermer that one can have religion without morality, and morality without religion.

Shermer begins his fifth chapter with an appeal to pathos. He describes to readers the massacre perpetrated at Columbine High School by Eric Harris and Dylan Klebold (141). His description of the event along with a photograph of the black-clad, angry-looking murderers gives the reader a glimpse of the terror that must have been experienced by those unfortunate enough to have been present at the massacre. In building up to proving his argument, Shermer appeals to readers' ability to reason by showing that outside influences do not cause a person to behave immorally. He explains that in the aftermath of the event, many theories were put forth to rationalize the cause of Harris and Klebold's murderous rampage. Included in these causes were use of prescription drugs, cult or gang influence, a fatherless home, homosexuality, and exposure to violence in video games (143-144). Shermer uses logic to point out that none of these causes were relevant, particularly the idea that video game violence may have been the cause. He makes mention of several newspapers that make such a claim, but dismisses the articles as having been written by "wannabe social commentators" and "ad hoc social scientists" and lacking in evidence (143). Shermer shows how ridiculous the notion of video games being the causal factor is by relaying testimony of other players of violent games. They all point out that they have not been driven to violence by their gaming habits (143). By presenting these testimonies, he appeals to our common sense and ability to reason as intelligent individuals to realize that if video games caused people to behave violently, all gamers who played violent games would exhibit violent behavior, which is certainly not the case. Shermer has thus far proved to readers that outside influences do not cause a person to abandon their morality.

Having logically dismantled the previous cases, Shermer turns his focus to the subject of gun control. He quips that those in favor of more gun control took advantage of the Columbine massacre by "squawking for more legislation" (146). His use of the word 'squawking' brings chickens to mind, and the great amount of noise they produce at the slightest provocation. I believe creating this visual was probably the intent behind his humorous choice of words.

Liberal gun control advocates thoroughly ridiculed, Shermer notes that conservatives answered the call for more gun control by insisting that guns were not the problem. The problem, as conservatives saw it, was the evil souls of the people who used them to commit evil deeds (146). I feel that Shermer purposefully saved mentioning the gun control issue for last because it deals with the ideas of evil, morality, and religion. He has taken much care in the preceding chapters to make it clear that he does not believe that evil exists, and that morality is not a product of religion. The issue of gun control seems a well-chosen topic from which to begin his argument of how morality is a thing separate from religion.

The first example of evidence Shermer offers in his argument is an excerpt from a letter read by Congressman Tom DeLay. He uses the excerpt to bring to readers' attention an argument that is commonly made to explain violent acts. It implies that as science provides evidence for questions that people once looked to religion to answer, people no longer feel obligated by a higher power to behave morally (147). Shermer disputes this argument by describing the case of another perpetrator of a school shooting. Rumors of the perpetrator being an atheist were quickly dispelled by the family priest, whose explanation was that the boy was a sinner but not an atheist, to which Shermer sarcastically quips "Thank God for that" (147). This remark demonstrates his disgust that the priest would imply that being a Christian murderer was less offensive than being an atheist. With this evidence, Shermer has supported his argument and demonstrated to his audience that religious people do not necessarily have morals.

For Shermer's next move, he takes into consideration the opinions of several credible people who believe that morality is impossible without religion. He utilizes quotes from the 103rd archbishop of Canterbury, Pope Pious XI, and the deeply religious Dostoyevsky who all fervently insist that religion is absolutely necessary for morality (149-150). Shermer then includes the religious views of Laura Schlessinger, his one-time colleague. He immediately diminishes her religious credibility by referring to her as a "self-appointed religious authority" (150). This implies to readers that although she is considered a 'religious authority' her opinions should not be taken too seriously. He points out that although Schlessinger claims to have grown up lacking morals due to an atheistic upbringing, she admits that her parents still managed to instill her with some degree of morality (151). This admission helps support his idea that non-religious people can have morals, but is the only part of Shermer's paragraphs about Schlessinger that appear to be relevant to his argument. He continues on about her, however, and it becomes apparent to readers that Shermer once admired her work but was taken aback by her conversion to Judaism. He further weakens her authority by poking fun at her, and readers (this reader, at least) cannot help but wonder if he only included these paragraphs about Schlessinger because he is still disgruntled about her defection from his cause.

Shermer has, through several quotes from religious authorities, demonstrated to his audience that religious people are adamant that religion is necessary for moral behavior. In an effort to prove that they are wrong, he refutes the claims of these authorities by serving up examples of religious people that committed atrocities while zealously practicing their religion. His go-to example is Hitler and the annihilation of the Jews in Germany. He illustrates for readers the religious fervor of Hitler by quoting him as saying "I believe today that I am acting in the sense of the Almighty Creator. By warding off the Jews I am fighting for the Lord's work" (qtd. on 153). By strategically using this quote, Shermer is proving to readers that not only did Hitler commit mass murder, he did so in the Lord's name. This example, more than any other, is meant to show that religion and morality are not related.

In perhaps his most convincing argument that one need not be religious to behave morally, Shermer gets personal. He asks readers the question "What would you do if there was no God?" (154). Now the reader must contemplate the point Shermer has been trying to make, but on an intimate level. He forces one to admit that if it was learned that God did not exist, the vast majority of people would continue to behave morally. Most people would not, free from fear of eternal reprisal, proceed to pillage, rape, and commit murder. After this degree of self-examination, it would be illogical to disagree that morality is not a creation of religion.

In his chapter "Can We Be Good Without God?", Shermer successfully proves that we can indeed be good without God. He appealed to readers' emotions by describing the nightmare that was the Columbine massacre and led his audience to logically conclude that no outside influences caused the perpetrators' behavior. Through the strategic use of quotes and examples, Shermer effectively demonstrated that contrary to the beliefs of religious authorities, deeply religious people are capable of behaving extremely immorally. Shermer ingeniously substantiated his point by asking readers to ponder what their own behavior might be like without God holding them accountable for their actions. I feel that this was his most convincing piece of evidence in support of his argument, it is hard to deny his logic when applying it to oneself. It can be assumed that most readers would continue to behave morally, and would agree with Shermer that we can be good without God.

Work Cited

Shermer, Michael. "Can We Be Good Without God?" *The Science of Good and Evil: Why People Cheat,*

Gossip, Care, Share, and Follow the Golden Rule. Henry Holt and Company, LLC, 2004, pp.141-156.

Toulmin's Argument Model

Stephen Toulmin, an English philosopher and logician, identified elements of a persuasive argument. These give useful categories by which an argument may be analyzed.

Claim

A claim is a statement that you are asking the other person to accept. This includes information you are asking them to accept as true or actions you want them to accept and enact.

For example:

You should use a hearing aid.

Many people start with a claim, but then find that it is challenged. If you just ask me to do something, I will not simply agree with what you want. I will ask why I should agree with you. I will ask you to prove your claim. This is where grounds become important.

Grounds

The grounds (or data) is the basis of real persuasion and is made up of data and hard facts, plus the reasoning behind the claim. It is the 'truth' on which the claim is based. Grounds may also include proof of expertise and the basic premises on which the rest of the argument is built.

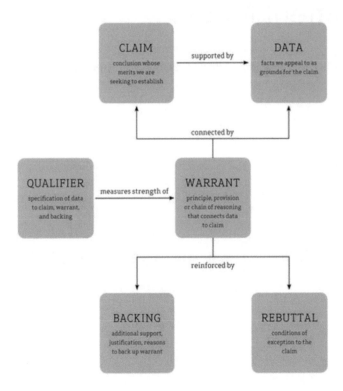

The actual truth of the data may be less that 100%, as much data are ultimately based on perception. We assume what we measure is true, but there may be problems in this measurement, ranging from a faulty measurement instrument to biased sampling.

It is critical to the argument that the grounds are not challenged because, if they are, they may become a claim, which you will need to prove with even deeper information and further argument.

For example:

> Over 70% of all people over 65 years have a hearing difficulty.

Information is usually a very powerful element of persuasion, although it does affect people differently. Those who are dogmatic, logical or rational will more likely to be persuaded by factual data. Those who argue emotionally and who are highly invested in their own position will challenge it or otherwise try to ignore it. It is often a useful test to give something factual to the other person that disproves their argument, and watch how they handle it. Some will accept it without question. Some will dismiss it out of hand. Others will dig deeper, requiring more explanation. This is where the warrant comes into its own.

Warrant

A warrant links data and other grounds to a claim, legitimizing the claim by showing the grounds to be relevant. The warrant may be explicit or unspoken and implicit. It answers the question 'Why does that data mean your claim is true?'

For example:

A hearing aid helps most people to hear better.

The warrant may be simple and it may also be a longer argument, with additional sub–(http://www.designmethodsandprocesses.co.uk/2011/03/the-jump/)elements including those described below.

Warrants may be based on *logos*, *ethos* or *pathos*, or values that are assumed to be shared with the listener.

In many arguments, warrants are often implicit and hence unstated. This gives space for the other person to question and expose the warrant, perhaps to show it is weak or unfounded.

Backing

The backing (or support) for an argument gives additional support to the warrant by answering different questions.

For example:

Hearing aids are available locally.

Qualifier

The qualifier (or modal qualifier) indicates the strength of the leap from the data to the warrant and may limit how universally the claim applies. They include words such as 'most', 'usually', 'always' or 'sometimes'. Arguments may hence range from strong assertions to generally quite floppy with vague and often rather uncertain kinds of statement.

For example:

Hearing aids help most people.

Another variant is the reservation, which may give the possibility of the claim being incorrect. Unless there is evidence to the contrary, hearing aids do no harm to ears.

Qualifiers and reservations are much used by advertisers who are constrained not to lie. Thus they slip 'usually', 'virtually', 'unless' and so on into their claims.

Rebuttal

Despite the careful construction of the argument, there may still be counter-arguments that can be used. These may be rebutted either through a continued dialogue, or by pre-empting the counter-argument by giving the rebuttal during the initial presentation of the argument.

For example:

There is a support desk that deals with technical problems.

Any rebuttal is an argument in itself, and thus may include a claim, warrant, backing and so on. It also, of course can have a rebuttal. Thus if you are presenting an argument, you can seek to understand both possible rebuttals and also rebuttals to the rebuttals.

See also:

Arrangement, Use of Language

Toulmin, S. (1969). The Uses of Argument, Cambridge, England: Cambridge University Press

http://changingminds.org/disciplines/argument/making_argument/toulmin.htm [accessed April 2011]

See more at: http://www.designmethodsandprocesses.co.uk/2011/03/toulmins-argument-model/#sthash.dwkAUTvh.dpuf

Toulmin's Schema

Stephen Edelston Toulmin (born March 25, 1922) is a British philosopher, author, and educator. Influenced by the Austrian philosopher Ludwig Wittgenstein, Toulmin devoted his works to the analysis of moral reasoning. Throughout his writings, he seeks to develop practical arguments which can be used effectively in evaluating the ethics behind moral issues. The Toulmin Model of Argumentation, a diagram containing six interrelated components used for analyzing arguments, was considered his most influential work, particularly in the field of rhetoric and communication, and in computer science.

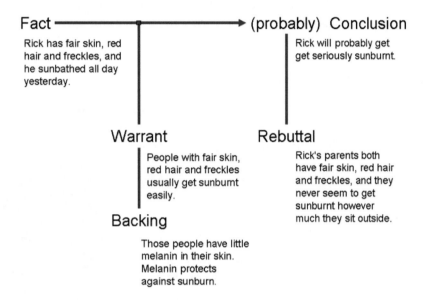

Stephen Toulmin is a British philosopher and educator who devoted to analyzing moral reasoning. Throughout his writings, he seeks to develop practical arguments which can be used effectively in evaluating the ethics behind moral issues. His most famous work was his Model of Argumentation(sometimes called "Toulmin's Schema," which is a method of analyzing an argument by breaking it down into six parts. Once an argument is broken down and examined, weaknesses in the argument can be found and addressed.

Toulmin's Schema:

1. Claim: conclusions whose merit must be established. For example, if a person tries to convince a listener that he is a British citizen, the claim would be "I am a British citizen."
2. Data: the facts appealed to as a foundation for the claim. For example, the person introduced in 1 can support his claim with the supporting data "I was born in Bermuda."
3. Warrant: the statement authorizing the movement from the data to the claim. In order to move from the data established in 2, "I was born in Bermuda," to the claim in 1, "I am a British citizen," the person must supply a warrant to bridge the gap between 1 & 2 with the statement "A man born in Bermuda will legally be a British Citizen." Toulmin stated that an argument is only as strong as its weakest warrant and if a warrant isn't valid, then the whole argument collapses. Therefore, it is important to have strong, valid warrants.
4. Backing: facts that give credibility to the statement expressed in the warrant; backing must be introduced when the warrant itself is not convincing enough to the readers or the listeners. For example, if the listener does not deem the warrant as credible, the speaker would supply legal documents as backing statement to show that it is true that "A man

born in Bermuda will legally be a British Citizen."

5. Rebuttal: statements recognizing the restrictions to which the claim may legitimately be applied. The rebuttal is exemplified as follows, "A man born in Bermuda will legally be a British citizen, unless he has betrayed Britain and become a spy of another country."

6. Qualifier: words or phrases expressing how certain the author/speaker is concerning the claim. Such words or phrases include "possible," "probably," "impossible," "certainly," "presumably," "as far as the evidence goes," or "necessarily." The claim "I am definitely a British citizen" has a greater degree of force than the claim "I am a British citizen, presumably."

7. The first three elements "claim," "data," and "warrant" are considered as the essential components of practical arguments, while the 4-6 "Qualifier," "Backing," and "Rebuttal" may not be needed in some arguments. When first proposed, this layout of argumentation is based on legal arguments and intended to be used to analyze arguments typically found in the courtroom; in fact, Toulmin did not realize that this layout would be applicable to the field of rhetoric and communication until later. 1

Here are a few more examples of Toulmin's Schema:

Suppose you see a one of those commercials for a product that promises to give you whiter teeth. Here are the basic parts of the argument behind the commercial:

1. Claim: You should buy our tooth-whitening product.
2. Data: Studies show that teeth are 50% whiter after using the product for a specified time.
3. Warrant: People want whiter teeth.
4. Backing: Celebrities want whiter teeth.
5. Rebuttal: Commercial says "unless you don't want to attract guys."
6. Qualifier: Fine print says "product must be used six weeks for results."

Notice that those commercials don't usually bother trying to convince you that you want whiter teeth; instead, they assume that you have bought into the value our culture places on whiter teeth. When an assumption—a warrant in Toulmin's terms—is unstated, it's called an implicit warrant. Sometimes, however, the warrant may need to be stated because it is a powerful part of the argument. When the warrant is stated, it's called an explicit warrant. 2

Another example:

1. Claim: People should probably own a gun.
2. Data: Studies show that people who own a gun are less likely to be mugged.
3. Warrant: People want to be safe.
4. Backing: May not be necessary. In this case, it is common sense that people want to be safe.
5. Rebuttal: Not everyone should own a gun. Children and those will mental disorders/problems should not own a gun.
6. Qualifier: The word "probably" in the claim.

1. Claim: Flag burning should be unconstitutional in most cases.
2. Data: A national poll says that 60% of Americans want flag burning unconstitutional
3. Warrant: People want to respect the flag.
4. Backing: Official government procedures for the disposal of flags.
5. Rebuttal: Not everyone in the U.S. respects the flag.
6. Qualifier: The phrase "in most cases"

Toulmin says that the weakest part of any argument is its weakest warrant. Remember that the warrant is the link between the data and the claim. If the warrant isn't valid, the argument collapses. 2

Sources

1. Stephen Toulmin (http://en.wikipedia.org/wiki/Stephen_Toulmin)

2. Toulmin's Analysis (http://owlet.letu.edu/contenthtml/research/toulmin.html)

Persuasion

LEARNING OBJECTIVES

- Determine the purpose and structure of persuasion in writing.
- Identify bias in writing.
- Assess various rhetorical devices.
- Distinguish between fact and opinion.
- Understand the importance of visuals to strengthen arguments.
- Write a persuasive essay.

The Purpose of Persuasive Writing

The purpose of persuasion in writing is to convince, motivate, or move readers toward a certain point of view, or opinion. The act of trying to persuade automatically implies more than one opinion on the subject can be argued.

The idea of an argument often conjures up images of two people yelling and screaming in anger. In writing, however, an argument is very different. An argument is a reasoned opinion supported and explained by evidence. To argue in writing is to advance knowledge and ideas in a positive way. Written arguments often fail when they employ ranting rather than reasoning.

TIP

Most of us feel inclined to try to win the arguments we engage in. On some level, we all want to be right, and we want others to see the error of their ways. More times than not, however, arguments in which both sides try to win end up producing losers all around. The more productive approach is to persuade your audience to consider your opinion as a valid one, not simply the right one.

The Structure of a Persuasive Essay

The following five features make up the structure of a persuasive essay:

1. Introduction and thesis
2. Opposing and qualifying ideas
3. Strong evidence in support of claim
4. Style and tone of language
5. A compelling conclusion

Creating an Introduction and Thesis

The persuasive essay begins with an engaging introduction that presents the general topic. The thesis typically appears somewhere in the introduction and states the writer's point of view.

TIP

Avoid forming a thesis based on a negative claim. For example, "The hourly minimum wage is not high enough for the average worker to live on." This is probably a true statement, but persuasive arguments should make a positive case. That is, the thesis statement should focus on how the hourly minimum wage is low or insufficient.

Acknowledging Opposing Ideas and Limits to Your Argument

Because an argument implies differing points of view on the subject, you must be sure to acknowledge those opposing ideas. Avoiding ideas that conflict with your own gives the reader the impression that you may be uncertain, fearful, or unaware of opposing ideas. Thus it is essential that you not only address counterarguments but also do so respectfully.

Try to address opposing arguments earlier rather than later in your essay. Rhetorically speaking, ordering your positive arguments last allows you to better address ideas that conflict with your own, so you can spend the rest of the essay countering those arguments. This way, you leave your reader thinking about your argument rather than someone else's. You have the last word.

Acknowledging points of view different from your own also has the effect of fostering more credibility between you and the audience. They know from the outset that you are aware of opposing ideas and that you are not afraid to give them space.

It is also helpful to establish the limits of your argument and what you are trying to accomplish. In effect, you are conceding early on that your argument is not the ultimate authority on a given topic. Such humility can go a long way toward earning credibility and trust with an audience. Audience members will know from the beginning that you are a reasonable writer, and audience members will trust your argument as a result. For example, in the following concessionary statement, the writer advocates for stricter gun control laws, but she admits it will not solve all of our problems with crime:

Although tougher gun control laws are a powerful first step in decreasing violence in our streets, such legislation alone cannot end these problems since guns are not the only problem we face.

Such a concession will be welcome by those who might disagree with this writer's argument in the first place. To effectively persuade their readers, writers need to be modest in their goals and humble in their approach to get readers to listen to the ideas. See Table 10.5 "Phrases of Concession" for some useful phrases of concession.

Table 10.5 Phrases of Concession

although	granted that
of course	still
though	yet

Bias in Writing

Everyone has various biases on any number of topics. For example, you might have a bias toward wearing black instead of brightly colored clothes or wearing jeans rather than formal wear. You might have a bias toward working at night rather than in the morning, or working by deadlines rather than getting tasks done in advance. These examples identify minor biases, of course, but they still indicate preferences and opinions.

Handling bias in writing and in daily life can be a useful skill. It will allow you to articulate your own points of view while also defending yourself against unreasonable points of view. The ideal in persuasive writing is to let your reader know your bias, but do not let that bias blind you to the primary components of good argumentation: sound, thoughtful evidence and a respectful and reasonable address of opposing sides.

The strength of a personal bias is that it can motivate you to construct a strong argument. If you are invested in the topic, you are more likely to care about the piece of writing. Similarly, the more you care, the more time and effort you are apt to put forth and the better the final product will be.

The weakness of bias is when the bias begins to take over the essay—when, for example, you neglect opposing ideas, exaggerate your points, or repeatedly insert yourself ahead of the subject by using *I* too often. Being aware of all three of these pitfalls will help you avoid them.

The Use of *I* in Writing

The use of *I* in writing is often a topic of debate, and the acceptance of its usage varies from instructor to instructor. It is difficult to predict the preferences for all your present and future instructors, but consider the effects it can potentially have on your writing.

Be mindful of the use of *I* in your writing because it can make your argument sound overly biased. There are two primary reasons:

1. Excessive repetition of any word will eventually catch the reader's attention—and usually not in a good way. The use of *I* is no different.
2. The insertion of *I* into a sentence alters not only the way a sentence might sound but also the composition of the sentence

itself. *I* is often the subject of a sentence. If the subject of the essay is supposed to be, say, smoking, then by inserting yourself into the sentence, you are effectively displacing the subject of the essay into a secondary position. In the following example, the subject of the sentence is underlined:

Smoking is bad.

I think smoking is bad.

In the first sentence, the rightful subject, *smoking*, is in the subject position in the sentence. In the second sentence, the insertion of *I* and *think* replaces *smoking* as the subject, which draws attention to *I* and away from the topic that is supposed to be discussed. Remember to keep the message (the subject) and the messenger (the writer) separate.

Checklist

Developing Sound Arguments

Does my essay contain the following elements?

- An engaging introduction
- A reasonable, specific thesis that is able to be supported by evidence
- A varied range of evidence from credible sources
- Respectful acknowledgement and explanation of opposing ideas
- A style and tone of language that is appropriate for the subject and audience
- Acknowledgement of the argument's limits
- A conclusion that will adequately summarize the essay and reinforce the thesis

Fact and Opinion

Facts are statements that can be definitely proven using objective data. The statement that is a fact is absolutely valid. In other words, the statement can be pronounced as true or false. For example, 2 + 2 = 4. This expression identifies a true statement, or a fact, because it can be proved with objective data.

Opinions are personal views, or judgments. An opinion is what an individual believes about a particular subject. However, an opinion in argumentation must have legitimate backing; adequate evidence and credibility should support the opinion. Consider the credibility of expert opinions. Experts in a given field have the knowledge and credentials to make their opinion meaningful to a larger audience.

For example, you seek the opinion of your dentist when it comes to the health of your gums, and you seek the opinion of your mechanic when it comes to the maintenance of your car. Both have knowledge and credentials in those respective fields, which is why their opinions matter to you. But the authority of your dentist may be greatly diminished should he or she offer an opinion about your car, and vice versa.

In writing, you want to strike a balance between credible facts and authoritative opinions. Relying on one or the other will likely lose more of your audience than it gains.

EXERCISE 2

On a separate sheet of paper, take three of the theses you formed in Note 10.94 "Exercise 1", and list the types of evidence you might use in support of that thesis.

EXERCISE 3

Using the evidence you provided in support of the three theses in Note 10.100 "Exercise 2", come up with at least one counterargument to each. Then write a concession statement, expressing the limits to each of your three arguments.

Using Visual Elements to Strengthen Arguments

Adding visual elements to a persuasive argument can often strengthen its persuasive effect. There are two main types of visual elements: quantitative visuals and qualitative visuals.

Quantitative visuals present data graphically. They allow the audience to see statistics spatially. The purpose of using quantitative visuals is to make logical appeals to the audience. For example, sometimes it is easier to understand the disparity in certain statistics if you can see how the disparity looks graphically. Bar graphs, pie charts, Venn diagrams, histograms, and line graphs are all ways of presenting quantitative data in spatial dimensions.

Qualitative visuals present images that appeal to the audience's emotions. Photographs and pictorial images are examples of qualitative visuals. Such images often try to convey a story, and seeing an actual example can carry more power than hearing or reading about the example. For example, one image of a child suffering from malnutrition will likely have more of an emotional impact than pages dedicated to describing that same condition in writing.

WRITING AT WORK

When making a business presentation, you typically have limited time to get across your idea. Providing visual elements for your audience can be an effective timesaving tool. Quantitative visuals in business presentations serve the same purpose as they do in persuasive writing. They should make logical appeals by showing numerical data in a spatial design. Quantitative visuals should be pictures that might appeal to your audience's emotions. You will find that many of the rhetorical devices used in writing are the same ones used in the workplace. For more information about visuals in presentations, see Chapter 14 "Creating Presentations: Sharing Your Ideas."

Writing a Persuasive Essay

Choose a topic that you feel passionate about. If your instructor requires you to write about a specific topic, approach the subject from an angle that interests you. Begin your essay with an engaging introduction. Your thesis should typically appear somewhere in your introduction.

Start by acknowledging and explaining points of view that may conflict with your own to build credibility and trust with your audience. Also state the limits of your argument. This too helps you sound more reasonable and honest to those who may naturally be inclined to disagree with your view. By respectfully acknowledging opposing arguments and conceding limitations to your own view, you set a measured and responsible tone for the essay.

Make your appeals in support of your thesis by using sound, credible evidence. Use a balance of facts and opinions from a wide range of sources, such as scientific studies, expert testimony, statistics, and personal anecdotes. Each piece of evidence should be fully explained and clearly stated.

Make sure that your style and tone are appropriate for your subject and audience. Tailor your language and word choice to these two factors, while still being true to your own voice.

Finally, write a conclusion that effectively summarizes the main argument and reinforces your thesis. See Chapter 15 "Readings: Examples of Essays" to read a sample persuasive essay.

EXERCISE 4

Choose one of the topics you have been working on throughout this section. Use the thesis, evidence, opposing argument, and concessionary statement as the basis for writing a full persuasive essay. Be sure to include an engaging introduction, clear explanations of all the evidence you present, and a strong conclusion.

KEY TAKEAWAYS

- The purpose of persuasion in writing is to convince or move readers toward a certain point of view, or opinion.
- An argument is a reasoned opinion supported and explained by evidence. To argue, in writing, is to advance knowledge and ideas in a positive way.
- A thesis that expresses the opinion of the writer in more specific terms is better than one that is vague.
- It is essential that you not only address counterarguments but also do so respectfully.

- It is also helpful to establish the limits of your argument and what you are trying to accomplish through a concession statement.
- To persuade a skeptical audience, you will need to use a wide range of evidence. Scientific studies, opinions from experts, historical precedent, statistics, personal anecdotes, and current events are all types of evidence that you might use in explaining your point.
- Make sure that your word choice and writing style is appropriate for both your subject and your audience.
- You should let your reader know your bias, but do not let that bias blind you to the primary components of good argumentation: sound, thoughtful evidence and respectfully and reasonably addressing opposing ideas.
- You should be mindful of the use of *I* in your writing because it can make your argument sound more biased than it needs to.
- Facts are statements that can be proven using objective data.
- Opinions are personal views, or judgments, that cannot be proven.
- In writing, you want to strike a balance between credible facts and authoritative opinions.
- Quantitative visuals present data graphically. The purpose of using quantitative visuals is to make logical appeals to the audience.
- Qualitative visuals present images that appeal to the audience's emotions.

CC licensed content, Shared previously

Jonathan Swift, A Modest Proposal

Access Jonathan Swift's satirical essay "A Modest Proposal" below. Read it—just not at lunchtime, fair adventurer, for then thoughts turn toward food. Answer the following questions:

1) What is the serious social problem Swift is actually trying to address? (Hint: The answer is not that there are too many Irish children!)

2) There are several details in the essay that speak to the viability of further exploiting humans—this time, as a food source. Cite one of the most effective of these examples.

3) What is the purpose of the detail in the example you noted in #2?

4) Restate Swift's satirical thesis. Remember, satire points out flaws in society with the (quite conservative) goal of getting us to a better way of being or of doing. (Your answer should discuss the real problems and the better way of being that Swift assumes.)

5) Lastly, what makes this a funny essay?

Skills

Reading tone

Separating text from subtext

Understanding a writer's purpose

Gauging the writer's strategy in achieving purpose

Analysis of the impact of details upon audiences

A MODEST PROPOSAL

For preventing the children of poor people in Ireland, from being a burden on their parents or country, and for making them beneficial to the publick.

by Dr. Jonathan Swift

1729

It is a melancholy object to those, who walk through this great town, or travel in the country, when they see the streets, the roads and cabbin-doors crowded with beggars of the female sex, followed by three, four, or six children, all in rags, and importuning every passenger for an alms. These mothers instead of being able to work for their honest livelihood, are forced to employ all their time in stroling to beg sustenance for their helpless infants who, as they grow up, either turn thieves for want of work, or leave their dear native country, to fight for the Pretender in Spain, or sell themselves to the Barbadoes.

I think it is agreed by all parties, that this prodigious number of children in the arms, or on the backs, or at the heels of their mothers, and frequently of their fathers, is in the present deplorable state of the kingdom, a very great additional grievance; and therefore whoever could find out a fair, cheap and easy method of making these children sound and useful members of the common-wealth, would deserve so well of the publick, as to have his statue set up for a preserver of the nation.

But my intention is very far from being confined to provide only for the children of professed beggars: it is of a much greater extent, and shall take in the whole number of infants at a certain age, who are born of parents in effect as little able to support them, as those who demand our charity in the streets.

As to my own part, having turned my thoughts for many years, upon this important subject, and maturely weighed the several schemes of our projectors, I have always found them grossly mistaken in their computation. It is true, a child just dropt from its dam, may be supported by her milk, for a solar year, with little other nourishment: at most not above the value of two shillings, which the mother may certainly get, or the value in scraps, by her lawful occupation of begging; and it is exactly at one year old that I propose to provide for them in such a manner, as, instead of being a charge upon their parents, or the parish, or wanting food and raiment for the rest of their lives, they shall, on the contrary, contribute to the feeding, and partly to the cloathing of many thousands.

There is likewise another great advantage in my scheme, that it will prevent those voluntary abortions, and that horrid practice of women murdering their bastard children, alas! too frequent among us, sacrificing the poor innocent babes, I doubt, more to avoid the expence than the shame, which would move tears and pity in the most savage and inhuman breast.

The number of souls in this kingdom being usually reckoned one million and a half, of these I calculate there may be about two hundred thousand couple whose wives are breeders; from which number I subtract thirty thousand couple, who are able to maintain their own children, (although I apprehend there cannot be so many, under the present distresses of the kingdom) but this being granted, there will remain an hundred and seventy thousand breeders. I again subtract fifty thousand, for those women who miscarry, or whose children die by accident or disease within the year. There only remain an hundred and twenty thousand children of poor parents annually born. The question therefore is, How this number shall be reared, and provided for? which, as I have already said, under the present situation of affairs, is utterly impossible by all the methods hitherto proposed. For we can neither employ them in handicraft or agriculture; they neither build houses, (I mean in the country) nor cultivate land: they can very seldom pick up a livelihood by stealing till they arrive at six years old; except where they are of towardly parts, although I confess they learn the rudiments much earlier; during which time they can however be properly looked upon only as probationers: As I have been informed by a principal gentleman in the county of Cavan, who protested to me, that he never knew above one or two instances under the age of six, even in a part of the kingdom so renowned for the quickest proficiency in that art.

I am assured by our merchants, that a boy or a girl before twelve years old, is no saleable commodity, and even when they come to this age, they will not yield above three pounds, or three pounds and half a crown at most, on the exchange; which cannot turn to account either to the parents or kingdom, the charge of nutriments and rags having been at least four times that value.

I shall now therefore humbly propose my own thoughts, which I hope will not be liable to the least objection.

I have been assured by a very knowing American of my acquaintance in London, that a young healthy child well nursed, is, at a year old, a most delicious nourishing and wholesome food, whether stewed, roasted, baked, or boiled; and I make no doubt that it will equally serve in a fricasie, or a ragoust.

I do therefore humbly offer it to publick consideration, that of the hundred and twenty thousand children, already computed, twenty thousand may be reserved for breed, whereof only one fourth part to be males; which is more than we allow to sheep, black cattle, or swine, and my reason is, that these children are seldom the fruits of marriage, a circumstance not much regarded by our savages, therefore, one male will be sufficient to serve four females. That the remaining hundred thousand may, at a year old, be offered in sale to the persons of quality and fortune, through the kingdom, always advising the mother to let them suck plentifully in the last month, so as to render them plump, and fat for a good table. A child will make two dishes at an entertainment for friends, and when the family dines alone, the fore or hind quarter will make a reasonable dish, and seasoned with a little pepper or salt, will be very good boiled on the fourth day, especially in winter.

I have reckoned upon a medium, that a child just born will weigh 12 pounds, and in a solar year, if tolerably nursed, encreaseth to 28 pounds.

I grant this food will be somewhat dear, and therefore very proper for landlords, who, as they have already devoured most of the parents, seem to have the best title to the children.

Infant's flesh will be in season throughout the year, but more plentiful in March, and a little before and after; for we are told by a grave author, an eminent French physician, that fish being a prolifick dyet, there are more children born in Roman Catholick countries about nine months after Lent, the markets will be more glutted than usual, because the number of Popish infants, is at least three to one in this kingdom, and therefore it will have one other collateral advantage, by lessening the number of Papists among us.

I have already computed the charge of nursing a beggar's child (in which list I reckon all cottagers, labourers, and four-fifths of the farmers) to be about two shillings per annum, rags included; and I believe no gentleman would repine to give ten shillings for the carcass of a good fat child, which, as I have said, will make four dishes of excellent nutritive meat, when he hath only some particular friend, or his own family to dine with him. Thus the squire will learn to be a good landlord, and grow popular among his tenants, the mother will have eight shillings neat profit, and be fit for work till she produces another child.

Those who are more thrifty (as I must confess the times require) may flea the carcass; the skin of which, artificially dressed, will make admirable gloves for ladies, and summer boots for fine gentlemen.

As to our City of Dublin, shambles may be appointed for this purpose, in the most convenient parts of it, and butchers we may be assured will not be wanting; although I rather recommend buying the children alive, and dressing them hot from the knife, as we do roasting pigs.

A very worthy person, a true lover of his country, and whose virtues I highly esteem, was lately pleased, in discoursing on this matter, to offer a refinement upon my scheme. He said, that many gentlemen of this kingdom, having of late destroyed their deer, he conceived that the want of venison might be well supply'd by the bodies of young lads and maidens, not exceeding fourteen years of age, nor under twelve; so great a number of both sexes in every country being now ready to starve for want of work and service: And these to be disposed of by their parents if alive, or otherwise by their nearest relations. But with due deference to so excellent a friend, and so deserving a patriot, I cannot be altogether in his sentiments; for as to the males, my American acquaintance assured me from frequent experience, that their flesh was generally tough and lean, like that of our school-boys, by continual exercise, and their taste disagreeable, and to fatten them would not answer the charge. Then as to the females, it would, I think, with humble submission, be a loss to the publick, because they soon would become breeders themselves: And besides, it is not improbable that some scrupulous people might be apt to censure such a practice, (although indeed very unjustly) as a little bordering upon cruelty, which, I confess, hath always been with me the strongest objection against any project, how well soever intended.

But in order to justify my friend, he confessed, that this expedient was put into his head by the famous Salmanaazor, a native of the island Formosa, who came from thence to London, above twenty years ago, and in conversation told my friend, that in his country, when any young person happened to be put to death, the executioner sold the carcass to persons of quality, as a prime dainty; and that, in his time, the body of a plump girl of fifteen, who was crucified for an attempt to poison the Emperor, was sold to his imperial majesty's prime minister of state, and other great mandarins of the court in joints from the gibbet, at four hundred crowns. Neither indeed can I deny, that if the same use were made of several plump young girls in this town, who without one single groat to their fortunes, cannot stir abroad without a chair, and appear at a play-house and assemblies in foreign fineries which they never will pay for; the kingdom would not be the worse.

Some persons of a desponding spirit are in great concern about that vast number of poor people, who are aged, diseased, or maimed; and I have been desired to employ my thoughts what course may be taken, to ease the nation of so grievous an incumbrance. But I am not in the least pain upon that matter, because it is very well known, that they are every day dying, and rotting, by cold and famine, and filth, and vermin, as fast as can be reasonably expected. And as to the young labourers, they are now in almost as hopeful a condition. They cannot get work, and consequently pine away from want of nourishment, to a degree, that if at any time they are accidentally hired to common labour, they have not strength to perform it, and thus the country and themselves are happily delivered from the evils to come.

I have too long digressed, and therefore shall return to my subject. I think the advantages by the proposal which I have made are obvious and many, as well as of the highest importance.

For first, as I have already observed, it would greatly lessen the number of Papists, with whom we are yearly over-run, being the principal breeders of the nation, as well as our most dangerous enemies, and who stay at home on purpose with a design to deliver the kingdom to the Pretender, hoping to take their advantage by the absence of so many good Protestants, who have chosen rather to leave their country, than stay at home and pay tithes against their conscience to an episcopal curate.

Secondly, The poorer tenants will have something valuable of their own, which by law may be made liable to a distress, and help to pay their landlord's rent, their corn and cattle being already seized, and money a thing unknown.

Thirdly, Whereas the maintainance of an hundred thousand children, from two years old, and upwards, cannot be computed at less than ten shillings a piece per annum, the nation's stock will be thereby encreased fifty thousand pounds per annum, besides the profit of a new dish, introduced to the tables of all gentlemen of fortune in the kingdom, who have any refinement in taste. And the money will circulate among our selves, the goods being entirely of our own growth and manufacture.

Fourthly, The constant breeders, besides the gain of eight shillings sterling per annum by the sale of their children, will be rid of the charge of maintaining them after the first year.

Fifthly, This food would likewise bring great custom to taverns, where the vintners will certainly be so prudent as to procure the best receipts for dressing it to perfection; and consequently have their houses frequented by all the fine gentlemen, who justly value themselves upon their knowledge in good eating; and a skilful cook, who understands how to oblige his guests, will contrive to make it as expensive as they please.

Sixthly, This would be a great inducement to marriage, which all wise nations have either encouraged by rewards, or enforced by laws and penalties. It would encrease the care and tenderness of mothers towards their children, when they were sure of a settlement for life to the poor babes, provided in some sort by the publick, to their annual profit instead of expence. We should soon see an honest emulation among the married women, which of them could bring the fattest child to the market. Men would become as fond of their wives, during the time of their pregnancy, as they are now of their mares in foal, their cows in calf, or sow when they are ready to farrow; nor offer to beat or kick them (as is too frequent a practice) for fear of a miscarriage.

Many other advantages might be enumerated. For instance, the addition of some thousand carcasses in our exportation of barrel'd beef: the propagation of swine's flesh, and improvement in the art of making good bacon, so much wanted among us by the great destruction of pigs, too frequent at our tables; which are no way comparable in taste or magnificence to a well grown, fat yearly child, which roasted whole will make a considerable figure at a Lord Mayor's feast, or any other publick entertainment. But this, and many others, I omit, being studious of brevity.

Supposing that one thousand families in this city, would be constant customers for infants flesh, besides others who might have it at merry meetings, particularly at weddings and christenings, I compute that Dublin would take off annually about twenty thousand carcasses; and the rest of the kingdom (where probably they will be sold somewhat cheaper) the remaining eighty thousand.

I can think of no one objection, that will possibly be raised against this proposal, unless it should be urged, that the number of people will be thereby much lessened in the kingdom. This I freely own, and 'twas indeed one principal design in offering it to the world. I desire the reader will observe, that I calculate my remedy for this one individual Kingdom of Ireland, and for no other that ever was, is, or, I think, ever can be upon Earth. Therefore let no man talk to me of other expedients: Of taxing our absentees at five shillings a pound: Of using neither cloaths, nor houshold furniture, except what is of our own growth and manufacture: Of utterly rejecting the materials and instruments that promote foreign luxury: Of curing the expensiveness of pride, vanity, idleness, and gaming in our women: Of introducing a vein of parsimony, prudence and temperance: Of learning to love our country, wherein we differ even from Laplanders, and the inhabitants of Topinamboo: Of quitting our animosities and factions, nor acting any longer like the Jews, who were murdering one another at the very moment their city was taken: Of being a little cautious not to sell our country and consciences for nothing: Of teaching landlords to have at least one degree of mercy towards their tenants. Lastly, of putting a spirit of honesty, industry, and skill into our shop-keepers, who, if a resolution could now be taken to buy only our native goods, would immediately unite to cheat and exact upon us in the price, the measure, and the goodness, nor could ever yet be brought to make one fair proposal of just dealing, though often and earnestly invited to it.

Therefore I repeat, let no man talk to me of these and the like expedients, 'till he hath at least some glympse of hope, that there will ever be some hearty and sincere attempt to put them into practice.

But, as to my self, having been wearied out for many years with offering vain, idle, visionary thoughts, and at length utterly despairing of success, I fortunately fell upon this proposal, which, as it is wholly new, so it hath something solid and real, of no expence and little trouble, full in our own power, and whereby we can incur no danger in disobliging England. For this kind of commodity will not bear exportation, and flesh being of too tender a consistence, to admit a long continuance in salt, although perhaps I could name a country, which would be glad to eat up our whole nation without it.

After all, I am not so violently bent upon my own opinion, as to reject any offer, proposed by wise men, which shall be found equally innocent, cheap, easy, and effectual. But before something of that kind shall be advanced in contradiction to my scheme, and offering a better, I desire the author or authors will be pleased maturely to consider two points. First, As things now stand, how they will be able to find food and raiment for a hundred thousand useless mouths and backs. And secondly, There being a round million of creatures in humane figure throughout this kingdom, whose whole subsistence put into a common stock, would leave them in debt two million of pounds sterling, adding those who are beggars by profession, to the bulk of farmers, cottagers and labourers, with their wives and children, who are beggars in effect; I desire those politicians who dislike my overture, and may perhaps be so bold to attempt an answer, that they will first ask the parents of these mortals, whether they would not at this day think it a great happiness to have been sold for food at a year old, in the manner I prescribe, and thereby have avoided such a perpetual scene of misfortunes, as they have since gone through, by the oppression of landlords, the impossibility of paying rent without money or trade, the want of common sustenance, with neither house nor cloaths to cover them from the inclemencies of the weather, and the most inevitable prospect of intailing the like, or greater miseries, upon their breed for ever.

I profess, in the sincerity of my heart, that I have not the least personal interest in endeavouring to promote this necessary work, having no other motive than the publick good of my country, by advancing our trade, providing for infants, relieving the poor, and giving some pleasure to the rich. I have no children, by which I can propose to get a single penny; the youngest being nine years old, and my wife past child-bearing.

Mark Twain, Two Ways of Seeing a River

As a writer, you have often done rhetorical analysis without naming it. When broken down, though, the assignment is all about noticing moves that work together. The trap is clear: Editorializing or writing about the content rather than about the form. This is not an essay about morality or violence.

Rhetorical analysis is all about form over content, moves rather than what is in the material. In our culture right now, people get a lot of mileage simply for thinking something. They believe others ought to have huge respect and a hands-off attitude just because something is believed–especially if it is believes strongly. This can stop discussion because people insist "It's true for me!" We also think that someone's beliefs must be more valid if they risk danger in holding those.

Both of these beliefs contain logical flaws. We're not right "just because we think so." What informs our reading–things we can point to, defend, and discuss–must matter. (At least, I think they should. . . get the joke?)

Your Task

Read Mark Twain's "Two Ways of Seeing a River" and then respond in a one-page Word document to its point how some people are deluded by ignorance into creating a deceptive reality.

Two Ways of Seeing a River (1883)

Now when I had mastered the language of this water and had come to know every trifling feature that bordered the great river as familiarly as I knew the letters of the alphabet, I had made a valuable acquisition. But I had lost something, too. I had lost something which could never be restored to me while I lived. All the grace, the beauty, the poetry, had gone out of the majestic river! I still kept in mind a certain wonderful sunset which I witnessed when steamboating was new to me. A broad expanse of the river was turned to blood; in the middle distance the red hue brightened into gold, through which a solitary log came floating, black and conspicuous; in one place a long, slanting mark lay sparkling upon the water; in another the surface was broken by boiling, tumbling rings that were as many-tinted as an opal; where the ruddy flush was faintest was a smooth spot that was covered with graceful circles and radiating lines, ever so delicately traced; the shore on our left was densely wooded, and the somber shadow that fell from this forest was broken in one place by a long, ruffled trail that shone like silver; and high above the forest wall a clean-stemmed dead tree waved a single leafy bough that glowed like a flame in the unobstructed splendor that was flowing from the sun. There were graceful curves, reflected images, woody heights, soft distances, and over the whole scene, far and near, the dissolving lights drifted steadily, enriching it every passing moment with new marvels of coloring.

I stood like one bewitched. I drank it in, in a speechless rapture. The world was new to me and I had never seen anything like this at home. But as I have said, a day came when I began to cease from noting the glories and the charms which the moon and the sun and the twilight wrought upon the river's face; another day came when I ceased altogether to note them. Then, if that sunset scene had been repeated, I should have looked upon it without rapture and should have commented upon it inwardly after this fashion: "This sun means that we are going to have wind tomorrow; that floating log means that the river is rising, small thanks to it; that slanting mark on the water refers to a bluff reef which is going to kill somebody's steamboat one of these nights, if it keeps on stretching out like that; those tumbling 'boils' show a dissolving bar and a changing channel there; the lines and circles in the slick water over yonder are a warning that that troublesome place is shoaling up dangerously; that silver streak in the shadow of the forest is the 'break' from a new snag and he has located himself in the very best place he could have found to fish for steamboats; that tall dead tree, with a single living branch, is not going to last long, and then how is a body ever going to get through this blind place at night without the friendly old landmark?"

No, the romance and beauty were all gone from the river. All the value any feature of it had for me now was the amount of usefulness it could furnish toward compassing the safe piloting of a steamboat. Since those days, I have pitied doctors from my heart. What does the lovely flush in a beauty's cheek mean to a doctor but a "break" that ripples above some deadly disease? Are not all her visible charms sown thick with what are to him the signs and symbols of hidden decay? Does he ever see her beauty at all, or doesn't he simply view her professionally and comment upon her unwholesome condition all to himself? And doesn't he sometimes wonder whether he has gained most or lost most by learning his trade?

Public domain content

- Mark Twain, Two Ways of Seeing a River. **Authored by**: Mark Twain. **Provided by**: Project Gutenberg. **Located at**: http://www.gutenberg.org/ebooks/245 (http://www.gutenberg.org/ebooks/245). **Project**: ENG 101. **License**: *Public Domain: No Known Copyright (https://creativecommons.org/about/pdm)*

James Gleick, What Defines a Meme?

Access the following link to read James Gleick's essay, "What Defines a Meme? (https://www.smithsonianmag.com/arts-culture/what-defines-a-meme-1904778/)"

Also read this comment on "What's in a Meme" by Mark A. Jordan which is from from *The Richard Dawkins Foundation* website (https://www.richarddawkins.net/2014/02/whats-in-a-meme/) and available (for print users) at: https://www.richarddawkins.net/2014/02/whats-in-a-meme/

Dawkins is the biologist most closely connected with the coining of this term *meme*.

Know Your Meme, used from Wikimedia Commons

CC licensed content, Original

- James Gleick, What Defines a Meme?. **Authored by**: James Gleick; Mark A. Jordan for the second link. **Provided by**: Smithsonian . **Located at**: https://www.smithsonianmag.com/arts-culture/what-defines-a-meme-1904778/ (https://www.smithsonianmag.com/arts-culture/what-defines-a-meme-1904778/). **Project**: ENG 101. **License**: *CC BY-SA: Attribution-ShareAlike (https://creativecommons.org/licenses/by-sa/4.0/)*

THE RESEARCH PROJECT

Audiences Know the Topic Well. . . . Alter Their Actions

Just a reminder: Research papers will need to show your side (obviously) as well as the opposition *and* refutals of the specific points from the other side. Refutals are counterargument sections where we respectfully and clearly prove the extent to which the other side is misguided. These are not reports we're writing. . .

Readers know the topic well, so you won't be able to get away with a lot of informing or basic overviews.

Similarly, yes/no "answers" probably reflect a lack of imagination or sufficient research.

It's better to reflect the fact that the ongoing debates that preceded your argument will continue after you write it. Locate those areas of genuine, ongoing disagreement. While the tone of the essay doesn't need to be combative (like the "winner take all" binary debates that make for good courtroom dramas), they should focus on the ways that the argument tends to be organized.

Where you can make the essay yours is in giving different emphasis to the reasons and refutals.

Avoid Oversimplifying in Essays

A key tendency when arguing definitions is to oversimplify inherently complex issues. Some of the claims so far seems scattered in that there are several reasons but they aren't being shown to fit the claim. The body paragraphs aren't being transitioned among or connected to the claim. Let's try and tighten up the coherence so that the flow is allowed while also letting readers know how each reason helps prove the claim.

All this can be done without resorting to the use of *you* or *I*. Remember that informed readers' ideas are being challenged to a greater or lesser extent by the claims, so those must be provable.

Some people are finding success in showing the conditions under which something works. That can seem fairly obvious as a move, though, so make sure that if you do this you are following up by locating arguable areas. For instance, if I were trying to modify an author's idea of the evolution of morals and tried showing that Stalin's killing of millions of his people was immoral (easy enough), I might do well to connect that to other atrocities. The fact that Stalin did this to his own countrymen might be something to talk about. The problem with equating evil like Stalin with Hitler's actions could be covered and its difficulties discussed. My point is that the details can be occasions for you to comment, to point out the ways definitions prove useful.

My fear is that, for too many years, most writers have gotten just to point out ideas as stand-ins for actually analyzing their aspects. There's a definition for this: passive writing! So let us comment carefully and as thoroughly as we can to earn points and alter readers' ideas.

CC licensed content, Original

The Qualities of a Good Research Question

Research = the physical process of **gathering information** + the mental process of **deriving the answer to your question** from the information you gathered.

Research writing = the process of **sharing the answer** to your research question along with the **evidence** on which your answer is based, the **sources** you used, and your own **reasoning** and **explanation**.

Developing a good research question is the foundation of a successful research project, so it is worth spending time and effort understanding what makes a good question.

1. **A research question is a question that CAN be answered in an objective way, at least partially and at least for now.**

   ◦ Questions that are purely values-based (such as "Should assisted suicide be legal?") cannot be answered objectively because the answer varies depending on one's values. Be wary of questions that include "should" or "ought" because those words often (although not always) indicate a values-based question.However, note that most values-based questions can be turned into research questions by judicious reframing. For instance, you could reframe "Should assisted suicide be legal?" as "What are the ethical implications of legalizing assisted suicide?" Using a "what are" frame turns a values-based question into a legitimate research question by moving it out of the world of debate and into the world of investigation.

2. **A good research question is one that can be answered using information that already exists or that can be collected.**

   ◦ The question, "Does carbon-based life exist outside of Earth's solar system?" is a perfectly good research question in the sense that it is not values-based and therefore could be answered in an objective way, IF it were possible to collect data about the presence of life outside of Earth's solar system. That is not yet possible with current technology; therefore, this is not (yet) a research question because it's not (now) possible to obtain the data that would be needed to answer it.

3. **A good research question is a question that hasn't already been answered, or hasn't been answered completely, or hasn't been answered for your specific context.**

   ◦ If the answer to the question is readily available in a good encyclopedia, textbook, or reference book, then it is a homework question, not a research question. It was probably a research question in the past, but if the answer is so thoroughly known that you can easily look it up and find it, then it is no longer an open question.However, it is important to remember that as new information becomes available, homework questions can sometimes be reopened as research questions. Equally important, a question may have been answered for one population or circumstance, but not for all populations or all circumstances.

Assessment: Research Question Task

First, review the 3 resources noted below.

1. This infographic about fantasy cover art illustrates one way of reporting data. From the accompanying notes, you will get a good idea of the research method used, and you should be able to infer (that is, make an informed guess based on relevant evidence) the research question.

    ◦ The Chart of Fantasy Art, 2009 (http://www.orbitbooks.net/2010/08/16/the-chart-of-fantasy-art-part-one/)

2. This research uses the same pool of sources (cover art from fantasy titles published by Orbit in 2008 and 2009) but collects different data (details of the visual representations of heroines) to answer a different research question. Again, you should be able to infer the question from the answer as represented in the infographic.

    ◦ Changing Fashion in Urban Fantasy (http://www.orbitbooks.net/2010/08/17/the-chart-of-fantasy-art-part-2-urban-fantasy/)

3. Meta-Analysis and Review of the LiteratureA meta-analysis is a form of research in which the researcher examines all of a certain type of artifact, in this case all the scientific articles on climate change published between November 2012 and December 2013 in peer-reviewed journals. The purpose of meta-analysis is to identify trends in the available data that would not be visible from any one article alone. A meta-analysis is similar to another type of research that begins by examining all the artifacts in a certain category: the review of the literature (aka literature review).

    ◦ Scientific Consensus on Anthropogenic Global Warming: A Pie Chart (http://www.jamespowell.org/index.html)

Then, complete this writing task.

Pick ONE of the above examples of research ("Fantasy Book Covers," "Heroines," or "Scientific Consensus on Anthropogenic Global Warming: A Pie Chart").

For the one you choose, state what you feel the research question was of the author in a single sentence. Then briefly explain what the research method used was. You may need to infer (that is, use evidence and logical reasoning to draw a conclusion about) the research method.

CC licensed content, Shared previously

Choosing A Manageable Research Topic

This is a link to a YouTube video called "Choosing a Manageable Research Topic" by PfauLibrary.   The end contains a few "test yourself" questions. Consider WHY the answers are the way they are as you watch.

- https://youtu.be/BDuqfJQhFeM

CC licensed content, Shared previously

- Composition II. **Authored by**: Alexis McMillan-Clifton. **Provided by**: Tacoma Community College. **Located at**: http://www.tacomacc.edu (http://www.tacomacc.edu). **Project**: Kaleidoscope Open Course Initiative. **License**: *CC BY: Attribution (https://creativecommons.org/licenses/by/4.0/)*
- Choosing a Manageable Research Topic. **Authored by**: PfauLibrary. **Located at**: https://youtu.be/BDuqfJQhFeM (https://youtu.be/BDuqfJQhFeM). **License**: *CC BY: Attribution (https://creativecommons.org/licenses/by/4.0/)*

Discussion: Potential Topics

This discussion is going to be in small groups, with 3–4 other people, in order to facilitate more direct interaction.

After finishing this unit's readings, as well as looking through the research essay prompt we'll use to guide us the rest of the quarter, what are your initial thoughts about possible topic ideas? Come up with at least 5 potential ideas. At least one of those should be something "light-hearted"—something you would normally never consider as a possible topic, but still think it'd be fun to play with for a while. Don't tell us which one the light-hearted topic is, though!

For each of the 5 ideas (or more!), tell us the following:

- 1-2 sentences about what it is and why it interests you
- 1-2 questions you have about the topic that **you don't already know the answers to**. These can be small questions or large ones—whatever you would like to find out.

Your post should be about 100-150 words. It doesn't have to be grammatically perfect, but should use standard English (no text-speak, please) and normal capitalization rules.

Respond to EVERYONE else in your group who has made a post before you. (That means that the first person to post doesn't have to reply to anyone. The earlier you post, the less work you have to do!)

Of the list of 5 your classmate has suggested, which do you like best as a paper topic? Why? What do you think the potential value of researching this idea further would be? Do you have any initial suggestions for research sources, or ways of narrowing down this idea further? Basically—we're helping one another brainstorm.

Replies should be at least 50 words long each. They should contain serious, thoughtful replies that directly correspond to what your classmate has written.

Diotima's Ladder Video: Check Out the Forms

Whether they term it idealism outright, the editors write a lot about the Forms (capitalized, big-deal abstractions they thought were primary to the imperfect versions we can observe with the senses). This basic Western, Platonic approach informs many of our topics. For instance, it's a Platonic move to have lawyers and judges inferring what the Founders might have thought of assault weapons or privacy. The Form (their thinking then) is being used to decide court cases on issues impacting us.

From a really neat series, *The History of Ideas*, here's *The Simpsons*' Harry Shearer narrating about Diotima's Ladder:

- https://youtu.be/xT6wjgssVK4?list=PLLiykcLllCgOof1XMu1gfUSlVdx8OtkJT

The one on "The Golden Ratio" is also neat! Beats some of the reading on these ideas, I can attest!

Charles Pierce, Greetings from Idiot America

Read this 2005 feature article from *Esquire*, "Greetings from Idiot America (http://jccweb.sunyjefferson.edu:2055/login.aspx?direct=true&db=a9h&AN=18624951&site=ehost-live)." We will focus upon its use of persuasion in our discussions. Access it either through the permalink below or by accessing either your library databases or by doing a search online.

Be sure to access the document with the images.

http://jccweb.sunyjefferson.edu:2055/login.aspx?direct=true&db=a9h&AN=18624951&site=ehost-live

RESEARCH PROPOSAL

Managing Your Research Project

LEARNING OBJECTIVES

By the end of this section, you will be able to:

1. Identify reasons for outlining the scope and sequence of a research project.
2. Recognize the steps of the research writing process.
3. Develop a plan for managing time and resources to complete the research project on time.
4. Identify organizational tools and strategies to use in managing the project.

The prewriting you have completed so far has helped you begin to plan the content of your research paper—your topic, research questions, and preliminary thesis. It is equally important to plan out the process of researching and writing the paper. Although some types of writing assignments can be completed relatively quickly, developing a good research paper is a complex process that takes time. Breaking it into manageable steps is crucial. Review the steps outlined at the beginning of this chapter.

Steps to Writing a Research Paper

1. Choose a topic.
2. Schedule and plan time for research and writing.
3. Conduct research.
4. Organize research
5. Draft your paper.
6. Revise and edit your paper.

You have already completed step 1. In this section, you will complete step 2. The remaining steps fall under two broad categories—the research phase of the project (steps 3 and 4) and the writing phase (steps 5 and 6). Both phases present challenges. Understanding the tasks involved and allowing enough time to complete each task will help you complete your research paper on time with a minimal amount of stress.

Planning Your Project

Each step of a research project requires time and attention. Careful planning helps ensure that you will keep your project running smoothly and produce your best work. Set up a project schedule that shows when you will complete each step. Think about *how* you will complete each step and what project resources you will use. Resources may include anything from library databases and word-processing software to interview subjects and writing tutors.

To develop your schedule, use a calendar and work backward from the date your final draft is due. Generally, it is wise to divide half of the available time on the research phase of the project and half on the writing phase. For example, if you have a month to work, plan for two weeks for each phase. If you have a full semester, plan to begin research early and to start writing by the middle of the term. You might think that no one really works that far ahead, but try it. You will probably be pleased with the quality of your work and with the reduction in your stress level.

As you plan, break down major steps into smaller tasks if necessary. For example, step 3, conducting research, involves locating potential sources, evaluating their usefulness and reliability, reading, and taking notes. Defining these smaller tasks makes the project more manageable by giving you concrete goals to achieve.

Jorge had six weeks to complete his research project. Working backward from a due date of May 2, he mapped out a schedule for completing his research by early April so that he would have ample time to write. Jorge chose to write his schedule in his weekly planner to help keep himself on track.

Review Jorge's schedule. Key target dates are shaded. Note that Jorge planned times to use available resources by visiting the library and writing center and by meeting with his instructor.

S	M	T	W	T	F	S
March 20	21	22 Choose Topic	23 Preliminary research	24 Write research questions and working thesis	25 Write research proposal	26
27	28 Research proposal due	29 Look for sources online	30 Library	31 Evaluate sources; make source cards	April 1 Take notes→	2
3 →	4	5 Finish note cards	6 Organize notes→	7	8 Write outline	9 →
10	11 Outline due	12 Write draft→	13	14	15 Off - Trip to NYC	16 Off - Trip to NYC
17	18 Conference with Prof. Habib 2:00	19 Finish writing draft	20	21 Revise draft→	22	23 Library?
24	25	26 Finish revising draft	27 Edit draft	28 Writing Center 4:30	29 Finish editing draft	30 Create Works Cited page
May 1	2 Final draft due	3	4	5	6	7

EXERCISE 1

1. Working backward from the date your final draft is due, create a project schedule. You may choose to write a sequential list of tasks or record tasks on a calendar.
2. Check your schedule to be sure that you have broken each step into smaller tasks and assigned a target

3. Review your target dates to make sure they are realistic. Always allow a little more time than you think you will actually need.

TIP

Plan your schedule realistically, and consider other commitments that may sometimes take precedence. A business trip or family visit may mean that you are unable to work on the research project for a few days. Make the most of the time you have available. Plan for unexpected interruptions, but keep in mind that a short time away from the project may help you come back to it with renewed enthusiasm. Another strategy many writers find helpful is to finish each day's work at a point when the next task is an easy one. That makes it easier to start again.

Writing at Work

When you create a project schedule at work, you set target dates for completing certain tasks and identify the resources you plan to use on the project. It is important to build in some flexibility. Materials may not be received on time because of a shipping delay. An employee on your team may be called away to work on a higher-priority project. Essential equipment may malfunction. You should always plan for the unexpected.

Staying Organized

Although setting up a schedule is easy, sticking to one is challenging. Even if you are the rare person who never procrastinates, unforeseen events may interfere with your ability to complete tasks on time. A self-imposed deadline may slip your mind despite your best intentions. Organizational tools—calendars, checklists, note cards, software, and so forth—can help you stay on track.

Throughout your project, organize both your time and your resources systematically. Review your schedule frequently and check your progress. It helps to post your schedule in a place where you will see it every day. Both personal and workplace e-mail systems usually include a calendar feature where you can record tasks, arrange to receive daily reminders, and check off completed tasks. Electronic devices such as smartphones have similar features.

Organize project documents in a binder or electronic folder, and label project documents and folders clearly. Use note cards or an electronic document to record bibliographical information for each source you plan to use in your paper. Tracking this information throughout the research process can save you hours of time when you create your references page.

EXERCISE 2

1. Revisit the schedule you created in Note 11.42 "Exercise 1." Transfer it into a format that will help you stay on track from day to day. You may wish to input it into your smartphone, write it in a weekly planner, post it by your

TIP

Some people enjoy using the most up-to-date technology to help them stay organized. Other people prefer simple methods, such as crossing off items on a checklist. The key to staying organized is finding a system you like enough to use daily. The particulars of the method are not important as long as you are consistent.

Anticipating Challenges

Do any of these scenarios sound familiar? You have identified a book that would be a great resource for your project, but it is currently checked out of the library. You planned to interview a subject matter expert on your topic, but she calls to reschedule your meeting. You have begun writing your draft, but now you realize that you will need to modify your thesis and conduct additional research. Or you have finally completed your draft when your computer crashes, and days of hard work disappear in an instant.

These troubling situations are all too common. No matter how carefully you plan your schedule, you may encounter a glitch or setback. Managing your project effectively means anticipating potential problems, taking steps to minimize them where possible, and allowing time in your schedule to handle any setbacks.

Many times a situation becomes a problem due only to lack of planning. For example, if a book is checked out of your local library, it might be available through interlibrary loan, which usually takes a few days for the library staff to process. Alternatively, you might locate another, equally useful source. If you have allowed enough time for research, a brief delay will not become a major setback.

You can manage other potential problems by staying organized and maintaining a take-charge attitude. Take a minute each day to save a backup copy of your work on a portable hard drive. Maintain detailed note cards and source cards as you conduct research—doing so will make citing sources in your draft infinitely easier. If you run into difficulties with your research or your writing, ask your instructor for help, or make an appointment with a writing tutor.

EXERCISE 3

1. Identify five potential problems you might encounter in the process of researching and writing your paper. Write them on a separate sheet of paper. For each problem, write at least one strategy for solving the problem or minimizing its effect on your project.

Writing at Work

In the workplace, documents prepared at the beginning of a project often include a detailed plan for risk management. When you manage a project, it makes sense to anticipate and prepare for potential setbacks. For example, to roll out a new product line, a software development company must strive to complete tasks on a schedule in order to meet the new product release date. The project manager may need to adjust the project plan if one or more tasks fall behind schedule.

KEY TAKEAWAYS

- To complete a research project successfully, a writer must carefully manage each phase of the process and break major steps into smaller tasks.
- Writers can plan a research project by setting up a schedule based on the deadline and by identifying useful project resources.
- Writers stay focused by using organizational tools that suit their needs.
- Anticipating and planning for potential setbacks can help writers avoid those setbacks or minimize their effect on the project schedule.

Steps in Developing a Research Proposal

Writing a good research paper takes time, thought, and effort. Although this assignment is challenging, it is manageable. Focusing on one step at a time will help you develop a thoughtful, informative, well-supported research paper.

Your first step is to choose a topic and then to develop research questions, a working thesis, and a written research proposal. Set aside adequate time for this part of the process. Fully exploring ideas will help you build a solid foundation for your paper.

Choosing a Topic

When you choose a topic for a research paper, you are making a major commitment. Your choice will help determine whether you enjoy the lengthy process of research and writing—and whether your final paper fulfills the assignment requirements. If you choose your topic hastily, you may later find it difficult to work with your topic. By taking your time and choosing carefully, you can ensure that this assignment is not only challenging but also rewarding.

Writers understand the importance of choosing a topic that fulfills the assignment requirements and fits the assignment's purpose and audience. (For more information about purpose and audience, see Chapter 6 "Writing Paragraphs: Separating Ideas and Shaping Content".) Choosing a topic that interests you is also crucial. You instructor may provide a list of suggested topics or ask that you develop a topic on your own. In either case, try to identify topics that genuinely interest you.

After identifying potential topic ideas, you will need to evaluate your ideas and choose one topic to pursue. Will you be able to find enough information about the topic? Can you develop a paper about this topic that presents and supports your original ideas? Is the topic too broad or too narrow for the scope of the assignment? If so, can you modify it so it is more manageable? You will ask these questions during this preliminary phase of the research process.

Identifying Potential Topics

Sometimes, your instructor may provide a list of suggested topics. If so, you may benefit from identifying several possibilities before committing to one idea. It is important to know how to narrow down your ideas into a concise, manageable thesis. You may also use the list as a starting point to help you identify additional, related topics. Discussing your ideas with your instructor will help ensure that you choose a manageable topic that fits the requirements of the assignment.

In this chapter, you will follow a writer named Jorge, who is studying health care administration, as he prepares a research paper. You will also plan, research, and draft your own research paper.

Jorge was assigned to write a research paper on health and the media for an introductory course in health care. Although a general topic was selected for the students, Jorge had to decide which specific issues interested him. He brainstormed a list of possibilities.

TIP

If you are writing a research paper for a specialized course, look back through your notes and course activities. Identify reading assignments and class discussions that especially engaged you. Doing so can help you identify topics to pursue.

Possible topics

1. Health Maintenance Organizations (HMOs) in the news
2. Sexual education programs
3. Hollywood and eating disorders
4. Americans' access to public health information
5. Media portrayal of the health care reform bill
6. Depictions of drugs on television
7. The effect of the Internet on mental health
8. Popularized diets (such as low-carbohydrate diets)
9. Fear of pandemics (bird flu, H1N1, SARS)
10. Electronic entertainment and obesity
11. Advertisements for prescription drugs
12. Public education and disease prevention

EXERCISE 1

Set a timer for five minutes. Use brainstorming or idea mapping to create a list of topics you would be interested in researching for a paper about the influence of the Internet on social networking. Do you closely follow the media coverage of a particular website, such as Twitter? Would you like to learn more about a certain industry, such as online dating? Which social networking sites do you and your friends use? List as many ideas related to this topic as you can.

Narrowing Your Topic

Once you have a list of potential topics, you will need to choose one as the focus of your essay. You will also need to narrow your topic. Most writers find that the topics they listed during brainstorming or idea mapping are broad—too broad for the scope of the assignment. Working with an overly broad topic, such as sexual education programs or popularized diets, can be frustrating and overwhelming. Each topic has so many facets that it would be impossible to cover them all in a college research paper. However, more specific choices, such as the pros and cons of sexual education in kids' television programs or the physical effects of the South Beach diet, are specific enough to write about without being too narrow to sustain an entire research paper.

A good research paper provides focused, in-depth information and analysis. If your topic is too broad, you will find it difficult to do more than skim the surface when you research it and write about it. Narrowing your focus is essential to making your topic manageable. To narrow your focus, explore your topic in writing, conduct preliminary research, and discuss both the topic and the research with others.

Exploring Your Topic in Writing

"How am I supposed to narrow my topic when I haven't even begun researching yet?" In fact, you may already know more than you realize. Review your list and identify your top two or three topics. Set aside some time to explore each one through freewriting. (For more information about freewriting, see Chapter 8 "The Writing Process: How Do I Begin?".) Simply taking the time to focus on your topic may yield fresh angles.

Jorge knew that he was especially interested in the topic of diet fads, but he also knew that it was much too broad for his assignment. He used freewriting to explore his thoughts so he could narrow his topic. Read Jorge's ideas.

> Our instructors are always saying that accurate, up-to-date information is crucial in encouraging people to make better choices about their health. I don't think the media does a very good job of providing that, though. Every time I go on the Internet, I see tons of ads for the latest "miracle food." One week it's acai berries, the next week it's green tea, and then six months later I see a news story saying all the fabulous claims about acai berries and green tea are overblown! Advice about weight loss is even worse. Think about all the diet books that are out there! Some say that a low-fat diet is best; some say you should cut down on carbs; and some make bizarre recommendations like eating half a grapefruit with every meal. I don't know how anyone is supposed to make an informed decision about what to eat when there's so much confusing, contradictory information. I bet even doctors, nurses, and dieticians have trouble figuring out what information is reliable and what is just the latest hype.

Conducting Preliminary Research

Another way writers may focus a topic is to conduct preliminary research. Like freewriting, exploratory reading can help you identify interesting angles. Surfing the web and browsing through newspaper and magazine articles are good ways to start. Find out what people are saying about your topic on blogs and online discussion groups. Discussing your topic with others can also inspire you. Talk about your ideas with your classmates, your friends, or your instructor.

Jorge's freewriting exercise helped him realize that the assigned topic of health and the media intersected with a few of his interests—diet, nutrition, and obesity. Preliminary online research and discussions with his classmates strengthened his impression that many people are confused or misled by media coverage of these subjects.

Jorge decided to focus his paper on a topic that had garnered a great deal of media attention—low-carbohydrate diets. He wanted to find out whether low-carbohydrate diets were as effective as their proponents claimed.

Writing at Work

At work, you may need to research a topic quickly to find general information. This information can be useful in understanding trends in a given industry or generating competition. For example, a company may research a competitor's prices and use the information when pricing their own product. You may find it useful to skim a variety of reliable sources and take notes on your findings.

TIP

The reliability of online sources varies greatly. In this exploratory phase of your research, you do not need to evaluate sources as closely as you will later. However, use common sense as you refine your paper topic. If you read a fascinating blog comment that gives you a new idea for your paper, be sure to check out other, more reliable sources as well to make sure the idea is worth pursuing.

EXERCISE 2

Review the list of topics you created in Note 11.18 "Exercise 1" and identify two or three topics you would like to explore further. For each of these topics, spend five to ten minutes writing about the topic without stopping. Then review your writing to identify possible areas of focus.

Set aside time to conduct preliminary research about your potential topics. Then choose a topic to pursue for your research paper.

Collaboration

Please share your topic list with a classmate. Select one or two topics on his or her list that you would like to learn more about and return it to him or her. Discuss why you found the topics interesting, and learn which of your topics your classmate selected and why.

A Plan for Research

Your freewriting and preliminary research have helped you choose a focused, manageable topic for your research paper. To work with your topic successfully, you will need to determine what exactly you want to learn about it—and later, what you want to say about it. Before you begin conducting in-depth research, you will further define your focus by developing a research question, a working thesis, and a research proposal.

Formulating a Research Question

In forming a research question, you are setting a goal for your research. Your main research question should be substantial enough to form the guiding principle of your paper—but focused enough to guide your research. A strong research question requires you not only to find information but also to put together different pieces of information, interpret and analyze them, and figure out what you think. As you consider potential research questions, ask yourself whether they would be too hard or too easy to answer.

To determine your research question, review the freewriting you completed earlier. Skim through books, articles, and websites and list the questions you have. (You may wish to use the 5WH strategy to help you formulate questions. See Chapter 8 "The Writing Process: How Do I Begin?" for more information about 5WH questions.) Include simple, factual questions and more complex questions that would require analysis and interpretation. Determine your main question—the primary focus of your paper—and several subquestions that you will need to research to answer your main question.

Here are the research questions Jorge will use to focus his research. Notice that his main research question has no obvious, straightforward answer. Jorge will need to research his subquestions, which address narrower topics, to answer his main question.

Topic: Low-carbohydrate diets

Main question: Are low-carbohydrate diets as effective as they have been portrayed to be by media sources?

Subquestions:

Who can benefit from following a low-carbohydrate diet?

What are the supposed advantages of following a low-carbohydrate diet?

When did low-carb diets become a "hot" topic in the media?

Where do average consumers get information about diet and nutrition?

Why has the low-carb approach received so much media attention?

How do low-carb diets work?

EXERCISE 3

Using the topic you selected in Note 11.24 "Exercise 2", write your main research question and at least four to five subquestions. Check that your main research question is appropriately complex for your assignment.

Constructing a Working Thesis

A working thesis concisely states a writer's initial answer to the main research question. It does not merely state a fact or present a subjective opinion. Instead, it expresses a debatable idea or claim that you hope to prove through additional research. Your working thesis is called a working thesis for a reason—it is subject to change. As you learn more about your topic, you may change your thinking in light of your research findings. Let your working thesis serve as a guide to your research, but do not be afraid to modify it based on what you learn.

Jorge began his research with a strong point of view based on his preliminary writing and research. Read his working thesis statement, which presents the point he will argue. Notice how it states Jorge's tentative answer to his research question.

Main research question: Are low-carb diets as effective as they have sometimes been portrayed to be by the mass media?

Working thesis statement: Low-carb diets do not live up to the media hype surrounding them.

TIP

One way to determine your working thesis is to consider how you would complete sentences such as *I believe* or *My opinion is*. However, keep in mind that academic writing generally does not use first-person pronouns. These statements are useful starting points, but formal research papers use an objective voice.

EXERCISE 4

Write a working thesis statement that presents your preliminary answer to the research question you wrote in Note 11.27 "Exercise 3". Check that your working thesis statement presents an idea or claim that could be supported or refuted by evidence from research.

Creating a Research Proposal

A research proposal is a brief document—no more than one typed page—that summarizes the preliminary work you have completed. Your purpose in writing it is to formalize your plan for research and present it to your instructor for feedback. In your research proposal, you will present your main research question, related subquestions, and working thesis. You will also briefly discuss the value of researching this topic and indicate how you plan to gather information.

When Jorge began drafting his research proposal, he realized that he had already created most of the pieces he needed. However, he knew he also had to explain how his research would be relevant to other future health care professionals. In addition, he wanted to form a general plan for doing the research and identifying potentially useful sources. Read Jorge's research proposal.

Jorge Ramirez

March 28, 2011

Health Care 101

Professor Habib

Research Proposal

In recent years, topics related to diet, nutrition, and weight loss have been covered extensively in the popular media. Different experts recommend various, often conflicting strategies for maintaining a healthy weight. One highly recommended approach, which forms the basis of many popular diet plans, is to limit consumption of carbohydrates. Yet experts disagree on the effectiveness and health benefits of this approach. What information should consumers consider when evaluating diet plans?

In my research, I will explore the claims made by proponents of the "low-carbohydrate lifestyle." My primary research question is: Are low-carbohydrate diets as effective for maintaining a healthy weight as they are portrayed to be? My secondary research questions are:

- Who can benefit from following a low-carbohydrate diet?
- What are the supposed advantages to following a low-carb diet?
- When did low-carb diets become a "hot" topic in the media?
- Where do average consumers get information about diet and nutrition?
- Why has the low-carb approach received so much media attention?
- How do low-carb diets work?

My working thesis is that low-carbohydrate diets do not live up to the media hype surrounding them. For this assignment, I will review general-interest and scholarly articles that discuss the relationship between low-carbohydrate diets, weight loss, and long-term health outcomes.

Writing at Work

Before you begin a new project at work, you may have to develop a project summary document that states the purpose of the project, explains why it would be a wise use of company resources, and briefly outlines the steps involved in completing the project. This type of document is similar to a research proposal. Both documents define and limit a project, explain its value, discuss how to proceed, and identify what resources you will use.

Writing Your Own Research Proposal

Now you may write your own research proposal, if you have not done so already. Follow the guidelines provided in this lesson.

KEY TAKEAWAYS

- Developing a research proposal involves the following preliminary steps: identifying potential ideas, choosing ideas to explore further, choosing and narrowing a topic, formulating a research question, and developing a working thesis.
- A good topic for a research paper interests the writer and fulfills the requirements of the assignment.
- Defining and narrowing a topic helps writers conduct focused, in-depth research.
- Writers conduct preliminary research to identify possible topics and research questions and to develop a

working thesis.

- A good research question interests readers, is neither too broad nor too narrow, and has no obvious answer.
- A good working thesis expresses a debatable idea or claim that can be supported with evidence from research.
- Writers create a research proposal to present their topic, main research question, subquestions, and working thesis to an instructor for approval or feedback.

CC licensed content, Shared previously

Persuasive Writing Differs Markedly from Previous Arguments

The differences between a documented essay and a research paper fall into several categories:

- complexity of topic
- breadth of discussion
- focus of the author
- formality of language
- number and diversity of sources consulted
- types and quality of sources used
- degree of integration and synthesis
- quality of processing of material by the writer, including explanations and interpretations
- achieved balance between writers' own voice and multiple voices of other writer

Avoid the "I didn't find any of the topics interesting" approach, please, and pick from the list. I'm restrictive about sources, only accepting websites if you clear them with me by email first. Mostly, we'll be using books and database articles for this paper. We will get several scholarly sources as well, so it's important not to let the decisions (topic, sources) wait too long. Since each of the topics must be narrowed (so you couldn't write a book about the research question or claim you create), it's all the more important that you begin.

CC licensed content, Original

WHAT IS RESEARCH?

Research Essay Project Overview

In the remainder of the course ahead, you will select a topic of personal interest to you, define a controversy within that topic, and examine that controversy at length. The final result will be a **2500-3000 word (approx. 10-12 page) persuasive research paper** that argues convincingly for one side of that controversy.

You will utilize **at least 7 sources** that will help you portray your argument. These sources must be incorporated correctly, used appropriately, and cited thoroughly using MLA standards. Sources should represent both the side that agrees with you and those that disagree with your own thesis. Your final draft will need to incorporate **at least one chart, table, or graph**, as well as **at least one pictorial component** (photo, drawing, etc).

You will be given more detailed assignments for each portion of the project as we move through the quarter. You're welcome to peek ahead at upcoming modules to get a sense of what the steps leading up to the final will be. The idea is that we do small chunks here and there, so that the last steps feel more like assembly than writing a huge paper all in one or two days.

What Is Research?

At its most basic level, research is anything you have to do to find out something you didn't already know. That definition might seem simple and obvious, but it contains some key assumptions that might not be as obvious. Understanding these assumptions is going to be essential to your success in this course (and in your life after college), so I'm going to spell them out here.

First, research is about acquiring new information or new knowledge, which means that it always begins from a gap in your knowledge—that is, something you don't know. More importantly, research is always goal-directed: that is, it always begins from a specific question you need to answer (a specific gap in your body of information that you need to fill) in order to accomplish some particular goal. If you are a very focused, driven person, this will seem obvious to you because you are probably already quite aware of yourself as someone who goes after the information you need in order to accomplish your goals. If you tend to be more laid-back and open to whatever experiences life brings you, you may not be as conscious of yourself as a goal-directed finder of information, but I hope to help you recognize the ways in which research is already embedded in your life.

Research (definition 1) = Anything you have to do to find out something you didn't already know.

Research Question = Your one-sentence statement of the thing-you-don't-know that motivates your research.

Sometimes the answer to your question or the information needed to fill your knowledge gap already exists in exactly the form you need. For example,

1. Does Columbus, Ohio, have a commercial airport?

The answer to this turns out to be yes, and the time to find the answer is about ten seconds. A Google search of "airports in Ohio" produces as its first hit a Wikipedia entry titled "List of airports in Ohio." A quick glance at the this document shows that Columbus does indeed have a commercial airport, and that it is one of the three largest airports in Ohio.

2. Do any airlines offer direct flights from Kansas City to Columbus?

The answer to this appears to be no, and the time to find the answer is about two minutes. Using Travelocity.com and searching for flights from MCI (Kansas City International Airport) to CMH (Port Columbus International Airport) gets the message "We've searched more than 400 airlines we sell and couldn't find any flights from Kansas City (MCI) ... [to] Columbus (CMH)." Doing the same search on Expedia.com and Orbitz.com yields the same answer. There appear to be no direct flights from Kansas City to Columbus, Ohio.

Often, however, the questions we need to have answered are more complicated than this, which means that answer comes with some assembly required.

3. What's the best way to get from Kansas City to Columbus, Ohio?

To answer this question requires a two stage process of gathering information about travel options and then evaluating the results based on parameters not stated in the question. We already know that it is possible to fly to Columbus, although no direct flights are available. A quick look at a map shows that is also a relatively straightforward drive of about 650 miles. That's the information gathering stage. Now we have to evaluate the results based on things like cost, time and effort required, practicality given the purpose of the trip, and the personal preferences of the traveler. For a business traveler for whom shortest possible travel time is more important than lowest cost, the final decision may be very different than for a college student with a large dog.

Although all three questions require information gathering, for the purposes of this course we are going to call questions like #1 and #2 "homework questions" (because you can find the answer just by going to a single reference source and looking it up) and save the designation "research question" for questions like #3 for which developing a fully functional answer requires both gathering relevant information and then assembling it in a meaningful way.

So for the purposes of this course, **research** (definition 2) **is the process of finding the information needed to answer your research question and then deriving or building the answer from the information you found.**

Research (definition 2) = *The physical process of **gathering information** + the mental process of **deriving the answer to your research question** from the information you gathered.*

Homework question = A question for which a definite answer exists and can easily be found by consulting the appropriate reference source.

Research question = A question that can be answered through a process of collecting relevant information and then building the answer from the relevant information.

How to Read Like a Writer

by Mike Bunn

In 1997, I was a recent college graduate living in London for six months and working at the Palace Theatre owned by Andrew Lloyd Webber. The Palace was a beautiful red brick, four-story theatre in the heart of London's famous West End, and eight times a week it housed a three-hour performance of the musical *Les Miserables*. Because of antiquated fire-safety laws, every theatre in the city was required to have a certain number of staff members inside watching the performance in case of an emergency.

My job (in addition to wearing a red tuxedo jacket) was to sit inside the dark theater with the patrons and make sure nothing went wrong. It didn't seem to matter to my supervisor that I had no training in security and no idea where we kept the fire extinguishers. I was pretty sure that if there *was* any trouble I'd be running down the back stairs, leaving the patrons to fend for themselves. I had no intention of dying in a bright red tuxedo.

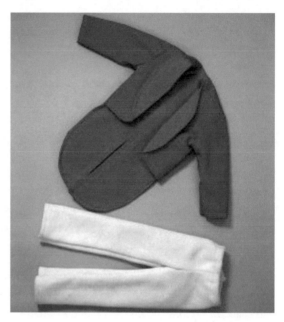

There was a Red Coat stationed on each of the theater's four floors, and we all passed the time by sitting quietly in the back, reading books with tiny flashlights. It's not easy trying to read in the dim light of a theatre—flashlight or no flashlight—and it's even tougher with shrieks and shouts and gunshots coming from the stage. I had to focus intently on each and every word, often rereading a single sentence several times. Sometimes I got distracted and had to re-read entire paragraphs. As I struggled to read in this environment, I began to realize that the way I was reading—one word at a time—was exactly the same way that the author had written the text. I realized writing is a word-by-word, sentence-by-sentence process. The intense concentration required to read in the theater helped me recognize some of the interesting ways that authors string words into phrases into paragraphs into entire books.

I came to realize that all writing consists of a series of choices.

I was an English major in college, but I don't think I ever thought much about reading. I read all the time. I read for my classes and on the computer and sometimes for fun, but I never really thought about the important connections between reading and writing, and how reading in a particular way could also make me a better writer.

What Does It Mean to Read Like a Writer?

When you Read Like a Writer (RLW) you work to identify some of the choices the author made so that you can better understand how such choices might arise in your own writing. The idea is to carefully examine the things you read, looking at the writerly techniques in the text in order to decide if you might want to adopt similar (or the same) techniques in your writing.

You are reading to learn about writing.

Instead of reading for content or to better understand the ideas in the writing (which you will automatically do to some degree anyway), you are trying to understand how the piece of writing was put together by the author and what you can learn about writing by reading a particular text. As you read in this way, you think about how the choices the author made and the techniques that he/she used are influencing your own responses as a reader. What is it about the way this text is written that makes you feel and respond the way you do?

The goal as you read like a writer is to locate what you believe are the most important writerly choices represented in the text—choices as large as the overall structure or as small as a single word used only once—to consider the effect of those choices on potential readers (including yourself). Then you can go one step further and imagine what *different* choices the author *might* have made instead, and what effect those different choices would have on readers.

Say you're reading an essay in class that begins with a short quote from President Barack Obama about the war in Iraq. As a writer, what do you think of this technique? Do you think it is effective to begin the essay with a quote? What if the essay began with a quote from someone else? What if it was a much *longer* quote from President Obama, or a quote from the President about something other than the war?

And here is where we get to the most important part: *Would you want to try this technique in your own writing?*

Would you want to start your own essay with a quote? Do you think it would be effective to begin your essay with a quote from President Obama? What about a quote from someone else? You could make yourself a list. What are the advantages and disadvantages of starting with a quote? What about the advantages and disadvantages of starting with a quote from the President? How would other readers respond to this technique? Would certain readers (say Democrats or liberals) appreciate an essay that started with a quote from President Obama better than other readers (say Republicans or conservatives)? What would be the advantages and disadvantages of starting with a quote from a *less* divisive person? What about starting with a quote from someone *more* divisive?

The goal is to carefully consider the choices the author made and the techniques that he or she used, and then decide whether you want to make those same choices or use those same techniques in your own writing. Author and professor Wendy Bishop explains how her reading process changed when she began to read like a writer:

> It wasn't until I claimed the sentence as my area of desire, interest, and expertise—until I wanted to be a writer writing better—that I had to look underneath my initial readings . . . I started asking, *how*—*how* did the writer get me to feel, *how* did the writer say something so that it remains in my memory when many other things too easily fall out, *how* did the writer communicate his/her intentions about genre, about irony? (119–20)

Bishop moved from simply reporting her personal reactions to the things she read to attempting to uncover *how* the author led her (and other readers) to have those reactions. This effort to uncover how authors build texts is what makes Reading Like a Writer so useful for student writers.

How Is RLW Different from "Normal" Reading?

Most of the time we read for information. We read a recipe to learn how to bake lasagna. We read the sports page to see if our school won the game, Facebook to see who has commented on our status update, a history book to learn about the Vietnam War, and the syllabus to see when the next writing assignment is due. Reading Like a Writer asks for something very different.

In 1940, a famous poet and critic named Allen Tate discussed two different ways of reading:

> There are many ways to read, but generally speaking there are two ways. They correspond to the two ways in which we may be interested in a piece of architecture. If the building has Corinthian columns, we can trace the origin and

development of Corinthian columns; we are interested as historians. But if we are interested as architects, we may or may not know about the history of the Corinthian style; we must, however, know all about the construction of the building, down to the last nail or peg in the beams. We have got to know this if we are going to put up buildings ourselves. (506)

While I don't know anything about Corinthian columns (and doubt that I will ever *want* to know anything about Corinthian columns), Allen Tate's metaphor of reading as if you were an architect is a great way to think about RLW. When you read like a writer, you are trying to figure out how the text you are reading was constructed so that you learn how to "build" one for yourself. Author David Jauss makes a similar comparison when he writes that "reading won't help you much unless you learn to read like a writer. You must look at a book the way a carpenter looks at a house someone else built, examining the details in order to see how it was made" (64).

Perhaps I should change the name and call this Reading Like an Architect, or Reading Like a Carpenter. In a way those names make perfect sense. You are reading to see how something was constructed so that you can construct something similar yourself.

Why Learn to Read Like a Writer?

For most college students RLW is a new way to read, and it can be difficult to learn at first. Making things even *more* difficult is that your college writing instructor may expect you to read this way for class but never actually teach you how to do it. He or she may not even tell you that you're supposed to read this way. This is because most writing instructors are so focused on teaching writing that they forget to show students how they want them to read.

That's what this essay is for.

In addition to the fact that your college writing instructor may expect you to read like a writer, this kind of reading is also one of the very best ways to learn how to write well. Reading like a writer can help you understand how the process of writing is a series of making choices, and in doing so, can help you recognize important decisions you might face and techniques you might want to use when working on your own writing. Reading this way becomes an opportunity to think and learn about writing.

Charles Moran, a professor of English at the University of Massachusetts, urges us to read like writers because:

> When we read like writers we understand and participate in the writing. We see the choices the writer has made, and we see how the writer has coped with the consequences of those choices . . . We "see" what the writer is doing because we read as writers; we see because we have written ourselves and know the territory, know the feel of it, know some of the moves ourselves. (61)

You are already an author, and that means you have a built-in advantage when reading like a writer. All of your previous writing experiences—inside the classroom and out—can contribute to your success with RLW. Because you "have written" things yourself, just as Moran suggests, you are better able to "see" the choices that the author is making in the texts that you read. This in turn helps you to think about whether you want to make some of those same choices in your own writing, and what the consequences might be for your readers if you do.

What Are Some Questions to Ask Before You Start Reading?

As I sat down to work on this essay, I contacted a few of my former students to ask what advice they would give to college students regarding how to read effectively in the writing classroom and also to get their thoughts on RLW. Throughout the rest of the essay I'd like to share some of their insights and suggestions; after all, who is better qualified to help you learn what you need to know about reading in college writing courses than students who recently took those courses themselves?

One of the things that several students mentioned to do first, before you even start reading, is to consider the *context* surrounding both the assignment and the text you're reading. As one former student, Alison, states: "The reading I did in college asked me to go above and beyond, not only in breadth of subject matter, but in depth, with regards to informed analysis and background information on *context*." Alison was asked to think about some of the factors that went into the creation of the text, as well as some of the factors influencing her own experience of reading—taken together these constitute the *context* of reading. Another former student, Jamie, suggests that students "learn about the historical context of the writings" they will read for class. Writing professor Richard Straub puts it this way: "You're not going to just read a text. You're going to read a text within a certain context, a set of circumstances . . . It's one kind of writing or another, designed for one audience and purpose or another" (138).

Among the contextual factors you'll want to consider before you even start reading are:

- Do you know the author's purpose for this piece of writing?
- Do you know who the intended audience is for this piece of writing?

It may be that you need to start reading before you can answer these first two questions, but it's worth trying to answer them before you start. For example, if you know at the outset that the author is trying to reach a very specific group of readers, then his or her writerly techniques may seem more or less effective than if he/she was trying to reach a more general audience. Similarly—returning to our earlier example of beginning an essay with a quote from President Obama about the war in Iraq—if you know that the author's purpose is to address some of the dangers and drawbacks of warfare, this may be a very effective opening. If the purpose is to encourage Americans to wear sunscreen while at the beach this opening makes no sense at all. One former student, Lola, explained that most of her reading assignments in college writing classes were designed "to provoke analysis and criticisms into the style, structure, and *purpose* of the writing itself."

In What Genre Is This Written?

Another important thing to consider before reading is the genre of the text. Genre means a few different things in college English classes, but it's most often used to indicate the *type* of writing: a poem, a newspaper article, an essay, a short story, a novel, a legal brief, an instruction manual, etc. Because the conventions for each genre can be very different (who ever heard of a 900-page newspaper article?), techniques that are effective for one genre may not work well in another. Many readers expect poems and pop songs to rhyme, for example, but might react negatively to a legal brief or instruction manual that did so. Another former student, Mike, comments on how important the genre of the text can be for reading:

I think a lot of the way I read, of course, depends on the type of text I'm reading. If I'm reading philosophy, I always look for signaling words (however, therefore, furthermore, despite) indicating the direction of the argument . . . when I read fiction or creative nonfiction, I look for how the author inserts dialogue or character sketches within narration or environmental observation. After reading To the Lighthouse [sic] last semester, I have noticed how much more attentive I've become to the types of narration (omniscient, impersonal, psychological, realistic, etc.), and how these different approaches are utilized to achieve an author's overall effect.

Although Mike specifically mentions what he looked for while reading a published novel, one of the great things about RLW is that it can be used equally well with either published or student-produced writing.

Is This a Published or a Student-Produced Piece of Writing?

As you read both kinds of texts you can locate the choices the author made and imagine the different decisions that he/she might have made. While it might seem a little weird at first to imagine how published texts could be written differently—after all, they were good enough to be published—remember that all writing can be improved. Scholar Nancy Walker believes that it's important for students to read published work using RLW because "the work ceases to be a mere artifact, a stone tablet, and becomes instead a living utterance with immediacy and texture. It could have been better or worse than it is had the author made different choices" (36). As Walker suggests, it's worth thinking about how the published text would be different—maybe even *better*—if the author had made different choices in the writing because you may be faced with similar choices in your own work.

Is This the Kind of Writing You Will Be Assigned to Write Yourself?

Knowing ahead of time what kind of writing assignments you will be asked to complete can really help you to read like a writer. It's probably impossible (and definitely too time consuming) to identify *all* of the choices the author made and *all* techniques an author used, so it's important to prioritize while reading. Knowing what you'll be writing yourself can help you prioritize. It may be the case that your instructor has assigned the text you're reading to serve as model for the kind of writing you'll be doing later. Jessie, a former student, writes, "In college writing classes, we knew we were reading for a purpose—to influence or inspire our own work. The reading that I have done in college writing courses has always been really specific to a certain type of writing, and it allows me to focus and experiment on that specific style in depth and without distraction."

If the text you're reading is a model of a particular style of writing—for example, highly-emotional or humorous—RLW is particularly helpful because you can look at a piece you're reading and think about whether you want to adopt a similar style in your own writing. You might realize that the author is trying to arouse sympathy in readers and examine what techniques he/she uses to do this; then you can decide whether these techniques might work well in your own writing. You might notice that the author keeps including jokes or funny stories and think about whether you want to include them in your writing—what would the impact be on your potential readers?

What Are Questions to Ask As You Are Reading?

It is helpful to continue to ask yourself questions *as* you read like a writer. As you're first learning to read in this new way, you may want to have a set of questions written or typed out in front of you that you can refer to while reading. Eventually—after plenty of practice—you will start to ask certain questions and locate certain things in the text almost automatically. Remember, for most students this is a new way of reading, and you'll have to train yourself to do it well. Also keep in mind that you're reading to understand how the text was *written*—how the house was built—more than you're trying to determine the meaning of the things you read or assess whether the texts are good or bad.

First, return to two of the same questions I suggested that you consider *before* reading:

- What is the author's purpose for this piece of writing?
- Who is the intended audience?

Think about these two questions again as you read. It may be that you couldn't really answer them before, or that your ideas will change while reading. Knowing *why* the piece was written and *who* it's for can help explain why the author might have made certain choices or used particular techniques in the writing, and you can assess those choices and techniques based in part on how effective they are in fulfilling that purpose and/or reaching the intended audience.

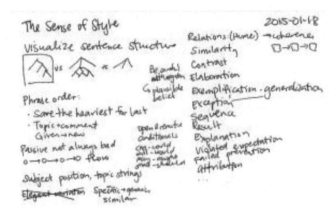

Beyond these initial two questions, there is an almost endless list of questions you might ask regarding writing choices and techniques. Here are some of the questions that one former student, Clare, asks herself:

> When reading I tend to be asking myself a million questions. If I were writing this, where would I go with the story? If the author goes in a different direction (as they so often do) from what I am thinking, I will ask myself, why did they do this? What are they telling me?

Clare tries to figure out why the author might have made a move in the writing that she hadn't anticipated, but even more importantly, she asks herself what *she* would do if she were the author. Reading the text becomes an opportunity for Clare to think about her own role as an author.

Here are some additional examples of the kinds of questions you might ask yourself as you read:

- How effective is the language the author uses? Is it too formal? Too informal? Perfectly appropriate?

Depending on the subject matter and the intended audience, it may make sense to be more or less formal in terms of language. As you begin reading, you can ask yourself whether the word choice and tone/ language of the writing seem appropriate.

- What kinds of evidence does the author use to support his/her claims? Does he/she use statistics? Quotes from famous people? Personal anecdotes or personal stories? Does he/she cite books or articles?
- How appropriate or effective is this evidence? Would a different type of evidence, or some combination of evidence, be more effective?

To some extent the kinds of questions you ask should be determined by the genre of writing you are reading. For example, it's probably worth examining the evidence that the author uses to support his/ her claims if you're reading an opinion column, but less important if you're reading a short story. An opinion column is often intended to convince readers of something, so the kinds of evidence used are often very important. A short story *may* be intended to convince readers of something, sometimes, but probably not in the same way. A short story rarely includes claims or evidence in the way that we usually think about them.

- Are there places in the writing that you find confusing? What about the writing in those places makes it unclear or confusing?

It's pretty normal to get confused in places while reading, especially while reading for class, so it can be helpful to look closely at the writing to try and get a sense of exactly what tripped you up. This way you can learn to avoid those same problems in your own writing.

- How does the author move from one idea to another in the writing? Are the transitions between the ideas effective? How else might he/she have transitioned between ideas instead?

Notice that in these questions I am encouraging you to question whether aspects of the writing are *appropriate* and *effective* in addition to deciding whether you liked or dislikedthem. You want to imagine how other readers might respond to the writing and the techniques you've identified. Deciding whether you liked or disliked something is only about you; considering whether a technique is appropriate or effective lets you contemplate what the author might have been trying to do and to decide whether a majority of readers would find the move successful. This is important because it's the same thing you should be thinking about while you are writing: how will readers respond to this technique I am using, to this sentence, to this word? As you read, ask yourself what the author is doing at each step of the way, and then consider whether the same choice or technique might work in your own writing.

What Should You Be Writing As You Are Reading?

The most common suggestion made by former students—mentioned by every single one of them—was to mark up the text, make comments in the margins, and write yourself notes and summaries both during and after reading. Often the notes students took while reading became ideas or material for the students to use in their own papers. It's important to read with a pen or highlighter in your hand so that you can mark—right on the text—all those spots where you identify an interesting choice the author has made or a writerly technique you might want to use. One thing that I like to do is to highlight and underline the passage in the text itself, and then try to answer the following three questions on my notepad:

- What is the technique the author is using here?
- Is this technique effective?
- What would be the advantages and disadvantages if I tried this same technique in my writing?

By utilizing this same process of highlighting and note taking, you'll end up with a useful list of specific techniques to have at your disposal when it comes time to begin your own writing.

What Does RLW Look Like in Action?

Let's go back to the opening paragraph of this essay and spend some time reading like writers as a way to get more comfortable with the process:

> In 1997, I was a recent college graduate living in London for six months and working at the Palace Theatre owned by Andrew Lloyd Webber. The Palace was a beautiful red brick, four-story theatre in the heart of London's famous West End, and eight times a week it housed a three-hour performance of the musical Les Miserables. Because of antiquated fire-safety laws, every theatre in the city was required to have a certain number of staff members inside watching the performance in case of an emergency.

Let's begin with those questions I encouraged you to try to answer *before* you start reading. (I realize we're cheating a little bit in this case since you've already read most of this essay, but this is just practice. When doing this on your own, you should attempt to answer these questions before reading, and then return to them as you read to further develop your answers.)

- Do you know the author's purpose for this piece of writing? I hope the purpose is clear by now; if it isn't, I'm doing a pretty lousy job of explaining how and why you might read like a writer.
- Do you know who the intended audience is? Again, I hope that you know this one by now.
- What about the genre? Is this an essay? An article? What would you call it?

- You know that it's published and not student writing. How does this influence your expectations for what you will read?
- Are you going to be asked to write something like this yourself? Probably not in your college writing class, but you can still use RLW to learn about writerly techniques that you might want to use in whatever you do end up writing.

Now ask yourself questions *as* you read.

In 1997, I was a recent college graduate living in London for six months and working at the Palace Theatre owned by Andrew Lloyd Webber. The Palace was a beautiful red brick, four-story theatre in the heart of London's famous West End, and eight times a week it housed a three-hour performance of the musical Les Miserables. *Because of antiquated fire-safety laws, every theatre in the city was required to have a certain number of staff members inside watching the performance in case of an emergency.*

Since this paragraph is the very first one, it makes sense to think about how it introduces readers to the essay. What technique(s) does the author use to begin the text? This is a personal story about his time working in London. What else do you notice as you read over this passage? Is the passage vague or specific about where he worked? You know that the author worked in a famous part of London in a beautiful theater owned by a well-known composer. Are these details important? How different would this opening be if instead I had written:

In 1997, I was living in London and working at a theatre that showed Les Miserables.

This is certainly shorter, and some of you may prefer this version. It's quick. To the point. But what (if anything) is lost by eliminating so much of the detail? I *chose* to include each of the details that the revised sentence omits, so it's worth considering why. Why did I mention where the theater was located? Why did I explain that I was living in London right after finishing college? Does it matter that it was after college? What effect might I have hoped the inclusion of these details would have on readers? Is this reference to college an attempt to connect with my audience of college students? Am I trying to establish my credibility as an author by announcing that I went to college? Why might I want the readers to know that this was a theater owned by Andrew Lloyd Weber? Do you think I am just trying to mention a famous name that readers will recognize? Will Andrew Lloyd Weber figure prominently in the rest of the essay?

These are all reasonable questions to ask. They are not necessarily the right questions to ask because there are no right questions. They certainly aren't the only questions you could ask, either. The goal is to train yourself to formulate questions as you read based on whatever you notice in the text. Your own reactions to what you're reading will help determine the kinds of questions to ask.

Now take a broader perspective. I begin this essay—an essay about *reading*—by talking about my job in a theater in London. Why? Doesn't this seem like an odd way to begin an essay about reading? If you read on a little further (feel free to scan back up at the top of this essay) you learn in the third full paragraph what the connection is between working in the theater and reading like a writer, but why include this information at all? What does this story add to the essay? Is it worth the space it takes up?

Think about what effect presenting this personal information might have on readers. Does it make it feel like a real person, some "ordinary guy," is talking to you? Does it draw you into the essay and make you want to keep reading?

What about the language I use? Is it formal or more informal? This is a time when you can really narrow your focus and look at particular words:

Because of antiquated fire-safety laws, every theatre in the city was required to have a certain number of staff members inside watching the performance in case of an emergency.

What is the effect of using the word "antiquated" to describe the firesafety laws? It certainly projects a negative impression; if the laws are described as antiquated it means I view them as old-fashioned or obsolete. This is a fairly uncommon word, so it stands out, drawing attention to my choice in using it. The word also sounds quite formal. Am I formal in the rest of this sentence?

I use the word "performance" when I just as easily could have written "show." For that matter, I could have written "old" instead of "antiquated." You can proceed like this throughout the sentence, thinking about alternative choices I could have made and what the effect would be. Instead of "staff members" I could have written "employees" or just "workers." Notice the difference if the sentence had been written:

> Because of old fire-safety laws, every theatre in the city was required to have a certain number of workers inside watching the show in case of an emergency.

Which version is more likely to appeal to readers? You can try to answer this question by thinking about the advantages and disadvantages of using formal language. When would you want to use formal language in your writing and when would it make more sense to be more conversational?

As you can see from discussing just this one paragraph, you could ask questions about the text forever. Luckily, you don't have to. As you continue reading like a writer, you'll learn to notice techniques that seem new and pay less attention to the ones you've thought about before. The more you practice the quicker the process becomes until you're reading like a writer almost automatically.

I want to end this essay by sharing one more set of comments by my former student, Lola, this time about what it means to her to read like a writer:

> Reading as a writer would compel me to question what might have brought the author to make these decisions, and then decide what worked and what didn't. What could have made that chapter better or easier to understand? How can I make sure I include some of the good attributes of this writing style into my own? How can I take aspects that I feel the writer failed at and make sure not to make the same mistakes in my writing?

Questioning why the author made certain decisions. Considering what techniques could have made the text better. Deciding how to include the best attributes of what you read in your own writing. This is what Reading Like a Writer is all about.

Are you ready to start reading?

Discussion

1. How is "Reading Like a Writer" similar to and/or different from the way(s) you read for other classes?
2. What kinds of choices do you make as a writer that readers might identify in your written work?
3. Is there anything you notice in this essay that you might like to try in your own writing? What is that technique or strategy? When do you plan to try using it?
4. What are some of the different ways that you can learn about the context of a text before you begin reading it?

Works Cited

Bishop, Wendy. "Reading, Stealing, and Writing Like a Writer." Elements of Alternate Style: Essays on Writing and Revision. Ed. Wendy Bishop. Portsmouth, NH: Boynton/Cook, 1997. Print.

Jauss, David. "Articles of Faith." Creative Writing in America: Theory and Pedagogy. Ed. Joseph Moxley. Urbana, IL: NCTE, 1989. Print.

Moran, Charles. "Reading Like a Writer." Vital Signs 1. Ed. James L. Collins. Portsmouth, NH: Boynton/Cook, 1990. Print.

Straub, Richard. "Responding—Really Responding—to Other Students' Writing." The Subject is Reading. Ed. Wendy Bishop. Portsmouth, NH: Boynton/Cook, 2000. Print.

Tate, Allen. "We Read as Writers." Princeton Alumni Weekly 40 (March 8, 1940): 505- 506. Print.

Walker, Nancy. "The Student Reader as Writer." ADE Bulletin 106 (1993) 35–37. Print.

Discussion: What Research Have You Done Lately?

In your life outside of school, think about some investigation you've done to satisfy your own curiosity. (Keep in mind the difference between "homework questions" and "research questions" as noted in What Is Research? (https://courses.lumenlearning.com/englishcomp2kscopexmaster/chapter/what-is-research/))

- What was your research question?
- What kind of information did you have to gather in order to answer it?
- What sources did you use to gather the information?
- Were you successful in answering the question?
- And, if you're willing to share, what was your answer?

Post 1: For your first post, answer the first 4 bullet points (and the last, if you're willing).

> Your post should be at least 150-200 words. It doesn't have to be grammatically perfect, but should use standard English (no text-speak, please) and normal capitalization rules.

Posts 2 and 3: Respond to at least two of your classmates' posts.

> Responses are weighed as heavily as your initial posting, and should be roughly as long (150-200 words) when combined. Responses should indicate you've read your classmates' posts carefully. Include specific details from the post you're responding to in your reply.

Research and Other Types of Source-based Writing

Some high school and first-year college writing courses use the term "research paper" or "research writing" to apply to any situation in which students use information from an outside source in writing a paper. The logic behind this is that if the writer has to go find information from a source, that action of going and finding information is similar to research, so it is convenient to call that kind of writing task a "research paper." However, it is only true research if it starts from a QUESTION to which the writer genuinely doesn't know the answer and if the writer then develops or builds the answer to the question through gathering and processing information.

To help keep that difference in mind, this module will use "**research**" to refer to the goal-directed process of gathering information and building the answer to a research question, and "**source-based writing**" to refer to the many other types of information gathering and source-based writing one might do.

One important indicator of the difference between research and other source-based writing tasks is when in the process you develop the thesis (main point) of your paper. In a research project, you begin with a question, gather the data from which you will derive or build the answer to the question, build the answer, and then state your answer in a single sentence. This one-sentence statement of your answer to your research question then becomes your thesis statement and serves as the main point of your paper. In the research writing process, therefore, stating your thesis happens at the pivot point between research and writing (so roughly half or two thirds of the way through the project, depending on the amount of time spent gathering and processing information).

Any assignment for which you begin by developing your thesis and then go out and gather information to support it is indeed be a source-based writing assignment, but it is not technically research because it begins from the answer instead of the question.

Being aware of this distinction is essential to your successful completion of both research projects and other source-based writing tasks. The work processes that lead to efficiency and success with research projects are very different from the work processes you may have used successfully for other types of source-based papers. Both offer valuable learning experiences, but it is important to understand which type of assignment you are being asked to do so that you can adjust your expectations accordingly.

Think of the most recent writing project you have done that required sources. Based on this definition, was it a research project or a source-based writing project?

- Composition II. **Authored by**: Janet Zepernick. **Provided by**: Pittsburg State University. **Located at**: http://www.pittstate.edu/ (http://www.pittstate.edu/). **Project**: Kaleidoscope Open Course Initiative. **License**: *CC BY: Attribution (https://creativecommons.org/licenses/by/4.0/)*

- Image of man using computer. **Authored by**: World Bank Photo Collection. **Located at**: https://flic.kr/p/cvL28d (https://flic.kr/p/cvL28d). **License**: *CC BY-NC-ND: Attribution-NonCommercial-NoDerivatives (https://creativecommons.org/licenses/by-nc-nd/4.0/)*

- Image of man with question mark. **Authored by**: Seth Capitulo. **Located at**: https://flic.kr/p/fnN1SJ (https://flic.kr/p/fnN1SJ). **License**: *CC BY: Attribution (https://creativecommons.org/licenses/by/4.0/)*

What Is Research Writing?

Research = the physical process of **gathering information** + the mental process of **deriving the answer to your question** from the information you gathered.

Research writing = the process of **sharing the answer** to your research question along with the **evidence** on which your answer is based, the **sources** you used, and your own **reasoning** and **explanation**.

The essential components or building blocks of research writing are the same no matter what kind of question you are answering or what kind of reader you are assuming as you share your answer.

The Essential Building Blocks of Research Writing

1. **Do real research**

    1. Begin from a question to which you don't know the answer and that can't be answered just by going to the appropriate reference source. That is, begin from a research question, not a homework question.
    2. Decide what kind of information or data will be needed in order to build the answer to the question.
    3. Gather information and/or collect data.
    4. Work with the information/data to derive or construct your answer.

    This is the *research process*, and it happens before you begin to write your paper. No research, no research writing, so don't shortchange this part of the process.

2. **Create a one-sentence answer to your research question.**

    1. This will be the thesis statement/main point/controlling idea of your research paper.

3. **Share your answer to research questions in a way that make it believable, understandable, and usable for your readers.** To do this

    1. Include plentiful and well-chosen examples from the data/information you gathered
    2. Indicate the validity of your data by accurately reporting your research method (field or lab research)
    3. Indicate the quality of your information by accurately citing your sources (source-based research)
    4. Provide the reasoning and explanation that will let your readers completely understand how the evidence adds up to your answer.

CC licensed content, Shared previously

- Composition II. **Authored by**: Janet Zepernick. **Provided by**: Pittsburg State University. **Located at**: http://www.pittstate.edu/ (http://www.pittstate.edu/). **Project**: Kaleidoscope Open Course Initiative. **License**: *CC BY: Attribution (https://creativecommons.org/licenses/by/4.0/)*
- Image of man using card catalog. **Authored by**: brewbooks. **Located at**: https://flic.kr/p/7NxJTd (https://flic.kr/p/7NxJTd). **License**: *CC BY-SA: Attribution-ShareAlike (https://creativecommons.org/licenses/by-sa/4.0/)*

Reading to Write Effectively

Reading to Write Effectively: Why you need a reading strategy before writing anything

Given all of the reading and writing that we are expected to accomplish as college/university students, it's important to be as efficient as possible when committing our time to these responsibilities. Three of the most important suggestions for approaching reading and, therefore, writing, efficiently are as follows:

read with a pen in hand; don't expect yourself to remember key concepts/ideas

- *most of us can't remember everything that we've read and then call it to memory when we're writing. Therefore, reading with a pen in hand prepares you to circle/underline key concepts/ideas in the text you're reading. This creates a way of "tracing" key concepts/ideas throughout the text so that when it's time to recall what you've read and use it to guide your writing, it will be much easier to condense the entire text into a unique, organized, written response. If you don't want to write in the text that you're reading, open a blank Word document for keeping track of key concepts/ideas (and page numbers).*

write while reading because it's an informal way of "conversing with" the author of the text (i.e. learning about how your writing can contribute something useful to "the conversation" of your resources)

- *in addition to circling/underlining key concepts/ideas throughout your reading process, it may also be helpful to keep a list of questions, connections with other texts/assignments/disciplines, etc. because this list can easily translate into "official" writing. For instance, even if your teacher isn't requiring a written assignment in response to the reading assignment, if you keep a working document with questions, connections, etc. regarding the reading assignment, you will likely be much better prepared to discuss the reading, not to mention that your notations can easily serve in the short-term as a Twitter/Facebook post (which is helpful for providing others' responses to your ideas) or in the long-term as an idea for a final paper. For most of us, it's much easier to have somewhere to start when, eventually, we need to complete a writing assignment based on the reading assignments of the course.*

develop research questions/research key words while reading; most of the time, it's fairly easy to identify research key words/ create unique research questions while reading actively

- *the notations you keep in the texts you're reading can help to prevent the frustration of figuring out "what to write about" when it comes time to interpret the reading assignments into unique written work. They give you something to start with — either in the sense that you can extend the ideas you have already written down, or challenge them by researching what's missing ... either way, you have something to work with, which helps to alleviate some of the anxiety of staring at a blank page.*

CC licensed content, Shared previously

- Reading to Write Effectively. **Provided by**: WritingCommons. **Located at**: http://writingcommons.org/blog-feed-home-page/657-reading-to-write-effectively-why-you-need-a-reading-strategy-before-writing-anything (http://writingcommons.org/blog-feed-home-page/657-reading-to-write-effectively-why-you-need-a-reading-strategy-before-writing-anything). **License**: *CC BY-NC-ND: Attribution-NonCommercial-NoDerivatives (https://creativecommons.org/licenses/by-nc-nd/4.0/)*

Assessment: Reading Notebook #1

This will be the first of several Reading Notebook entries you'll be asked to create this quarter. Each will follow a similar format.

Typically, you'll be finding your own sources for Reading Notebook entries, but for this first one, we'll all be looking at the same source.

- **Please review the article "How to Read Like a Writer" by Mike Bunn (https://courses.candelalearning.com/englishcomp2kscopexmaster/chapter/how-to-read-like-a-writer/) for this exercise.**

In this article, you learned several tools to get more out of your reading activities for schoolwork. We'll amend the first bullet point's advice slightly to "read with a *computer keyboard* in hand" for our purposes.

While reading the "How to Read Like a Writer" source, put this first strategy of "reading with a keyboard in hand" to work. Create a document that includes any or all of the following:

- questions you had while reading
- emotional reactions to the text
- key terms that seem important to you
- what you think the thesis or main idea of this source is
- what you think the intended audience for this source is
- how effective you think this source is
- anything else that comes to mind

This is an informal assignment. Your writing can be in complete sentences, or bullet points or fragments, as you see appropriate. Editing isn't vital for this work, though it should be proofread to the point that obvious typos or misspellings are addressed and corrected. Target word count is 150-300 words for this entry.

EVALUATING SOURCES

The Seven Steps of the Research Process

The following seven steps outline a simple and effective strategy for finding information for a research paper and documenting the sources you find. Depending on your topic and your familiarity with the library, you may need to rearrange or recycle these steps. Adapt this outline to your needs. We are ready to help you at every step in your research.

STEP 1: IDENTIFY AND DEVELOP YOUR TOPIC

SUMMARY: State your topic as a question. For example, if you are interested in finding out about use of alcoholic beverages by college students, you might pose the question, "What effect does use of alcoholic beverages have on the health of college students?" Identify the main concepts or keywords in your question.

More details on how to identify and develop your topic. (http://olinuris.library.cornell.edu/ref/research/topic.html)

STEP 2: FIND BACKGROUND INFORMATION

SUMMARY: Look up your keywords in the indexes to subject encyclopedias. Read articles in these encyclopedias to set the context for your research. Note any relevant items in the bibliographies at the end of the encyclopedia articles. Additional background information may be found in your lecture notes, textbooks, and reserve readings.

More suggestions on how to find background information. (http://olinuris.library.cornell.edu/ref/research/background.html)

STEP 3: USE CATALOGS TO FIND BOOKS AND MEDIA

SUMMARY: Use guided keyword searching to find materials by topic or subject. Print or write down the citation (author, title,etc.) and the location information (call number and library). Note the circulation status. When you pull the book from the shelf, scan the bibliography for additional sources. Watch for book-length bibliographies and annual reviews on your subject; they list citations to hundreds of books and articles in one subject area. Check the standard subject subheading "—BIBLIOGRAPHIES," or titles beginning with Annual Review of... in the Cornell Library Classic Catalog.

More detailed instructions for using catalogs to find books. (http://olinuris.library.cornell.edu/ref/research/books.html)

Finding media (audio and video) titles (http://olinuris.library.cornell.edu/ref/research/mediafind.html).

- https://youtu.be/R1yNDvmjqaE

STEP 4: USE INDEXES TO FIND PERIODICAL ARTICLES

SUMMARY: Use periodical indexes and abstracts to find citations to articles. The indexes and abstracts may be in print or computer-based formats or both. Choose the indexes and format best suited to your particular topic; ask at the reference desk if you need help figuring out which index and format will be best. You can find periodical articles by the article author, title, or keyword by using the periodical indexes in theLibrary home page. If the full text is not linked in the index you are using, write down the citation from the index and search for the title of the periodical in the Cornell Library Classic Catalog. The catalog lists the print, microform, and electronic versions of periodicals at Cornell.

How to find and use periodical indexes at Cornell. (http://olinuris.library.cornell.edu/ref/research/periodical.html)

STEP 5: FIND INTERNET RESOURCES

SUMMARY: Use search engines. Check to see if your class has a bibliography or research guide created by librarians.

Finding Information on the Internet (http://www.lib.berkeley.edu/TeachingLib/Guides/Internet/FindInfo.html): A thorough tutorial from UC Berkeley.

STEP 6: EVALUATE WHAT YOU FIND

SUMMARY: See How to Critically Analyze Information Sources and Distinguishing Scholarly from Non-Scholarly Periodicals: A Checklist of Criteria for suggestions on evaluating the authority and quality of the books and articles you located.

- https://youtu.be/uDGJ2CYfY9A
- https://youtu.be/QAiJL5B5esM

If you have found too many or too few sources, you may need to narrow or broaden your topic. Check with a reference librarian or your instructor. When you're ready to write, here is an annotated list of books to help you organize, format, and write your paper.

STEP 7: CITE WHAT YOU FIND USING A STANDARD FORMAT

Give credit where credit is due; cite your sources.

Citing or documenting the sources used in your research serves two purposes, it gives proper credit to the authors of the materials used, and it allows those who are reading your work to duplicate your research and locate the sources that you have listed as references.

Knowingly representing the work of others as your own is plagarism. (See Cornell's Code of Academic Integrity (http://cuinfo.cornell.edu/Academic/AIC.html)). Use one of the styles listed below or another style approved by your instructor. Handouts summarizing the APA and MLA styles are available at Uris and Olin Reference.

Available online:

RefWorks (http://encompass.library.cornell.edu/cgi-bin/checkIP.cgi?access=gateway_standard%26url=http://www.refworks.com/refworks)is a web-based program that allows you to easily collect, manage, and organize bibliographic references by interfacing with databases. RefWorks also interfaces directly with Word, making it easy to import references and incorporate them into your writing, properly formatted according to the style of your choice.

See our guide to citation tools and styles (http://www.library.cornell.edu/services/citing.html).

Format the citations in your bibliography using examples from the following Library help pages: Modern Language Association (MLA) examples (http://www.library.cornell.edu/resrch/citmanage/mla) and American Psychological Association (APA) examples (http://www.library.cornell.edu/resrch/citmanage/apa).

- Style guides in print (book) format:
- **MLA Handbook for Writers of Research Papers**. 7th ed. New York: MLA, 2009. This handbook is based on the MLA Style Manual and is intended as an aid for college students writing research papers. Included here is information on selecting a topic, researching the topic, note taking, the writing of footnotes and bibliographies, as well as sample pages of a research paper. Useful for the beginning researcher.
- **Publication Manual of the American Psychological Association**. 6th ed. Washington: APA, 2010. The authoritative style

manual for anyone writing in the field of psychology. Useful for the social sciences generally. Chapters discuss the content and organization of a manuscript, writing style, the American Psychological Association citation style, and typing, mailing and proofreading.

If you are writing an annotated bibliography, see How to Prepare an Annotated Bibliography (http://olinuris.library.cornell.edu/ref/research/skill28.htm).

RESEARCH TIPS:

- WORK FROM THE GENERAL TO THE SPECIFIC. Find background information first, then use more specific and recent sources.
- RECORD WHAT YOU FIND AND WHERE YOU FOUND IT. Record the complete citation for each source you find; you may need it again later.
- TRANSLATE YOUR TOPIC INTO THE SUBJECT LANGUAGE OF THE INDEXES AND CATALOGS YOU USE. Check your topic words against a thesaurus or subject heading list.

CC licensed content, Shared previously

- The Seven Steps. **Provided by**: Research & Learning Services Olin Library Cornell University Library Ithaca, NY, USA. **Located at**: http://guides.library.cornell.edu/sevensteps (http://guides.library.cornell.edu/sevensteps). **License**: *CC BY-NC-SA: Attribution-NonCommercial-ShareAlike (https://creativecommons.org/licenses/by-nc-sa/4.0/)*. **License Terms**: Lumen Learning has received permission from Olin & Uris Libraries to reproduce this and adapt it for our own use
- Research Minutes: How to Identify Scholarly Journal Articles. **Authored by**: Olin & Uris Libraries, Cornell University. **Located at**: https://youtu.be/uDGJ2CYfY9A (https://youtu.be/uDGJ2CYfY9A). **License**: *All Rights Reserved*. **License Terms**: Standard YouTube License

All rights reserved content

- Research Minutes: How to Read Citations. **Authored by**: Olin & Uris Libraries, Cornell University. **Located at**: https://youtu.be/R1yNDvmjqaE (https://youtu.be/R1yNDvmjqaE). **License**: *All Rights Reserved*. **License Terms**: Standard YouTube License
- Research Minutes: How to Identify Substantive News Articles. **Authored by**: Olin & Uris Libraries, Cornell University. **Located at**: https://youtu.be/QAiJL5B5esM (https://youtu.be/QAiJL5B5esM). **License**: *All Rights Reserved*. **License Terms**: Standard YouTube License

Understanding Bias

Bias

Bias means presenting facts and arguments in a way that consciously favours one side or other in an argument. Is bias bad or wrong?

No! Everyone who argues strongly for something is biased. So it's not enough, when you are doing a language analysis, to merely spot some bias and say..."This writer is biased" or "This speaker is biased."

Let's begin by reading a biased text.

Hypocrites gather to feed off Daniel's tragic death

The death of two-year-old Daniel Valerio at the hands of his step-father brought outrage from the media.

Daniel suffered repeated beatings before the final attack by Paul Alton, who was sentenced in Melbourne in February to 22 years jail.

Rupert Murdoch's Herald-Sun launched a campaign which included a public meeting of hundreds of readers. Time magazine put Daniel on its front cover. The Herald-Sun summed up their message:

The community has a duty to protect our children from abuse – if necessary by laws that some people regard as possibly harsh or unnecessary.

But laws – like making it compulsory for doctors and others to report suspected abuse – cannot stop the violence.

Last year, 30 children were murdered across Australia. Babies under one are more likely to be killed than any other social group.

Daniel's murder was not a horrific exception but the product of a society that sends some of its members over the edge into despairing violence.

The origin of these tragedies lies in the enormous pressures on families, especially working class families.

The media and politicians wring their hands over a million unemployed. But they ignore the impact that having no job, or a stressful poorly paid job, can have.

Child abuse can happen in wealthy families. But generally it is linked to poverty.

A survey in 1980 of "maltreating families" showed that 56.5 per cent were living in poverty and debt. A further 20 per cent expressed extreme anxiety about finances.

A study in Queensland found that all the children who died from abuse came from working class families.

Police records show that school holidays – especially Xmas – are peak times for family violence. "The sad fact is that when families are together for longer than usual, there tends to be more violence", said one Victorian police officer.

Most people get by. Family life may get tense, but not violent.

But a minority cannot cope and lash out at the nearest vulnerable person to hand – an elderly person, a woman, or a child.

Compulsory reporting of child abuse puts the blame on the individual parents rather than the system that drives them to this kind of despair.

Neither is it a solution. Daniel was seen by 21 professionals before he was killed. Nonetheless, the Victorian Liberal government has agreed to bring it in.

Their hypocrisy is breathtaking.

This is the same government that is sacking 250 fire-fighters, a move that will lead to more deaths.

A real challenge to the basis of domestic violence means a challenge to poverty.

Yet which side were the media on when Labor cut the under-18 dole, or when Jeff Kennett[1] added $30 a week to the cost of sending a child to kindergarten?

To really minimise family violence, we need a fight for every job and against every cutback.

– by David Glanz, *The Socialist*, April 1993

There are good and bad aspects of bias.

1. It is good to be open about one's bias. For example, the article about Daniel Valerio's tragic death is written for *The Socialist* newspaper. Clearly socialists will have a bias against arguments that blame only the individual for a crime when it could be argued that many other factors in society contributed to the crime and need to be changed. Focusing on the individual, from the socialist's point of view, gets "the system" off the hook when crimes happen. The socialist's main reason for writing is to criticise the capitalist system. So David Glanz is not pretending to not be biased, because he has published his article in a partisan[2] newspaper.

   ◦ Here are some ways to be open about your bias, but still be naughty.

     - (a) Deliberately avoid mentioning any of the opposing arguments.
     - (b) Deliberately avoid mentioning relevant facts or information that would undermine your own case.
     - (c) Get into hyperbole.
     - (d) Make too much use of emotive language.
     - (e) Misuse or distort statistics.
     - (f) Use negative adjectives when talking about people you disagree with, but use positive adjectives when talking about people you agree with.
     - Can you find examples of any of these "naughty" ways to be biased in Glaz's article?

2. You mustn't assume that because a person writes with a particular bias he/she is not being sincere, or that he/she has not really thought the issue through. The person is not just stating what he/she thinks, he/she is trying to persuade you about something.

Bias can result from the way you have organised your experiences in your own mind. You have lumped some experiences into the 'good' box and some experiences into the 'bad' box. Just about everybody does this[3]. The way you have assembled and valued experiences in your mind is called your *Weltanschauung* (Velt-arn-shao-oong). If through your own experience, plus good thinking about those experiences, you have a better understanding of something, your bias is indeed a good thing.

For example, if you have been a traffic policeman, and have seen lots of disasters due to speed and alcohol, it is not 'wrong' for you to biased against fast cars and drinking at parties and pubs. Your bias is due to your better understanding of the issue, *but you still have to argue logically.*

Really naughty bias

4. If you pretend to be objective, to not take sides, but actually use techniques that tend to support one side of an argument, in that case you are being naughty. There are subtle ways to do this.

(a) If the support for one side of the argument is mainly at the top of the article, and the reasons to support the opposite side of the issue are mainly at the bottom end of the article; that might be subtle bias – especially if it was written by a journalist. Journalists are taught that many readers only read the first few paragraphs of an article before moving on to reading another article, so whatever is in the first few paragraphs will be what sticks in the reader's mind.

(b) Quotes from real people are stronger emotionally than just statements by the writer. This is especially true if the person being quoted is an 'authority' on the subject, or a 'celebrity'. So if one side of the issue is being supported by lots of quotes, and the other side isn't, that is a subtle form of bias.

(c) If when one person is quoted as saying X, but the very next sentence makes that quote sound silly or irrational, that is a subtle form of bias too.

Common sense tells us that if someone is making money out of something, he/she will be biased in favour of it.

For example, a person who makes money out of building nuclear reactors in Europe or China could be expected to support a change in policy in Australia towards developing nuclear energy.

A manufacturer of cigarettes is unlikely to be in favour of health warnings on cigarette packets or bans on smoking in pubs.

Nonetheless, logically speaking, **we cannot just assume** a person who is making money out of something will always take sides with whomever or whatever will make him/her more money.

We have to listen to the arguments as they come up. **Assuming** someone is biased is not logically okay. You have to **show** that someone is biased and use **evidence** to support your assertion that he/she is biased.

[1] Jeff Kennett was the leader of the Liberal party in Victoria at that time.

[2] When you are a **partisan** you have **taken sides** in an argument, or a battle, or a war.

[3] Learning critical thinking (which is what you are learning in Year 11 and 12 English) is aimed at getting you to do more, and better, thinking than that.

- Image of Assume Nothing. **Authored by**: David Gallagher. **Located at**: https://flic.kr/p/5wZECN (https://flic.kr/p/5wZECN). **License**: *CC BY-NC: Attribution-NonCommercial (https://creativecommons.org/licenses/by-nc/4.0/)*

Public domain content

- Bias. **Authored by**: nenifoofer. **Located at**: http://www.docstoc.com/docs/4644737/Understanding%20Bias (http://www.docstoc.com/docs/4644737/Understanding%20Bias). **License**: *Public Domain: No Known Copyright (https://creativecommons.org/about/pdm)*

Anatomy of a Journal Article

Academic papers are essentially reports that scholars write to their peers—present and

future—about what they've done in their research, what they've found, and why they think

it's important. Thus, in a lot of fields they often have a structure reminiscent of the lab

reports you've written for science classes:

1. *Abstract*: A one-paragraph summary of the article: its purpose, methods, findings,

   and significance.

2. *Introduction*: An overview of the key question or problem that the paper addresses, why it is important, and the key
   conclusion(s) (i.e., thesis or theses) of the paper.

3. *Literature review*: A synthesis of all the relevant prior research (the so-called "academic

   literature" on the subject) that explains why the paper makes an original and important contribution to the body of
   knowledge.

4. *Data and methods*: An explanation of what data or information the author(s) used and what they did with it.

5. *Results*: A full explanation of the key findings of the study.

6. *Conclusion/discussion*: Puts the key findings or insights from the paper into their broader context; explains why they
   matter.

Not all papers are so "sciencey." For example, a historical or literary analysis doesn't necessarily

have a "data and methods" section; but they do explain and justify the research

question, describe how the authors' own points relate to those made in other relevant

articles and books, develop the key insights yielded by the analysis, and conclude by explaining

their significance. Some academic papers are review articles, in which the "data"

are published papers and the "findings" are key insights, enduring lines of debate, and/or

remaining unanswered questions.

Scholarly journals use a peer-review process to decide which articles merit publication. First, hopeful authors send their article manuscript to the journal editor, a role filled by some prominent scholar in the field. The editor reads over the manuscript and decides whether it seems worthy of peer-review. If it's outside the interests of the journal or is clearly inadequate, the editor will reject it outright. If it looks appropriate and sufficiently high quality, the editor will recruit a few other experts in the field to act as anonymous peer reviewers.

The editor will send the manuscript (scrubbed of identifying information) to the reviewers who will read it closely and provide a thorough critique. Is the research question driving the paper timely and important? Does the paper sufficiently and accurately review all of the relevant prior research? Are the information sources believable and the research methods rigorous? Are the stated results fully justified by the findings? Is the significance of the research clear? Is it well written? Overall, does the paper add new, trustworthy, and important knowledge to the field?

Reviewers send their comments to the editor who then decides whether to (1) reject the manuscript, (2) ask the author(s) to revise and resubmit the manuscript7, or (3) accept it for publication.

Editors send the reviewers' comments (again, with no identifying information) to authors along with their decisions.

A manuscript that has been revised and resubmitted usually goes out for peer-review again; editors often try to get reviews from one or two first-round reviewers as well as a new reviewer. The whole process, from start to finish, can easily take a year, and it is often another year before the paper appears in print.

Understanding the academic publication process and the structure of scholarly articles tells

you a lot about how to find, read and use these sources:

1. *Find them quickly.* Instead of paging through mountains of dubious web content, go right to the relevant scholarly article databases in order to quickly find the highest quality sources.
2. *Use the abstracts.* Abstracts tell you immediately whether or not the article you're holding is relevant or useful to the paper you're assigned to write. You shouldn't ever have the experience of reading the whole paper just to discover it's not useful.
3. *Read strategically.* Knowing the anatomy of a scholarly article tells you what you should be reading for in each section. For example, you don't necessarily need to understand every nuance of the literature review. You can just focus on why the authors claim that their own study is distinct from the ones that came before.
4. *Don't sweat the technical stuff.* Not every social scientist understands the intricacies of log-linear modeling of quantitative survey data; however, the reviewers definitely do, and they found the analysis to be well constructed. Thus, you can accept the findings as legitimate and just focus on the passages that explain the findings and their significance in plainer language.
5. *Use one article to find others.* If you have one really good article that's a few years old, you can use article databases to find newer articles that cited it in their own literature reviews. That immediately tells you which ones are on the same topic and offer newer findings. On the other hand, if your first source is very recent, the literature review section will describe the other papers in the same line of research.

You can look them up directly.

CC licensed content, Shared previously

Assessment: Investigating Your Source

For the source you've chosen—and it can be **anything** that relates to your final research essay topic—complete the following questionnaire. *It's important to note that not all of these answers may prove helpful to actually drafting the Evaluation Essay.* Instead, you're brainstorming possible content for that essay, and then picking what seems to be the most important features about your source from this initial exploration.

Source Evaluation Questionnaire

Title of Source:

How you found it:

1. Who wrote/presented this information? (If not an individual, who is responsible for publishing it?) Do a websearch on this individual or group. What do you learn?
2. Where was this source published or made available? What other types of articles, etc., does this publication have on offer?
3. Note one particular fact or bit of data that is included, here. Try to verify this fact by checking other sources. What do you learn?
4. Does the author seem to have any bias? In what way? Why do you suspect this? (Review the Understanding Bias page (https://courses.lumenlearning.com/englishcomp2kscopexmaster/chapter/understanding-bias/)to help.)
5. Does the source publication have any bias? In what way? Why do you suspect this?
6. What is this source's thesis or prevailing idea?
7. How does this source promote this main idea? In other words, how does it support its argument?
8. What does this source's primary audience seem to be? How do you know?
9. What is its primary rhetorical mode (logic, emotion, ethics)?
10. Does this source support, oppose, or remain neutral on your own paper's thesis?

Library Research as Problem-Solving

You'll probably engage the subscription article databases at different points in the process. For example, imagine you've been assigned a research paper that can focus on any topic relevant to the course. Imagine further that you don't have a clue about where to start and aren't entirely sure what counts as an appropriate topic in this discipline. A great approach is to find the top journals in the specific field of your course and browse through recent issues to see what people are publishing on. For example, when I assign an open-topic research paper in my Introduction to Sociology course, I suggest that students looking for a topic browse recent issues of *Social Problems* or *American Journal of Sociology* and find an article that looks interesting. They'll have a topic and—booyah!—their first source. An instructor of a class on kinesiology might recommend browsing *Human Movement Science*, the *Journal of Strength and Conditioning Research*, or *Perceptual and Motor Skills*.

When you have a topic and are looking for a set of sources, your biggest challenge is finding the right keywords. You'll never find the right sources without them. You'll obviously start with words and phrases from the assignment prompt, but you can't stop there.

As explained above, lower tier sources (such as Wikipedia) or the top-tier sources you already have are great for identifying alternative keywords, and librarians and other library staff are also well practiced at finding new approaches to try. Librarians can also point you to the best
databases for your topic as well.

As you assess your evidence and further develop your thesis through the writing process, you may need to seek additional sources. For example, imagine you're writing a paper about the added risks adolescents face when they have experienced their parents' divorce. As you synthesize the evidence about negative impacts, you begin to wonder if scholars have documented some positive impacts as well. Thus you delve back into the literature to look for more articles, find some more concepts and keywords (such as *resiliency*), assess new evidence, and revise your thinking to account for these broader perspectives. Your instructor may have asked you to turn in a bibliography weeks before the final paper draft.
You can check with your professor, but he or she is probably perfectly fine with you seeking additional sources as your thinking evolves. That's how scholars write.

Finding good sources is a much more creative task than it seems on the face of it. It's an extended problem-solving exercise, an iterative cycle of questions and answers. Go ahead and use Wikipedia to get broadly informed if you want. It won't corrupt your brain. But use it, and all other sources, strategically. You should eventually arrive at a core set of Tier 1 sources that will enable you to make a well informed and thoughtful argument in support of your thesis. It's also a good sign when you find yourself deciding that some of the first sources you found are no longer relevant to your thesis; that likely means that you have revised and specified your thinking and are well on your way to constructing the kind of self-driven in-depth analysis that your professor is looking for.

INTEGRATING SOURCES

Quotation Marks

Quotation marks (" ") set off a group of words from the rest of the text. Use quotation marks to indicate direct quotations of another person's words or to indicate a title. Quotation marks always appear in pairs.

Direct Quotations

A direct quotation is an exact account of what someone said or wrote. To include a direct quotation in your writing, enclose the words in quotation marks. An indirect quotation is a restatement of what someone said or wrote. An indirect quotation does not use the person's exact words. You do not need to use quotation marks for indirect quotations.

Direct quotation: Carly said, **"I'm not ever going back there again."**

Indirect quotation: Carly said that she would never go back there.

Writing at Work

Most word processing software is designed to catch errors in grammar, spelling, and punctuation. While this can be a useful tool, it is better to be well acquainted with the rules of punctuation than to leave the thinking to the computer. Properly punctuated writing will convey your meaning clearly. Consider the subtle shifts in meaning in the following sentences:

- The client said he thought our manuscript was garbage.
- The client said, "He thought our manuscript was garbage."

The first sentence reads as an indirect quote in which the client does not like the manuscript. But did he actually use the word "garbage"? (This would be alarming!) Or has the speaker paraphrased (and exaggerated) the client's words?

The second sentence reads as a direct quote from the client. But who is "he" in this sentence? Is it a third party?

Word processing software would not catch this because the sentences are not grammatically incorrect. However, the meanings of the sentences are not the same. Understanding punctuation will help you write what you mean, and in this case, could save a lot of confusion around the office!

Punctuating Direct Quotations

Quotation marks show readers another person's exact words. Often, you will want to identify who is speaking. You can do this at the beginning, middle, or end of the quote. Notice the use of commas and capitalized words.

Beginning: Madison said, **"L**et's stop at the farmers market to buy some fresh vegetables for dinner."

Middle: "Let's stop at the farmers market," Madison said, "to buy some fresh vegetables for dinner."

End: "Let's stop at the farmers market to buy some fresh vegetables for dinner," Madison said.

Speaker not identified: "Let's stop at the farmers market to buy some fresh vegetables for dinner."

Always capitalize the first letter of a quote even if it is not the beginning of the sentence. When using identifying words in the middle of the quote, the beginning of the second part of the quote does not need to be capitalized.

Use commas between identifying words and quotes. Quotation marks must be placed *after* commas and periods. Place quotation marks after question marks and exclamation points only if the question or exclamation is part of the quoted text.

Question is part of quoted text: The new employee asked, "When is lunch**?"**

Question is not part of quoted text: Did you hear her say you were "the next Picasso"**?**

Exclamation is part of quoted text: My supervisor beamed, "Thanks for all of your hard work!"

Exclamation is not part of quoted text: He said I "single-handedly saved the company thousands of dollars"!

Quotations within Quotations

Use single quotation marks (' ') to show a quotation within in a quotation.

Theresa said, "I wanted to take my dog to the festival, but the man at the gate said, 'No dogs allowed.'"

"When you say, 'I can't help it,' what exactly does that mean?"

"The instructions say, 'Tighten the screws one at a time.'"

Titles

Use quotation marks around titles of short works of writing, such as essays, songs, poems, short stories, and chapters in books. Usually, titles of longer works, such as books, magazines, albums, newspapers, and novels, are italicized.

"Annabelle Lee" is one of my favorite romantic poems.

The *New York Times* has been in publication since 1851.

Writing at Work

In many businesses, the difference between exact wording and a paraphrase is extremely important. For legal purposes, or for the purposes of doing a job correctly, it can be important to know exactly what the client, customer, or supervisor said. Sometimes, important details can be lost when instructions are paraphrased. Use quotes to indicate exact words where needed, and let your coworkers know the source of the quotation (client, customer, peer, etc.).

KEY TAKEAWAYS

- Use quotation marks to enclose direct quotes and titles of short works.
- Use single quotation marks to enclose a quote within a quote.
- Do not use any quotation marks for indirect quotations.

EXERCISES

1. Copy the following sentences onto your own sheet of paper, and correct them by adding quotation marks where necessary. If the sentence does not need any quotation marks, write *OK*.

- Yasmin said, I don't feel like cooking. Let's go out to eat.
- Where should we go? said Russell.
- Yasmin said it didn't matter to her.
- I know, said Russell, let's go to the Two Roads Juice Bar.
- Perfect! said Yasmin.
- Did you know that the name of the Juice Bar is a reference to a poem? asked Russell.
- I didn't! exclaimed Yasmin. Which poem?
- The Road Not Taken, by Robert Frost Russell explained.
- Oh! said Yasmin, Is that the one that starts with the line, Two roads diverged in a yellow wood?
- That's the one said Russell.

CC licensed content, Shared previously

Quotations

What this handout is about

Used effectively, quotations can provide important pieces of evidence and lend fresh voices and perspectives to your narrative. Used ineffectively, however, quotations clutter your text and interrupt the flow of your argument. This handout will help you decide when and how to quote like a pro.

When should I quote?

Use quotations at strategically selected moments. You have probably been told by teachers to provide as much evidence as possible in support of your thesis. But packing your paper with quotations will not necessarily strengthen your argument. The majority of your paper should still be your original ideas in your own words (after all, it's your paper). And quotations are only one type of evidence: well-balanced papers may also make use of paraphrases, data, and statistics. The types of evidence you use will depend in part on the conventions of the discipline or audience for which you are writing. For example, papers analyzing literature may rely heavily on direct quotations of the text, while papers in the social sciences may have more paraphrasing, data, and statistics than quotations.

1. Discussing specific arguments or ideas.

Sometimes, in order to have a clear, accurate discussion of the ideas of others, you need to quote those ideas word for word. Suppose you want to challenge the following statement made by John Doe, a well-known historian:

"At the beginning of World War Two, almost all Americans assumed the war would end quickly."

If it is especially important that you formulate a counterargument to this claim, then you might wish to quote the part of the statement that you find questionable and establish a dialogue between yourself and John Doe:

Historian John Doe has argued that in 1941 "almost all Americans assumed the war would end quickly" (Doe 223). Yet during the first six months of U.S. involvement, the wives and mothers of soldiers often noted in their diaries their fear that the war would drag on for years.

2. Giving added emphasis to a particularly authoritative source on your topic.

There will be times when you want to highlight the words of a particularly important and authoritative source on your topic. For example, suppose you were writing an essay about the differences between the lives of male and female slaves in the U.S. South. One of your most provocative sources is a narrative written by a former slave, Harriet Jacobs. It would then be appropriate to quote some of Jacobs's words:

Harriet Jacobs, a former slave from North Carolina, published an autobiographical slave narrative in 1861. She exposed the hardships of both male and female slaves but ultimately concluded that "slavery is terrible for men; but it is far more terrible for women."

In this particular example, Jacobs is providing a crucial first-hand perspective on slavery. Thus, her words deserve more exposure than a paraphrase could provide. Jacobs is quoted in Harriet A. Jacobs, Incidents in the Life of a Slave Girl, ed. Jean Fagan Yellin (Cambridge: Harvard University Press, 1987).

3. Analyzing how others use language.

This scenario is probably most common in literature and linguistics courses, but you might also find yourself writing about the use of language in history and social science classes. If the use of language is your primary topic, then you will obviously need to quote users of that language.

Examples of topics that might require the frequent use of quotations include:

Southern colloquial expressions in William Faulkner's Light in August

Ms. and the creation of a language of female empowerment

A comparison of three British poets and their use of rhyme

4. Spicing up your prose.

In order to lend variety to your prose, you may wish to quote a source with particularly vivid language. All quotations, however, must closely relate to your topic and arguments. Do not insert a quotation solely for its literary merits.

One example of a quotation that adds flair:

Calvin Coolidge's tendency to fall asleep became legendary. As H. L. Mencken commented in the American Mercury in 1933, "Nero fiddled, but Coolidge only snored."

How do I set up and follow up a quotation?

Once you've carefully selected the quotations that you want to use, your next job is to weave those quotations into your text. The words that precede and follow a quotation are just as important as the quotation itself. You can think of each quote as the filling in a sandwich: it may be tasty on its own, but it's messy to eat without some bread on either side of it. Your words can serve as the "bread" that helps readers digest each quote easily. Below are four guidelines for setting up and following up quotations.

In illustrating these four steps, we'll use as our example, Franklin Roosevelt's famous quotation, "The only thing we have to fear is fear itself."

1. Provide a context for each quotation.

Do not rely on quotations to tell your story for you. It is your responsibility to provide your reader with a context for the quotation. The context should set the basic scene for when, possibly where, and under what circumstances the quotation was spoken or written. So, in providing a context for our above example, you might write:

When Franklin Roosevelt gave his inaugural speech on March 4, 1933, he addressed a nation weakened and demoralized by economic depression.

2. Attribute each quotation to its source.

Tell your reader who is speaking. Here is a good test: try reading your text aloud. Could your reader determine without looking at your paper where your quotations begin? If not, you need to attribute the quote more noticeably.

Avoid getting into the "he/she said" attribution rut! There are many other ways to attribute quotes besides this construction. Here are a few alternative verbs, usually followed by "that":

add	remark	exclaim
announce	reply	state
comment	respond	estimate
write	point out	predict
argue	suggest	propose
declare	criticize	proclaim
note	complain	opine
observe	think	note

Different reporting verbs are preferred by different disciplines, so pay special attention to these in your disciplinary reading. If you're unfamiliar with the meanings of any of these words or others you find in your reading, consult a dictionary before using them.

3. Explain the significance of the quotation.

Once you've inserted your quotation, along with its context and attribution, don't stop! Your reader still needs your assessment of why the quotation holds significance for your paper. Using our Roosevelt example, if you were writing a paper on the first one-hundred days of FDR's administration, you might follow the quotation by linking it to that topic:

With that message of hope and confidence, the new president set the stage for his next one-hundred days in office and helped restore the faith of the American people in their government.

4. Provide a citation for the quotation.

All quotations, just like all paraphrases, require a formal citation. For more details about particular citation formats, see the UNC Library's citation tutorial (http://www2.lib.unc.edu/instruct/citations/). In general, you should remember one rule of thumb: Place the parenthetical reference or footnote/endnote number after—not within—the closed quotation mark.

Roosevelt declared, "The only thing we have to fear is fear itself" (Roosevelt, Public Papers 11).

Roosevelt declared, "The only thing we have to fear is fear itself."[1]

How much should I quote?

As few words as possible. Remember, your paper should primarily contain your own words, so quote only the most pithy and memorable parts of sources. Here are three guidelines for selecting quoted material judiciously.

1. Excerpt fragments.

Sometimes, you should quote short fragments, rather than whole sentences. Suppose you interviewed Jane Doe about her reaction to John F. Kennedy's assassination. She commented:

"I couldn't believe it. It was just unreal and so sad. It was just unbelievable. I had never experienced such denial. I don't know why I felt so strongly. Perhaps it was because JFK was more to me than a president. He represented the hopes of young people everywhere."

You could quote all of Jane's comments, but her first three sentences are fairly redundant. You might instead want to quote Jane when she arrives at the ultimate reason for her strong emotions:

Jane Doe grappled with grief and disbelief. She had viewed JFK, not just as a national figurehead, but as someone who "represented the hopes of young people everywhere."

2. Excerpt those fragments carefully!

Quoting the words of others carries a big responsibility. Misquoting misrepresents the ideas of others. Here's a classic example of a misquote:

John Adams has often been quoted as having said: "This would be the best of all possible worlds if there were no religion in it."

John Adams did, in fact, write the above words. But if you see those words in context, the meaning changes entirely. Here's the rest of the quotation:

Twenty times, in the course of my late reading, have I been on the point of breaking out, 'this would be the best of all possible worlds, if there were no religion in it!!!!' But in this exclamation, I should have been as fanatical as Bryant or Cleverly. Without religion, this world would be something not fit to be mentioned in public company—I mean hell.

As you can see from this example, context matters!

This example is from Paul F. Boller, Jr. and John George, They Never Said It: A Book of Fake Quotes, Misquotes, and Misleading Attributions (Oxford University Press, 1989).

3. Use block quotations sparingly.

There may be times when you need to quote long passages. However, you should use block quotations only when you fear that omitting any words will destroy the integrity of the passage. If that passage exceeds four lines (some sources say five), then set it off as a block quotation.

Here are a few general tips for setting off your block quotation—to be sure you are handling block quotes correctly in papers for different academic disciplines, check the index of the citation style guide you are using:

1. Set up a block quotation with your own words followed by a colon.
2. Indent. You normally indent 4-5 spaces for the start of a paragraph. When setting up a block quotation, indent the entire paragraph once from the left-hand margin.

3. Single space or double space within the block quotation, depending on the style guidelines of your discipline (MLA, CSE, APA, Chicago, etc.).
4. Do not use quotation marks at the beginning or end of the block quote—the indentation is what indicates that it's a quote.
5. Place parenthetical citation according to your style guide (usually after the period following the last sentence of the quote).
6. Follow up a block quotation with your own words.

So, using the above example from John Adams, here's how you might include a block quotation:

After reading several doctrinally rigid tracts, John Adams recalled the zealous ranting of his former teacher, Joseph Cleverly, and minister, Lemuel Bryant. He expressed his ambivalence toward religion in an 1817 letter to Thomas Jefferson:

> Twenty times, in the course of my late reading, have I been on the point of breaking out, 'this would be the best of all possible worlds, if there were no religion in it!!!!' But in this exclamation, I should have been as fanatical as Bryant or Cleverly. Without religion, this world would be something not fit to be mentioned in public company—I mean hell.

Adams clearly appreciated religion, even if he often questioned its promotion.

How do I combine quotation marks with other punctuation marks?

It can be confusing when you start combining quotation marks with other punctuation marks. You should consult a style manual for complicated situations, but the following two rules apply to most cases:

1) Keep periods and commas within quotation marks.

So, for example:

According to Professor Jones, Lincoln "feared the spread of slavery," but many of his aides advised him to "watch and wait."

In the above example, both the comma and period were enclosed in the quotation marks. The main exception to this rule involves the use of internal citations, which always precede the last period of the sentence. For example:

According to Professor Jones, Lincoln "feared the spread of slavery," but many of his aides advised him to "watch and wait" (Jones 143).

Note, however, that the period remains inside the quotation marks when your citation style involved superscript footnotes or endnotes. For example:

According to Professor Jones, Lincoln "feared the spread of slavery," but many of his aides advised him to "watch and wait."[2]

2) Place all other punctuation marks (colons, semicolons, exclamation marks, question marks) outside the quotation marks, except when they were part of the original quotation.

Take a look at the following examples:

The student wrote that the U. S. Civil War "finally ended around 1900"!

The coach yelled, "Run!"

In the first example, the author placed the exclamation point outside the quotation mark because she added it herself to emphasize the absurdity of the student's comment. The student's original comment had not included an exclamation mark. In the second example, the exclamation mark remains within the quotation mark because it is indicating the excited tone in which the coach yelled the command. Thus, the exclamation mark is considered to be part of the original quotation.

How do I indicate quotations within quotations?

If you are quoting a passage that contains a quotation, then you use single quotation marks for the internal quotation. Quite rarely, you quote a passage that has a quotation within a quotation. In that rare instance, you would use double quotation marks for the second internal quotation.

Here's an example of a quotation within a quotation:

In "The Emperor's New Clothes," Hans Christian Andersen wrote, "'But the Emperor has nothing on at all!' cried a little child."

Remember to consult your style guide to determine how to properly cite a quote within a quote.

When do I use those three dots (. . .)?

Whenever you want to leave out material from within a quotation, you need to use an ellipsis, which is a series of three periods, each of which should be preceded and followed by a space. So, an ellipsis in this sentence would look like . . . this. There are a few rules to follow when using ellipses:

1. Be sure that you don't fundamentally change the meaning of the quotation by omitting material.

Take a look at the following example: "The Writing Center is located on the UNC campus and serves the entire UNC community."

"The Writing Center . . . serves the entire UNC community."

The reader's understanding of the Writing Center's mission to serve the UNC community is not affected by omitting the information about its location.

2. Do not use ellipses at the beginning or ending of quotations, unless it's important for the reader to know that the quotation was truncated.

For example, using the above example, you would NOT need an ellipsis in either of these situations:

"The Writing Center is located on the UNC campus . . ."

The Writing Center " . . . serves the entire UNC community."

3. Use punctuation marks in combination with ellipses when removing material from the end of sentences or clauses.

For example, if you take material from the end of a sentence, keep the period in as usual.

"The boys ran to school, forgetting their lunches and books. Even though they were out of breath, they made it on time."

"The boys ran to school. . . . Even though they were out of breath, they made it on time."

Likewise, if you excerpt material at the end of clause that ends in a comma, retain the comma.

"The red car came to a screeching halt that was heard by nearby pedestrians, but no one was hurt."

"The red car came to a screeching halt . . . , but no one was hurt."

Is it ever okay to insert my own words or change words in a quotation?

Sometimes it is necessary for clarity and flow to alter a word or words within a quotation. You should make such changes rarely. In order to alert your reader to the changes you've made, you should always bracket the altered words. Here are a few examples of situations when you might need brackets.

1. Changing verb tense or pronouns in order to be consistent with the rest of the sentence.

Suppose you were quoting a woman who, when asked about her experiences immigrating to the United States, commented "nobody understood me." You might write:

Esther Hansen felt that when she came to the United States "nobody understood [her]."

In the above example, you've changed "me" to "her" in order to keep the entire passage in third person. However, you could avoid the need for this change by simply rephrasing:

"Nobody understood me," recalled Danish immigrant Esther Hansen.

2. Including supplemental information that your reader needs in order to understand the quotation.

For example, if you were quoting someone's nickname, you might want to let your reader know the full name of that person in brackets.

"The principal of the school told Billy [William Smith] that his contract would be terminated."

Similarly, if a quotation referenced an event with which the reader might be unfamiliar, you could identify that event in brackets.

"We completely revised our political strategies after the strike [of 1934]."

3. Indicating the use of nonstandard grammar or spelling.

In rare situations, you may quote from a text that has nonstandard grammar, spelling, or word choice. In such cases, you may want to insert [sic], which means "thus" or "so" in Latin. Using [sic] alerts your reader to the fact that this nonstandard language is not the result of a typo on your part. Always italicize "sic" and enclose it in brackets. There is no need to put a period at the end. Here's an example of when you might use [sic]:

Twelve-year-old Betsy Smith wrote in her diary, "Father is afraid that he will be guilty of beach [*sic*] of contract."

Here [*sic*] indicates that the original author wrote "beach of contract," not breach of contract, which is the accepted terminology.

4. Do not overuse brackets!

For example, it is not necessary to bracket capitalization changes that you make at the beginning of sentences. For example, suppose you were going to use part of this quotation:

"We never looked back, but the memory of our army days remained with us the rest of our lives."

If you wanted to begin a sentence with an excerpt from the middle of this quotation, there would be no need to bracket your capitalization changes.

"The memory of our army days remained with us the rest of our lives," commented Joe Brown, a World War II veteran.

Not

"[T]he memory of our army days remained with us the rest of our lives," commented Joe Brown, a World War II veteran.

Works consulted

We consulted these works while writing the original version of this handout. This is not a comprehensive list of resources on the handout's topic, and we encourage you to do your own research to find the latest publications on this topic. Please do not use this list as a model for the format of your own reference list, as it may not match the citation style you are using. For guidance on formatting citations, please see the UNC Library's citation tutorial (http://www2.lib.unc.edu/instruct/citations/).

Barzun, Jacques and Henry F. Graff. The Modern Researcher. 6th Edition. Harcourt Brace Jovanovich, 2004.

Booth, Wayne C., Gregory G. Colomb, and Joseph M. Williams. The Craft of Research, 2nd Edition. Chicago: University of Chicago Press, 2003.

Gibaldi, Joseph. MLA Handbook for Writers of Research Papers, 6th Edition. New York: The Modern Language Association of America, 2003.

Turabian, Kate L. A Manual for Writers of Term Papers, Theses, and Dissertations. 6th Edition. Chicago: University of Chicago Press, 1996.

Introduction of Borrowed Material

The basic idea is that you need to set up your quotes or paraphrases. Establish the credibility of your source. By reading your paragraph aloud, you will notice how well you have done this. Trust your ear. You will hear whether you have set up the quote at all—or whether you have used the same patterns of introduction over and over.

- Fit in the used material smoothly.
- Parenthetical citations are meant to be brief, so that they wont distract readers.
- Use brackets [like this] to indicate that you added words to the original quote.
- Avoid taking a quote out of context. The examples in the handbook illustrate awkward and revised source usage.
- Vary the verbs while still maintaining accuracy. Readers will notice such little touches.

Writers who fail to realize their options often end up with papers that are boring collections of quotes from others.

By varying verbs, first words of sentences, and types of sentences (simple, compound, complex), you will tend to write stronger papers. Such flexibility and variety—hallmarks of strong writing—are also necessary ingredients when integrating borrowed material.

CC licensed content, Original

A Typical Body Paragraph Pattern

(Remember, though, that this is not a formula. Vary your paragraphs, sentences, details, appeals, etc.)

1. Transition.
2. Topic sentence. This is your own. **Avoid** starting w/quote
3. Signal phrase: This is the setup for source use (1-3 sentences)
4. Source use (quote then cite, **or paraphrase one sentence** then cite)
5. Direct interpretation of the quote's words or the paraphrase's meaning(s) (1-4 sentences, right?)
6. Analyze, interpret, challenge, elaborate on, evaluate the cited material.

If you have space you might reproduce 3-5 all over again with another bit of cited material.

7. Craft a paragraph closing/transition/restated topic sentence/link to thesi

Make sure you nearly always end the paragraph on your own.

CC licensed content, Original

Transition Placemats

Using Sources Blending Source Material with Your Own Work

When working with sources, many students worry they are simply regurgitating ideas that others formulated. That is why it is important for you to develop your own assertions, organize your findings so that your own ideas are still the thrust of the paper, and take care not to rely too much on any one source, or your paper's content might be controlled too heavily by that source.

In practical terms, some ways to develop and back up your assertions include:

Blend sources with your assertions. Organize your sources before and as you write so that they blend, even within paragraphs. Your paper—both globally and at the paragraph level—should reveal relationships among your sources, and should also reveal the relationships between your own ideas and those of your sources.

Write an original introduction and conclusion. As much as is practical, make the paper's introduction and conclusion your own ideas or your own synthesis of the ideas inherent in your research. Use sources minimally in your introduction and conclusion.

Open and close paragraphs with originality. In general, use the openings and closing of your paragraphs to reveal your work—"enclose" your sources among your assertions. At a minimum, create your own topic sentences and wrap-up sentences for paragraphs.

Use transparent rhetorical strategies. When appropriate, outwardly practice such rhetorical strategies as analysis, synthesis, comparison, contrast, summary, description, definition, hierarchical structure, evaluation, hypothesis, generalization, classification, and even narration. Prove to your reader that you are thinking as you write.

Also, you must clarify where your own ideas end and the cited information begins. Part of your job is to help your reader draw the line between these two things, often by the way you create context for the cited information. A phrase such as "A 1979 study revealed that . . ." is an obvious announcement of citation to come. Another recommended technique is the insertion of the author's name into the text to announce the beginning of your cited information. You may worry that you are not allowed to give the actual names of sources you have studied in the paper's text, but just the opposite is true. In fact, the more respectable a source you cite, the more impressed your reader is likely to be with your material while reading. If you note that the source is the NASA Science website or an article by Stephen Jay Gould or a recent edition of *The Wall Street Journal* right in your text, you offer your readers immediate context without their having to guess or flip to the references page to look up the source.

What follows is an excerpt from a political science paper that clearly and admirably draws the line between writer and cited information:

The above political upheaval illuminates the reasons behind the growing Iranian hatred of foreign interference; as a result of this hatred, three enduring geopolitical patterns have evolved in Iran, as noted by John Limbert. First . . .

Note how the writer begins by redefining her previous paragraph's topic (political upheaval), then connects this to Iran's hatred of foreign interference, then suggests a causal relationship and ties her ideas into John Limbert's analysis—thereby announcing that a synthesis of Limbert's work is coming. This writer's work also becomes more credible and meaningful because, right in the text, she announces the name of a person who is a recognized authority in the field. Even in this short excerpt, it is obvious that this writer is using proper citation and backing up her own assertions with confidence and style.

The Paragraph Body: Supporting Your Ideas

Whether the drafting of a paragraph begins with a main idea or whether that idea surfaces in the revision process, once you have that main idea, you'll want to make sure that the idea has enough support. The job of the paragraph body is to develop and support the topic. Here's one way that you might think about it:

• Topic sentence: what is the main claim of your paragraph; what is the most important idea that you want your readers to take away from this paragraph?
• Support in the form of evidence: how can you prove that your claim or idea is true (or important, or noteworthy, or relevant)?
• Support in the form of analysis or evaluation: what discussion can you provide that helps your readers see the connection between the evidence and your claim?
• Transition: how can you help your readers move from the idea you're currently discussing to the next idea presented? (For more specific discussion about transitions, see the following section on "Developing Relationships between Ideas").

For more on methods of development that can help you to develop and organize your ideas within paragraphs, see "Patterns of Organization and Methods of Development" later in this section of this text.

Types of support might include
• Reasons.
• Facts.
• Statistics.
• Quotations.
• Examples.

Now that we have a good idea what it means to develop support for the main ideas of your paragraphs, let's talk about how to make sure that those supporting details are solid and convincing.

Good vs. Weak Support

What questions will your readers have? What will they need to know? What makes for good supporting details? Why might readers consider some evidence to be weak?

If you're already developing paragraphs, it's likely that you already have a plan for your essay, at least at the most basic level. You know what your topic is, you might have a working thesis, and you probably have at least a couple of supporting ideas in mind that will further develop and support your thesis.

So imagine you're developing a paragraph on one of these supporting ideas and you need to make sure that the support that you develop for this idea is solid. Considering some of the points about understanding and appealing to your audience (from the Audience and Purpose and the Prewriting sections of this text) can also be helpful in determining what your readers will consider good support and what they'll consider to be weak. Here are some tips on what to strive for and what to avoid when it comes to supporting details.

Good support
• Is relevant and focused (sticks to the point).
• Is well developed.

- Provides sufficient detail.
- Is vivid and descriptive.
- Is well organized.
- Is coherent and consistent.
- Highlights key terms and ideas.

Weak Support
- Lacks a clear connection to the point that it's meant to support.
- Lacks development.
- Lacks detail or gives too much detail.
- Is vague and imprecise.
- Lacks organization.
- Seems disjointed (ideas don't clearly relate to each other).
- Lacks emphasis of key terms and ideas.

Breaking, Combining, or Beginning New Paragraphs

Like sentence length, paragraph length varies. There is no single ideal length for "the perfect paragraph." There are some general guidelines, however. Some writing handbooks or resources suggest that a paragraph should be at least three or four sentences; others suggest that 100 to 200 words is a good target to shoot for. In academic writing, paragraphs tend to be longer, while in less formal or less complex writing, such as in a newspaper, paragraphs tend to be much shorter. Two-thirds to three-fourths of a page is usually a good target length for paragraphs at your current level of college writing. If your readers can't see a paragraph break on the page, they might wonder if the paragraph is ever going to end or they might lose interest.

The most important thing to keep in mind here is that the amount of space needed to develop one idea will likely be different than the amount of space needed to develop another. So when is a paragraph complete? The answer is, when it's fully developed. The guidelines above for providing good support should help.

Some signals that it's time to end a paragraph and start a new one include that
- You're ready to begin developing a new idea.
- You want to emphasize a point by setting it apart.
- You're getting ready to continue discussing the same idea but in a different way (e.g. shifting from comparison to contrast).
- You notice that your current paragraph is getting too long (more than three-fourths of a page or so), and you think your writers will need a visual break.
Some signals that you may want to combine paragraphs include that
- You notice that some of your paragraphs appear to be short and choppy.
- You have multiple paragraphs on the same topic.
- You have undeveloped material that needs to be united under a clear topic.

Finally, paragraph number is a lot like paragraph length. You may have been asked in the past to write a five paragraph essay. There's nothing inherently wrong with a five-paragraph essay, but just like sentence length and paragraph length, the number of paragraphs in an essay depends upon what's needed to get the job done. There's really no way to know that until you start writing. So try not to worry too much about the proper length and number of things. Just start writing and see where the essay and the paragraphs take you. There will be plenty of time to sort out the organization in the revision process. You're not trying to fit pegs into holes here. You're letting your ideas unfold. Give yourself—and them—the space to let that happen.

Developing Relationships Between Ideas

So you have a main idea, and you have supporting ideas, but how can you be sure that your readers will understand the relationships between them? How are the ideas tied to each other? One way to emphasize these relationships is through the use of clear transitions between ideas. Like every other part of your essay, transitions have a job to do. They form logical connections between the ideas presented in an essay or paragraph, and they give readers clues that reveal how you want them to think about (process, organize, or use) the topics presented.

Why are Transitions Important?

Transitions signal the order of ideas, highlight relationships, unify concepts, and let readers know what's coming next or remind them about what's already been covered. When instructors or peers comment that your writing is choppy, abrupt, or needs to "flow better," those are some signals that you might need to work on building some better transitions into your writing. If a reader comments that she's not sure how something relates to your thesis or main idea, a transition is probably the right tool for the job.

When Is the Right Time to Build in Transitions?

There's no right answer to this question. Sometimes transitions occur spontaneously, but just as often (or maybe even more often) good transitions are developed in revision. While drafting, we often write what we think, sometimes without much reflection about how the ideas fit together or relate to one another. If your thought process jumps around a lot (and that's okay), it's more likely that you will need to pay careful attention to reorganization and to providing solid transitions as you revise.

When you're working on building transitions into an essay, consider the essay's overall organization. Consider using reverse outlining and other organizational strategies presented in this text to identify key ideas in your essay and to get a clearer look at how the ideas can be best organized. This can help you determine where transitions are needed.

Let's take some time to consider the importance of transitions at the sentence level and transitions between paragraphs.

Sentence-Level Transitions

Transitions between sentences often use "connecting words" to emphasize relationships between one sentence and another. A friend and coworker suggests the "something old something new" approach, meaning that the idea behind a transition is to introduce something new while connecting it to something old from an earlier point in the essay or paragraph. Here are some examples of ways that writers use connecting words (highlighted with red text and italicized) to show connections between ideas in adjacent sentences:

To Show Similarity
When I was growing up, my mother taught me to say "please" and "thank you" as one small way that I could show appreciation and respect for others. *In the same way*, I have tried to impress the importance of manners onmy own children.
Other connecting words that show similarity include also, similarly, and likewise.

To Show Contrast

Some scientists take the existence of black holes for granted; however, in 2014, a physicist at the University of North Carolina claimed to have mathematically proven that they do not exist.

Other connecting words that show contrast include in spite of, on the other hand, in contrast, and yet.

To Exemplify

The cost of college tuition is higher than ever, so students are becoming increasingly motivated to keep costs as low as possible. For example, a rising number of students are signing up to spend their first two years at a less costly community college before transferring to a more expensive four-year school to finish their degrees.

Other connecting words that show example include for instance, specifically, and to illustrate.

To Show Cause and Effect

Where previously painters had to grind and mix their own dry pigments with linseed oil inside their studios, in the 1840s, new innovations in pigments allowed paints to be premixed in tubes. Consequently, this new technology facilitated the practice of painting outdoors and was a crucial tool for impressionist painters, such as Monet, Cezanne, Renoir, and Cassatt.

Other connecting words that show cause and effect include therefore, so, and thus.

To Show Additional Support

When choosing a good trail bike, experts recommend 120–140 millimeters of suspension travel; that's the amount that the frame or fork is able to flex or compress. Additionally, they recommend a 67–69 degree head-tube angle, as a steeper head-tube angle allows for faster turning and climbing.

Other connecting words that show additional support include also, besides, equally important, and in addition.

A Word of Caution

Single-word or short-phrase transitions can be helpful to signal a shift in ideas within a paragraph, rather than between paragraphs (see the discussion below about transitions between paragraphs). But it's also important to understand that these types of transitions shouldn't be frequent within a paragraph. As with anything else that happens in your writing, they should be used when they feel natural and feel like the right choice. Here are some examples to help you see the difference between transitions that feel like they occur naturally and transitions that seem forced and make the paragraph awkward to read:

Too Many Transitions: The Impressionist painters of the late 19th century are well known for their visible brush strokes, for their ability to convey a realistic sense of light, and for their everyday subjects portrayed in outdoor settings. In spite of this fact, many casual admirers of their work are unaware of the scientific innovations that made it possible this movement in art to take place. Then, In 1841, an American painter named John Rand invented the collapsible paint tube. To illustrate the importance of this invention, pigments previously had to be ground and mixed in a fairly complex process that made it difficult for artists to travel with them. For example, the mixtures were commonly stored in pieces of pig bladder to keep the paint from drying out. In addition, when working with their palettes, painters had to puncture the bladder, squeeze out some paint, and then mend the bladder again to keep the rest of the paint mixture from drying out. Thus, Rand's collapsible tube freed the painters from these cumbersome and messy processes, allowing artists to be more mobile and to paint in the open air.

Subtle Transitions that Aid Reader Understanding: The Impressionist painters of the late 19th century are well known for their visible brush strokes, for their ability to convey a realistic sense of light, for their everyday subjects portrayed in outdoor settings. However, many casual admirers of their work are unaware of the scientific innovations that made it possible for this movement in art to take place. In 1841, an American painter named John Rand invented the collapsible paint tube. Before this invention, pigments had to be ground and mixed in a fairly complex process that made it difficult for artists to travel with them. The mixtures were commonly stored in pieces of pig bladder to keep the paint from drying out. When working with their palettes, painters had to puncture the bladder, squeeze out some paint, and then mend the bladder again to keep the rest of the paint mixture from drying out. Rand's collapsible tube freed the painters from these cumbersome and messy processes, allowing artists to be more mobile and to paint in the open air.

Transitions between Paragraphs and Sections

It's important to consider how to emphasize the relationships not just between sentences but also between paragraphs in your essay. Here are a few strategies to help you show your readers how the main ideas of your paragraphs relate to each other and also to your thesis.

Use Signposts

Signposts are words or phrases that indicate where you are in the process of organizing an idea; for example, signposts might indicate that you are introducing a new concept, that you are summarizing an idea, or that you are concluding your thoughts. Some of the most common signposts include words and phrases like first, then, next, finally, in sum, and in conclusion. Be careful not to overuse these types of transitions in your writing. Your readers will quickly find them tiring or too obvious. Instead, think of more creative ways to let your readers know where they are situated within the ideas presented in your essay. You might say, "The first problem with this practice is…" Or you might say, "The next thing to consider is…" Or you might say, "Some final thoughts about this topic are…."

Use Forward-Looking Sentences at the End of Paragraphs

Sometimes, as you conclude a paragraph, you might want to give your readers a hint about what's coming next. For example, imagine that you're writing an essay about the benefits of trees to the environment and you've just wrapped up a paragraph about how trees absorb pollutants and provide oxygen. You might conclude with a forward-looking sentence like this: "Trees benefits to local air quality are important, but surely they have more to offer our communities than clean air." This might conclude a paragraph (or series of paragraphs) and then prepare your readers for additional paragraphs to come that cover the topics of trees' shade value and ability to slow water evaporation on hot summer days. This transitional strategy can be tricky to employ smoothly. Make sure that the conclusion of your paragraph doesn't sound like you're leaving your readers hanging with the introduction of a completely new or unrelated topic.

Use Backward-Looking Sentences at the Beginning of Paragraphs

Rather than concluding a paragraph by looking forward, you might instead begin a paragraph by looking back. Continuing with the example above of an essay about the value of trees, let's think about how we might begin a new paragraph or section by first taking a moment to look back. Maybe you just concluded a paragraph on the topic of trees' ability to decrease soil erosion and you're getting ready to talk about how they provide habitats for urban wildlife. Beginning the opening of a new paragraph or section of the essay with a backward-looking transition might look something like this: "While their benefits to soil and water conservation are great, the value that trees provide to our urban wildlife also cannot be overlooked."

Evaluate Transitions for Predictability or Conspicuousness

Finally, the most important thing about transitions is that you don't want them to become repetitive or too obvious. Reading your draft aloud is a great revision strategy for so many reasons, and revising your essay for transitions is no exception to this rule. If you read your essay aloud, you're likely to hear the areas that sound choppy or abrupt. This can help you make note of areas where transitions need to be added. Repetition is another problem that can be easier to spot if you read your essay aloud. If you notice yourself using the same transitions over and over again, take time to find some alternatives. And if the transitions frequently stand out as you read aloud, you may want to see if you can find some subtler strategies.

CC licensed content, Shared previously

- The Paragraph Body from The Word on College Reading and Writing. **Authored by**: Monique Babin, Clackamas Community College Carol Burnell, Clackamas Community College Susan Pesznecker, Portland State University. **Provided by**: Open Textbook Library. **Located at**: https://open.umn.edu/opentextbooks/BookDetail.aspx?bookId=471 (https://open.umn.edu/opentextbooks/BookDetail.aspx?bookId=471). **Project**: Center for Open Education. **License**: *CC BY-NC: Attribution-NonCommercial (https://creativecommons.org/licenses/by-nc/4.0/)*

Using Sources Creatively

Using Sources Creatively

Heather Logan

(printable version here (http://writing2.richmond.edu/writing/wweb/creatsrcprint.html))

When writing papers that require the use of outside source material, it is often tempting to cite only direct quotations from your sources. If, however, this is the only method of citation you choose, your paper will become nothing more than a series of quotations linked together by a few connecting words. Your paper will seem to be a collection of others' thoughts and will contain little thinking on your part.

To avoid falling into this trap, follow a few simple pointers:

- **Avoid using long quotations merely as space-fillers**. While this is an attractive option when faced with a ten-page paper, the overuse of long quotations gives the reader the impression you cannot think for yourself.
- **Don't use only direct quotations**. Try using paraphrases in addition to your direct quotations. To the reader, the effective use of paraphrases indicates that you took the time to think about the meaning behind the quote's words. (For further assistance see our materials on "Using Paraphrases (http://writing2.richmond.edu/writing/wweb/paraphrs.html).")
- When introducing direct quotations, try to **use a variety of verbs in your signal phrases**. Don't always rely on stock verbs such as "states" or "says." Think for a little while about the purpose of your quotation and then choose a context-appropriate verb.

Also, when using direct quotations try qualifying them in a novel or interesting manner. Depending on the system of documentation you're using, the signal phrases don't always have to introduce the quotation.

For example, instead of saying:

> "None of them knew the color of the sky" is the opening line of Stephen Crane's short story, "The Open Boat" (339). This implies the idea that "all sense of certainty" in the lives of these men is gone (Wolford 18).

Try saying:

> "None of them knew the color of the sky," the opening line of Stephen Crane's, "The Open Boat," implies that "all sense of certainty" in the lives of these men is gone (Crane 339; Wolford 18).

The combination of these two sentences into one is something different. It shows thought on the writer's part in how to combine direct quotations in an interesting manner.

CC licensed content, Shared previously

Assessment: Practice Quoting

Responsible academic writing involves a good deal of direct quotation from sources. Let's practice that now, to make sure that we've got the finer points figured out by the time the essay is due.

Find a quote from the original article that you think will serve you well in your Source Evaluation Essay.

- Include an introductory "signal" phrase that cues us in on the context for the quote, and then the quote itself. Follow this quote with a phrase or sentence in your own words that summarizes, interprets, or explains the quote in your own words.

This 3-step process is sometimes referred to as a **"quote sandwich"** and is useful for every time you'd like to incorporate a quote into an academic essay you're writing.

If you have any questions at all about using quotations in your writing, please include them in your submission.

This work is just a draft—you may choose to use it or not in the final version of your essay at your discretion.

CC licensed content, Shared previously

- Composition II. **Authored by**: Alexis McMillan-Clifton. **Provided by**: Tacoma Community College. **Located at**: http://www.tacomacc.edu (http://www.tacomacc.edu). **Project**: Kaleidoscope Open Course Initiative. **License**: *CC BY: Attribution (https://creativecommons.org/licenses/by/4.0/)*
- Image of sandwich. **Authored by**: James Yu. **Located at**: https://flic.kr/p/ki52 (https://flic.kr/p/ki52). **License**: *CC BY-NC-SA: Attribution-NonCommercial-ShareAlike (https://creativecommons.org/licenses/by-nc-sa/4.0/)*

When to Quote & When to Paraphrase

"When to Quote and When to Paraphrase" was written by Brianna Jerman

Academic writing requires authors to connect information from outside sources to their own ideas in order to establish credibility and produce an effective argument.

Sometimes, the rules surrounding source integration and plagiarism may seem confusing, so many new writers err on the side of caution by using the simplest form of integration: direct quotation. However, using direct quotes is not always the best way to use a source. Paraphrasing or summarizing a text is sometimes a more effective means of supporting a writer's argument than directly quoting. Taking into consideration the purpose of their own writing and the purpose of utilizing the outside source, authors should seek to vary the ways in which they work sources into their own writing.

Paraphrasing and quoting are two of the three ways an author can integrate sources. The two methods are closely related, and therefore, can sometimes be confused with one another. Quoting borrows the exact wording used in a source and is indicated by placing quotes around the borrowed material. Paraphrasing, on the other hand, borrows an idea found in a shorter passage but communicates this idea using different words and word order. While it is acceptable to loosely follow a similar structure, paraphrasing requires more than simply changing a few of the original words to synonyms. Both paraphrasing and directly quoting have their merit, but they should be used at different times for different purposes. An author chooses to use one of these strategies depending on why the source is being used and what information the source provides.

When to Paraphrase

Paraphrasing provides an author the opportunity to tailor the passage for the purpose of his or her own essay, which cannot always be done when using a direct quote. Paraphrasing should be used to

- Further explain or simplify a passage that may be difficult to understand. It could be that the topic, such as the process of extracting stem cells, is particularly difficult to follow, or that the author has used language that further complicates the topic. In such situations, paraphrasing allows an author to clarify or simplify a passage so the audience can better understand the idea.
- Establish the credibility of the author. In connection to the above point, paraphrasing a complicated passage can help the author establish trust with his or her audience. If an author directly quotes a difficult passage without analysis or further explanation, it may appear that he or she does not understand the idea. Paraphrasing not only clarifies the idea in the passage but also illustrates that the writer, since he or she can articulate this difficult message to the reader, is knowledgeable about the topic and should be trusted.
- Maintain the flow of the writing. Each author has a unique voice, and using direct quotes can interrupt this voice. Too many quotes can make an essay sound choppy and difficult to follow. Paraphrasing can help communicate an important idea in a passage or source without interrupting the flow of the essay.
- Eliminate less relevant information. Since paraphrasing is written using the author's own words, he or she can be more selective in what information from a passage should be included or omitted. While an author should not manipulate a passage unnecessarily, paraphrasing allows an author to leave out unrelated details that would have been part of a direct quote.
- Communicate relevant statistics and numerical data. A lot of times, sources offer statistical information about a topic that an author may find necessary to developing his or her own argument. For example, statistics about the percentage of mothers who work more than one job may be useful to explaining how the economy has affected children rearing practices. Directly quoting statistics such as this should be avoided.

When to Quote

Direct quotes should be used sparingly, but when they are used, they can be a powerful rhetorical tool. As a rule, avoid using long quotes when possible, especially those longer than three lines. When quotes are employed, they should be used to

- Provide indisputable evidence of an incredible claim. Directly quoting a source can show the audience exactly what the source says so there is not suspicion of misinterpretation on the author's part.
- Communicate an idea that is stated in a particularly striking or unique way. A passage should be quoted if the source explains an idea in the best way possible or in a way that cannot be reworded. Additionally, quoting should be used when the original passage is particularly moving or striking.
- Serve as a passage for analysis. If an author is going to analyze the quote or passage, the exact words should be included in the essay either before or following the author's analysis.
- Provide direct evidence for or proof of an author's own claim. An author can use a direct quote as evidence for a claim he or she makes. The direct quote should follow the author's claim and a colon, which indicates that the following passage is evidence of the statement that precedes it.
- Support or clarify information you've already reported from a source. Similar to the above principle, an author can use a direct quote as further evidence or to emphasize a claim found in the source. This strategy should be used when an idea from a source is particularly important to an author's own work.
- Provide a definition of a new or unfamiliar term or phrase. When using a term that is used or coined by the source's author or that is unfamiliar to most people, use direct quotes to show the exact meaning of the phrase or word according to the original source.

CC licensed content, Shared previously

- When to Quote and When to Paraphrase. **Authored by**: Brianna Jerman. **Provided by**: WritingCommons. **Located at**: http://writingcommons.org/open-text/research-methods-methodologies/integrate-evidence/summarize-paraphrase-sources/692-when-to-quote-and-when-to-paraphrase (http://writingcommons.org/open-text/research-methods-methodologies/integrate-evidence/summarize-paraphrase-sources/692-when-to-quote-and-when-to-paraphrase). **License**: *CC BY-NC-ND: Attribution-NonCommercial-NoDerivatives (https://creativecommons.org/licenses/by-nc-nd/4.0/)*

Discussion: Practice Paraphrasing

Academic writing also involves heavy use of paraphrasing sources. Paraphrasing is actually much more common than quoting, particularly in APA-style writing.

Paraphrasing has several advantages:

- it lets you keep a consistent tone and voice throughout the essay
- it demonstrates your mastery of the concepts coming from outside sources
- it lets you be flexible in wording and vocabulary to best meet the needs of your readers

Paraphrasing seems simple on the surface: it's just putting another author's ideas into your own original words. In practice, though, this is one of the most challenging aspects of writing academic work.

To help us all feel more comfortable and confident with our paraphrasing skills, let's practice it here.

In your post, copy and paste the original wording (a direct quote) from the source you're using for the Source Evaluation Essay. Be sure to include the title of the source and a link to it, if possible, and put the quote inside of quotation marks.

Beneath this quote, draft a paraphrase that states the idea of the quotation in unique language. The paraphrase should include a "signal" phrase, so that we have some context for where it's coming from. Guidance about how to draft a paraphrase can be found in earlier module contents.

Your post should be about 100-200 words. It doesn't have to be grammatically perfect, but should use standard English (no text-speak, please) and normal capitalization rules.

You will also need to return to this Discussion to **reply to at least two** of your classmates' posts. Content could include, but is not limited to, any of the following: Commenting on the style or quality of your classmate's paraphrase. Be sure to point out if the paraphrase contains too much borrowed language from the original article that your classmate may not have noticed.

Responses are weighed as heavily as your initial posting, and should be roughly as long (100-200 words) when combined. Responses should indicate you've read your classmate's post carefully. Include specific details from the post you're responding to in your reply.

Signal Phrases

For us to Appreciate Your Thinking, Use These!

If readers cannot tell where a source begins or ends—forget about whether or not it's credible—then the paper will feature serious problems. At all points, make it clear where you begin or end. Some of the drafts rely on summaries where it's not clear where the writer's source use starts.

Other papers—and this is common—start with setup, show a summary (after which there's no citation) and then have the writer's interpretation *and then more source material*. The problem here would be that the best part is the writer's interpretation and it's hidden between two citations. . . only there's just one citation where there should be two. So readers get distracted both by the lack of clarity and the missing citation.

Check for this in one's writing. Thanks!

> The following link from the Shepard Academy overviews signal phrases (http://shepardacademyjuniorblockspring.weebly.com/integrating-research-into-your-essay.html) and offers some useful models.

Lastly, remember that using no signal phrases is also a choice which signals something to readers: that you either didn't know the source context/credibility or could not be bothered to let the audience know!

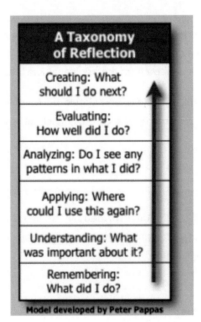

Assessment: Signalling/Paraphrasing/Quoting

Directions:

1. Find any 4 pieces of information that you have found from your research. This information should come from at least four different sources that you have found to be credible and useful to your research. Once you have identified these sources, do the following:

2. Copy one paragraph from the source that includes information that you might want to use in your research paper. Type the section out EXACTLY as it is written in the original. **(1 point)**

3. Take **one piece** of specific information from the original information and write a direct quote using those exact words The direct quote needs to contain a **signal phrases and use MLA in-text citations. (2 points)**

4. Take the **same** information that you've just quoted and write it again,**paraphrasing** it into your own words. **Remember to use MLA in-text citations. (2 points)**

Example (Using MLA In-text citation rules):

Original

About half of the rise in sea level is due to thermal expansion. In addition oceans are rising because ice is melting. So far, most of that water has come from mountain glaciers and ice caps. If the Greenland ice sheet were to melt completely, it would release enough water to raise the sea level by 7 meters. West Antarctica's melting would raise sea level by over 5 meters and East Antarctica by 50 meters. If the Earth were to lose just 8% of its ice, the consequences would be horrific. New York, London, Shanghai, and other low-lying cities would be submerged.

Direct Quote

According to Lonnie G. Thompson and Gioietta Kuo in the article, "Climate Change" "If the Earth were to lose just 8% of its ice, the consequences would be horrific. New York, London, Shanghai, and other low-lying cities would be submerged."

Paraphrase

According to Lonnie G. Thompson and Gioetta Kuo in the article, "Climate Change" even if the earth lost only 8% of its frozen waters, many cities below sea level would be engulfed under water.

> You will **repeat this process 4 times,** for a total of 4 sets of quotes & paraphrases.

Integration Tips in Preparation for Peer Editing or Editing

The following comments can be applied either to one's paper or others' work. Each challenge appears enough that it is worth noting generally.

We shouldn't be seeing many quotes at the starts or ends of paragraphs for the obvious reason that they would not get integrated.

You're not complimenting a reader's intelligence if you define, say, drug use or what a computer game is. That would be filler.

Sometimes, students pad papers by overusing long quotes. Avoid this. Those quotes are rarely that well-worded. Mostly, they are used for filler. Summarize so you can set up interpretations and commentary instead..

Consider that the default source use option isn't quoting, but paraphrase. With that in mind, we should see drafts which contain paraphrases.

Topic Sentences Related to the Thesis? Where are These Legendary Creatures?

Early in semesters, students get caught deferring—passively letting sources take over—far too much. I cannot tell what your topic sentences are, much less the causes—even much less the ways that those causes *relate* to the claim you are making. Partly, this is because the thesis statements were too broad and didn't argue much. A valid thesis must be an arguable opinion about which others may disagree. It's not a fact. If the claim you're working with is one on which a book could be based, it's too broad!

Consider recognizing the boring, obvious causes outright in your introduction, but then pivoting to make some claim about lesser-known causes that must be known if the topic is to be understood properly. *You* provide those lesser-known causes while acknowledging the ones most other people immediately think about. Again, show that you know how to get beyond the obvious. (Read a few papers and see if anyone's causes taught you anything or were surprising in how they were combined with the other causes.) The claims must change so that you show how the causes work together—which are relatively more or less important.

Oh, and add transitions . . . . there ought to be a logic that you provide to readers as to how the causes are ordered. Causes being time-based, that should be easy, but you can focus on importance as well. Not all causes are equally important, so not all causes get equal attention.

Setup is Something Critical Readers Expect

Provide a signal phrase. It's a must. Readers need to know that you know why a source is valid. Don't just name drop. If you say that Robinson says _____ about video games, who are good readers to care about Robinson yet? The *yet* is the key. It's for you to establish. Use a signal phrase that does this.

- Save author's name for the in-text citation if there's no page to put in there, as there wouldn't be a page with a HTML database article or a website. There would be a page for a book or PDF article.
- Establish the credentials and context in a signal phrase. **Example:** In his acclaimed 1991 book on Africa's migration crisis, Harvard researcher Tudo Bom notes

That example has time, status, context, and name all folded in. See how much better this is than "cold quoting"—starting a sentence with a quote. If you compound the problem by not following up with any interpretation, readers are checked out and your impressive quote has utterly backfired. This is what we expect at the college level.

Interpretation: Comment to Varying Extents and Adopt Tones

Readers are less interested in a quote than in what the writer does with it.

Do more writing around the quote (signal phrase, interpretation) than the quote is long. If you can start there, you might have an integrated paragraph. There are writing moves that ought to occur after a quote.

Statistics and misleadingly vivid, atypical cases got overused in too many people's drafts. Instead of marshaling support for your side, they erode credibility.

"In other words," is a common after-citation move.

Relate the cited material to the topic sentence and/or the thesis claim. Do something afterwards!

In no case should I be seeing over 60% of any paragraph coming from sources. (Summaries, remember, are from "them" and are theirs.)

These are not skill-based issues, folks. They are attentiveness challenges. We are overlooking the basics and filling space. Having errors like the extra spaces in the heading, around the title, between paragraphs, etc., will lead to automatic letter-grade deductions by most instructors. The topics will become more arguable if you break them down.

Why not note that "In discussions of the supposed link between video games and violence, television media have tended to suppose _____ and _____; this paper instead focuses on _____." Set apart your paper. In my example, too, you'll see that some people in D1 entirely mistook the purpose and ended up supporting those mistaken media presumptions rather than arguing anything of their own.

Think about what you think here. Read aloud the work you have. You'll notice gaps in logic, areas needing transitions, and unfounded presumptions needing reworking. You can do it!

CC licensed content, Original

Proper Source Use in Paragraphs

Function of Source Use

You use sources as a form of backup for what you write. They support your claims. This means that you own your paper

Consequences of the String of Pearls Effect

Using a single source several times in a row and then moving on as if some writing occurred is a common writing problem. How great a percentage of an average body paragraph should come from the source? Answers vary, of course, depending on your purpose and the sophistication of your topic. However, if you consistently let the sources take over more than one-third of your body paragraphs, you will not be a successful arguer, thinker, or writer.

If you consistently string together a bunch of quotes, then readers are left with unused material. If you have two or three quotes in a row, that means you did not interpret them. For some reason, many writers think that the quotation marks are magic, as if the quotes speak–or mean something–for themselves. They don't. If you think of the quotes as excuses for you to discuss their meaning, you will be much better off.

We call the stringing together of paraphrases or quotes "the string of pearls effect." What is the effect on readers of such lists?

I usually tell students that readers need lots of prompts and reminders. Say things again, even if you think the quote did a good job of making meaning. Tell readers what something means–just don't use "I" or "you" as you follow up on the quote. The ends of paragraphs are where things tend to fall apart, I think. Succeed in synthesizing your source, in using it and proving the meaning of source information.

With cited material, follow up by

1. linking the paraphrase/quote to the paragraph's topic sentence,
2. linking the cited information to the thesis
3. restating the relevance, credibility, or context of the source material
4. setting up a transition to the upcoming paragraph(s)
5. using a signal phrase like "In other words, . . ." and launching into a direct interpretation of the cited bit

Use your options. Take an active approach so papers–especially the research essay–actually use the sources actively.

A Typical Paragraph Pattern

(Remember, though, that this is not a formula. Vary your paragraphs, sentences, details, appeals, etc.)

> Topic sentence. This is your own. **Avoid** starting w/quote (Why is this so?)
>
> setup for source use (1-3 sentences)
>
> source use (quote then cite, **or paraphrase one sentence** then cite)
>
> direct interpretation of the quote's words or the paraphrase's meaning(s) (1-4 sentences, right?)
>
> paragraph closing/transition/restated topic sentence/link to thesis
>
> End the paragraph on your own with emphasis and power.

In large part, how well you do from here on out depends on how well you learn MLA citing and the standards of writing academic arguments. If we're stuck with poorly-written paragraphs, the papers will only reach a certain level of quality.

CC licensed content, Original

- Proper Source Use in Paragraphs. **Authored by**: Joshua Dickinson. **Provided by**: Jefferson Community College. **Located at**: http://www.sunyjefferson.edu (http://www.sunyjefferson.edu). **Project**: ENG 101. **License**: *CC BY-SA: Attribution-ShareAlike (https://creativecommons.org/licenses/by-sa/4.0/)*

CITING SOURCES

Citing and Referencing Techniques

LEARNING OBJECTIVE

By the end of this section, you will be able to:

- Apply American Psychological Association (APA) style formatting guidelines for citations.

This section covers the nitty-gritty details of in-text citations. You will learn how to format citations for different types of source materials, whether you are citing brief quotations, paraphrasing ideas, or quoting longer passages. You will also learn techniques you can use to introduce quoted and paraphrased material effectively. Keep this section handy as a reference to consult while writing the body of your paper.

Formatting Cited Material: The Basics

As noted in previous sections of this book, in-text citations usually provide the name of the author(s) and the year the source was published. For direct quotations, the page number must also be included. Use past-tense verbs when introducing a quote—"Smith found..." and not "Smith finds...."

Formatting Brief Quotations

For brief quotations—fewer than forty words—use quotation marks to indicate where the quoted material begins and ends, and cite the name of the author(s), the year of publication, and the page number where the quotation appears in your source. Remember to include commas to separate elements within the parenthetical citation. Also, avoid redundancy. If you name the author(s) in your sentence, do not repeat the name(s) in your parenthetical citation. Review following the examples of different ways to cite direct quotations.

Chang (2008) emphasized that "engaging in weight-bearing exercise consistently is one of the single best things women can do to maintain good health" (p. 49).

The author's name can be included in the body of the sentence or in the parenthetical citation. Note that when a parenthetical citation appears at the end of the sentence, it comes **after** the closing quotation marks and **before** the period. The elements within parentheses are separated by commas.

Weight Training for Women (Chang, 2008) claimed that "engaging in weight-bearing exercise consistently is one of the single best things women can do to maintain good health" (p. 49).

Weight Training for Women claimed that "engaging in weight-bearing exercise consistently is one of the single best things women can do to maintain good health" (Chang, 2008, p. 49).

Including the title of a source is optional.

In Chang's 2008 text *Weight Training for Women*, she asserts, "Engaging in weight-bearing exercise is one of the single best things women can do to maintain good health" (p. 49).

The author's name, the date, and the title may appear in the body of the text. Include the page number in the parenthetical citation. Also, notice the use of the verb *asserts* to introduce the direct quotation.

"Engaging in weight-bearing exercise," Chang asserts, "is one of the single best things women can do to maintain good health" (2008, p. 49).

You may begin a sentence with the direct quotation and add the author's name and a strong verb before continuing the quotation.

Formatting Paraphrased and Summarized Material

When you paraphrase or summarize ideas from a source, you follow the same guidelines previously provided, except that you are not required to provide the page number where the ideas are located. If you are summing up the main findings of a research article, simply providing the author's name and publication year may suffice, but if you are paraphrasing a more specific idea, consider including the page number.

Read the following examples.

Chang (2008) pointed out that weight-bearing exercise has many potential benefits for women.

Here, the writer is summarizing a major idea that recurs throughout the source material. No page reference is needed.

Chang (2008) found that weight-bearing exercise could help women maintain or even increase bone density through middle age and beyond, reducing the likelihood that they will develop osteoporosis in later life (p. 86).

Although the writer is not directly quoting the source, this passage paraphrases a specific detail, so the writer chose to include the page number where the information is located.

TIP

Although APA style guidelines do not require writers to provide page numbers for material that is not directly quoted, your instructor may wish you to do so when possible.

Check with your instructor about his or her preferences.

Formatting Longer Quotations

When you quote a longer passage from a source—forty words or more—use a different format to set off the quoted material. Instead of using quotation marks, create a block quotation by starting the quotation on a new line and indented five spaces from the margin. Note that in this case, the parenthetical citation comes **after** the period that ends the sentence. Here is an example:

> In recent years, many writers within the fitness industry have emphasized the ways in which women can benefit from weight-bearing exercise, such as weightlifting, karate, dancing, stair climbing, hiking, and jogging. Chang (2008) found that engaging in weight-bearing exercise regularly significantly reduces women's risk of developing osteoporosis. Additionally, these exercises help women maintain muscle mass and overall strength, and many common forms of weight-bearing exercise, such as brisk walking or stair climbing, also provide noticeable cardiovascular benefits. (p. 93)

If you are quoting a passage that continues into a second paragraph, indent five spaces again in the first line of the second paragraph. Here is an example:

> In recent years, many writers within the fitness industry have emphasized the ways in which women can benefit from weight-bearing exercise, such as weightlifting, karate, dancing, stair climbing, hiking, and jogging. Chang (2008) found that engaging in weight-bearing exercise regularly significantly reduces women's risk of developing osteoporosis. Additionally, these exercises help women maintain muscle mass and overall strength, and many common forms of weight-bearing exercise, such as brisk walking or stair climbing, also provide noticeable cardiovascular benefits.
>
> It is important to note that swimming cannot be considered a weight-bearing exercise, since the water supports and cushions the swimmer. That doesn't mean swimming isn't great exercise, but it should be considered one part of an integrated fitness program. (p. 93)

TIP

Be wary of quoting from sources at length. Remember, your ideas should drive the paper, and quotations should be used to support and enhance your points. Make sure any lengthy quotations that you include serve a clear purpose. Generally, no more than 10–15 percent of a paper should consist of quoted material.

Introducing Cited Material Effectively

Including an introductory phrase in your text, such as "Jackson wrote" or "Copeland found," often helps you integrate source material smoothly. This citation technique also helps convey that you are actively engaged with your source material. Unfortunately, during the process of writing your research paper, it is easy to fall into a rut and use the same few dull verbs repeatedly, such as "Jones said," "Smith stated," and so on.

Punch up your writing by using strong verbs that help your reader understand how the source material presents ideas. There is a world of difference between an author who "suggests" and one who "claims," one who "questions" and one who "criticizes." You do not need to consult your thesaurus every time you cite a source, but do think about which verbs will accurately represent the ideas and make your writing more engaging. The following chart shows some possibilities.

Strong Verbs for Introducing Cited Material		
ask	suggest	question
explain	assert	claim
recommend	compare	contrast
propose	hypothesize	believe
insist	argue	find
determine	measure	assess
evaluate	conclude	study
warn	point out	sum up

Writing at Work

It is important to accurately represent a colleague's ideas or communications in the workplace. When writing professional or academic papers, be mindful of how the words you use to describe someone's tone or ideas carry certain connotations. Do not say a source *argues* a particular point unless an argument is, in fact, presented. Use lively language, but avoid language that is emotionally charged. Doing so will ensure you have represented your colleague's words in an authentic and accurate way.

Formatting In-Text Citations for Other Source Types

These sections discuss the correct format for various types of in-text citations. Read them through quickly to get a sense of what is covered, and then refer to them again as needed.

Print Sources

This section covers books, articles, and other print sources with one or more authors.

A Work by One Author

For a print work with one author, follow the guidelines provided in "Formatting a Research Paper." (https://courses.candelalearning.com/englishforbusiness/chapter/14-1-formatting-a-research-paper/) Always include the author's name and year of publication. Include a page reference whenever you quote a source directly. (See also the guidelines presented earlier in this chapter about when to include a page reference for paraphrased material.)

Chang (2008) emphasized that "engaging in weight-bearing exercise consistently is one of the single best things women can do to maintain good health" (p. 49).

Chang (2008) pointed out that weight-bearing exercise has many potential benefits for women.

Two or More Works by the Same Author

At times, your research may include multiple works by the same author. If the works were published in different years, a standard in-text citation will serve to distinguish them. If you are citing multiple works by the same author published in the same year, include a lowercase letter immediately after the year. Rank the sources in the order they appear in your references section. The source listed first includes an *a* after the year, the source listed second includes a *b*, and so on.

Rodriguez (2009a) criticized the nutrition-supplement industry for making unsubstantiated and sometimes misleading claims about the benefits of taking supplements. Additionally, he warned that consumers frequently do not realize the potential harmful effects of some popular supplements (Rodriguez, 2009b).

TIP

If you have not yet created your references section, you may not be sure which source will appear first. See "Creating a References Section" (https://courses.candelalearning.com/englishforbusiness/chapter/14-3-creating-a-references-section/) for guidelines—or assign each source a temporary code and highlight the in-text citations so you remember to double-check them later on.

Works by Authors with the Same Last Name

If you are citing works by different authors with the same last name, include each author's initials in your citation, whether you mention them in the text or in parentheses. Do so even if the publication years are different.

J. S. Williams (2007) believes nutritional supplements can be a useful part of some diet and fitness regimens. C. D. Williams (2008), however, believes these supplements are overrated.

According to two leading researchers, the rate of childhood obesity exceeds the rate of adult obesity (K. Connelley, 2010; O. Connelley, 2010).

Studies from both A. Wright (2007) and C. A. Wright (2008) confirm the benefits of diet and exercise on weight loss.

A Work by Two Authors

When two authors are listed for a given work, include both authors' names each time you cite the work. If you are citing their names in parentheses, use an ampersand (&) between them. (Use the word *and*, however, if the names appear in your sentence.)

As Garrison and Gould (2010) pointed out, "It is never too late to quit smoking. The health risks associated with this habit begin to decrease soon after a smoker quits" (p. 101).

As doctors continue to point out, "It is never too late to quit smoking. The health risks associated with this habit begin to decrease soon after a smoker quits" (Garrison & Gould, 2010, p. 101).

A Work by Three to Five Authors

If the work you are citing has three to five authors, list all the authors' names the first time you cite the source. In subsequent citations, use the first author's name followed by the abbreviation et al. (*Et al.* is short for *et alia*, the Latin phrase for "and others.")

Henderson, Davidian, and Degler (2010) surveyed 350 smokers aged 18 to 30.

One survey, conducted among 350 smokers aged 18 to 30, included a detailed questionnaire about participants' motivations for smoking (Henderson, Davidian, & Degler, 2010).

Note that these examples follow the same ampersand conventions as sources with two authors. Again, use the ampersand only when listing authors' names in parentheses.

As Henderson et al. (2010) found, some young people, particularly young women, use smoking as a means of appetite suppression.

Disturbingly, some young women use smoking as a means of appetite suppression (Henderson et al., 2010).

Note how the phrase *et al.* is punctuated. No period comes after *et*, but *al.* gets a period because it is an abbreviation for a longer Latin word. In parenthetical references, include a comma after *et al.* but not before. Remember this rule by mentally translating the citation to English: "Henderson and others, 2010."

A Work by Six or More Authors

If the work you are citing has six or more authors, list only the first author's name, followed by *et al.*, in your in-text citations. The other authors' names will be listed in your references section.

Researchers have found that outreach work with young people has helped reduce tobacco use in some communities (Costello et al., 2007).

A Work Authored by an Organization

When citing a work that has no individual author(s) but is published by an organization, use the organization's name in place of the author's name. Lengthy organization names with well-known abbreviations can be abbreviated. In your first citation, use the full name, followed by the abbreviation in square brackets. Subsequent citations may use the abbreviation only.

It is possible for a patient to have a small stroke without even realizing it (American Heart Association [AHA], 2010).

Another cause for concern is that even if patients realize that they have had a stroke and need medical attention, they may not know which nearby facilities are best equipped to treat them (AHA, 2010).

A Work with No Listed Author

If no author is listed and the source cannot be attributed to an organization, use the title in place of the author's name. You may use the full title in your sentence or use the first few words—enough to convey the key ideas—in a parenthetical reference. Follow standard conventions for using italics or quotations marks with titles:

- Use italics for titles of books or reports.
- Use quotation marks for titles of articles or chapters.

"Living With Diabetes: Managing Your Health" (2009) recommends regular exercise for patients with diabetes.

Regular exercise can benefit patients with diabetes ("Living with Diabetes," 2009).

Rosenhan (1973) had mentally healthy study participants claim to be experiencing hallucinations so they would be admitted to psychiatric hospitals.

A Work Cited within Another Work

To cite a source that is referred to within another secondary source, name the first source in your sentence. Then, in parentheses, use the phrase *as cited in* and the name of the second source author.

Rosenhan's study "On Being Sane in Insane Places" (as cited in Spitzer, 1975) found that psychiatrists diagnosed schizophrenia in people who claimed to be experiencing hallucinations and sought treatment—even though these patients were, in fact, imposters.

Two or More Works Cited in One Reference

At times, you may provide more than one citation in a parenthetical reference, such as when you are discussing related works or studies with similar results. List the citations in the same order they appear in your references section, and separate the citations with a semicolon.

Some researchers have found serious flaws in the way Rosenhan's study was conducted (Dawes, 2001; Spitzer, 1975).

Both of these researchers authored works that support the point being made in this sentence, so it makes sense to include both in the same citation.

A Famous Text Published in Multiple Editions

In some cases, you may need to cite an extremely well-known work that has been repeatedly republished or translated. Many works of literature and sacred texts, as well as some classic nonfiction texts, fall into this category. For these works, the original date of publication may be unavailable. If so, include the year of publication or translation for your edition. Refer to specific parts or chapters if you need to cite a specific section. Discuss with your instructor whether he or she would like you to cite page numbers in this particular instance.

In *New Introductory Lectures on Psycho-Analysis*, Freud explains that the "manifest content" of a dream—what literally takes place—is separate from its "latent content," or hidden meaning (trans. 1965, lecture XXIX).

Here, the student is citing a classic work of psychology, originally written in German and later translated to English. Since the book is a collection of Freud's lectures, the student cites the lecture number rather than a page number.

An Introduction, Foreword, Preface, or Afterword

To cite an introduction, foreword, preface, or afterword, cite the author of the material and the year, following the same format used for other print materials.

Electronic Sources

Whenever possible, cite electronic sources as you would print sources, using the author, the date, and where appropriate, a page number. For some types of electronic sources—for instance, many online articles—this information is easily available. Other times, however, you will need to vary the format to reflect the differences in online media.

Online Sources without Page Numbers

If an online source has no page numbers but you want to refer to a specific portion of the source, try to locate other information you can use to direct your reader to the information cited. Some websites number paragraphs within published articles; if so, include the paragraph number in your citation. Precede the paragraph number with the abbreviation for the word *paragraph* and the number of the paragraph (e.g., para. 4).

As researchers have explained, "Incorporating fresh fruits and vegetables into one's diet can be a challenge for residents of areas where there are few or no easily accessible supermarkets" (Smith & Jones, 2006, para. 4).

Even if a source does not have numbered paragraphs, it is likely to have headings that organize the content. In your citation, name the section where your cited information appears, followed by a paragraph number.

The American Lung Association (2010) noted, "After smoking, radon exposure is the second most common cause of lung cancer" (What Causes Lung Cancer? section, para. 2).

This student cited the appropriate section heading within the website and then counted to find the specific paragraph where the cited information was located.

If an online source has no listed author and no date, use the source title and the abbreviation *n.d.* in your parenthetical reference.

It has been suggested that electromagnetic radiation from cellular telephones may pose a risk for developing certain cancers ("Cell Phones and Cancer," n.d.).

Personal Communication

For personal communications, such as interviews, letters, and e-mails, cite the name of the person involved, clarify that the material is from a personal communication, and provide the specific date the communication took place. Note that while in-text citations correspond to entries in the references section, personal communications are an exception to this rule. They are cited only in the body text of your paper.

J. H. Yardley, M.D., believes that available information on the relationship between cell phone use and cancer is inconclusive (personal communication, May 1, 2009).

Writing at Work

At work, you may sometimes share information resources with your colleagues by photocopying an interesting article or forwarding the URL of a useful website. Your goal in these situations and in formal research citations is the same. The goal is to provide enough information to help your professional peers locate and follow up on potentially useful information. Provide as much specific information as possible to achieve that goal, and consult with your professor as to what specific style he or she may prefer.

KEY TAKEAWAY

- In APA papers, in-text citations include the name of the author(s) and the year of publication whenever possible.
- Page numbers are always included when citing quotations. It is optional to include page numbers when citing paraphrased material; however, this should be done when citing a specific portion of a work.
- When citing online sources, provide the same information used for print sources if it is available.
- When a source does not provide information that usually appears in a citation, in-text citations should provide readers with alternative information that would help them locate the source material. This may include the title of the source, section headings and paragraph numbers for websites, and so forth.
- When writing a paper, discuss with your professor what particular standards he or she would like you to follow.

EXERCISES

1. Review the places in your paper where you cited, quoted, and paraphrased material from a source with a single author. Edit your citations to ensure that

- each citation includes the author's name, the date of publication, and, where appropriate, a page reference;
- parenthetical citations are correctly formatted;
- longer quotations use the block-quotation format.

2. Review the citations in your paper once again. This time, look for places where you introduced source material using a signal phrase in your sentence.

- Highlight the verbs used in your signal phrases, and make note of any that seem to be overused throughout the paper.

- Identify at least three places where a stronger verb could be used.
- Make the edits to your draft.

3. Review the places in your paper where you cited material from a source with multiple authors or with an organization as the author. Edit your citations to ensure that each citation follows APA guidelines for the inclusion of the authors' names, the use of ampersands and *et al.*, the date of publication, and, where appropriate, a page reference.

CC licensed content, Shared previously

- Successful Writing. **Authored by**: Anonymous. **Provided by**: Anonymous. **Located at**: http://2012books.lardbucket.org/books/successful-writing/s17-02-citing-and-referencing-techniq.html (http://2012books.lardbucket.org/books/successful-writing/s17-02-citing-and-referencing-techniq.html). **License**: *CC BY-NC-SA: Attribution-NonCommercial-ShareAlike (https://creativecommons.org/licenses/by-nc-sa/4.0/)*

Academic Integrity Tutorial

The University of Maryland University College maintains a well-known academic integrity tutorial (http://www.umuc.edu/current-students/learning-resources/academic-integrity/tutorial/interactive.html). It has many valuable tips and should refresh your skills in these areas.

MLA Checklist

OWL Excelsior, an online writing lab with many other good pages, has the following checklist for MLA (http://owl.excelsior.edu/ citation-and-documentation/mla-style/mla-checklist/). Access it and use this when you're writing the essays.

CC licensed content, Shared previously

- MLA Checklist. **Authored by**: OWL Excelsior Writing Lab. **Provided by**: Excelsior College. **Located at**: http://owl.excelsior.edu/citation-and-documentation/mla-style/mla-checklist/ (http://owl.excelsior.edu/citation-and-documentation/mla-style/mla-checklist/). **Project**: OWL Excelsior. **License**: *CC BY: Attribution (https://creativecommons.org/ licenses/by/4.0/)*

Read: Acknowledging Sources and Avoiding Plagiarism

Acknowledgment of Sources is a Rhetorical Act

To an inexperienced writer, citing and documenting sources may seem like busywork. Yet, when you cite your external sources in the text of your paper and when you document them at the end of your piece in a list of works cited or a bibliography, you are performing a rhetorical act. Complete and accurate citing and documenting of all external sources help writers achieve three very important goals:

1. It enhances your credibility as a writer. By carefully and accurately citing your external sources in the text and by documenting them at the end of your paper you show your readers that you are serious about your subject, your research, and the argument which you are making in your paper. You demonstrate that you have studied your subject in sufficient depth, and by reading credible and authoritative sources.

2. It helps you to avoid plagiarism. Plagiarism is trying to pass someone else's ideas or writing as your own. It is a serious offense that can damage the reputation of a writer forever and lead to very serious consequences if committed in an academic or professional setting. Later on in the chapter, we will discuss plagiarism and ways to avoid it in detail.

3. The presence of complete citations of sources in your paper will help you demonstrate to your readers that you are an active participant in the community of readers, writers, researchers, and learners. It shows that you are aware of the conversations that are going on among writers and researchers in your field and that you are willing to enter those conversations by researching and writing about the subjects that interest you. By providing enough information about the sources which you used in you own research and writing, you give other interested readers the opportunity to find out more about your subject and, thus, to enter in a conversation with you.

The Logic and Structure of a Source Citation

Every time writers cite and document their sources, they do it in two places in the paper—in the text itself and at the end of the paper, in a list of works cited or bibliography. A citation is incomplete and, by and large, useless to the readers, if either of the parts is missing. Consider the following example, in which I cite an academic journal article using the Modern Language Association citation system. Please note that I give this example at this point in the chapter only to demonstrate the two parts of a citation. Later on, we will discuss how to cite and document different kinds of sources using different documentation systems, in full detail.

In-text citations

In-text citations are also known as parenthetical citations or parenthetical references because, at the end of the citation, parentheses are used. In her essay "If Winston Weather Would Just Write to Me on E-mail," published in the journal College Composition and Communication, writer and teacher Wendy Bishop shares her thoughts on the nature of writing: "[I see...writing as a mixture of mess and self-discipline, of self-history [and] cultural history." (101).

The Citation in the List of Works Cited

Bishop, Wendy. "If Winston Weather Would Just Write to Me on E-mail." College Composition and Communication. 46.1 (1995): 97-103.

The reason why each citation, regardless of the type of source and the documentation system being used, has two parts is simple. Writers acknowledge and document external sources for several reasons. One of these reasons is to give their readers enough information and enable them, if necessary, to find the same source which the paper mentions. Therefore, if we look at the kinds of information provided in the citation (page numbers, titles, authors, publishers, and publication dates), it becomes clear that this information is sufficient to locate the source in the library, bookstore, or online.

When to Cite and Document Sources

The brief answer to this question is "always." Every time you use someone else's ideas, arguments, opinions, or data, you need to carefully acknowledge their author and source. Keep in mind that you are not just borrowing others' words when you use sources in your writing. You are borrowing ideas. Therefore, even if you are not directly citing the source, but paraphrase or summarize it, you still need to cite it both in the text and at the end of the paper in a list of works cited or in a list of references.

The only exception is when you are dealing with what is known as "common knowledge." Common knowledge consists of facts that are so widely known that they do not require a source reference. For instance, if you say in your writing that the Earth rotates around the Sun or that Ronald Reagan was a US President, you do not need to cite the sources of this common knowledge formally.

Avoiding Plagiarism

Plagiarism is a problem that exists not only on college, university, and high school campuses. In recent years, several high profile cases, some involving famous writers and journalists have surfaced, in which the these writers were accused of either presenting someone else work as their own or fabricating works based on fictitious or unreliable research. With the advent of the Internet, it has become relatively easy to download complete papers. Various people and organizations, sometimes masquerading as "writing consultants" promise students that they would write a paper on any subject and of any level of complexity for a hefty fee. Clearly, the use of such services by student writers is dishonest and dishonorable. If your college or university is like mine, it probably has adopted strict policies for dealing with plagiarizing writers. Punishments for intentional plagiarism are severe and may include not only a failing grade for the class but even an expulsion from the university.

In addition to intentional plagiarism, there is also the unintentional kind. Experience shows that beginning writers' work sometimes include passages which could be called plagiarized because such writers often do not know how to cite and document external sources properly or do not understand that importance of following proper citation practices.

Observing the following practices will help you avoid plagiarism:

As you research, keep careful notes of your sources. As you take notes for your research project, keep track of what materials in those notes comes from external sources and what material is yours. Keep track of all your sources, including interviews and surveys, photographs and drawings, personal e-mails and conversations. Be sure to record the following information:

- Author
- Title
- Date of publication
- Publisher

Remember that when you use external sources, you are borrowing not the words of another writer, but his or her ideas, theories, and opinions. Therefore, even if you summarize or paraphrase a source, be sure to give it full credit. Writers used to have to record this information on separate note cards. However, with the proliferation of online and other electronic tools which allow us to keep track of our research, the task of recording and reflecting on source-related information has become easier.

Anti-Plagiarism Activity

Read the following four paragraphs. They are from a research source, an article in *The New Yorker* magazine. The other three are from student papers which attempt to use the article as an external source. As you read consider the following questions:

- Would you call the student's passage or its parts plagiarized from the original? Why or why not?
- If any parts of the student's passages are plagiarized what needs to be changed in order to avoid plagiarism? Keep in mind that you may need to rewrite the whole Paragraph and not just make changes in separate sentences.
- Which of the student passages will require more significant rewriting than others and why?

Source Paragraph (from the article "Personality Plus," by Malcolm Gladwell. *New Yorker*, Sept 20, 2004). One of the most popular personality tests in the world is the Myers-Briggs Type Indicator (MBTI), a psychologicalassessment system based on Carl Jung's notion that people make sense of the world through a series or psychological frames. Some people are extraverts, some are introverts. Some process information through logical thought. Some are directed by their feelings. Some make sense of the world through intuitive leaps. Others collect data through their senses.

Student Paragraph 1

The Myers-Briggs Test is a very popular way to assess someone's personality type. Philosopher Carl Jung believed that people make sense of the world in different ways. Some are extraverts and some and introverts. According to this idea, people process information either by logical reasoning or through intuition or feelings.

Student Paragraph 2

According to writer Malcolm Gladwell, One of the most popular personality tests in the world is the Myers-Briggs Type Indicator (MBTI), a psychological-assessment system based on Carl Jung's notion that people make sense of the world through a series or psychological frames. Gladwell states that the test is based on the idea by Carl Jung that people make sense of the world through a series of psychological frames. According to Jung, some people are extroverts and some are introverts. Some process information through logical input, and some through feelings. Some make sense of the world through intuitive leaps. Others collect data through their senses.

Student Paragraph 3

One of the most popular personality tests in the world is the Myers-Briggs Type Indicator (MBTI), a psychological assessment system based on Carl Jung's notion that people make sense of the world through a series or psychological frames (Gladwell 43). The test is based on Jung's theory that people understand the world differently. This is why we have extroverts and introverts and people who act either based on reasoning or feelings (Gladwell).

Major Citation Systems

In this part of the chapter, I will explain the major citation and documentation systems which you are likely to encounter in your writing for college classes and beyond. The information in this section is not meant to be memorized. Instead, I encourage you to use this material as a reference source, when you are writing a paper and need to cite and document sources correctly, using one of the systems described below, refer to this chapter.

Please note that the following sections include only the basic information about each of the citation styles. There are plenty of excellent sources explaining and illustrating the differences between citation systems. I recommend the cite of the Online Writing Center at Purdue University (https://owl.english.purdue.edu/).

Conclusion

Avoiding plagiarism and acknowledging your external sources completely and accurately are vital parts of the writing process. Your credibility as a writer and the reception that you work will receive from readers may depend on how well you acknowledge your sources. By following the guidelines presented in this chapter and by seeking out more knowledge about the rules of citing and documenting from the publications listed in this chapter, you will become a more competent, more professional, and more credible writer. This chapter covers only the basics of source citing and documenting. For more resources this topic and the various styles of documentation, see the Appendix to this book.

CC licensed content, Shared previously

- Chapter 5: Acknowledging Sources and Avoiding Plagiarism. **Provided by**: Saylor.org. **Located at**: http://www.saylor.org/site/wp-content/uploads/2011/01/Acknowledging-Sources-and-Avoiding-Plagiarism.pdf (http://www.saylor.org/site/wp-content/uploads/2011/01/Acknowledging-Sources-and-Avoiding-Plagiarism.pdf). **License**: *CC BY: Attribution (https://creativecommons.org/licenses/by/4.0/)*

Assessment: MLA & APA Game Response

APA (American Psychological Association) and MLA (Modern Language Association) are two very common types of citation formatting used in higher education. There are others, as well, but we'll be talking specifically about APA and MLA this quarter.

APA is typically used for science courses, including nursing. MLA, on the other hand, is the usual style for humanities and social science courses. You'll probably be asked to use both of them during your time in college, so I want you to be prepared to handle each of them when need be.

First, visit the APA and MLA Citation Game Home Page (http://depts.washington.edu/trio/quest/citation/apa_mla_citation_game/index.htm) by the University of Washington's TRIO Training program.

Then, complete the writing task below.

For this assignment, I'd like you to write a 2-paragraph (3+ sentences per paragraph) commentary on your familiarity with APA and MLA right now.

- In the first paragraph, describe your reaction to the citation work you've done so far in your academic life. Which style have you used more often so far? Which style seems more natural to you? Which style is more likely to be the one used in your degree program?
- In the second paragraph, discuss the mechanics of APA and MLA citation as you understand them right now. Did the questions in this game make sense to you? Do you have questions about why things are formatted in citations the way they are? Do you have comments about what information needs to be included in a citation, and why that information is necessary?

Extra Credit Opportunity: While the overall quiz is pretty accurate, it does contain a few minor mistakes in the way it lists authors and dates. You can earn 1 extra credit point for each inaccuracy you find, up to 5 points maximum.

For each extra point, you must tell me

- which page of the quiz the error is on
- what specifically is wrong
- what the correct format should be instead

CC licensed content, Shared previously

- Composition II. **Authored by**: Alexis McMillan-Clifton. **Provided by**: Tacoma Community College. **Located at**: http://www.tacomacc.edu (http://www.tacomacc.edu). **Project**: Kaleidoscope Open Course Initiative. **License**: *CC BY: Attribution (https://creativecommons.org/licenses/by/4.0/)*

When & How To Use MLA In-Text Citation

Download this PDF file to see a Decision Tree for When & How to use MLA in-text citation (https://s3-us-west-2.amazonaws.com/oerfiles/Composition/WhenHowToUseMLAInTextCitation.pdf).

CC licensed content, Shared previously

Assessment: Five Potential Sources

Locate 5 potential research sources for the topic you submitted as your final choice for the Research Essay. At least one of these needs to come from the school's library (electronic databases are fine).

These are just to get you started. You won't have to use them in the final draft of the essay if they turn out to be duds.

These should be 5 NEW sources. Don't include ones you've used for previous assignments, even if they relate to your chosen topic.

You don't have to tell me anything about the contents of these sources. Instead, I want you to **create BOTH Works Cited (MLA) citations and References (APA) citations for each of the 5 sources you've found**.

You're welcome to use the pre-formatted citations available in the library databases, if you find your sources there. Other good helpful tools for building citations are Son of Citation Machine (http://www.citationmachine.net/index2.php) and EasyBib (http://www.easybib.com/).

> All of the automated citation generators have their unique, problematic quirks. Be sure to compare what they give you with what the handbooks say your citation should look like, so you can learn to spot the problems with machine-generated citations.

How to Cite YouTube

For information on how to cite YouTube using APA style, view the "Quick Answers" article directly from the APA (http://www.apastyle.org/learn/quick-guide-on-references.aspx).

How to Cite a YouTube Video in MLA

As more information is introduced via the Web, students and instructors must come to expect an increase in the number of online citations included in research papers. YouTube videos are among the content one should learn to handle. Continue reading for specific instructions and examples concerning how to cite a YouTube video in MLA format.

Method 1 of 4: In-Text Citation

1. **Type a portion of the title in parentheses.**[1] Follow quoted, paraphrased, or summarized information included in the text with the video's full title or a shortened version of the title. Enclose the title in parentheses, and place any punctuation marks on the outside of the parentheses.

   ◦ Maru is a famous cat known for a variety of antics ("Maru Greatest Hits").

2. **Introduce the title in the sentence.** Instead of including the title inside parentheses, you can also introduce the video's full title or a shortened form directly in the sentence when you write out the borrowed information. Surround the title in quotation marks.

   ◦ As seen in "Maru Greatest Hits," Maru is a famous cat known for a variety of antics.

3. **Include the creator's name when applicable.** If you know the name of the director or the person otherwise responsible for creating the content of the video, state the last name of that individual. A YouTube username can be used if no real name is provided. The name can either be included in the parentheses or introduced directly within the sentence containing the cited information.

   ◦ The man responsible for holding the three Cleveland women captive has been arrested along with two other suspects (Associated Press, "3 Women").
   ◦ As stated in "3 Women," the man responsible for holding the three Cleveland women captive has been arrested along with two other suspects (Associated Press).
   ◦ According the the Associated Press, the man responsible for holding the three Cleveland women captive has been arrested along with two other suspects ("3 Women").
   ◦ In "3 Women," the Associated Press explains that the man responsible for holding the three Cleveland women captive has been arrested along with two other suspects.

Method 2 of 4: Works Cited Page with Creator Name

Mention the name or username of the creator.[2] Use the real name of the director, editor, or compiler when available. Write it out in *LastName, FirstName*format. If citing a video from an organization or if the creator's real name is not available, cite the name of the organization or the username associated with that YouTube account. Regardless of the name you use, follow it with a period.

- Associated Press.
- Tofield, Simon.

State the full title of the video. Write the title exactly as it is typed online. Never abbreviate it; write the full title out since multiple videos may be abbreviated in similar ways. Type a period after the final word and enclose it all in double quotation marks.

- Associated Press. "3 Women, Missing for Years, Found Alive in Ohio."
- Tofield, Simon. "Screen Grab – Simon's Cat."

Name the website. In this case, the name of the website is simply "YouTube." Italicize the website name and follow it with a period.

- Associated Press. "3 Women, Missing for Years, Found Alive in Ohio." *YouTube.*
- Tofield, Simon. "Screen Grab – Simon's Cat." *Youtube.*

Name the sponsor/publisher.[3] The sponsor refers to the official legal name of the corporation or entity responsible for the website. In this case, it would be "YouTube." Do not enclose it in quotation marks or italicize it. Instead of following it with a period, use a comma.

- Associated Press. "3 Women, Missing for Years, Found Alive in Ohio." *YouTube.* YouTube,
- Tofield, Simon. "Screen Grab – Simon's Cat." *Youtube.* YouTube,

State when the video was created. The date that the video was posted should be written in *Day Month Year* format. Follow it with a period.

- Associated Press. "3 Women, Missing for Years, Found Alive in Ohio." *YouTube.* YouTube, 6 May 2013.
- Tofield, Simon. "Screen Grab – Simon's Cat." *Youtube.* YouTube, 12 April 2013.

Mention the publishing medium. For all YouTube videos, the medium should be listed as "Web." This, too, should be followed with a period.

- Associated Press. "3 Women, Missing for Years, Found Alive in Ohio." *YouTube.* YouTube, 6 May 2013. Web.
- Tofield, Simon. "Screen Grab – Simon's Cat." *Youtube.* YouTube, 12 April 2013. Web.

Include the date of access. The date of access refers to the first date that you went to that video for the sake of using it as a citation source. List the date in *Day Month Year* format. Conclude with a period.

- Associated Press. "3 Women, Missing for Years, Found Alive in Ohio." *YouTube.* YouTube, 6 May 2013. Web. 7 May 2013.
- Tofield, Simon. "Screen Grab – Simon's Cat." *Youtube.* YouTube, 12 April 2013. Web. 7 May 2013.

Type the URL, when requested. The URL is not a standard part of MLA citation style for online videos. Nonetheless, many instructors still request it. If your instructor does request the URL, enclose it in carrot brackets and follow the ending bracket with a period.

- Associated Press. "3 Women, Missing for Years, Found Alive in Ohio." *YouTube.* YouTube, 6 May 2013. Web. 7 May 2013. <http://www.youtube.com/watch?v=W9ZXoHnzbcA (http://www.youtube.com/watch?v=W9ZXoHnzbcA)>.
- Tofield, Simon. "Screen Grab – Simon's Cat." *Youtube.* YouTube, 12 April 2013. Web. 7 May 2013. <http://www.youtube.com/watch?v=LpHpm_b0vRY (http://www.youtube.com/watch?v=LpHpm_b0vRY)>.

Method 3 of 4: Works Cited Page with No Creator Name

Write out the full title of the video. If video footage is reposted by a YouTube user who is not the original creator of the footage, and if the name of the original creator is not listed, the first piece of information is the title of the video. Do not list the name or username of the YouTube channel responsible for reposting the video. Enclose the full title in double quotation marks, and follow the final word of the title with a period.

- "Maru Greatest Hits V1."

Indicate the name of the website. For all YouTube videos, the name of the website should simply be "YouTube." Italicize the word and follow it with another period.

- "Maru Greatest Hits V1." *YouTube*.

State the name of the sponsor. The official, legal name of the corporation that owns YouTube should also be indicated. Type "YouTube," and follow the name with a comma.

- "Maru Greatest Hits V1." *YouTube*. YouTube,

Include a posting date. Specify the original date that the video was posted on the YouTube channel you used to access it. Arrange the date in *Day Month Year* format and place another period after the year.

- "Maru Greatest Hits V1." *YouTube*. YouTube, 29 April 2009.

State the publishing medium. For a YouTube video, the publishing medium will always be "Web." Follow it with yet another period.

- "Maru Greatest Hits V1." *YouTube*. YouTube, 29 April 2009. Web.

Type an access date. The access date is the day, month, and year on which you first accessed the video with the intention of citing it among your research. Write the date in *Day Month Year* format and conclude with a period.

- "Maru Greatest Hits V1." *YouTube*. YouTube, 29 April 2009. Web. 7 May 2013.

Include the URL only when requested. The video URL is not a standard part of MLA format and may be marked as wrong if you include it. Oftentimes, however, an instructor will specifically ask for the URL of any online source to be included, in which case, you should enclose the URL in carrot brackets and conclude the entire thing with a final period.

- "Maru Greatest Hits V1." *YouTube*. YouTube, 29 April 2009. Web. 7 May 2013. <http://www.youtube.com/watch?v=8uDuIs5TyNE (http://www.youtube.com/watch?v=8uDuIs5TyNE)>.

Method 4 of 4: Works Cited Page when Citing YouTube Directly

State the creator as "YouTube." This applies to any video that was uploaded to the official YouTube channel. Write the name out and follow it with a period.

- YouTube.

Include the full title of the video. Make sure to include the full title to minimize the odds of citing a duplicate or similar title. Follow the title with a period and enclose it in parentheses.

- YouTube. "Rewind YouTube Style 2012."

Specify the name of the website. Even though "YouTube" is already listed once as the creator of the video, you must also list it a second time as the publisher. Note, however, that you do not need to list it a third time as an official corporation. Only italicize the name of the website here, and follow it with another period.

- YouTube. "Rewind YouTube Style 2012." *YouTube*.

Indicate the date of publication. Specify the date that the video was originally updated in *Day Month Year* format. Follow the year with a period.

- YouTube. "Rewind YouTube Style 2012." *YouTube*. 17 Dec. 2012.

State the publishing medium. The publishing medium for any YouTube video will be "Web." Type a period after this information.

- YouTube. "Rewind YouTube Style 2012." *YouTube*. 17 Dec. 2012. Web.

Include a date of access. Write the day on which you first accessed or viewed the video with the intention of using it as a resource. Type it out in *Day Month Year*format.

- YouTube. "Rewind YouTube Style 2012." *YouTube*. 17 Dec. 2012. Web. 7 May 2013.

Write the URL if directly requested. Official MLA guidelines do not list the URL as vital information, but if your instructor asks for it, include the URL in carrot brackets and follow the end bracket with a concluding period.

- YouTube. "Rewind YouTube Style 2012." *YouTube*. 17 Dec. 2012. Web. 7 May 2013. <http://www.youtube.com/watch?v=iCkYw3cRwLo (http://www.youtube.com/watch?v=iCkYw3cRwLo)>[4]

Tips

- Ask your instructor if he or she has a preference regarding the way that YouTube videos are cited. Some instructors prefer students to include the URL of online sources, while many do not. Moreover, since there is no official set of guidelines governing the citation of YouTube videos in MLA format, these details can be considered somewhat subjective.
- Check the MLA citation guidelines to verify that the above information is accurate and complete. These guidelines change periodically.

Sources and Citations

1. http://citesource.trincoll.edu/mla/mlavideoweb_002.pdf (http://citesource.trincoll.edu/mla/mlavideoweb_002.pdf)
2. http://valenciacollege.edu/library/documents/youtube.pdf (http://valenciacollege.edu/library/documents/youtube.pdf)
3. http://www.bibme.org/citation-guide/MLA/website (http://www.bibme.org/citation-guide/MLA/website)
4. http://elmo.academyart.edu/reference-help/mla_citation_guide.html (http://elmo.academyart.edu/reference-help/mla_citation_guide.html)

- How to Cite a YouTube Video in MLA. **Provided by**: WikiHow. **Located at**: http://www.wikihow.com/Cite-a-YouTube-Video-in-MLA (http://www.wikihow.com/Cite-a-YouTube-Video-in-MLA). **License**: *CC BY-NC-SA: Attribution-NonCommercial-ShareAlike (https://creativecommons.org/licenses/by-nc-sa/4.0/)*

Paragraph Menu Settings Use No Extra Vertical Spaces

MLA calls for double-spacing with no extra spaces (around titles, heading, between paragraphs). Avoid getting a significant penalty for multiple MLA errors.

Here's a screen shot of the proper Paragraph menu settings in Word:

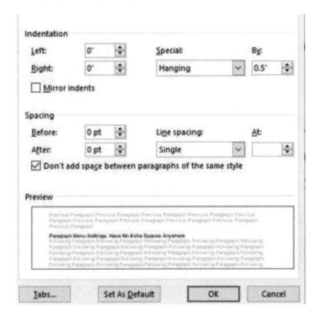

When managing the works cited page, use the Paragraph menu to create the hanging indent that indent the second or third lines of a given works cited entry.

CC licensed content, Original

- Paragraph Menu Settings Use No Extra Vertical Spaces. **Authored by**: Joshua Dickinson. **Provided by**: Jefferson Community College. **Located at**: http://www.sunyjefferson.edu (http://www.sunyjefferson.edu). **Project**: ENG 101. **License**: *CC BY-SA: Attribution-ShareAlike (https://creativecommons.org/licenses/by-sa/4.0/)*

Avoid Word Templates for Citations

When citing in the text of your paper or preparing your works cited list, be sure to avoid the "handy" Word templates. They invariably go wrong. Citation engines can help, but again they're going to lead to errors. For instance, they have cute colored fonts, bold, and bigger text for the title of the page.

We want this to be 100% correct. Any errors degrade our credibility.

CC licensed content, Original

Works Cited Entries: What to Include

The Indian River State College Library pages have many useful pages covering MLA style and how to approach it. I like this page on what goes into a works cited entry (http://irsc.libguides.com/mla/whattoinclude) for the way it reminds us that the entries have common elements we should remember.

Public domain content

- Works Cited Entries: What to Include. **Authored by**: IRSC. **Provided by**: Indian River State College. **Located at**: http://irsc.libguides.com/friendly.php?s=MLA (http://irsc.libguides.com/friendly.php?s=MLA). **Project**: ENG 101. **License**: *CC BY-SA: Attribution-ShareAlike (https://creativecommons.org/licenses/by-sa/4.0/)*

ANNOTATED BIBLIOGRAPHIES

Assessment: Annotated Bibliography

The Annotated Bibliography   100 points

"An annotated bibliography provides specific information about each source you have used. As a researcher, you have become an expert on your topic and have the ability both to explain the content and to assess the usefulness of your sources for those not in the know. Think of your paper as part of a conversation with others interested in the same things you are; the annotated bibliography allows you to tell readers what to check out, what might be worth checking out in some situations, and what might not be worth spending the time on. It's kind of like providing a list of good movies for your classmates to watch and then going over the list with them, telling them why this movie is better than that one or why one student in your class might like a particular movie better than another student would. You want to give your audience enough information to understand basically what the movies are about and to make an informed decision about where to spend their money based on their interests" ("Annotated Bibliography").

Essentially, this assignment consists of two elements that will be blended together:

- A Works Cited page in MLA format that lists all of the research sources you have found and evaluated thus far for your final paper
- A 3-4 sentence-long mini-evaluation immediately following each of these source's citation that shows how and why this source will be useful to your final project (or not). This evaluation should include your interpretation of the source's thesis or overall focus.

An MLA example, using the source for the above quote:

"Annotated Bibliography." _Handouts and Links._ The Writing Center, University of North Carolina at Chapel Hill, 2007. Web. 12 Feb. 2010.   This source is a handout made available by a reputable university's writing center, and describes with great detail and examples what an annotated bibliography is and what purpose it serves. It contains an extensive list of works consulted that could lead me towards additional sources as needed.

The Nuts and Bolts

Your final Annotated Bibliography will have **12 sources** listed. Of those,

- at least 5 will be academic journal article sources, retrieved from the school or a public library
- at least 2 will be book-length, either physical books or ebooks from the Library or online
- at least 1 will be an online media source, such as a YouTube video, podcast, or interactive presentation
- The remaining 4 sources will be "wild card" slots—anything you want to include.
- at least 2 sources (of any of the above formats) must contain elements that DISAGREE with your own position on the matter

The remaining sources may fall into whichever category you choose. You may single-space both the citations and evaluations to make it more reader-friendly. Entries should be organized in alphabetical order. **We are using MLA formatting,** for the Bibliography as well as the final Research Essay.

Remember, this is just an assignment to demonstrate the range of research you'll be doing for your final essay. You won't be expected to use all of these sources in your final paper, and if you find more after you've turned this in, you can use those instead. The Annotated Bibliography is a snapshot of where you are in the research process at this particular point in time.

You're also more than welcome to recycle sources you've used in earlier assignments.

CC licensed content, Shared previously

Video: Annotated Bibliographies An Illustrated Guide

A quick tour of the what, why, and how of an annotated bibliography. Created to support information literacy instruction at Lincoln Memorial University.

- https://youtu.be/-LpgXJvQnEc

All rights reserved content

Annotated Bibliographies

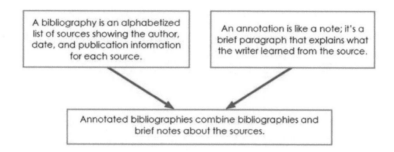

Writers often create annotated bibliographies as a part of a research project, as a means of recording their thoughts and deciding which sources to actually use to support the purpose of their research. Some writers include annotated bibliographies at the end of a research paper as a way of offering their insights about the source's usability to their readers.

Instructors in college often assign annotated bibliographies as a means of helping students think through their source's quality and appropriateness to their research question or topic.

Although it may take a while to complete the annotated bibliography, the annotations themselves are relatively brief.

Annotations may include three things:

1. A brief summary of the information in that source.
2. A brief evaluation of the quality of the source's information.
3. A brief evaluation of whether the source is useful for the purpose of the research.

NOTE: Although there is a basic structure to annotated bibliographies that most professors will follow, your professor may require something a little different. Be sure to follow your assignment instructions, as each professor may have expectations that are slightly different.
The Excelsior OWL site also has a sample annotated bibliography in APA style (http://owl.excelsior.edu/research/annotated-bibliographies/).

STRUCTURE & OUTLINING

Academic Writing Review

Remember these items as you edit your essay. They can make a big difference. I hope this sort of things helps. It's incomplete, but it's a start.

Think of the purpose of your paper, and of how each paragraph helps you fulfill it. As I mentioned elsewhere, the essays in the book aren't pure models for the academic writing we will be doing. What we write should look more solid, even if it is less flashy. You'll need to cite details and quickly follow up on their meanings through strong interpretation of the cited material. Topic sentences and transitions are key elements as well.

Thesis/Introduction

- Set up your thesis; it's best to place it near/at the end of the introduction.
- Two-part introductions or other types of unconventional introductions tend not to work. Why? The writer tends not to do the jobs of the introduction. These include previewing the rest of the essay, setting up the thesis (and showing other sides to the point you're trying to prove).
- Make sure your introduction promises what you'll do. (Don't say "In this essay I'll. . ." or "First, I'll discuss," though. Just go ahead and start previewing the paper.)
- Avoid using "I" as much as possible.
- "Don't use don't." Avoid contractions—as I haven't in this posting!
- "Oh, I almost forgot." Be careful of the formal writing voice you need to use. Don't sound chatty. I want you to write more formally than you are in your postings.

Thesis Checklist

With the thesis statement, keep the following questions in mind. They might work for most academic writing. Get good at asking follow-up questions of your own so that you can edit your work.

- Is it a statement?
- Is it a complex sentence? (Most good thesis statements provide an overview of what you'll go into. Therefore, most good thesis statements need to be complex sentences.)
- Does it take into account your 2-3 main reasons? (These are usually your body paragraph topics, right?)
- Does it take different sides into account? You want to appear fair, and the thesis is a great place for you to frame the merits and weak points of contending sides.
- Where will you locate this statement? Usually, though not always, we put the thesis either at the end of the introduction, or near the end. This allows us to set up the thesis carefully. Your introduction should take care to preview what you'll get into in the body paragraphs, just as the conclusion reviews what you did.

Paragraphing

- Starting/ending paragraphs with quotes is often a warning sign. Why is that?
- When editing, check for strong topic sentences. Are they there? (Go a step further: did your major topics make it into the introduction as preview material, and into the conclusion as review?)
- Citing properly matters. If readers are wondering where a source begins or ends, they are not attending to the content you chose to cite. Their job of appreciating what you brought to the essay is made impossible by citing problems.
- Do interpret between quotes. Avoid stacking two or three quotes. I'm more interested in what you have to write about the

quotes than what's in the quotes.

- Fix the problems with Smart Quotes. (See that mini-lecture in Module 1.)
- Are your paragraphs connected directly to the thesis? How? (Is the connection clear enough?)
- End paragraphs well. (Consider **transitions** as well as restatement of topic sentence.)

Interpretation

Perhaps the biggest frustration is that many of you include great quotes. They're promising, they're useful, they're. . . sitting there! Use the words in the quote. Get readers to see their meaning. If you aren't doing some work at this level, then you aren't interpreting. Good readers are waiting for you to prove your points through close reading of the text. (Sell us on what the words mean. That takes some time.)

Conclusion

- Lack of a conclusion will seriously affect your readers' reactions to the essay (and thus, your grade).
- I value strong conclusions that restate your points and remind readers about *how* you proved your claim(s).
- Do not add new information to the conclusion.
- Restate your thesis at a strategic point. Otherwise, readers will not remember your work soon afterwards—or a week from now.
- Be detailed: this is where you remind us of what you did.
- Don't write two or three sentences and "be done with it."

Classical Essay Structure

The following videos provide an explanation of the classical model of structuring a persuasive argument. You can access the slides alone, without narration, here (https://docs.google.com/presentation/d/1ziU11K7VmGX0BueQIZ6sI6i8fk6PUk7HmCNw8X1V4gl/pub?start=false&loop=false&delayms=3000).

- https://youtu.be/kraJ2Juub5U
- https://youtu.be/3m_EP-BPsBs

CC licensed content, Shared previously

- Composition II. **Authored by**: Alexis McMillan-Clifton. **Provided by**: Tacoma Community College. **Located at**: http://www.tacomacc.edu (http://www.tacomacc.edu). **Project**: Kaleidoscope Open Course Initiative. **License**: *CC BY: Attribution (https://creativecommons.org/licenses/by/4.0/)*

All rights reserved content

- 102 S11 Classical I. **Authored by**: Alexis McMillan-Clifton. **Located at**: https://youtu.be/kraJ2Juub5U (https://youtu.be/kraJ2Juub5U). **License**: *All Rights Reserved*. **License Terms**: Standard YouTube License
- 102 S11 Classical II. **Authored by**: Alexis McMillan-Clifton. **Located at**: https://youtu.be/3m_EP-BPsBs (https://youtu.be/3m_EP-BPsBs). **License**: *All Rights Reserved*. **License Terms**: Standard YouTube License

Writing for Success: Outlining

LEARNING OBJECTIVES

By the end of this section, you will be able to:

- Identify the steps in constructing an outline.
- Construct a topic outline and a sentence outline.

Your prewriting activities and readings have helped you gather information for your assignment. The more you sort through the pieces of information you found, the more you will begin to see the connections between them. Patterns and gaps may begin to stand out. But only when you start to organize your ideas will you be able to translate your raw insights into a form that will communicate meaning to your audience.

TIP

Longer papers require more reading and planning than shorter papers do. Most writers discover that the more they know about a topic, the more they can write about it with intelligence and interest.

Organizing Ideas

When you write, you need to organize your ideas in an order that makes sense. The writing you complete in all your courses exposes how analytically and critically your mind works. In some courses, the only direct contact you may have with your instructor is through the assignments you write for the course. You can make a good impression by spending time ordering your ideas.

Order refers to your choice of what to present first, second, third, and so on in your writing. The order you pick closely relates to your purpose for writing that particular assignment. For example, when telling a story, it may be important to first describe the background for the action. Or you may need to first describe a 3-D movie projector or a television studio to help readers visualize the setting and scene. You may want to group your support effectively to convince readers that your point of view on an issue is well reasoned and worthy of belief.

In longer pieces of writing, you may organize different parts in different ways so that your purpose stands out clearly and all parts of the paper work together to consistently develop your main point.

Methods of Organizing Writing

The three common methods of organizing writing are chronological order, spatial order, and order of importance. You will learn more about these in Chapter 8 "Writing Essays: From Start to Finish"; however, you need to keep these methods of organization in mind as you plan how to arrange the information you have gathered in an outline. An outline is a written plan that serves as a skeleton for the paragraphs you write. Later, when you draft paragraphs in the next stage of the writing process, you will add support to create "flesh" and "muscle" for your assignment.

When you write, your goal is not only to complete an assignment but also to write for a specific purpose—perhaps to inform, to explain, to persuade, or for a combination of these purposes. Your purpose for writing should always be in the back of your mind, because it will help you decide which pieces of information belong together and how you will order them. In other words, choose the order that will most effectively fit your purpose and support your main point.

Table 7.1 "Order versus Purpose" shows the connection between order and purpose.

Table 7.1 Order versus Purpose

Order	Purpose
Chronological Order	To explain the history of an event or a topic
	To tell a story or relate an experience
	To explain how to do or make something
	To explain the steps in a process
Spatial Order	To help readers visualize something as you want them to see it
	To create a main impression using the senses (sight, touch, taste, smell, and sound)
Order of Importance	To persuade or convince
	To rank items by their importance, benefit, or significance

Writing a Thesis Statement

One legitimate question readers always ask about a piece of writing is "What is the big idea?" (You may even ask this question when you are the reader, critically reading an assignment or another document.) Every nonfiction writing task—from the short essay to the ten-page term paper to the lengthy senior thesis—needs a big idea, or a controlling idea, as the spine for the work. The controlling idea is the main idea that you want to present and develop.

TIP

For a longer piece of writing, the main idea should be broader than the main idea for a shorter piece of writing. Be sure to frame a main idea that is appropriate for the length of the assignment. Ask yourself, "How many pages will it take for me to explain and explore this main idea in detail?" Be reasonable with your estimate. Then expand or trim it to fit the required length.

The big idea, or controlling idea, you want to present in an essay is expressed in a thesis statement. A thesis statement is often one sentence long, and it states your point of view. The thesis statement is not the topic of the piece of writing but rather what you have to say about that topic and what is important to tell readers.

Table 7.2 "Topics and Thesis Statements" compares topics and thesis statements.

Table 7.2 Topics and Thesis Statements

Topic	Thesis Statement
Music piracy	The recording industry fears that so-called music piracy will diminish profits and destroy markets, but it cannot be more wrong.
The number of consumer choices available in media gear	Everyone wants the newest and the best digital technology, but the choices are extensive, and the specifications are often confusing.
E-books and online newspapers increasing their share of the market	E-books and online newspapers will bring an end to print media as we know it.
Online education and the new media	Someday, students and teachers will send avatars to their online classrooms.

The first thesis statement you write will be a preliminary thesis statement, or a working thesis statement. You will need it when you begin to outline your assignment as a way to organize it. As you continue to develop the arrangement, you can limit your working thesis statement if it is too broad or expand it if it proves too narrow for what you want to say.

TIP

You will make several attempts before you devise a working thesis statement that you think is effective. Each draft of the thesis statement will bring you closer to the wording that expresses your meaning exactly.

Writing an Outline

For an essay question on a test or a brief oral presentation in class, all you may need to prepare is a short, informal outline in which you jot down key ideas in the order you will present them. This kind of outline reminds you to stay focused in a stressful situation and to include all the good ideas that help you explain or prove your point.

For a longer assignment, like an essay or a research paper, many college instructors require students to submit a formal outline before writing a major paper as a way to be sure you are on the right track and are working in an organized manner. A formal outline is a detailed guide that shows how all your supporting ideas relate to each other. It helps you distinguish between ideas that are of equal importance and ones that are of lesser importance. You build your paper based on the framework created by the outline.

TIP

Instructors may also require you to submit an outline with your final draft to check the direction of the assignment and the logic of your final draft. If you are required to submit an outline with the final draft of a paper, remember to revise the outline to reflect any changes you made while writing the paper.

There are two types of formal outlines: the topic outline and the sentence outline. You format both types of formal outlines in the same way.

- Place your introduction and thesis statement at the beginning, under roman numeral I.
- Use roman numerals (II, III, IV, V, etc.) to identify main points that develop the thesis statement.

- Use capital letters (A, B, C, D, etc.) to divide your main points into parts.
- Use arabic numerals (1, 2, 3, 4, 5, etc.) if you need to subdivide any As, Bs, or Cs into smaller parts.
- End with the final roman numeral expressing your idea for your conclusion.

Here is what the skeleton of a traditional formal outline looks like. The indention helps clarify how the ideas are related.

1. IntroductionThesis statement
2. Main point 1 → *becomes the topic sentence of body paragraph 1*
    1. Supporting detail → *becomes a support sentence of body paragraph 1*

        1. Subpoint
        2. Subpoint
    2. Supporting detail

        1. Subpoint
        2. Subpoint
    3. Supporting detail

        1. Subpoint
        2. Subpoint
3. Main point 2 → *becomes the topic sentence of body paragraph 2*

    1. Supporting detail
    2. Supporting detail
    3. Supporting detail
4. Main point 3 → *becomes the topic sentence of body paragraph 3*

    1. Supporting detail
    2. Supporting detail
    3. Supporting detail
5. Conclusion

TIP

In an outline, any supporting detail can be developed with subpoints. For simplicity, the model shows them only under the first main point.

TIP

Formal outlines are often quite rigid in their organization. As many instructors will specify, you cannot subdivide one point if it is only one part. For example, for every roman numeral I, there must be a For every A, there must be a B. For every arabic numeral 1, there must be a 2. See for yourself on the sample outlines that follow.

Constructing Topic Outlines

A topic outline is the same as a sentence outline except you use words or phrases instead of complete sentences. Words and phrases keep the outline short and easier to comprehend. All the headings, however, must be written in parallel structure. (For more information on parallel structure, see "Refining Your Writing: How Do I Improve My Writing Technique?" (https://courses.candelalearning.com/englishforbusiness/chapter/chapter-6-refining-your-writing-how-do-i-improve-my-writing-technique/).)

Here is the topic outline that Mariah constructed for the essay she is developing. Her purpose is to inform, and her audience is a general audience of her fellow college students. Notice how Mariah begins with her thesis statement. She then arranges her main points and supporting details in outline form using short phrases in parallel grammatical structure.

I.   Introduction
     · Thesis statement: Everyone wants the newest and the best digital technology, but the choices are many, and the specifications are often confusing.
II. E-book readers and the way that people read
     A. Books easy to access and carry around
        1. Electronic downloads
        2. Storage in memory for hundreds of books
     B. An expanding market
        1. E-book readers from booksellers
        2. E-book readers from electronics and computer companies
     C. Limitations of current e-book readers
        1. Incompatible features from one brand to the next
        2. Borrowing and sharing e-books
III. Film cameras replaced by digital cameras
     A. Three types of digital cameras
        1. Compact digital cameras
        2. Single lens reflex cameras, or SLRs
        3. Cameras that combine the best features of both
     B. The confusing "megapixel wars"
     C. The zoom lens battle
IV. The confusing choice among televisions
     A. 1080p vs. 768p
     B. Plasma screens vs. LCDs
     C. Home media centers
V.   Conclusion
     · How to be a wise consumer

Checklist

Writing an Effective Topic Outline

This checklist can help you write an effective topic outline for your assignment. It will also help you discover where you may need to do additional reading or prewriting.

- Do I have a controlling idea that guides the development of the entire piece of writing?
- Do I have three or more main points that I want to make in this piece of writing? Does each main point connect to my controlling idea?
- Is my outline in the best order—chronological order, spatial order, or order of importance—for me to present my main points? Will this order help me get my main point across?
- Do I have supporting details that will help me inform, explain, or prove my main points?
- Do I need to add more support? If so, where?
- Do I need to make any adjustments in my working thesis statement before I consider it the final version?

WRITING AT WORK

Word processing programs generally have an automatic numbering feature that can be used to prepare outlines. This feature automatically sets indents and lets you use the tab key to arrange information just as you would in an outline. Although in business this style might be acceptable, in college your instructor might have different requirements. Teach yourself how to customize the levels of outline numbering in your word-processing program to fit your instructor's preferences.

Constructing Sentence Outlines

A sentence outline is the same as a topic outline except you use complete sentences instead of words or phrases. Complete sentences create clarity and can advance you one step closer to a draft in the writing process.

Here is the sentence outline that Mariah constructed for the essay she is developing.

I. Introduction
   - Thesis statement: Everyone wants the newest and the best digital technology, but the choices are many, and the specifications are often confusing.
II. E-book readers are changing the way people read.
   A. E-book readers make books easy to access and to carry.
      1. Books can be downloaded electronically.
      2. Devices can store hundreds of books in memory.
   B. The market expands as a variety of companies enter it.
      1. Booksellers sell their own e-book readers.
      2. Electronics and computer companies also sell e-book readers.
   C. Current e-book readers have significant limitations.
      1. The devices are owned by different brands and may not be compatible.
      2. Few programs have been made to fit the other way Americans read: by borrowing books from libraries.
III. Digital cameras have almost totally replaced film cameras.
   A. The first major choice is the type of digital camera.
      1. Compact digital cameras are light but have fewer megapixels.
      2. Single lens reflex cameras, or SLRs, may be large and heavy but can be used for many functions.
      3. Some cameras combine the best features of compacts and SLRs.
   B. Choosing the camera type involves the confusing "megapixel wars."
   C. The zoom lens battle also determines the camera you will buy.
IV. Nothing is more confusing to me than choosing among televisions.
   A. In the resolution wars, what are the benefits of 1080p and 768p?
   B. In the screen-size wars, what do plasma screens and LCD screens offer?
   C. Does every home really need a media center?
V. Conclusion
   - The solution for many people should be to avoid buying on impulse. Consumers should think about what they really need, not what is advertised.

TIP

The information compiled under each roman numeral will become a paragraph in your final paper. In the previous example, the outline follows the standard five-paragraph essay arrangement, but longer essays will require more paragraphs and thus more roman numerals. If you think that a paragraph might become too long or stringy, add an additional paragraph to your outline, renumbering the main points appropriately.

WRITING AT WORK

PowerPoint presentations, used both in schools and in the workplace, are organized in a way very similar to formal outlines. PowerPoint presentations often contain information in the form of talking points that the presenter develops with more details and examples than are contained on the PowerPoint slide.

KEY TAKEAWAYS

- Writers must put their ideas in order so the assignment makes sense. The most common orders are chronological order, spatial order, and order of importance.
- After gathering and evaluating the information you found for your essay, the next step is to write a working, or preliminary, thesis statement.
- The working thesis statement expresses the main idea that you want to develop in the entire piece of writing. It can be modified as you continue the writing process.
- Effective writers prepare a formal outline to organize their main ideas and supporting details in the order they will be presented.
- A topic outline uses words and phrases to express the ideas.
- A sentence outline uses complete sentences to express the ideas.
- The writer's thesis statement begins the outline, and the outline ends with suggestions for the concluding paragraph.

EXERCISES

1. Using the topic you selected in "Apply Prewriting Models," (https://courses.candelalearning.com/englishforbusiness/chapter/7-1-apply-prewriting-models/) develop a working thesis statement that states your controlling idea for the piece of writing you are doing. On a sheet of paper, write your working thesis statement.

2. Using the working thesis statement you wrote in #1 and the reading you did in "Apply Prewriting Models," (https://courses.candelalearning.com/englishforbusiness/chapter/7-1-apply-prewriting-models/) construct a topic outline for your essay. Be sure to observe correct outline form, including correct indentions and the use of Roman and arabic numerals and capital letters. Please share with a classmate and compare your outline. Point out areas of interest from their outline and what you would like to learn more about.

3. Expand the topic outline you prepared #2 to make it a sentence outline. In this outline, be sure to include multiple supporting points for your main topic even if your topic outline does not contain them. Be sure to observe correct outline form, including correct indentions and the use of Roman and arabic numerals and capital letters.

CC licensed content, Shared previously

Introductions

WHAT THIS HANDOUT IS ABOUT

This handout will explain the functions of introductions, offer strategies for writing effective ones, help you check your drafted introductions, and provide you with examples of introductions to be avoided.

THE ROLE OF INTRODUCTIONS

Introductions and conclusions can be the most difficult parts of papers to write. Usually when you sit down to respond to an assignment, you have at least some sense of what you want to say in the body of your paper. You might have chosen a few examples you want to use or have an idea that will help you answer the main question of your assignment: these sections, therefore, are not as hard to write. But these middle parts of the paper can't just come out of thin air; they need to be introduced and concluded in a way that makes sense to your reader.

Your introduction and conclusion act as bridges that transport your readers from their own lives into the "place" of your analysis. If your readers pick up your paper about education in the autobiography of Frederick Douglass, for example, they need a transition to help them leave behind the world of Chapel Hill, television, e-mail, and the The Daily Tar Heel and to help them temporarily enter the world of nineteenth-century American slavery. By providing an introduction that helps your readers make a transition between their own world and the issues you will be writing about, you give your readers the tools they need to get into your topic and care about what you are saying. Similarly, once you've hooked your reader with the introduction and offered evidence to prove your thesis, your conclusion can provide a bridge to help your readers make the transition back to their daily lives. (See our handout on conclusions (http://writingcenter.unc.edu/handouts/conclusions/).)

WHY BOTHER WRITING A GOOD INTRODUCTION?

You never get a second chance to make a first impression. The opening paragraph of your paper will provide your readers with their initial impressions of your argument, your writing style, and the overall quality of your work. A vague, disorganized, error-filled, off-the-wall, or boring introduction will probably create a negative impression. On the other hand, a concise, engaging, and well-written introduction will start your readers off thinking highly of you, your analytical skills, your writing, and your paper. This impression is especially important when the audience you are trying to reach (your instructor) will be grading your work.

Your introduction is an important road map for the rest of your paper. Your introduction conveys a lot of information to your readers. You can let them know what your topic is, why it is important, and how you plan to proceed with your discussion. In most academic disciplines, your introduction should contain a thesis that will assert your main argument. It should also, ideally, give the reader a sense of the kinds of information you will use to make that argument and the general organization of the paragraphs and pages that will follow. After reading your introduction, your readers should not have any major surprises in store when they read the main body of your paper.

Ideally, your introduction will make your readers want to read your paper. The introduction should capture your readers' interest, making them want to read the rest of your paper. Opening with a compelling story, a fascinating quotation, an interesting question, or a stirring example can get your readers to see why this topic matters and serve as an invitation for them to join you for an interesting intellectual conversation.

STRATEGIES FOR WRITING AN EFFECTIVE INTRODUCTION

Start by thinking about the question (or questions) you are trying to answer. Your entire essay will be a response to this question, and your introduction is the first step toward that end. Your direct answer to the assigned question will be your thesis, and your thesis will be included in your introduction, so it is a good idea to use the question as a jumping off point. Imagine that you are assigned the following question:

Education has long been considered a major force for American social change, righting the wrongs of our society. Drawing on theNarrative of the Life of Frederick Douglass, discuss the relationship between education and slavery in 19th-century America. Consider the following: How did white control of education reinforce slavery? How did Douglass and other enslaved African Americans view education while they endured slavery? And what role did education play in the acquisition of freedom? Most importantly, consider the degree to which education was or was not a major force for social change with regard to slavery.

You will probably refer back to your assignment extensively as you prepare your complete essay, and the prompt itself can also give you some clues about how to approach the introduction. Notice that it starts with a broad statement, that education has been considered a major force for social change, and then narrows to focus on specific questions from the book. One strategy might be to use a similar model in your own introduction —start off with a big picture sentence or two about the power of education as a force for change as a way of getting your reader interested and then focus in on the details of your argument about Douglass. Of course, a different approach could also be very successful, but looking at the way the professor set up the question can sometimes give you some ideas for how you might answer it.

Decide how general or broad your opening should be. Keep in mind that even a "big picture" opening needs to be clearly related to your topic; an opening sentence that said "Human beings, more than any other creatures on earth, are capable of learning" would be too broad for our sample assignment about slavery and education. If you have ever used Google Maps or similar programs, that experience can provide a helpful way of thinking about how broad your opening should be. Imagine that you're researching Chapel Hill. If what you want to find out is whether Chapel Hill is at roughly the same latitude as Rome, it might make sense to hit that little "minus" sign on the online map until it has zoomed all the way out and you can see the whole globe. If you're trying to figure out how to get from Chapel Hill to Wrightsville Beach, it might make more sense to zoom in to the level where you can see most of North Carolina (but not the rest of the world, or even the rest of the United States). And if you are looking for the intersection of Ridge Road and Manning Drive so that you can find the Writing Center's main office, you may need to zoom all the way in. The question you are asking determines how "broad" your view should be. In the sample assignment above, the questions are probably at the "state" or "city" level of generality. But the introductory sentence about human beings is mismatched—it's definitely at the "global" level. When writing, you need to place your ideas in context—but that context doesn't generally have to be as big as the whole galaxy! (See our handout on understanding assignments (http://writingcenter.unc.edu/handouts/understanding-assignments/) for additional information on the hidden clues in assignments.)

Try writing your introduction last. You may think that you have to write your introduction first, but that isn't necessarily true, and it isn't always the most effective way to craft a good introduction. You may find that you don't know what you are going to argue at the beginning of the writing process, and only through the experience of writing your paper do you discover your main argument. It is perfectly fine to start out thinking that you want to argue a particular point, but wind up arguing something slightly or even dramatically different by the time you've written most of the paper. The writing process can be an important way to organize your ideas, think through complicated issues, refine your thoughts, and develop a sophisticated argument. However, an introduction written at the beginning of that discovery process will not necessarily reflect what you wind up with at the end. You will need to revise your paper to make sure that the introduction, all of the evidence, and the conclusion reflect the argument you intend. Sometimes it's easiest to just write up all of your evidence first and then write the introduction last—that way you can be sure that the introduction will match the body of the paper.

Don't be afraid to write a tentative introduction first and then change it later. Some people find that they need to write some kind of introduction in order to get the writing process started. That's fine, but if you are one of those people, be sure to return to your initial introduction later and rewrite if necessary.

Open with an attention grabber. Sometimes, especially if the topic of your paper is somewhat dry or technical, opening with something catchy can help. Consider these options:

1. an intriguing example (for example, the mistress who initially teaches Douglass but then ceases her instruction as she learns more about slavery)
2. a provocative quotation (Douglass writes that "education and slavery were incompatible with each other")
3. a puzzling scenario (Frederick Douglass says of slaves that "[N]othing has been left undone to cripple their intellects, darken their minds, debase their moral nature, obliterate all traces of their relationship to mankind; and yet how wonderfully they have sustained the mighty load of a most frightful bondage, under which they have been groaning for centuries!" Douglass clearly asserts that slave owners went to great lengths to destroy the mental capacities of slaves, yet his own life story proves that these efforts could be unsuccessful.)
4. a vivid and perhaps unexpected anecdote (for example, "Learning about slavery in the American history course at Frederick Douglass High School, students studied the work slaves did, the impact of slavery on their families, and the rules that governed their lives. We didn't discuss education, however, until one student, Mary, raised her hand and asked, 'But when did they go to school?' That modern high school students could not conceive of an American childhood devoid of formal education speaks volumes about the centrality of education to American youth today and also suggests the significance of the deprivation of education in past generations.")
5. a thought-provoking question (given all of the freedoms that were denied enslaved individuals in the American South, why does Frederick Douglass focus his attentions so squarely on education and literacy?)

Pay special attention to your first sentence. Start off on the right foot with your readers by making sure that the first sentence actually says something useful and that it does so in an interesting and error-free way.

Be straightforward and confident. Avoid statements like "In this paper, I will argue that Frederick Douglass valued education." While this sentence points toward your main argument, it isn't especially interesting. It might be more effective to say what you mean in a declarative sentence. It is much more convincing to tell us that "Frederick Douglass valued education" than to tell us that you are going to say that he did. Assert your main argument confidently. After all, you can't expect your reader to believe it if it doesn't sound like you believe it!

HOW TO EVALUATE YOUR INTRODUCTION DRAFT

Ask a friend to read it and then tell you what he or she expects the paper will discuss, what kinds of evidence the paper will use, and what the tone of the paper will be. If your friend is able to predict the rest of your paper accurately, you probably have a good introduction.

FIVE KINDS OF LESS EFFECTIVE INTRODUCTIONS

1. The place holder introduction. When you don't have much to say on a given topic, it is easy to create this kind of introduction. Essentially, this kind of weaker introduction contains several sentences that are vague and don't really say much. They exist just to take up the "introduction space" in your paper. If you had something more effective to say, you would probably say it, but in the meantime this paragraph is just a place holder.

Example: Slavery was one of the greatest tragedies in American history. There were many different aspects of slavery. Each created different kinds of problems for enslaved people.

2. The restated question introduction. Restating the question can sometimes be an effective strategy, but it can be easy to stop at JUST restating the question instead of offering a more specific, interesting introduction to your paper. The professor or teaching assistant wrote your questions and will be reading ten to seventy essays in response to them—he or she does not need to read a whole paragraph that simply restates the question. Try to do something more interesting.

Example: Indeed, education has long been considered a major force for American social change, righting the wrongs of our society. The Narrative of the Life of Frederick Douglass discusses the relationship between education and slavery in 19th century America, showing how white control of education reinforced slavery and how Douglass and other enslaved African Americans viewed education while they endured. Moreover, the book discusses the role that education played in the acquisition of freedom. Education was a major force for social change with regard to slavery.

3. The Webster's Dictionary introduction. This introduction begins by giving the dictionary definition of one or more of the words in the assigned question. This introduction strategy is on the right track—if you write one of these, you may be trying to establish the important terms of the discussion, and this move builds a bridge to the reader by offering a common, agreed-upon definition for a key idea. You may also be looking for an authority that will lend credibility to your paper. However, anyone can look a word up in the dictionary and copy down what Webster says—it may be far more interesting for you (and your reader) if you develop your own definition of the term in the specific context of your class and assignment, or if you use a defintion from one of the sources you've been reading for class. Also recognize that the dictionary is also not a particularly authoritative work—it doesn't take into account the context of your course and doesn't offer particularly detailed information. If you feel that you must seek out an authority, try to find one that is very relevant and specific. Perhaps a quotation from a source reading might prove better? Dictionary introductions are also ineffective simply because they are so overused. Many graders will see twenty or more papers that begin in this way, greatly decreasing the dramatic impact that any one of those papers will have.

Example: Webster's dictionary defines slavery as "the state of being a slave," as "the practice of owning slaves," and as "a condition of hard work and subjection."

4. The "dawn of man" introduction. This kind of introduction generally makes broad, sweeping statements about the relevance of this topic since the beginning of time. It is usually very general (similar to the place holder introduction) and fails to connect to the thesis. You may write this kind of introduction when you don't have much to say—which is precisely why it is ineffective.

Example: Since the dawn of man, slavery has been a problem in human history.

5. The book report introduction. This introduction is what you had to do for your elementary school book reports. It gives the name and author of the book you are writing about, tells what the book is about, and offers other basic facts about the book. You might resort to this sort of introduction when you are trying to fill space because it's a familiar, comfortable format. It is ineffective because it offers details that your reader already knows and that are irrelevant to the thesis.

Example: Frederick Douglass wrote his autobiography, Narrative of the Life of Frederick Douglass, An American Slave, in the 1840s. It was published in 1986 by Penguin Books. In it, he tells the story of his life.

WORKS CONSULTED

We consulted these works while writing the original version of this handout. This is not a comprehensive list of resources on the handout's topic, and we encourage you to do your own research to find the latest publications on this topic. Please do not use this list as a model for the format of your own reference list, as it may not match the citation style you are using. For guidance on formatting citations, please see the UNC Libraries citation tutorial (http://www.lib.unc.edu/instruct/citations/).

All quotations are from Frederick Douglass, *Narrative of the Life of Frederick Douglass, An American Slave*, edited and with introduction by Houston A. Baker, Jr., New York: Penguin Books, 1986.

CC licensed content, Shared previously

- Introductions. **Provided by**: UNC Writing Center. **Located at**: http://writingcenter.unc.edu/handouts/introductions/ (http://writingcenter.unc.edu/handouts/introductions/). **License**: *CC BY-NC-ND: Attribution-NonCommercial-NoDerivatives (https://creativecommons.org/licenses/by-nc-nd/4.0/)*

Conclusions

WHAT THIS HANDOUT IS ABOUT

This handout will explain the functions of conclusions, offer strategies for writing effective ones, help you evaluate your drafted conclusions, and suggest conclusion strategies to avoid.

ABOUT CONCLUSIONS

Introductions and conclusions can be the most difficult parts of papers to write. While the body is often easier to write, it needs a frame around it. An introduction and conclusion frame your thoughts and bridge your ideas for the reader.

Just as your introduction acts as a bridge that transports your readers from their own lives into the "place" of your analysis, your conclusion can provide a bridge to help your readers make the transition back to their daily lives. Such a conclusion will help them see why all your analysis and information should matter to them after they put the paper down.

Your conclusion is your chance to have the last word on the subject. The conclusion allows you to have the final say on the issues you have raised in your paper, to synthesize your thoughts, to demonstrate the importance of your ideas, and to propel your reader to a new view of the subject. It is also your opportunity to make a good final impression and to end on a positive note.

Your conclusion can go beyond the confines of the assignment. The conclusion pushes beyond the boundaries of the prompt and allows you to consider broader issues, make new connections, and elaborate on the significance of your findings.

Your conclusion should make your readers glad they read your paper. Your conclusion gives your reader something to take away that will help them see things differently or appreciate your topic in personally relevant ways. It can suggest broader implications that will not only interest your reader, but also enrich your reader's life in some way. It is your gift to the reader.

STRATEGIES FOR WRITING AN EFFECTIVE CONCLUSION

One or more of the following strategies may help you write an effective conclusion.

- Play the "So What" Game. If you're stuck and feel like your conclusion isn't saying anything new or interesting, ask a friend to read it with you. Whenever you make a statement from your conclusion, ask the friend to say, "So what?" or "Why should anybody care?" Then ponder that question and answer it. Here's how it might go:You: *Basically, I'm just saying that education was important to Douglass.*

  Friend: *So what?*

  You: *Well, it was important because it was a key to him feeling like a free and equal citizen.*

  Friend: *Why should anybody care?*

  You: *That's important because plantation owners tried to keep slaves from being educated so that they could maintain control. When Douglass obtained an education, he undermined that control personally.*

  You can also use this strategy on your own, asking yourself "So What?" as you develop your ideas or your draft.
- Return to the theme or themes in the introduction. This strategy brings the reader full circle. For example, if you begin by describing a scenario, you can end with the same scenario as proof that your essay is helpful in creating a new

understanding. You may also refer to the introductory paragraph by using key words or parallel concepts and images that you also used in the introduction.

- Synthesize, don't summarize: Include a brief summary of the paper's main points, but don't simply repeat things that were in your paper. Instead, show your reader how the points you made and the support and examples you used fit together. Pull it all together.
- Include a provocative insight or quotation from the research or reading you did for your paper.
- Propose a course of action, a solution to an issue, or questions for further study. This can redirect your reader's thought process and help her to apply your info and ideas to her own life or to see the broader implications.
- Point to broader implications. For example, if your paper examines the Greensboro sit-ins or another event in the Civil Rights Movement, you could point out its impact on the Civil Rights Movement as a whole. A paper about the style of writer Virginia Woolf could point to her influence on other writers or on later feminists.

STRATEGIES TO AVOID

- Beginning with an unnecessary, overused phrase such as "in conclusion," "in summary," or "in closing." Although these phrases can work in speeches, they come across as wooden and trite in writing.
- Stating the thesis for the very first time in the conclusion.
- Introducing a new idea or subtopic in your conclusion.
- Ending with a rephrased thesis statement without any substantive changes.
- Making sentimental, emotional appeals that are out of character with the rest of an analytical paper.
- Including evidence (quotations, statistics, etc.) that should be in the body of the paper.

FOUR KINDS OF INEFFECTIVE CONCLUSIONS

1. The "That's My Story and I'm Sticking to It" Conclusion. This conclusion just restates the thesis and is usually painfully short. It does not push the ideas forward. People write this kind of conclusion when they can't think of anything else to say. Example: In conclusion, Frederick Douglass was, as we have seen, a pioneer in American education, proving that education was a major force for social change with regard to slavery.

2. The "Sherlock Holmes" Conclusion. Sometimes writers will state the thesis for the very first time in the conclusion. You might be tempted to use this strategy if you don't want to give everything away too early in your paper. You may think it would be more dramatic to keep the reader in the dark until the end and then "wow" him with your main idea, as in a Sherlock Holmes mystery. The reader, however, does not expect a mystery, but an analytical discussion of your topic in an academic style, with the main argument (thesis) stated up front. Example: (After a paper that lists numerous incidents from the book but never says what these incidents reveal about Douglass and his views on education): So, as the evidence above demonstrates, Douglass saw education as a way to undermine the slaveholders' power and also an important step toward freedom.

3. The "America the Beautiful"/"I Am Woman"/"We Shall Overcome" Conclusion. This kind of conclusion usually draws on emotion to make its appeal, but while this emotion and even sentimentality may be very heartfelt, it is usually out of character with the rest of an analytical paper. A more sophisticated commentary, rather than emotional praise, would be a more fitting tribute to the topic. Example: Because of the efforts of fine Americans like Frederick Douglass, countless others have seen the shining beacon of light that is education. His example was a torch that lit the way for others. Frederick Douglass was truly an American hero.

4. The "Grab Bag" Conclusion. This kind of conclusion includes extra information that the writer found or thought of but couldn't integrate into the main paper. You may find it hard to leave out details that you discovered after hours of research and thought, but adding random facts and bits of evidence at the end of an otherwise-well-organized essay can just create confusion. Example: In addition to being an educational pioneer, Frederick Douglass provides an interesting case study for masculinity in the American South. He also offers historians an interesting glimpse into slave resistance when he confronts Covey, the overseer. His relationships with female relatives reveal the importance of family in the slave

community.

WORKS CONSULTED

We consulted these works while writing the original version of this handout. This is not a comprehensive list of resources on the handout's topic, and we encourage you to do your own research to find the latest publications on this topic. Please do not use this list as a model for the format of your own reference list, as it may not match the citation style you are using. For guidance on formatting citations, please see the UNC Libraries citation tutorial (http://www.lib.unc.edu/instruct/citations/).

All quotations are from:

Douglass, Frederick. *Narrative of the Life of Frederick Douglass, an American Slave*, edited and with introduction by Houston A. Baker, Jr., New York: Penguin Books, 1986.

Strategies for Writing a Conclusion. Literacy Education Online, St. Cloud State University. 18 May 2005 <http://leo.stcloudstate.edu/acadwrite/conclude.html>.

Conclusions. Nesbitt-Johnston Writing Center, Hamilton College. 17 May 2005 <http://www.hamilton.edu/academic/Resource/WC/SampleConclusions.html>.

Discussion: Argument and Counterargument

This will be a small group discussion—you'll only see posts from a smaller group of people.

Previously you did some great work identifying your target audience for your research project. The whole fun of writing a persuasive paper is to pick an audience who disagrees with you, or at least is undecided about the matter. Then you use charm, wit, and raw intelligence to prove that they're absolutely silly for thinking what they do, and that they better come over to your side or else the world will end.

In being persuasive and winning the fight, it helps a lot to remember that your target audience has reasons for their position on the issue. Those reasons may not be GOOD ones, of course, but they have some motivation for thinking or feeling the way they do. (I still don't like eating at Jack in the Box because a friend of mine had a really bad experience there years ago, in another state. Not a very rational reason, I admit, but it does shape my behavior when it comes to fast food.)

In order to be truly persuasive, you have to understand what people's motivations are, and acknowledge those in your essay. If you don't, then readers will think one of two things: 1) you don't know what the other side thinks, and are therefore ignorant, or 2) you know what they think, but you just don't have any good response for it and are avoiding it.

I'd like you to visit POWA's "Anticipating Opposition" article (http://www.powa.org/index.php/convince/anticipating-opposition)and read the content there. Then, return to this discussion and build your own pro/con chart, using your thesis as the "proposition." It'll be easier to create a list, rather than a chart, given our constraints in the discussion forum platform.

Then look at one or two of your "con" statements in more detail. How will you acknowledge these arguments in your own essay, and what will you say to your reader to counter them? For instance, if I were trying to talk myself into eating at Jack in the Box again, I'd acknowledge that finding a bug in your food is yes, a traumatic event. But it was an isolated incident, and in no way reflects the standards of the chain overall. I'd go into food safety data and possibly relate the health scores of the local franchises recently. Maybe I'd even embark on a smear campaign and talk about similar events that have occurred at other fast food chains, to show it's not particular to one brand.

Your post should be at least 150-200 words. It doesn't have to be grammatically perfect, but should use standard English (no text-speak, please) and normal capitalization rules.

You will also need to return to this Discussion to reply to at least one of your group members' posts. Content could include, but is not limited to, any of the following: Suggest further elements that could be added either to the Pro or Con side of their chart. Indicate what it would take for you to be convinced, if you were on the con side of the argument.

Responses are weighed as heavily as your initial posting, and should be roughly as long (150-200 words). Responses should indicate you've read your classmate's post carefully. Include specific details from the post you're responding to in your reply.

Synthesizing and Supporting Refutals

Definition

Refutals, or counterarguments, break down the other side's claims and reasons. Refutals are typically placed at the ends of the other side's paragraphs. Because it takes time to disprove—partially or total—another side's views, refutals must be well developed. A few generalizations that turn away the other side's readers will not do!

Why Refutals Matter

It is not enough for writers to show that they disagree. In academic writing and especially in the research project, nobody gives much credit for the existence of another's point of view. You must do more than show *that* they are misguided; the refutals are an area where you can strike back at the underdone or overdone claims of your opposition.

Refuting well shows the audience that you know more than just your side. A well-researched point of view will have taken into account several sides. (There are more than two sides to your topic, correct?) Skilled writers think strategically about how they will respond to the other side. Because each side has stronger and weaker points, you must show fairness in giving ground to those opposition points which carry weight; conversely, you can be more aggressive in undercutting their points if they lack value. Such variety shows readers that you know which of their points are valid.

Just Doing What A Virus Does. . .

Viruses interrupt cell activity, hijacking the cell and making copies of themselves. The virus metaphor in writing goes like this: Source support is needed, but it's an interruption of your voice, your ideas. We work at integrating and subordinating the support so that it remains in a backing role. However, when writing refutals we try to be like viruses. We take over "their" paragraph and interrupt its flow. We bring in reasons why what they say is wrong, to some greater or lesser extent. We end with our ideas, not theirs. (In a weird way, some of our bad high-school habits of interrupting and switching focus, undercutting progress, can help us as we deal with the other side! Be specific and professional as you do this, though. Your refutal section fails if it sounds like a newspaper editorial (all generalized talk and no support). Save some of your best cited material for this job of blunting the other side's progress. **The key reminder is that you have to show their ideas fairly. You cannot distort their ideas in this strange process.**

"Don't You Take that Tone with Me, Missy/Mister!"

Tone is the author's attitude toward the material. It can be given away in diction, detail level, or even the amount of attention taken with a given idea. Work on wording your refutals so that you are not utterly demolishing the other side's views. Keep the conversation going. **Refutals move from their ideas to yours to where you want the audience to be; this is a tough series of moves to make!**Read your work aloud to gauge its tone and the effects it creates.

Cited Support

At the high-school level, writers often get away with uninterpreted citations. Cited, supported, well-integrated refutals are expected. If you are telling someone that they are wrong, do them the courtesy of backing it up. Because people often wait till last to do refutals, they often turn into the worst-written parts of papers. Refutals are the true test of the health of your argument; any lack of research will show through plainly.

Signal Phrases

"So Smith said _____. Who cares?" Signal phrases hand off the material from you to the source. Citations end the source use. Signal phrases also build source credibility. Tell us why so-and-so matters. Give use the context for their summary/paraphrase/quote. Hopefully, you can see why signal phrases are that much more important in the delicate refutal sections. **Work through source bias and credibility in the ways you deal with the setup of support.**

Transitions

"Which side is she on?" This is an ominous question that can appear if writers do not use transitions well enough. Use lists of transitions (found easily enough, you researchers) to make it clear when you are moving from arguing the opposition to arguing against the opposition. If a paragraph or two contains the con reason and the refutals, be sure we know where you switch from con to refutal. Similarly, signal when you are moving from one idea to the next.

Refutals often point toward areas of common ground or compromise. Think about how your refutals might alter/qualify/limit your thesis claim. The thesis should be available for revision throughout the writing process.

What To Do Now

- Using your sources, go through highlighted material and locate support for your citations. Decide on the extent to which each opposing reason is valid.
- Place your refutals within the opposing side's paragraphs. Set them up and the interpret them.
- Link the cited support to your idea that the opposing reason is misguided. (Remember the logical fallacies; they should provide a pattern by which you can refute the other side's moves.)

CC licensed content, Original

- Synthesizing and Supporting Refutals. **Authored by**: Joshua Dickinson. **Provided by**: Jefferson Community College. **Located at**: http://www.sunyjefferson.edu (http://www.sunyjefferson.edu). **Project**: College Writing Handbook. **License**: *CC BY-SA: Attribution-ShareAlike (https://creativecommons.org/licenses/by-sa/4.0/)*

Logical Fallacies

Logical Fallacies

Logical fallacies are errors in reasoning. The Excelsior OWL site has several of the main fallacies (http://owl.excelsior.edu/argument-and-critical-thinking/logical-fallacies/) outlined. If you become familiar with them, you can identify logical fallacies in others' arguments. You can also avoid using logical fallacies in your own writing. . . or, if you're very clever, use them to your advantage to convince of something. Beware! If a good reader catches the writer committing a fallacy, they will likely read with an edge, becoming an adversary of the writer. It's just logical that they would do so.

Wouldn't Mr. Spock would agree?

CC licensed content, Original

- Logical Fallacies. **Authored by**: Joshua Dickinson. **Provided by**: Jefferson Community College. **Located at**: http://www.sunyjefferson.edu (http://www.sunyjefferson.edu). **Project**: ENG 101. **License**: *CC BY-SA: Attribution-ShareAlike (https://creativecommons.org/licenses/by-sa/4.0/)*

Logical Fallacies Handlist

Logical Fallacies Handlist:

Fallacies are statements that might sound reasonable or superficially true but are actually flawed or dishonest. When readers detect them, these logical fallacies backfire by making the audience think the writer is (a) unintelligent or (b) deceptive. It is important to avoid them in your own arguments, and it is also important to be able to spot them in others' arguments so a false line of reasoning won't fool you. Think of this as intellectual *kung-fu*: the vital art of self-defense in a debate. For extra impact, learn both the Latin terms and the English equivalents. You can click here to download a PDF version of this material (https://web.cn.edu/kwheeler/documents/Logic_Fallacies_List.pdf).

In general, one useful way to organize fallacies is by category. We have below **fallacies of relevance (https://web.cn.edu/ kwheeler/fallacies_list.html#fallacies_of_relevance_anchor), component fallacies (https://web.cn.edu/kwheeler/ fallacies_list.html#component_fallacies_anchor), fallacies of ambiguity (https://web.cn.edu/kwheeler/ fallacies_list.html#fallacies_of_ambiguity_anchor)**, and **fallacies of omission (https://web.cn.edu/kwheeler/ fallacies_list.html#fallacies_of_omission_anchor)**. We will discuss each type in turn. The last point to discuss is **Occam's Razor** (https://web.cn.edu/kwheeler/logic_occam.html).

FALLACIES OF RELEVANCE: These fallacies appeal to evidence or examples that are not relevant to the argument at hand.

Appeal to Force (*Argumentum Ad Baculum* or the "Might-Makes-Right" Fallacy): This argument uses force, the threat of force, or some other unpleasant backlash to make the audience accept a conclusion. It commonly appears as a last resort when evidence or rational arguments fail to convince a reader. If the debate is about whether or not 2+2=4, an opponent's argument that he will smash your nose in if you don't agree with his claim doesn't change the truth of an issue. Logically, this consideration has nothing to do with the points under consideration. The fallacy is not limited to threats of violence, however. The fallacy includes threats of any unpleasant backlash—financial, professional, and so on. Example: "Superintendent, you should cut the school budget by $16,000. I need not remind you that past school boards have fired superintendents who cannot keep down costs." While intimidation may force the superintendent to conform, it does not convince him that the choice to cut the budget was the most beneficial for the school or community. Lobbyists use this method when they remind legislators that they represent so many thousand votes in the legislators' constituencies and threaten to throw the politician out of office if he doesn't vote the way they want. Teachers use this method if they state that students should hold the same political or philosophical position as the teachers or risk failing the class. Note that it is isn't a logical fallacy, however, to assert that students must fulfill certain requirements in the course or risk failing the class!

Genetic Fallacy: The genetic fallacy is the claim that an idea, product, or person must be untrustworthy because of its racial, geographic, or ethnic origin. "That car can't possibly be any good! It was made in Japan!" Or, "Why should I listen to her argument? She comes from California, and we all know those people are flakes." Or, "Ha! I'm not reading that book. It was published in Tennessee, and we know all Tennessee folk are hillbillies and rednecks!" This type of fallacy is closely related to the fallacy of *argumentum ad hominem* or **personal attack (https://web.cn.edu/kwheeler/ fallacies_list.html#personal_attack_anchor)**, appearing immediately below.

Personal Attack (*Argumentum Ad Hominem*, literally, "argument toward the man." Also called "Poisoning the Well"): Attacking or praising the people who make an argument, rather than discussing the argument itself. This practice is fallacious because the personal character of an individual is logically irrelevant to the truth or falseness of the argument itself. The statement "2+2=4" is true regardless if it is stated by criminals, congressmen, or pastors. There are two subcategories:

> **(1) Abusive**: To argue that proposals, assertions, or arguments must be false or dangerous because they originate with atheists, Christians, Muslims, communists, capitalists, the John Birch Society, Catholics, anti-Catholics, racists, anti-racists, feminists, misogynists (or any other group) is fallacious. This persuasion comes from irrational psychological transference rather than from an appeal to evidence or logic concerning the issue at hand. This is similar to the **genetic fallacy (https://web.cn.edu/kwheeler/ fallacies_list.html#genetic_fallacy_anchor)**, and only an anti-intellectual would argue otherwise.

> **(2) Circumstantial**: To argue that an opponent should accept or reject an argument because of circumstances in his or her life. If one's adversary is a clergyman, suggesting that he should accept a particular argument because not to do so would be incompatible with the scriptures is such a fallacy. To argue that, because the reader is a Republican or Democrat, she must vote for a specific measure is likewise a circumstantial fallacy. The opponent's special circumstances have no control over the truth or untruth of a specific contention. The speaker or writer must find additional evidence beyond that to make a strong case. This is also similar to the **genetic fallacy (https://web.cn.edu/kwheeler/ fallacies_list.html#genetic_fallacy_anchor)** in some ways. If you are a college student who wants to learn rational thought, you simply must avoid circumstantial fallacies.

Argumentum ad Populum (Literally "Argument to the People"): Using an appeal to popular assent, often by arousing the feelings and enthusiasm of the multitude rather than building an argument. It is a favorite device with the propagandist, the demagogue, and the advertiser. An example of this type of argument is Shakespeare's version of Mark Antony's funeral oration for Julius Caesar. There are three basic approaches:

(1) **Bandwagon Approach**: "Everybody is doing it." This *argumentum ad populum* asserts that, since the majority of people believes an argument or chooses a particular course of action, the argument must be true, or the course of action must be followed, or the decision must be the best choice. For instance, "85% of consumers purchase IBM computers rather than Macintosh; all those people can't be wrong. IBM must make the best computers." Popular acceptance of any argument does not prove it to be valid, nor does popular use of any product necessarily prove it is the best one. After all, 85% of people may once have thought planet earth was flat, but that majority's belief didn't mean the earth really *was* flat when they believed it! Keep this in mind, and remember that everybody should avoid this type of logical fallacy.

(2) **Patriotic Approach**: "Draping oneself in the flag." This argument asserts that a certain stance is true or correct because it is somehow patriotic, and that those who disagree are unpatriotic. It overlaps with *pathos (https://web.cn.edu/kwheeler/pathos.html)* and *argumentum ad hominem (https://web.cn.edu/kwheeler/ fallacies_list.html#personal_attack_anchor)* to a certain extent. The best way to spot it is to look for emotionally charged terms like Americanism, rugged individualism, motherhood, patriotism, godless communism, etc. A true American would never use this approach. And a truly free man will exercise his American right to drink beer, since beer belongs in this great country of ours. This approach is unworthy of a good citizen.

(3) **Snob Approach**: This type of *argumentum ad populum (https://web.cn.edu/ kwheeler/fallacies_list.html#argumentum_ad_populum_anchor)* doesn't assert "everybody is doing it," but rather that "all the best people are doing it." For instance, "Any true intellectual would recognize the necessity for studying logical fallacies." The implication is that anyone who fails to recognize the truth of the author's assertion is not an intellectual, and thus the reader had best recognize that necessity.

In all three of these examples, the rhetorician does not supply evidence that an argument is true; he merely makes assertions about people who agree or disagree with the argument. For Christian students in religious schools like Carson-Newman, we might add a fourth category, "**Covering Oneself in the Cross**." This argument asserts that a certain political or denominational stance is true or correct because it is somehow "Christian," and that anyone who disagrees is behaving in an "un-Christian" or "godless" manner. (It is similar to the **patriotic approach** (https://web.cn.edu/kwheeler/ fallacies_list.html#patriotic_approach_anchor) except it substitutes a gloss of piety instead of patriotism.) Examples include the various "Christian Voting Guides" that appear near election time, many of them published by non-Church related organizations with hidden financial/political agendas, or the stereotypical crooked used-car salesman who keeps a pair of bibles on his dashboard in order to win the trust of those he would fleece. Keep in mind Moliere's question in *Tartuffe*: "Is not a face quite different than a mask?" Is not the appearance of Christianity quite different than actual Christianity? Christians should beware of such manipulation since they are especially vulnerable to it.

Appeal to Tradition (*Argumentum Ad Traditionem; aka Argumentum Ad Antiquitatem*): This line of thought asserts that a premise must be true because people have always believed it or done it. For example, "We know the earth is flat because generations have thought that for centuries!" Alternatively, the appeal to tradition might conclude that the premise has always worked in the past and will thus always work in the future: "Jefferson City has kept its urban growth boundary at six miles for the past thirty years. That has been good enough for thirty years, so why should we change it now? If it ain't broke, don't fix it." Such an argument is appealing in that it seems to be common sense, but it ignores important questions. Might an alternative policy work even better than the old one? Are there drawbacks to that long-standing policy? Are circumstances changing from the way they were thirty years ago? Has new evidence emerged that might throw that long-standing policy into doubt?

Appeal to Improper Authority (*Argumentum Ad Verecundium*, literally "argument from that which is improper"): An appeal to an improper authority, such as a famous person or a source that may not be reliable or who might not know anything about the topic. This fallacy attempts to capitalize upon feelings of respect or familiarity with a famous individual. It is not fallacious to refer to an admitted authority if the individual's expertise is within a strict field of knowledge. On the other hand, to cite Einstein to settle an argument about education or economics is fallacious. To cite Darwin, an authority on biology, on religious matters is fallacious. To cite Cardinal Spellman on legal problems is fallacious. The worst offenders usually involve movie stars and psychic hotlines. A subcategory is the **Appeal to Biased Authority**. In this sort of appeal, the authority is one who actually *is* knowledgeable on the matter, but one who may have professional or personal motivations that render his professional judgment suspect: for instance, "To determine whether fraternities are beneficial to this campus, we interviewed all the frat presidents." Or again, "To find out whether or not sludge-mining really is endangering the Tuskogee salamander's breeding grounds, we interviewed the owners of the sludge-mines, who declared there is no problem." Indeed, it is important to get "both viewpoints" on an argument, but basing a substantial part of your argument on a source that has personal, professional, or financial interests at stake may lead to biased arguments. As Upton Sinclair once stated, "It's difficult to get a man to understand something when his salary depends upon his not understanding it." Sinclair is pointing out that even a knowledgeable authority might not be entirely rational on a topic when he has economic incentives that bias his thinking.

Appeal to Emotion (*Argumentum Ad Misericordiam*, literally, "argument from pity"): An emotional appeal concerning what should be a logical issue during a debate. While ***pathos*** (*https://web.cn.edu/kwheeler/pathos.html*) generally works to reinforce a reader's sense of duty or outrage at some abuse, if a writer tries to use emotion merely for the sake of getting the reader to accept what should be a logical conclusion, the argument is a fallacy. For example, in the 1880s, prosecutors in a Virginia court presented overwhelming proof that a boy was guilty of murdering his parents with an ax. The defense presented a "not-guilty" plea for on the grounds that the boy was now an orphan, with no one to look after his interests if the court was not lenient. This appeal to emotion obviously seems misplaced, and the argument is irrelevant to the question of whether or not he did the crime.

Argument from Adverse Consequences: Asserting that an argument must be false because the implications of it being true would create negative results. For instance, "The medical tests show that Grandma has advanced cancer. However, that *can't* be true because then she would die! I refuse to believe it!" The argument is illogical because truth and falsity are not contingent based upon how much we like or dislike the consequences of that truth. Grandma, indeed, might have cancer, in spite of how negative that fact may be or how cruelly it may affect us.

Argument from Personal Incredulity: Asserting that opponent's argument must be false because you personally don't understand it or can't follow its technicalities. For instance, one person might assert, "I don't understand that engineer's argument about how airplanes can fly. Therefore, I cannot believe that airplanes are able to fly." *Au contraire*, that speaker's own mental limitations do not limit the physical world—so airplanes may very well be able to fly in spite of a person's inability to understand how they work. One person's comprehension is not relevant to the truth of a matter.

COMPONENT FALLACIES: Component fallacies are errors in inductive and deductive reasoning or in syllogistic terms that fail to overlap.

Begging the Question (also called *Petitio Principii*, this term is sometimes used interchangeably with **Circular Reasoning** (https://web.cn.edu/kwheeler/fallacies_list.html#circular_reasoning_anchor)): If writers assume as evidence for their argument the very conclusion they are attempting to prove, they engage in the fallacy of begging the question. The most common form of this fallacy is when the first claim is initially loaded with the very conclusion one has yet to prove. For instance, suppose a particular student group states, "Useless courses like English 101 should be dropped from the college's curriculum." The members of the student group then immediately move on in the argument, illustrating that spending money on a useless course is something nobody wants. Yes, we all agree that spending money on useless courses is a bad thing. However, those students never did prove that English 101 was *itself* a useless course—they merely "begged the question" and moved on to the next "safe" part of the argument, skipping over the part that's the real controversy, the heart of the matter, the most important component. Begging the question is often hidden in the form of a **complex question** (https://web.cn.edu/kwheeler/fallacies_list.html#complex_question_anchor) (see below).

Circular Reasoning is closely related to **begging the question** (https://web.cn.edu/kwheeler/fallacies_list.html#begging_the_question_anchor). Often the writers using this fallacy word take one idea and phrase it in two statements. The assertions differ sufficiently to obscure the fact that that the same proposition occurs as both a premise and a conclusion. The speaker or author then tries to "prove" his or her assertion by merely repeating it in different words. Richard Whately wrote in *Elements of Logic* (London 1826): "To allow every man unbounded freedom of speech must always be on the whole, advantageous to the state; for it is highly conducive to the interest of the community that each individual should enjoy a liberty perfectly unlimited of expressing his sentiments." Obviously the premise is not logically irrelevant to the conclusion, for if the premise is true the conclusion must also be true. It is, however, logically irrelevant in *proving* the conclusion. In the example, the author is repeating the same point in different words, and then attempting to "prove" the first assertion with the second one. A more complex but equally fallacious type of circular reasoning is to create a circular chain of reasoning like this one: "God exists." "How do you know that God exists?" "The Bible says so." "Why should I believe the Bible?" "Because it's the inspired word of God." If we draw this out as a chart, it looks like this:

CIRCULAR REASONING

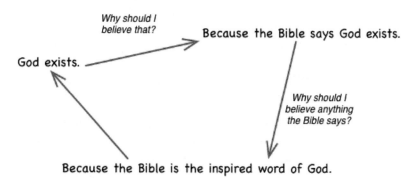

The so-called "final proof" relies on unproven evidence set forth initially as the subject of debate. Basically, the argument goes in an endless circle, with each step of the argument relying on a previous one, which in turn relies on the first argument yet to be proven. Surely God deserves a more intelligible argument than the circular reasoning proposed in this example!

Hasty Generalization (*Dicto Simpliciter*, also called "Jumping to Conclusions," "Converse Accident"): Mistaken use of inductive reasoning when there are too few samples to prove a point. Example: "Susan failed Biology 101. Herman failed Biology 101.

Egbert failed Biology 101. I therefore conclude that most students who take Biology 101 will fail it." In understanding and characterizing general situations, a logician cannot normally examine every single example. However, the examples used in inductive reasoning should be typical of the problem or situation at hand. Maybe Susan, Herman, and Egbert are exceptionally poor students. Maybe they were sick and missed too many lectures that term to pass. If a logician wants to make the case that most students will fail Biology 101, she should (a) get a very large sample—at least one larger than three—or (b) if that isn't possible, she will need to go out of his way to prove to the reader that her three samples are somehow representative of the norm. If a logician considers only exceptional or dramatic cases and generalizes a rule that fits these alone, the author commits the fallacy of hasty generalization.

One common type of hasty generalization is the **Fallacy of Accident**. This error occurs when one applies a general rule to a particular case when accidental circumstances render the general rule inapplicable. For example, in Plato's *Republic*, Plato finds an exception to the general rule that one should return what one has borrowed: "Suppose that a friend when in his right mind has deposited arms with me and asks for them when he is not in his right mind. Ought I to give the weapons back to him? No one would say that I ought or that I should be right in doing so. . . ." What is true in general may not be true universally and without qualification. So remember, generalizations are bad. All of them. Every single last one. Except, of course, for those that are not.

Another common example of this fallacy is the **misleading statistic**. Suppose an individual argues that women must be incompetent drivers, and he points out that last Tuesday at the Department of Motor Vehicles, 50% of the women who took the driving test failed. That would seem to be compelling evidence from the way the statistic is set forth. However, if only two women took the test that day, the results would be far less clear-cut. Incidentally, the cartoon *Dilbert* makes much of an incompetent manager who cannot perceive misleading statistics. He does a statistical study of when employees call in sick and cannot come to work during the five-day work week. He becomes furious to learn that 40% of office "sick-days" occur on Mondays (20%) and Fridays (20%)—just in time to create a three-day weekend. Suspecting fraud, he decides to punish his workers. The irony, of course, is that these two days compose 40% of a five day work week, so the numbers are completely average. Similar nonsense emerges when parents or teachers complain that "50% of students perform at or below the national average on standardized tests in mathematics and verbal aptitude." Of course they do! The very nature of an average implies that!

False Cause: This fallacy establishes a cause/effect relationship that does not exist. There are various Latin names for various analyses of the fallacy. The two most common include these types:

(1) **Non Causa Pro Causa** (Literally, "Not the cause for a cause"): A general, catch-all category for mistaking a false cause of an event for the real cause.

(2) **Post Hoc, Ergo Propter Hoc** (Literally: "After this, therefore because of this"): This type of false cause occurs when the writer mistakenly assumes that, because the first event preceded the second event, it must mean the first event caused the later one. Sometimes it does, but sometimes it doesn't. It is the honest writer's job to establish clearly that connection rather than merely assert it exists. Example: "A black cat crossed my path at noon. An hour later, my mother had a heart-attack. Because the first event occurred earlier, it must have caused the bad luck later." This is how superstitions begin.

> The most common examples are arguments that viewing a particular movie or show, or listening to a particular type of music "caused" the listener to perform an antisocial act–to snort coke, shoot classmates, or take up a life of crime. These may be potential suspects for the cause, but the mere fact that an individual did these acts and subsequently behaved in a certain way does not yet conclusively rule out other causes. Perhaps the listener had an abusive home-life or school-life, suffered from a chemical imbalance leading to depression and paranoia, or made a bad choice in his companions. Other potential causes must be examined before asserting that only one event or circumstance alone earlier in time *caused* a event or behavior later. For more information, see **correlation and causation** (https://web.cn.edu/kwheeler/logic_causation.html).

Irrelevant Conclusion (*Ignorantio Elenchi*): This fallacy occurs when a rhetorician adapts an argument purporting to establish a particular conclusion and directs it to prove a different conclusion. For example, when a particular proposal for housing legislation is under consideration, a legislator may argue that decent housing for all people is desirable. Everyone, presumably, will agree. However, the question at hand concerns a particular measure. The question really isn't, "Is it good to have decent housing?" The question really is, "Will this particular measure actually provide it or is there a better alternative?" This type of fallacy is a common one in student papers when students use a shared assumption–such as the fact that decent housing is a desirable thing to have–and then spend the bulk of their essays focused on that fact rather than the real question at issue. It's similar to **begging the question** (https://web.cn.edu/kwheeler/fallacies_list.html#begging_the_question_anchor), above.

One of the most common forms of *Ignorantio Elenchi* is the "**Red Herring**." A red herring is a deliberate attempt to change the subject or divert the argument from the real question at issue to some side-point; for instance, "Senator Jones should not be held accountable for cheating on his income tax. After all, there are other senators who have done far worse things." Another example: "I should not pay a fine for reckless driving. There are many other people on the street who are dangerous criminals and rapists, and the police should be chasing them, not harassing a decent tax-paying citizen like me." Certainly, worse criminals do exist, but that it is another issue! The questions at hand are (1) did the speaker drive recklessly, and (2) should he pay a fine for it?

Another similar example of the red herring is the fallacy known as *Tu Quoque* (Latin for "And you too!"), which asserts that the advice or argument must be false simply because the person presenting the advice doesn't consistently follow it herself. For instance, "Susan the yoga instructor claims that a low-fat diet and exercise are good for you–but I saw her last week pigging out on oreos, so her argument must be a load of hogwash." Or, "Reverend Jeremias claims that theft is wrong, but how can theft be wrong if Jeremias himself admits he stole objects when he was a child?" Or "Thomas Jefferson made many arguments about equality and liberty for all Americans, but he himself kept slaves, so we can dismiss any thoughts he had on those topics."

Straw Man Argument: A subtype of the **red herring** (https://web.cn.edu/kwheeler/fallacies_list.html#red_herring_anchor), this fallacy includes any lame attempt to "prove" an argument by overstating, exaggerating, or over-simplifying the arguments of the opposing side. Such an approach is building a straw man argument. The name comes from the idea of a boxer or fighter who meticulously fashions a false opponent out of straw, like a scarecrow, and then easily knocks it over in the ring before his admiring audience. His "victory" is a hollow mockery, of course, because the straw-stuffed opponent is incapable of fighting back. When a writer makes a cartoon-like caricature of the opposing argument, ignoring the real or subtle points of contention, and then proceeds to knock down each "fake" point one-by-one, he has created a straw man argument.

For instance, one speaker might be engaged in a debate concerning welfare. The opponent argues, "Tennessee should increase funding to unemployed single mothers during the first year after childbirth because they need sufficient money to provide medical care for their newborn children." The second speaker retorts, "My opponent believes that some parasites who don't work should get a free ride from the tax money of hard-working honest citizens. I'll show you why he's wrong . . ." In this example, the second speaker is engaging in a straw man strategy, distorting the opposition's statement about medical care for newborn children into an oversimplified form so he can more easily appear to "win." However, the second speaker is only defeating a dummy-argument rather than honestly engaging in the real nuances of the debate.

Non Sequitur (literally, "It does not follow"): A *non sequitur* is any argument that does not follow from the previous statements. Usually what happened is that the writer leaped from A to B and then jumped to D, leaving out step C of an argument she thought through in her head, but did not put down on paper. The phrase is applicable in general to any type of logical fallacy, but logicians use the term particularly in reference to syllogistic errors such as the **undistributed middle term (https://web.cn.edu/kwheeler/fallacies_list.html#undistributed_term_anchor)**, *non causa pro causa* (https://web.cn.edu/ kwheeler/fallacies_list.html#false_cause_anchor), and *ignorantio elenchi (https://web.cn.edu/kwheeler/ fallacies_list.html#irrelevant_conclusion_anchor)*. A common example would be an argument along these lines: "Giving up our nuclear arsenal in the 1980's weakened the United States' military. Giving up nuclear weaponry also weakened China in the 1990s. For this reason, it is wrong to try to outlaw pistols and rifles in the United States today." There's obviously a step or two missing here.

The "Slippery Slope" Fallacy (also called "The Camel's Nose Fallacy") is a *non sequitur (https://web.cn.edu/kwheeler/ fallacies_list.html#non_sequitur_anchor)* in which the speaker argues that, once the first step is undertaken, a second or third step will inevitably follow, much like the way one step on a slippery incline will cause a person to fall and slide all the way to the bottom. It is also called "the Camel's Nose Fallacy" because of the image of a sheik who let his camel stick its nose into his tent on a cold night. The idea is that the sheik is afraid to let the camel stick its nose into the tent because once the beast sticks in its nose, it will inevitably stick in its head, and then its neck, and eventually its whole body. However, this sort of thinking does not allow for any possibility of stopping the process. It simply assumes that, once the nose is in, the rest must follow—that the sheik can't stop the progression once it has begun—and thus the argument is a logical fallacy. For instance, if one were to argue, "If we allow the government to infringe upon our right to privacy on the Internet, it will then feel free to infringe upon our privacy on the telephone. After that, FBI agents will be reading our mail. Then they will be placing cameras in our houses. We must not let any governmental agency interfere with our Internet communications, or privacy will completely vanish in the United States." Such thinking is fallacious; no logical proof has been provided yet that infringement in one area will necessarily lead to infringement in another, no more than a person buying a single can of Coca-Cola in a grocery store would indicate the person will inevitably go on to buy every item available in the store, helpless to stop herself. So remember to avoid the slippery slope fallacy; once you use one, you may find yourself using more and more logical fallacies.

Either/Or Fallacy (also called "the Black-and-White Fallacy," "Excluded Middle," "False Dilemma," or "False Dichotomy"): This fallacy occurs when a writer builds an argument upon the assumption that there are only two choices or possible outcomes when actually there are several. Outcomes are seldom so simple. This fallacy most frequently appears in connection to sweeping generalizations: "Either we must ban X or the American way of life will collapse." "We go to war with Canada, or else Canada will eventually grow in population and overwhelm the United States." "Either you drink Burpsy Cola, or you will have no friends and no social life." Either you must avoid either/or fallacies, or everyone will think you are foolish.

Faulty Analogy: Relying only on comparisons to prove a point rather than arguing deductively and inductively. For example, "education is like cake; a small amount tastes sweet, but eat too much and your teeth will rot out. Likewise, more than two years of education is bad for a student." The analogy is only acceptable to the degree a reader thinks that education is similar to cake. As you can see, faulty analogies are like flimsy wood, and just as no carpenter would build a house out of flimsy wood, no writer should ever construct an argument out of flimsy material.

Undistributed Middle Term: A specific type of error in deductive reasoning in which the minor premise and the major premise of a **syllogism** (https://web.cn.edu/kwheeler/logic_syllogism.html) might or might not overlap. Consider these two examples: (1)

"All reptiles are cold-blooded. All snakes are reptiles. All snakes are cold-blooded." In the first example, the middle term "snakes" fits in the categories of both "reptile" and "things-that-are-cold-blooded." (2) "All snails are cold-blooded. All snakes are cold-blooded. All snails are snakes." In the second example, the middle term of "snakes" does not fit into the categories of both "things-that-are-cold-blooded" and "snails." Sometimes, **equivocation** (https://web.cn.edu/kwheeler/ fallacies_list.html#equivocation_anchor) (see below) leads to an undistributed middle term.

Contradictory Premises (also known as a logical paradox): Establishing a premise in such a way that it contradicts another, earlier premise. For instance, "If God can do anything, he can make a stone so heavy that he can't lift it." The first premise establishes a deity that has the irresistible capacity to move other objects. The second premise establishes an immovable object impervious to any movement. If the first object capable of moving anything exists, by definition, the immovable object cannot exist, and *vice-versa*.

Closely related is the fallacy of **Special Pleading**, in which the writer creates a universal principle, then insists that principle does not for some reason apply to the issue at hand. For instance, "Everything must have a source or creator. Therefore God must exist and he must have created the world. What? Who created God? Well, God is eternal and unchanging—He has no source or creator." In such an assertion, either God must have His own source or creator, or else the universal principle of everything having a source or creator must be set aside—the person making the argument can't have it both ways.

FALLACIES OF AMBIGUITY: These errors occur with ambiguous words or phrases, the meanings of which shift and change in the course of discussion. Such more or less subtle changes can render arguments fallacious.

Equivocation: Using a word in a different way than the author used it in the original premise, or changing definitions halfway through a discussion. When we use the same word or phrase in different senses within one line of argument, we commit the fallacy of equivocation. Consider this example: "Plato says the end of a thing is its perfection; I say that death is the end of life; hence, death is the perfection of life." Here the word *end* means "goal" in Plato's usage, but it means "last event" or "termination" in the author's second usage. Clearly, the speaker is twisting Plato's meaning of the word to draw a very different conclusion. Compare with *amphiboly* (https://web.cn.edu/kwheeler/fallacies_list.html#amphiboly_anchor), below.

Amphiboly (from the Greek word "indeterminate"): This fallacy is similar to equivocation. Here, the ambiguity results from grammatical construction. A statement may be true according to one interpretation of how each word functions in a sentence and false according to another. When a premise works with an interpretation that is true, but the conclusion uses the secondary "false" interpretation, we have the fallacy of *amphiboly* on our hands. In the command, "Save soap and waste paper," the amphibolous use of "waste" results in the problem of determining whether "waste" functions as a verb or as an adjective.

Composition: This fallacy is a result of reasoning from the properties of the parts of the whole to the properties of the whole itself—it is an inductive error. Such an argument might hold that, because every individual part of a large tractor is lightweight, the entire machine also must be lightweight. This fallacy is similar to **Hasty Generalization** (https://web.cn.edu/kwheeler/ fallacies_list.html#hasty_generalization_anchor) (see above), but it focuses on parts of a single whole rather than using too few examples to create a categorical generalization. Also compare it with **Division (https://web.cn.edu/kwheeler/ fallacies_list.html#division_anchor)** (see below).

Division: This fallacy is the reverse of **composition** (https://web.cn.edu/kwheeler/fallacies_list.html#composition_anchor). It is the misapplication of deductive reasoning. One fallacy of division argues falsely that what is true of the whole must be true of individual parts. Such an argument notes that, "Microtech is a company with great influence in the California legislature. Egbert Smith works at Microtech. He must have great influence in the California legislature." This is not necessarily true. Egbert might work as a graveyard shift security guard or as the copy-machine repairman at Microtech—positions requiring little interaction with the California legislature. Another fallacy of division attributes the properties of the whole to the individual member of the whole: "Sunsurf is a company that sells environmentally safe products. Susan Jones is a worker at Sunsurf. She must be an environmentally minded individual." (Perhaps she is motivated by money alone?)

Fallacy of Reification (Also called "**Fallacy of Misplaced Concreteness**" by Alfred North Whitehead): The fallacy of treating a word or an idea as equivalent to the actual thing represented by that word or idea, or the fallacy of treating an abstraction or process as equivalent to a concrete object or thing. In the first case, we might imagine a reformer trying to eliminate illicit lust by banning all mention of extra-marital affairs or certain sexual acts in publications. The problem is that eliminating the words for these deeds is not the same as eliminating the deeds themselves. In the second case, we might imagine a person or declaring "a war on poverty." In this case, the fallacy comes from the fact that "war" implies a concrete struggle with another concrete entity which can surrender or be exterminated. "Poverty," however is an abstraction that cannot surrender or sign peace treaties, cannot be shot or bombed, etc. Reification of the concept merely muddles the issue of what policies to follow and leads to sloppy thinking about the best way to handle a problem. It is closely related to and overlaps with **faulty analogy (https://web.cn.edu/kwheeler/fallacies_list.html#faulty_analogy_anchor)** and **equivocation** (https://web.cn.edu/kwheeler/fallacies_list.html#equivocation_anchor).

FALLACIES OF OMISSION: These errors occur because the logician leaves out necessary material in an argument or misdirects others from missing information.

Stacking the Deck: In this fallacy, the speaker "stacks the deck" in her favor by ignoring examples that disprove the point and listing only those examples that support her case. This fallacy is closely related to hasty generalization, but the term usually implies deliberate deception rather than an accidental logical error. Contrast it with the **straw man argument** (https://web.cn.edu/kwheeler/fallacies_list.html#straw_man_anchor).

'No True Scotsman' Fallacy: Attempting to **stack the deck** (https://web.cn.edu/kwheeler/fallacies_list.html#stacking_the_deck_anchor) specifically by defining terms in such a narrow or unrealistic manner as to exclude or omit relevant examples from a sample. For instance, suppose speaker #1 asserts, "The Scottish national character is brave and patriotic. No Scottish soldier has ever fled the field of battle in the face of the enemy." Speaker #2 objects, "Ah, but what about Lucas MacDurgan? He fled from German troops in World War I." Speaker #1 retorts, "Well, obviously he doesn't count as a true Scotsman because he did not live up to Scottish ideals, thus he forfeited his Scottish identity." By this fallacious reasoning, any individual who would serve as evidence contradicting the first speaker's assertion is conveniently and automatically dismissed from consideration. We commonly see this fallacy when a company asserts that it cannot be blamed for one of its particularly unsafe or shoddy products because that particular one doesn't live up to its normally high standards, and thus shouldn't "count" against its fine reputation. Likewise, defenders of Christianity as a positive historical influence in their zeal might argue the atrocities of the eight Crusades do not "count" in an argument because the Crusaders weren't living up to Christian ideals, and thus aren't really Christians, etc. So, remember this fallacy. Philosophers and logicians never use it, and anyone who does use it by definition is not really a philosopher or logician.

Argument from the Negative: Arguing from the negative asserts that, since one position is untenable, the opposite stance must be true. This fallacy is often used interchangeably with *Argumentum Ad Ignorantium (https://web.cn.edu/kwheeler/fallacies_list.html#argumentum_ad_ignorantium_anchor)* (listed below) and the *either/or fallacy (https://web.cn.edu/kwheeler/fallacies_list.html#either_or_fallacy)* (listed above). For instance, one might mistakenly argue that, since the Newtonian theory of mathematics is not one hundred percent accurate, Einstein's theory of relativity must be true. Perhaps not. Perhaps the theories of quantum mechanics are more accurate, and Einstein's theory is flawed. Perhaps they are all wrong. Disproving an opponent's argument does not necessarily mean your own argument must be true automatically, no more than disproving your opponent's assertion that 2+2=5 would automatically mean your argument that 2+2=7 must be the correct one. Keeping this mind, students should remember that arguments from the negative are bad, arguments from the positive must automatically be good.

Appeal to a Lack of Evidence (*Argumentum Ad Ignorantium*, literally "Argument from Ignorance"): Appealing to a lack of information to prove a point, or arguing that, since the opposition cannot disprove a claim, the opposite stance must be true. An example of such an argument is the assertion that ghosts must exist because no one has been able to prove that they do not exist. Logicians know this is a logical fallacy because no competing argument has yet revealed itself.

Hypothesis Contrary to Fact (*Argumentum Ad Speculum*): Trying to prove something in the real world by using imaginary examples alone, or asserting that, if hypothetically *X* had occurred, *Y* would have been the result. For instance, suppose an individual asserts that if Einstein had been aborted *in utero*, the world would never have learned about relativity, or that if Monet had been trained as a butcher rather than going to college, the impressionistic movement would have never influenced modern art. Such hypotheses are misleading lines of argument because it is often possible that some other individual would have solved the relativistic equations or introduced an impressionistic art style. The speculation might make an interesting thought-experiment, but it is simply useless when it comes to actually proving anything about the real world. A common example is the idea that one "owes" her success to another individual who taught her. For instance, "You owe me part of your increased salary. If I hadn't taught you how to recognize logical fallacies, you would be flipping hamburgers at McDonald's for minimum wages right now instead of taking in hundreds of thousands of dollars as a lawyer." Perhaps. But perhaps the audience would have learned about logical fallacies elsewhere, so the hypothetical situation described is meaningless.

Complex Question (Also called the "Loaded Question"): Phrasing a question or statement in such as way as to imply another unproven statement is true without evidence or discussion. This fallacy often overlaps with **begging the question** (https://web.cn.edu/kwheeler/fallacies_list.html#begging_the_question_anchor) (above), since it also presupposes a definite answer to a previous, unstated question. For instance, if I were to ask you "Have you stopped taking drugs yet?" my hidden supposition is that you *have* been taking drugs. Such a question cannot be answered with a simple yes or no answer. It is not a simple question but consists of several questions rolled into one. In this case the unstated question is, "Have you taken drugs in the past?" followed by, "If you have taken drugs in the past, have you stopped taking them now?" In cross-examination, a lawyer might ask a flustered witness, "Where did you hide the evidence?" or "when did you stop beating your wife?" The intelligent procedure when faced with such a question is to analyze its component parts. If one answers or discusses the prior, implicit question first, the explicit question may dissolve.

Complex questions appear in written argument frequently. A student might write, "Why is private development of resources so much more efficient than any public control?" The rhetorical question leads directly into his next argument. However, an observant reader may disagree, recognizing the prior, implicit question remains unaddressed. That question is, of course, whether private development of resources really *is* more efficient in all cases, a point which the author is skipping entirely and merely assuming to be true without discussion.

To master logic more fully, become familiar with the tool of **Occam's Razor** (https://web.cn.edu/kwheeler/logic_occam.html).

How does The Witch Sketch Work Logically?

How does "The Witch Sketch" Work Logically?

Given their deep academic backgrounds, the Pythons (aka Monty Python), a British comedy troupe of the 60s and 70s, featured many logical fallacies in their work. (YouTube "the cheese shop sketch" or "the pet shop sketch" or "the argument clinic sketch" with the Python search modifier to see some of this. One of my favorites is "Confuse a Cat"—and not just because it prefigures our fascination with silly cat videos!)

One of the most famous scenes from *Monty Python and the Search for the Holy Grail* is the witch sketch. It delineates some logic for figuring out how someone is a witch.

* https://youtu.be/zrzMhU_4m-g

Enjoy! See if you can relate this to our problems of arguing definition.

REVISING & EDITING

Revision Strategies

When you revise and are spending time thinking about how well your content works in your essay, there are some strategies to keep in mind that can help. First and foremost, during the revision process, you should **seek outside feedback**. It's especially helpful if you can find someone to review your work who disagrees with your perspective. This can help you better understand the opposing view and can help you see where you may need to strengthen your argument.

If you're in a writing class, chances are you'll have some kind of **peer review** for your argument. It's important to take advantage of any peer review you receive on your essay. Even if you don't take all of the advice you receive in a peer review, having advice to consider is going to help you as a writer.

Finally, in addition to the outside feedback, there are some revision strategies that you can engage in on your own. **Read your essay carefully** and think about the lessons you have learned about logic, fallacies, and audience. For an example of the revision process, check out this first **video** (http://owl.excelsior.edu/research-and-citations/revising-and-editing-a-research-paper/revising-and-editing-see-it-in-practice/) on revising from the **Research & Citations (http://owl.excelsior.edu/research-and-citations/)** area of the OWL.

A **post draft outline** can also help you during the revision process. A post draft outline can help you quickly see where you went with your essay and can help you more easily see if you need to make broad changes to content or to organizations.

For more information on creating a post draft outline, you can view the Prezi linked here (http://owl.excelsior.edu/argument-and-critical-thinking/revising-your-argument/revising-your-argument-revision-strategies/). (It will take you to the writing lab's site where you can then click on the Prezi to run it.) Be sure the volume is turned up on your computer!

Revising and Editing

Revising and editing are the two tasks you undertake to significantly improve your essay. Both are very important elements of the writing process. You may think that a completed first draft means little improvement is needed. However, even experienced writers need to improve their drafts and rely on peers during revising and editing. You may know that athletes miss catches, fumble balls, or overshoot goals. Dancers forget steps, turn too slowly, or miss beats. For both athletes and dancers, the more they practice, the stronger their performance will become. Web designers seek better images, a more clever design, or a more appealing background for their web pages. Writing has the same capacity to profit from improvement and revision.

Understanding the Purpose of Revising and Editing

Revising and editing allow you to examine two important aspects of your writing separately, so that you can give each task your undivided attention.

- When you revise, you take a second look at your ideas. You might add, cut, move, or change information in order to make your ideas clearer, more accurate, more interesting, or more convincing.
- When you edit, you take a second look at how you expressed your ideas. You add or change words. You fix any problems in grammar, punctuation, and sentence structure. You improve your writing style. You make your essay into a polished, mature piece of writing, the end product of your best efforts.

TIP

How do you get the best out of your revisions and editing? Here are some strategies that writers have developed to look at their first drafts from a fresh perspective. Try them throughout this course; then keep using the ones that bring results.

- Take a break. You are proud of what you wrote, but you might be too close to it to make changes. Set aside your writing for a few hours or even a day until you can look at it objectively.
- Ask someone you trust for feedback and constructive criticism.
- Pretend you are one of your readers. Are you satisfied or dissatisfied? Why?
- Use the resources that your college provides. Find out where your school's writing lab is located and ask about the assistance they provide online and in person.

Many people hear the words *critic*, *critical*, and *criticism* and pick up only negative vibes that provoke feelings that make them blush, grumble, or shout. However, as a writer and a thinker, you need to learn to be critical of yourself in a positive way and have high expectations for your work. You also need to train your eye and trust your ability to fix what needs fixing. For this, you need to teach yourself where to look.

Creating Unity and Coherence

Following your outline closely offers you a reasonable guarantee that your writing will stay on purpose and not drift away from the controlling idea. However, when writers are rushed, are tired, or cannot find the right words, their writing may become less than they want it to be. Their writing may no longer be clear and concise, and they may be adding information that is not needed to develop the main idea.

When a piece of writing has unity, all the ideas in each paragraph and in the entire essay clearly belong and are arranged in an order that makes logical sense. When the writing has coherence, the ideas flow smoothly. The wording clearly indicates how one idea leads to another within a paragraph and from paragraph to paragraph.

TIP

Reading your writing aloud will often help you find problems with unity and coherence. Listen for the clarity and flow of your ideas. Identify places where you find yourself confused, and write a note to yourself about possible fixes.

Creating Unity

Sometimes writers get caught up in the moment and cannot resist a good digression. Even though you might enjoy such detours when you chat with friends, unplanned digressions usually harm a piece of writing.

Mariah stayed close to her outline when she drafted the three body paragraphs of her essay she tentatively titled "Digital Technology: The Newest and the Best at What Price?" But a recent shopping trip for an HDTV upset her enough that she digressed from the main topic of her third paragraph and included comments about the sales staff at the electronics store she visited. When she revised her essay, she deleted the off-topic sentences that affected the unity of the paragraph.

Read the following paragraph twice, the first time without Mariah's changes, and the second time with them.

Nothing is more confusing to me than choosing among televisions. It confuses lots of people who want a new high-definition digital television (HDTV) with a large screen to watch sports and DVDs on. ~~You could listen to the guys in the electronics store, but word has it they know little more than you do. They want to sell you what they have in stock, not what best fits your needs.~~ You face decisions you never had to make with the old, bulky picture-tube televisions. Screen resolution means the number of horizontal scan lines the screen can show. This resolution is often 1080p, or full HD, or 768p. The trouble is that if you have a smaller screen, 32 inches or 37 inches diagonal, you won't be able to tell the difference with the naked eye. ~~The 1080p televisions cost more, though, so those are what the salespeople want you to buy. They get bigger commissions.~~ The ~~other~~ important decision you face as you walk around the sales floor is whether to get a plasma screen or an LCD screen. ~~Now here the salespeople may finally give you decent info.~~ Plasma flat-panel television screens can be much larger in diameter than their LCD rivals. Plasma screens show truer blacks and can be viewed at a wider angle than current LCD screens. ~~But be careful and tell the salesperson you have budget constraints.~~ Large flat-panel plasma screens are much more expensive than flat-screen LCD models. Don't ~~let someone make you~~ buy more television than you need!

TIP

When you reread your writing to find revisions to make, look for each type of problem in a separate sweep. Read it straight through once to locate any problems with unity. Read it straight through a second time to find problems with coherence. You may follow this same practice during many stages of the writing process.

Writing at Work

Many companies hire copyeditors and proofreaders to help them produce the cleanest possible final drafts of large writing projects. Copyeditors are responsible for suggesting revisions and style changes; proofreaders check documents for any errors in capitalization, spelling, and punctuation that have crept in. Many times, these tasks are done on a freelance basis, with one freelancer working for a variety of clients.

Creating Coherence

Careful writers use transitions to clarify how the ideas in their sentences and paragraphs are related. These words and phrases help the writing flow smoothly. Adding transitions is not the only way to improve coherence, but they are often useful and give a mature feel to your essays. Table 7.3 "Common Transitional Words and Phrases" groups many common transitions according to their purpose.

Table 7.3 Common Transitional Words and Phrases

Transitions That Show Sequence or Time		
after	before	later
afterward	before long	meanwhile
as soon as	finally	next
at first	first, second, third	soon
at last	in the first place	then
Transitions That Show Position		
above	across	at the bottom
at the top	behind	below
beside	beyond	inside
near	next to	opposite
to the left, to the right, to the side	under	where
Transitions That Show a Conclusion		
indeed	hence	in conclusion
in the final analysis	therefore	thus
Transitions That Continue a Line of Thought		
consequently	furthermore	additionally
because	besides the fact	following this idea further
in addition	in the same way	moreover
looking further	considering…, it is clear that	
Transitions That Change a Line of Thought		
but	yet	however
nevertheless	on the contrary	on the other hand
Transitions That Show Importance		
above all	best	especially
in fact	more important	most important
most	worst	
Transitions That Introduce the Final Thoughts in a Paragraph or Essay		
finally	last	in conclusion
most of all	least of all	last of all
All-Purpose Transitions to Open Paragraphs or to Connect Ideas Inside Paragraphs		
admittedly	at this point	certainly

granted	it is true	generally speaking
in general	in this situation	no doubt
no one denies	obviously	of course
to be sure	undoubtedly	unquestionably
Transitions that Introduce Examples		
for instance	for example	
Transitions That Clarify the Order of Events or Steps		
first, second, third	generally, furthermore, finally	in the first place, also, last
in the first place, furthermore, finally	in the first place, likewise, lastly	

After Maria revised for unity, she next examined her paragraph about televisions to check for coherence. She looked for places where she needed to add a transition or perhaps reword the text to make the flow of ideas clear. In the version that follows, she has already deleted the sentences that were off topic.

TIP

Many writers make their revisions on a printed copy and then transfer them to the version on-screen. They conventionally use a small arrow called a caret (^) to show where to insert an addition or correction.

Finally,
^Nothing is more confusing to me than choosing among televisions. It confuses lots of

people who want a new high-definition digital television (HDtelevision) with a large
                  There's good reason for this confusion:
screen to watch sports and DVDs on. ^You face decisions you never had to make with the
            The first big decision is the screen resolution you want.
old, bulky picture-tube televisions. ^Screen resolution means the number of horizontal

scan lines the screen can show. This resolution is often 1080p, or full HD, or 768p.

The trouble is that if you have a smaller screen, 32 inches or 37 inches diagonal, you
                                                        second
won't be able to tell the difference with the naked eye. The ^~~other~~ important decision

you face as you walk around the sales floor is whether to get a plasma screen or an LCD
Along with the choice of display type, a further decision buyers face is screen size
and features.
screen. ^ Plasma flat-panel television screens can be much larger in diameter than their

LCD rivals. Plasma screens show truer blacks and can be viewed at a wider angle than
                  However,
current LCD screens. ^ Large flat-panel plasma screens are much more expensive than

flat-screen LCD models. Don't buy more television than you need!

Being Clear and Concise

Some writers are very methodical and painstaking when they write a first draft. Other writers unleash a lot of words in order to get out all that they feel they need to say. Do either of these composing styles match your style? Or is your composing style somewhere in between? No matter which description best fits you, the first draft of almost every piece of writing, no matter its author, can be made clearer and more concise.

If you have a tendency to write too much, you will need to look for unnecessary words. If you have a tendency to be vague or imprecise in your wording, you will need to find specific words to replace any overly general language.

Identifying Wordiness

Sometimes writers use too many words when fewer words will appeal more to their audience and better fit their purpose. Here are some common examples of wordiness to look for in your draft. Eliminating wordiness helps all readers, because it makes your ideas clear, direct, and straightforward.

- **Sentences that begin with**
  There is
  or
  There are
  Wordy: There are two major experiments that the Biology Department sponsors.**Revised:** The Biology Department sponsors two major experiments.
- **Sentences with unnecessary modifiers.Wordy:** Two extremely famous and well-known consumer advocates spoke eloquently in favor of the proposed important legislation.**Revised:** Two well-known consumer advocates spoke in favor of the proposed legislation.
- **Sentences with deadwood phrases that add little to the meaning.** Be judicious when you use phrases such as *in terms of*, *with a mind to*, *on the subject of*, *as to whether or not*, *more or less*, *as far as...is concerned*, and similar expressions. You can usually find a more straightforward way to state your point.**Wordy:** As a world leader in the field of green technology, the company plans to focus its efforts in the area of geothermal energy.A report as to whether or not to use geysers as an energy source is in the process of preparation.**Revised:** As a world leader in green technology, the company plans to focus on geothermal energy.A report about using geysers as an energy source is in preparation.
- **Sentences in the passive voice or with forms of the verb** *to be*. Sentences with passive-voice verbs often create confusion, because the subject of the sentence does not perform an action. Sentences are clearer when the subject of the sentence performs the action and is followed by a strong verb. Use strong active-voice verbs in place of forms of *to be*, which can lead to wordiness. Avoid passive voice when you can.**Wordy:** It might perhaps be said that using a GPS device is something that is a benefit to drivers who have a poor sense of direction.**Revised:** Using a GPS device benefits drivers who have a poor sense of direction.
- **Sentences with constructions that can be shortened.Wordy:** The e-book reader, which is a recent invention, may become as commonplace as the cell phone.My over-sixty uncle bought an e-book reader, and his wife bought an e-book reader, too.**Revised:** The e-book reader, a recent invention, may become as commonplace as the cell phone.My over-sixty uncle and his wife both bought e-book readers.

Choosing Specific, Appropriate Words

Most college essays should be written in formal English suitable for an academic situation. Follow these principles to be sure that your word choice is appropriate.

- **Avoid slang.** Find alternatives to *bummer*, *kewl*, and *rad*.

- **Avoid language that is overly casual.** Write about "men and women" rather than "girls and guys" unless you are trying to create a specific effect. A formal tone calls for formal language.
- **Avoid contractions.** Use *do not* in place of *don't*, *I am* in place of *I'm*, *have not* in place of *haven't*, and so on. Contractions are considered casual speech.
- **Avoid clichés.** Overused expressions such as *green with envy*, *face the music*, *better late than never*, and similar expressions are empty of meaning and may not appeal to your audience.
- **Be careful when you use words that sound alike but have different meanings.** Some examples are *allusion/illusion*, *complement/compliment*, *council/counsel*, *concurrent/consecutive*, *founder/flounder*, and *historic/historical*. When in doubt, check a dictionary.
- **Choose words with the connotations you want.** Choosing a word for its connotations is as important in formal essay writing as it is in all kinds of writing. Compare the positive connotations of the word *proud* and the negative connotations of *arrogant* and *conceited*.
- **Use specific words rather than overly general words.** Find synonyms for *thing*, *people*, *nice*, *good*, *bad*, *interesting*, and other vague words. Or use specific details to make your exact meaning clear.

Now read the revisions Mariah made to make her third paragraph clearer and more concise. She has already incorporated the changes she made to improve unity and coherence.

confuses buyers more than purchasing

Finally, nothing ^ ~~is more confusing to me than choosing among televisions. It confuses~~ ~~lots of people who want~~ a new high-definition digital television (HDTV), ~~with a large~~

and with

~~screen to watch sports~~ and DVDs ~~on.~~ ^ ~~There's~~ good reason. ~~for this confusion. You face~~ ~~decisions you never had to make with the old, bulky picture-tube televisions.~~ The first

involves   which

big decision ~~is~~^ ~~the~~ screen resolution, ~~you want.~~ ^~~Screen resolution~~ means the number of horizontal scan lines the screen can show. This resolution is often expressed as 1080p,

as   on

or full HD, or ^768p, which is half that. The trouble is that^ ~~if you have~~ a smaller

screen, viewers will not   between them

~~screen,~~ 32-inch or 37-inch diagonal ^~~you won't~~ be able to tell the difference^ with the naked eye. The second important decision ~~you face as you walk around the sales~~ ~~floor~~ is whether to get a plasma screen or an LCD screen. ~~Along with the choice of~~ ~~display type, a further decision buyers face is screen size and features.~~ Plasma flat-panel television screens can be much larger in diameter than their LCD rivals. Plasma

deeper

screens show ~~truer~~ ^blacks and can be viewed at a wider angle than current LCD screens. However, large flat-panel plasma screens are much more expensive than flat-screen LCD

Only after buyers are totally certain they know what they want should they open their wallets.

models. ^~~Don't buy more television than you need!!~~

Completing a Peer Review

After working so closely with a piece of writing, writers often need to step back and ask for a more objective reader. What writers most need is feedback from readers who can respond only to the words on the page. When they are ready, writers show their drafts to someone they respect and who can give an honest response about its strengths and weaknesses.

You, too, can ask a peer to read your draft when it is ready. After evaluating the feedback and assessing what is most helpful, the reader's feedback will help you when you revise your draft. This process is called peer review.

You can work with a partner in your class and identify specific ways to strengthen each other's essays. Although you may be uncomfortable sharing your writing at first, remember that each writer is working toward the same goal: a final draft that fits the audience and the purpose. Maintaining a positive attitude when providing feedback will put you and your partner at ease. The box that follows provides a useful framework for the peer review session.

Questions for Peer Review

Title of essay: _____

Date: _____

Writer's name: _____

Peer reviewer's name: _____

1. This essay is about_____.
2. Your main points in this essay are_____.
3. What I most liked about this essay is_____.
4. These three points struck me as your strongest:

   1. Point: _____Why:
      _____

   2. Point: _____Why:
      _____

   3. Point: _____Why:
      _____

5. These places in your essay are not clear to me:

   1. Where: _____Needs improvement
      because_____

   2. Where: _____Needs improvement because
      _____

   3. Where: _____Needs improvement because
      _____

6. The one additional change you could make that would improve this essay significantly is
   _____.

Writing at Work

One of the reasons why word-processing programs build in a reviewing feature is that workgroups have become a common feature in many businesses. Writing is often collaborative, and the members of a workgroup and their supervisors often critique group members' work and offer feedback that will lead to a better final product.

Using Feedback Objectively

The purpose of peer feedback is to receive constructive criticism of your essay. Your peer reviewer is your first real audience, and you have the opportunity to learn what confuses and delights a reader so that you can improve your work before sharing the final draft with a wider audience (or your intended audience).

It may not be necessary to incorporate every recommendation your peer reviewer makes. However, if you start to observe a pattern in the responses you receive from peer reviewers, you might want to take that feedback into consideration in future assignments. For example, if you read consistent comments about a need for more research, then you may want to consider including more research in future assignments.

Using Feedback from Multiple Sources

You might get feedback from more than one reader as you share different stages of your revised draft. In this situation, you may receive feedback from readers who do not understand the assignment or who lack your involvement with and enthusiasm for it.

You need to evaluate the responses you receive according to two important criteria:

1. Determine if the feedback supports the purpose of the assignment.
2. Determine if the suggested revisions are appropriate to the audience.

Then, using these standards, accept or reject revision feedback.

Editing Your Draft

If you have been incorporating each set of revisions as Mariah has, you have produced multiple drafts of your writing. So far, all your changes have been content changes. Perhaps with the help of peer feedback, you have made sure that you sufficiently supported your ideas. You have checked for problems with unity and coherence. You have examined your essay for word choice, revising to cut unnecessary words and to replace weak wording with specific and appropriate wording.

The next step after revising the content is editing. When you edit, you examine the surface features of your text. You examine your spelling, grammar, usage, and punctuation. You also make sure you use the proper format when creating your finished assignment.

TIP

Editing often takes time. Budgeting time into the writing process allows you to complete additional edits after revising. Editing and proofreading your writing helps you create a finished work that represents your best efforts. Here are a few more tips to remember about your readers:

- Readers do not notice correct spelling, but they *do* notice misspellings.
- Readers look past your sentences to get to your ideas—unless the sentences are awkward, poorly constructed, and frustrating to read.
- Readers notice when every sentence has the same rhythm as every other sentence, with no variety.
- Readers do not cheer when you use *there*, *their*, and *they're* correctly, but they notice when you do not.
- Readers will notice the care with which you handled your assignment and your attention to detail in the delivery of an error-free document.

The last section of this book offers a useful review of grammar, mechanics, and usage. Use it to help you eliminate major errors in your writing and refine your understanding of the conventions of language. Do not hesitate to ask for help, too, from peer tutors in your academic department or in the college's writing lab. In the meantime, use the checklist to help you edit your writing.

Checklist

Editing Your Writing

Grammar

- Are some sentences actually sentence fragments?
- Are some sentences run-on sentences? How can I correct them?
- Do some sentences need conjunctions between independent clauses?
- Does every verb agree with its subject?
- Is every verb in the correct tense?
- Are tense forms, especially for irregular verbs, written correctly?
- Have I used subject, object, and possessive personal pronouns correctly?
- Have I used *who* and *whom* correctly?
- Is the antecedent of every pronoun clear?
- Do all personal pronouns agree with their antecedents?
- Have I used the correct comparative and superlative forms of adjectives and adverbs?
- Is it clear which word a participial phrase modifies, or is it a dangling modifier?

Sentence Structure

- Are all my sentences simple sentences, or do I vary my sentence structure?
- Have I chosen the best coordinating or subordinating conjunctions to join clauses?
- Have I created long, overpacked sentences that should be shortened for clarity?
- Do I see any mistakes in parallel structure?

Punctuation

- Does every sentence end with the correct end punctuation?
- Can I justify the use of every exclamation point?
- Have I used apostrophes correctly to write all singular and plural possessive forms?
- Have I used quotation marks correctly?

Mechanics and Usage

- Can I find any spelling errors? How can I correct them?
- Have I used capital letters where they are needed?
- Have I written abbreviations, where allowed, correctly?
- Can I find any errors in the use of commonly confused words, such as *to/too/two*?

TIP

Be careful about relying too much on spelling checkers and grammar checkers. A spelling checker cannot recognize that you meant to write *principle* but wrote *principal* instead. A grammar checker often queries constructions that are perfectly correct. The program does not understand your meaning; it makes its check against a general set of formulas that might not apply in each instance. If you use a grammar checker, accept the suggestions that make sense, but consider why the suggestions came up.

If you need additional proofreading help, ask a reliable friend, a classmate, or a peer tutor to make a final pass on your paper to look for anything you missed.

Formatting

Remember to use proper format when creating your finished assignment. Sometimes an instructor, a department, or a college will require students to follow specific instructions on titles, margins, page numbers, or the location of the writer's name. These requirements may be more detailed and rigid for research projects and term papers, which often observe the American Psychological Association (APA) or Modern Language Association (MLA) style guides, especially when citations of sources are included.

To ensure the format is correct and follows any specific instructions, make a final check before you submit an assignment.

EXERCISES

1.Answer the following two questions about Mariah's paragraph in "Creating Unity" above:

- Do you agree with Mariah's decision to make the deletions she made? Did she cut too much, too little, or just enough? Explain.
- Is the explanation of what screen resolution means a digression? Or is it audience friendly and essential to understanding the paragraph? Explain.

Please share with a classmate and compare your answers.

2. Now start to revise the first draft of the essay you wrote. Reread it to find any statements that affect the unity of your writing. Decide how best to revise.

3. Answer the following questions about Mariah's revised paragraph in "Creating Coherence."

- Do you agree with the transitions and other changes that Mariah made to her paragraph? Which would you keep and which were unnecessary? Explain.
- What transition words or phrases did Mariah add to her paragraph? Why did she choose each one?
- What effect does adding additional sentences have on the coherence of the paragraph? Explain. When you read both versions aloud, which version has a more logical flow of ideas? Explain.

4. Now return to the first draft of the essay you wrote and revise it for coherence. Add transition words and phrases where they are needed, and make any other changes that are needed to improve the flow and connection between ideas.

5. Answer the following questions about Mariah's revised paragraph:

- Read the unrevised and the revised paragraphs aloud. Explain in your own words how changes in word choice have affected Mariah's writing.
- Do you agree with the changes that Mariah made to her paragraph? Which changes would you keep and which were unnecessary? Explain. What other changes would you have made?
- What effect does removing contractions and the pronoun *you* have on the tone of the paragraph? How would you characterize the tone now? Why?

6. Now return once more to your essay in progress. Read carefully for problems with word choice. Be sure that your draft is written in formal language and that your word choice is specific and appropriate.

7. Exchange essays with a classmate and complete a peer review of each other's draft in progress. Remember to give positive feedback and to be courteous and polite in your responses. Focus on providing one positive comment and one question for more information to the author.

8. Work with two partners. Go back to #3 in this lesson and compare your responses about Mariah's paragraph with your partners'. Recall Mariah's purpose for writing and her audience. Then, working individually, list where you agree and where you disagree about revision needs.

9. With the help of the checklist, edit and proofread your essay.

CC licensed content, Shared previously

- English for Business Success. **Authored by**: Anonymous. **Provided by**: Anonymous. **Located at**:

Peer Editing

The OWL Excelsior Writing Lab site contains useful information on the writing process. This page on peer editing (http://owl.excelsior.edu/writing-process/revising-and-editing/revising-and-editing-peer-review/) is particularly helpful in reminding us to be positive but specific when engaging with peers' writing.

CC licensed content, Shared previously

General Revision Points to Consider

LEARNING OBJECTIVES

By the end of this section, you will be able to:

- Discuss the process of revision
- List three general elements of every document that require revision

Just when you think the production of your document is done, the revision process begins. Runners often refer to "the wall," where the limits of physical exertion are met and exhaustion is imminent. The writing process requires effort, from overcoming writer's block to the intense concentration composing a document often involves. It is only natural to have a sense of relief when your document is drafted from beginning to end. This relief is false confidence, though. Your document is not complete, and in its current state it could, in fact, do more harm than good. Errors, omissions, and unclear phrases may lurk within your document, waiting to reflect poorly on you when it reaches your audience. Now is not time to let your guard down, prematurely celebrate, or to mentally move on to the next assignment. Think of the revision process as one that hardens and strengthens your document, even though it may require the sacrifice of some hard-earned writing.

General revision requires attention to content, organization, style, and readability. These four main categories should give you a template from which to begin to explore details in depth. A cursory review of these elements in and of itself is insufficient for even the briefest review. Across this chapter we will explore ways to expand your revision efforts to cover the common areas of weakness and error. You may need to take some time away from your document to approach it again with a fresh perspective. Writers often juggle multiple projects that are at different stages of development. This allows the writer to leave one document and return to another without losing valuable production time. Overall, your goal is similar to what it was during your writing preparation and production: a clear mind.

Evaluate Content

Content is only one aspect of your document. Let's say you were assigned a report on the sales trends for a specific product in a relatively new market. You could produce a one-page chart comparing last year's results to current figures and call it a day, but would it clearly and concisely deliver content that is useful and correct? Are you supposed to highlight trends? Are you supposed to spotlight factors that contributed to the increase or decrease? Are you supposed to include projections for next year? Our list of questions could continue, but for now let's focus on content and its relationship to the directions. Have you included the content that corresponds to the given assignment, left any information out that may be necessary to fulfill the expectations, or have you gone beyond the assignment directions? Content will address the central questions of who, what, where, when, why and how within the range and parameters of the assignment.

Evaluate Organization

Organization is another key aspect of any document. Standard formats that include an introduction, body, and conclusion may be part of your document, but did you decide on a direct or indirect approach? Can you tell? A direct approach will announce the main point or purpose at the beginning, while an indirect approach will present an introduction before the main point. Your document may use any of a wide variety of organizing principles, such as chronological, spatial, compare/contrast. Is your organizing principle clear to the reader?

Beyond the overall organization, pay special attention to transitions. Readers often have difficulty following a document if the writer makes the common error of failing to make one point relevant to the next, or to illustrate the relationships between the points. Finally, your conclusion should mirror your introduction and not introduce new material.

Evaluate Style

Style is created through content and organization, but also involves word choice and grammatical structures. Is your document written in an informal or formal tone, or does it present a blend, a mix, or an awkward mismatch? Does it provide a coherent and unifying voice with a professional tone? If you are collaborating on the project with other writers or contributors, pay special attention to unifying the document across the different authors' styles of writing. Even if they were all to write in a professional, formal style, the document may lack a consistent voice. Read it out loud—can you tell who is writing what? If so, that is a clear clue that you need to do more revising in terms of style.

Evaluate Readability

Readability refers to the reader's ability to read and comprehend the document. A variety of tools are available to make an estimate of a document's reading level, often correlated to a school grade level. If this chapter has a reading level of 11.8, it would be appropriate for most readers in the eleventh grade. But just because you are in grade thirteen, eighteen, or twenty-one doesn't mean that your audience, in their everyday use of language, reads at a postsecondary level. As a business writer, your goal is to make your writing clear and concise, not complex and challenging.

You can often use the "Tools" menu of your word processing program to determine the approximate reading level of your document. The program will evaluate the number of characters per word, add in the number of words per sentence, and come up with a rating. It may also note the percentage of passive sentences, and other information that will allow you to evaluate readability. Like any computer-generated rating, it should serve you as one point of evaluation, but not the only point. Your concerted effort to choose words you perceive as appropriate for the audience will serve you better than any computer evaluation of your writing.

KEY TAKEAWAY

The four main categories—content, organization, style, and readability—provide a template for general revision.

EXERCISES

1. Select a document, such as an article from a Web site, newspaper, magazine, or a piece of writing you have completed for a course. Evaluate the document according to the four main categories described in this section. Could the document benefit from revision in any of these areas? Discuss your findings with your classmates.

2. Interview a coworker or colleague and specifically ask how much time and attention they dedicate to the revision process of their written work. Compare your results with classmates.

3. Find a particularly good example of writing according to the above criteria. Review it and share it with your classmates.

4. Find a particularly bad example of writing according to the above criteria. Review it and share it with your classmates.

Specific Revision Points to Consider

LEARNING OBJECTIVE

By the end of this section, you will be able to:

- List six specific elements of every document to check for revision

---

When revising your document, it can be helpful to focus on specific points. When you consider each point in turn, you will be able to break down the revision process into manageable steps. When you have examined each point, you can be confident that you have avoided many possible areas for errors. Specific revision requires attention to the following:

- Format
- Facts
- Names
- Spelling
- Punctuation
- Grammar

Let's examine these characteristics one by one.

Format

Format is an important part of the revision process. Format involves the design expectations of author and audience. If a letter format normally designates a date at the top, or the sender's address on the left side of the page before the salutation, the information should be in the correct location. Formatting that is messy or fails to conform to the company style will reflect poorly on you before the reader even starts to read it. By presenting a document that is properly formatted according to the expectations of your organization and your readers, you will start off making a good impression.

Facts

Another key part of the revision process is checking your facts. Did you know that news organizations and magazines employ professional fact-checkers? These workers are responsible for examining every article before it gets published and consulting original sources to make sure the information in the article is accurate. This can involve making phone calls to the people who were interviewed for the article—for example, "Mr. Diaz, our report states that you are thirty-nine years old. Our article will be published on the fifteenth. Will that be your correct age on that date?" Fact checking also involves looking facts up in encyclopedias, directories, atlases, and other standard reference works; and, increasingly, in online sources.

While you can't be expected to have the skills of a professional fact-checker, you do need to reread your writing with a critical eye to the information in it. Inaccurate content can expose you and your organization to liability, and will create far more work than a simple revision of a document. So, when you revise a document, ask yourself the following:

- Does my writing contain any statistics or references that need to be verified?
- Where can I get reliable information to verify it?

It is often useful to do independent verification—that is, look up the fact in a different source from the one where you first got it. For example, perhaps a colleague gave you a list of closing averages for the Dow Jones Industrial on certain dates. You still have the list, so you can make sure your document agrees with the numbers your colleague provided. But what if your colleague made a mistake? The Web sites of the *Wall Street Journal* and other major newspapers list closings for "the Dow," so it is reasonably easy for you to look up the numbers and verify them independently.

Names

There is no more embarrassing error in business writing than to misspell someone's name. To the writer, and to some readers, spelling a name "Michelle" instead of "Michele" may seem like a minor matter, but to Michele herself it will make a big difference. Attribution is one way we often involve a person's name, and giving credit where credit is due is essential. There are many other reasons for including someone's name, but regardless of your reasons for choosing to focus on them, you need to make sure the spelling is correct. Incorrect spelling of names is a quick way to undermine your credibility; it can also have a negative impact on your organization's reputation, and in some cases it may even have legal ramifications.

Spelling

Correct spelling is another element essential for your credibility, and errors will be glaringly obvious to many readers. The negative impact on your reputation as a writer, and its perception that you lack attention to detail or do not value your work, will be hard to overcome. In addition to the negative personal consequences, spelling errors can become factual errors and destroy the value of content. This may lead you to click the "spell check" button in your word processing program, but computer spell-checking is not enough. Spell checkers have improved in the years since they were first invented, but they are not infallible. They can and do make mistakes.

Typically, your incorrect word may in fact be a word, and therefore, according to the program, correct. For example, suppose you wrote, "The major will attend the meeting" when you meant to write "The mayor will attend the meeting." The program would miss this error because "major" is a word, but your meaning would be twisted beyond recognition.

Punctuation

Punctuation marks are the traffic signals, signs, and indications that allow us to navigate the written word. They serve to warn us in advance when a transition is coming or the complete thought has come to an end. A period indicates the thought is complete, while a comma signals that additional elements or modifiers are coming. Correct signals will help your reader follow the thoughts through sentences and paragraphs, and enable you to communicate with maximum efficiency while reducing the probability of error (Strunk & White, 1979).

Table 12.1 "Punctuation Marks" lists twelve punctuation marks that are commonly used in English in alphabetical order along with an example of each.

Table 12.1 Punctuation Marks

	Symbol	Example
Apostrophe	'	Michele's report is due tomorrow.
Colon	:	This is what I think: you need to revise your paper.

	Symbol	Example
Comma	,	The report advised us when to sell, what to sell, and where to find buyers.
Dash	—	This is more difficult than it seems—buyers are scarce when credit is tight.
Ellipsis	...	Lincoln spoke of "a new nation...dedicated to the proposition that all men are created equal."
Exclamation Point	!	How exciting!
Hyphen	-	The question is a many-faceted one.
Parentheses	( )	To answer it (or at least to begin addressing it) we will need more information.
Period	.	The answer is no. Period. Full stop.
Question Mark	?	Can I talk you into changing your mind?
Quotation Marks	" "	The manager told him, "I will make sure Renée is available to help you."
Semicolon	;	Theresa was late to the meeting; her computer had frozen and she was stuck at her desk until a tech rep came to fix it.

It may be daunting to realize that the number of possible punctuation errors is as extensive as the number of symbols and constructions available to the author. Software program may catch many punctuation errors, but again it is the committed writer that makes the difference. Here we will provide details on how to avoid mistakes with three of the most commonly used punctuation marks: the comma, the semicolon, and the apostrophe.

Commas

The comma is probably the most versatile of all punctuation marks. This means you as a writer can use your judgment in many cases as to whether you need a comma or not. It also means that the possible errors involving commas are many. Commas are necessary some of the time, but careless writers often place a comma in a sentence where it is simply not needed.

Commas are used to separate two independent clauses joined by a conjunction like "but," "and," and "or."

Example
The advertising department is effective, but don't expect miracles in this business climate.

Commas are not used simply to join two independent clauses. This is known as the comma splice error, and the way to correct it is to insert a conjunction after the comma.

Examples
The advertising department is effective, the sales department needs to produce more results.
The advertising department is effective, *but* the sales department needs to produce more results.

Commas are used for introductory phrases and to offset clauses that are not essential to the sentence. If the meaning would remain intact without the phrase, it is considered nonessential.

Examples
After the summary of this year's sales, the sales department had good reason to celebrate.
The sales department, *last year's winner of the most productive award*, celebrated their stellar sales success this year.
The sales department celebrated their stellar sales success this year.

Commas are used to offset words that help create unity across a sentence like "however" and "therefore."

Examples
The sales department discovered, *however*, that the forecast for next year is challenging.
However, the sales department discovered that the forecast for next year is challenging.

Commas are often used to separate more than one adjective modifying a noun.

Example
The sales department discovered the *troublesome, challenging* forecast for next year.

Commas are used to separate addresses, dates, and titles; they are also used in dialogue sequences.

Examples
John is from Ancud, Chile.
Katy was born on August 2, 2002.
Mackenzie McLean, D. V., is an excellent veterinarian.
Lisa said, "When writing, omit needless words."

Semicolons

Semicolons have two uses. First, they indicate relationships among groups of items in a series when the individual items are separated by commas. Second, a semicolon can be used to join two independent clauses; this is another way of avoiding the comma splice error mentioned above. Using a semicolon this way is often effective if the meaning of the two independent clauses is linked in some way, such as a cause-effect relationship.

Examples
Merchandise on order includes women's wear such as sweaters, skirts, and blouses; men's wear such as shirts, jackets, and slacks; and outwear such as coats, parkas, and hats.
The sales campaign was successful; without its contributions our bottom line would have been dismal indeed.

Apostrophes

The apostrophe, like the semicolon, has two uses: it replaces letters omitted in a contraction, and it often indicates the possessive.

Because contractions are associated with an informal style, they may not be appropriate for some professional writing. The business writer will—as always—evaluate the expectations and audience of the given assignment.

Examples
It's great news that sales were up. *It is* also good news that *we've* managed to reduce our advertising costs.

When you indicate possession, pay attention to the placement of the apostrophe. Nouns commonly receive "'s" when they are made possessive. But plurals that end in "s" receive a hanging apostrophe when they are made possessive, and the word "it" forms the possessive ("its") with no apostrophe at all.

Examples
Mackenzie's sheep are ready to be sheared.
The parents' meeting is scheduled for Thursday.
We are willing to adopt a dog that has already had its shots.

Grammar

Learning to use good, correct standard English grammar is more of a practice than an event, or even a process. Grammar involves the written construction of meaning from words and involves customs that evolve and adapt to usage over time. Because grammar is always evolving, none of us can sit back and rest assured that we "know" how to write with proper grammar. Instead, it is important to write and revise with close attention to grammar, keeping in mind that grammatical errors can undermine your credibility, reflect poorly on your employer, and cause misunderstandings.

Jean Wyrick has provided a list of common errors in grammar to watch out for, which we have adapted here for easy reference (Wyrick, 2008). In each case, the error is in *italics* and the *[correct form]* is italicized within square bracket.

Subject-Verb Agreement

The subject and verb should agree on the number under consideration. In faulty writing, a singular subject is sometimes mismatched with a plural verb form, or vice versa.

Examples
Sales have not been consistent and they *doesn't [do not]* reflect your hard work and effort.
The president appreciates your hard work and *wish [wishes]* to thank you.

Verb Tense

Verb tense refers to the point in time where action occurs. The most common tenses are past, present, and future. There is nothing wrong with mixing tenses in a sentence if the action is intended to take place at different times. In faulty or careless writing, however, they are often mismatched illogically.

Examples
Sharon was under pressure to finish the report, so she *uses [used]* a shortcut to paste in the sales figures.
The sales department holds a status meeting every week, and last week's meeting *will be [was]* at the Garden Inn.

Split Infinitive

The infinitive form of verb is one without a reference to time, and in its standard form it includes the auxiliary word "to," as in "to write is to revise." It has been customary to keep the "to" next to the verb; to place an adverb between them is known as splitting the infinitive. Some modern writers do this all the time (for example, "to boldly go…"), and since all grammar is essentially a set of customs that govern the written word, you will need to understand what the custom is where you work. If you are working with colleagues trained across the last fifty years, they may find split infinitives annoying. For this reason, it's often best to avoid splitting an infinitive wherever you can do so without distorting the meaning of the sentence.

Examples
The Marketing Department needs assistance *to accurately understand our readers [to understand our readers accurately]*.
David pondered *how to best revise [how best to revise]* the sentence.

Double Negative

A double negative uses two negatives to communicate a single idea, duplicating the negation. In some languages, such as Spanish, when the main action in the sentence is negative, it is correct to express the other elements in the sentence negatively as well. However, in English, this is incorrect. In addition to sounding wrong (you can often hear the error if you read the sentence out loud), a double negative in English causes an error in logic, because two negatives cancel each other out and yield a positive. In fact, the wording of ballot measures is often criticized for confusing voters with double negatives.

Examples
John *doesn't need no [any]* assistance with his sales presentation. [Or *John needs no assistance with his sales presentation*.]
Jeri *could not find no [any]* reason to approve the request. [Or *Jeri could find no reason to approve the request*.]

Irregular Verbs

Most verbs represent the past with the addition of the suffix "ed," as in "ask" becomes "asked." Irregular verbs change a vowel or convert to another word when representing the past tense. Consider the irregular verb "to go"; the past tense is "went," not "goed."

Examples
The need *arised [arose]* to seek additional funding.
Katy *leaped [leapt]* onto the stage to introduce the presentation.

Commas in a Series

A comma is used to separate the items in a series, but in some writing styles the comma is omitted between the final two items of the series, where the conjunction joins the last and next-to-last items. The comma in this position is known as the "serial comma." The serial comma is typically required in academic writing and typically omitted in journalism. Other writers omit the serial comma if the final two items in the series have a closer logical connection than the other items. In business writing, you may use it or omit it according to the prevailing style in your organization or industry. Know your audience and be aware of the rule.

Examples
Lisa is an amazing wife, mother, teacher, *gardener, and editor*.
Lisa is an amazing wife, mother teacher, *gardener and editor*.
Lisa is an amazing teacher, editor, gardener, *wife and mother*.

Faulty Comparisons

When comparing two objects by degree, there should be no mention of "est," as in "biggest" as all you can really say is that one is bigger than the other. If you are comparing three or more objects, then "est" will accurately communicate which is the "biggest" of them all.

Examples
Between the twins, Mackenzie is the *fastest [faster]* of the two.
Among our three children, Mackenzie is the *tallest*.

Dangling Modifiers

Modifiers describe a subject in a sentence or indicate how or when the subject carried out the action. If the subject is omitted, the modifier intended for the subject is left dangling or hanging out on its own without a clear relationship to the sentence. Who is doing the seeing in the first sentence?

Examples
Seeing the light at the end of the tunnel, celebrations were in order.
Seeing the light at the end of the tunnel, *we decided* that celebrations were in order.

Misplaced Modifiers

Modifiers that are misplaced are not lost, they are simply in the wrong place. Their unfortunate location is often far from the word or words they describe, making it easy for readers to misinterpret the sentence.

Examples
Trying to avoid the deer, *the tree hit my car.*
My car hit the tree when I tried to avoid a deer in the road.

KEY TAKEAWAY

By revising for format, facts, names, spelling, punctuation, and grammar, you can increase your chances of correcting many common errors in your writing.

EXERCISES

1. Select a news article from a news Web site, newspaper, or magazine. Find as many facts in the article as you can that could require fact-checking. Then check as many of these facts as you can, using sources available to you in the library and on the Internet. Did you find any errors in the article? Discuss your findings with your classmates.

2. Find an example of an assertion without attribution and share it with classmates.

3. Find an example of an error in a published document and share it with classmates.

4. Interview a coworker or colleague and specifically ask them to share a story where an error got past them during the revision process and made it to print or publication. How did they handle it? How much time did it take to correct? What did they learn from the experience? Compare your results with classmates.

"Breaking Up is Hard to Do"

Not a great song. . .

One of the toughest aspects of writing research projects—besides avoiding the completion of things at the last minute—is the breaking up of tasks.

If split apart, each task might take ten to thirty minutes. Sure, we can get into a two-hour writing jag where things work so well we don't have to slow down, but that's incredibly rare, even for published authors. I once wrote a twenty page paper on early Roman writing instruction in one sitting, but I don't even know how I did that.

Anyway, the idea is that we can break up the tasks. Of course, we'll have to do some tasks several times. We might be looking for that great source even as we are editing. Writing is a recursive process. Now, this could mean we swear again and again, but really it means that it curves back upon itself (like those early recurve bows which gain power from the curled shape and the lamination layers). The layering and ordering really doesn't matter. Those linear thinkers tend to get frustrated with writing because it's inherently chaotic.

The idea is to know what works for you. Have several options for when things fall through (as in tests). You should know several prewriting techniques and search tricks for those times when you are stymied. There is a frustration factor to be managed and even used for your advantage.

The papers with which I get annoyed are those where the person never returns to the process. For instance, a writer might get the first five sources that turn up in the first search they conduct. Or, they might be so focused on their own experiences that they do without research. Of course, there is often someone who entirely fails to reread—or even read fully—the essay directions. (You should see the number of literature essays where the sheet says the audience knows the story involved, yet the writer still only retells the plot of the thing!)

Try and work in a time and place that are going to allow you to be successful. (Sure, I'm one to talk. . . three little ones are doing art around me right now. I'm certainly not the still life model. . .)

Don't forget to add in annotating and highlighting of sources for prospective paraphrases, quotes, summaries. The beginnings and endings of sources tend to pack in important information, so go there. Don't forget the middles, though.

I'd like to see what you think about this breaking up of a seemingly overwhelming task into workable bits.

Page One in an Essay Abounds in Pitfalls for Errors

So that we all avoid any issues, here are the most common page one problems in order of appearance:

- Pagination appears in a header and is in the same font as the rest of the essay.
- Titles get centered but have no extra spaces above/below.
- In the heading, don't have Essay 1 listed. Also avoid having Essay 1 as the title.
- Avoid assuming audiences don't know what rhetoric or irony are. Only define terms you believe they may not know or whose wording is important to set forward and use.
- Make sure the first body paragraph features a topic sentence (somewhere . . . but usually first) that relates directly to the proving of your claim. Too often, we begin with the first "thing" of interest in the chapter or summarize the chapter in ways that don't obviously further the thesis' proving.
- Articles or essays are not novels or stories, so don't misidentify the title, misspell the author's (or my) name, or neglect to indicate which topic you're analyzing.
- Why it matters is called *exigency* in writing. Convey some sense of why it matters that we understand your thesis.

CC licensed content, Original

FINAL DRAFTS

Sample Definition Essay (MLA Style)

Essay is being shared with student's permission. In its original form, it had proper hanging indents, no extra spaces between double-spaced paragraphs, and MLA pagination.

Liana Monnat

English 101

Instructor: Joshua Dickinson

6 November 2016

Defining Evil

Oftentimes, when people think of the word *evil*, it may call to mind frightening images of demonic entities. These entities- beasts composed of scaly skin, glowing red eyes, and enormous wickedly pointed teeth- are thought to take possession of hapless humans, causing them to commit deeds they would otherwise never even contemplate. This is an image well-illustrated by Ante-Nicene theologian Lactanius who, in his *Divine Institutes*, claims that bringers of evil "wander over the earth seeking destruction of men, clinging to individuals and occupying whole houses, where they terrify human souls with dreams and harass their minds with frenzies" (qtd. in White 486). These ideas of evil give it presence; they turn it into a 'physical something' that has influence over the thoughts and actions of men. However, if one takes the time to truly contemplate the nature of evil, it becomes clear that *evil* has a much more logical definition, and thus does not exist as a thing unto itself.

In his book *The Science of Good and Evil*, publisher of *Skeptic* magazine and renowned author Dr. Michael Shermer defines evil as "A descriptive term for a range of environmental events and human behaviors that we describe and interpret as bad, wrong, awful, undesirable, or whatever appropriately descriptive adjective or synonym for evil is chosen" (69). He is expressing that evil is not the hypothetical tiny devil standing on a person's shoulder, cajoling them to behave immorally, evil is simply the adjective used to describe events or behavior that people think of as "'bad.'" Having clearly defined evil as a descriptive term, Shermer often uses it in his book to describe immoral behavior. This definition of evil as a description for immoral behavior, rather than an entity that causes harm, is the one that will be expounded upon in this essay.

In defining a person as evil, one is referring to someone who behaves immorally with intent to significantly harm others, without suffering guilt or remorse over the consequences of their actions (White 491). Such a person feels no moral responsibility and has no empathy for their victim. Most often, a person capable of committing an evil act seems perfectly normal under ordinary circumstances. Consider a 2015 case in which a man was prosecuted and charged for murdering his daughter fifteen years prior to his conviction. The man simply had no desire to be a father or pay child support to the mother of his daughter. One afternoon in 2000, after gaining visitation rights, he picked his four-year-old daughter up from school, took her hiking, and tossed the unwary child off a cliff (Shortland). This heinous act of murder was committed free of demonic influence and of his own volition, with no regard for the value of the young girl's life or for the devastated mother she left behind. The man did not take into consideration the terror that his little daughter must have experienced in her final moments. He had no empathy for her heartbroken mother and stepfather. The man was simply pleased to be free from making child support payments. With his lack of empathy and moral detachment from murdering his own child, the man perfectly illustrates the definition of evil as developed in this essay.

Perhaps the most notorious act of evil in modern history was perpetuated by Adolf Hitler and his lackeys, who followed his orders without so much as raising an eyebrow in question of their morality. If one contemplates humanism, which is the opposite of evil in that all people are acknowledged as worthy and deserving of respect, one can see how Hitler's deeds were considered evil (White 497). Not only did Adolf Hitler think the Jews were inferior to racially German people, he blamed his beloved Germany's defeat in World War I on a non-existent Jewish conspiracy, instead of bringing himself to admit that Germany was defeated due to its weaknesses (Calder 123). Thus, when he became the leader of Germany he set about systematically destroying German Jews in a mass genocide that still horrifies people to this day.

Per Hitler's evil orders, Jewish people were dragged from their homes and loaded onto trains without regard as to whether families were being separated. Husbands were parted from wives, children from parents. These unfortunate people were packed into train cars like cattle, with barely enough room to stand, heading for destinations about which they could only fearfully speculate. No empathy was given to the Jews for their hunger, thirst, and fear. No one cared if they were too hot or too cold, or if they had to relieve themselves. They were coldly denied even the most basic of human rights on the hellish train ride that whisked them away to their fates.

As bad as conditions on the train cars were, circumstances only became far worse when they reached their destinations and were unloaded into concentration camps that were surrounded by tall, barbed-wire-topped fences. Although German officers told them that the camps were only temporary holding areas, these death camps were the final stop for millions of innocent Jews. Locked behind fences with no way of escape, they were given scarcely any food or water; many starved to death and the ones who did not became horrifyingly emaciated. Living in deplorable conditions with no clean clothes or opportunity to bathe, the Jews became filthy, their clothing tattered. When finally given an opportunity to 'shower' in what seemed to be an unexpected act of grace by the German officers, they were grateful for the opportunity to wash some of the filth from their bodies. The officers led them, with no remorse, into what were not large showers but custom-built gas chambers. While anticipating warm water and a chance to get clean, the unsuspecting Jews, children and adults alike, were mass executed by the application of toxic gas. Their bodies were then carted to buildings that were built specifically as crematoriums, and burned to ash. As the crematoriums became too backlogged to handle the number of bodies being presented for burning, large pits had to be excavated and utilized as a means of disposing of bodies. Countless corpses were tossed into these mass unmarked graves, one atop another, then buried under tons of dirt with no more regard than one gives garbage.

In those final days of their lives, Jewish people were treated with contempt and as less than animals by German officers who would go home at the end of their shifts, sit down to hot meals with their wives and children, and enjoy the trivialities of daily life. Day after day they would impose starvation and suffering, commit mass murder, then be welcomed home by loving families, without a thought for the families they had helped destroy. Adolf Hitler, the mastermind behind the attempted Jewish genocide and responsible for the deaths of millions of innocent people, never even had to get his artsy little hands dirty. In doing what he thought was best for the betterment of his beloved country, Hitler was in fact perpetuating one of the most horrifyingly evil events in history.

In better understanding what evil is, one could contemplate its opposite. As aforementioned, humanism could be considered the opposite of evil. This belief "cherishes the worthiness of all individuals" (White 497). Unlike evil concepts such as the racism and hatred practiced by Hitler and his Nazi regime, those who practice humanism believe all humans were created equal and are worthy of respect and consideration. This anti-evil concept is practiced in the religion of Buddhism, where instead of causing harm to others or persecuting them for having different beliefs, the focus is on being in harmony with all of humanity and improving one's own inner tranquility (Fenchel 83). Buddhists welcome all people as fellow humans instead of viewing them as strangers or less worthy in some way, even if their beliefs are contradictory to the Buddhist's. As evil represents immoral behavior that harms others, selfishness, and lack of empathy, humanism represents having empathy for others, being selfless, and striving to behave in a way that does not cause harm to others.

Evil, as defined in this essay, includes immoral thoughts, behaviors, or actions that lead to the intentional significant harm of others. One can perpetrate an evil act directly, as illustrated by the example of the father who threw his four-year-old daughter off a cliff to rid himself of fatherly responsibility. Evil acts can also be masterminded by one person and carried out by many others, as demonstrated by the cruelty of Hitler and his Nazi regime. Both were examples in which pain and suffering were purposely inflicted upon the innocent, done without remorse or even acknowledging that the actions were immoral- and perfectly embody the definition of evil.

Works Cited

Calder, Todd. "Evil and Its Opposite." *Journal of Value Inquiry*, vol. 49, no. ½, 2015, pp 113-130. *Humanities Source* DOI: 10.1007/s10790-014-9456-7

Fenchel, Gerd. "Good and Evil." *Issues in Psychoanalytic Psychology*, vol. 35, 2013, pp 78-87.

Shermer, Michael. *The Science of Good and Evil: Why People Cheat, Gossip, Care, Share, and Follow the Golden Rule*. Holt, 2004.

Shortland, Gail. "Father Threw His 4-year-old Daughter Off a Cliff After Being Ordered to Pay Child Support By the Court; When Cameron Brown Was Ordered To Pay Care For the Child He Didn't Want, His Actions Were Beyond Evil." *Daily Mirror,* Nov. 2015. *General OneFile,* go. Galegroup.com

White, Thomas. "The Hollow Men: Moral Evil as Privatized Self." *Crosscurrents*, vol. 65, no. 4, 2015, pp 485-536. *Humanities Source* DOI: 10.1111/cros.12168

Sample Final Research Essay Drafts

Some of these samples were written with slightly different assignment criteria, but all provide good examples of what possible successful completion of this essay can look like.

Sample #1: Pro Organic Food (https://docs.google.com/document/d/19RjKYhgFRfCt3sXxzQuUSN7lvW6h-q0D6-YhK0zrx4k/edit) (Google Doc Link)

Sample #2: Anti Wireless Access Availability for Teenagers (https://docs.google.com/document/d/1ygTcH8iyT9yRDGG1lk7KmAX1xqOZL5q8lYy0r8KqYAA/edit) (Google Doc Link)

Sample #3: Anti Use of Term "Psychopath" in Media (https://docs.google.com/document/d/16K5bn1ki146TPxq6d3ap8MDYaaWlDET28PgRtUCD2SU/edit) (Google Doc Link)

Sample #4: Anti TV Show "Teen Mom" (https://docs.google.com/document/d/10eKmRJO_dY7eq47mfM46Gyztir4r2jhMtqusaff4Zr8/edit) (Google Doc Link)

CC licensed content, Shared previously

Coherence: What do People Mean When They Say My Writing Doesn't Flow

Coherence: What do People Mean When They Say My Writing Doesn't Flow

Before You Read

Write 750 to 1,000 words in response to this prompt, keeping in mind that you're going to be working with this piece of writing extensively in the coming days—not only in this chapter but in other chapters related to style:

As a public university that receives substantial support from the state legislature, the U has an obligation to serve the people of the state of Utah. However, there can be disagreements on what that service means. On one hand, it can mean admitting as many Utah residents as possible in order to increase the state's population of college-educated citizens. On the other hand, it can mean increasing admission requirements to fulfill the U's position as the "flagship" university in the state. Where do you come down?

Coherence, or "Flow"—An Overview

Many (student) writers have turned in papers only to have their readers (more often than not, their teachers) hand the papers back with comments that the writing doesn't "flow."

Unfortunately, teachers may not always be explicit about what they mean—just that it doesn't "read" or "sound" right or that the ideas don't progress from one to another. This chapter is about what "flow" actually means and how to make sure your writing does it.

By "flow," most readers mean what grammarians and linguists call **coherence**—the property of a text to hold together at the level of sentences and paragraphs. Of course, cohesion is good in any communication medium, and each medium can present challenges for it. If you're sending text messages back and forth to a friend and the network sends them out of order, the result can be confusing: you might have written "thank GOD" in response to some piece of news, but your friend might not have gotten your message until after she texted "gotta go." Oops. If you're speaking to someone on a train or bus and something outside the window catches your attention, you might say something about it, and the other person might say, "wait—what?"

But in both those cases, you can quickly and easily clear up the confusion. Speech and texting are more or less **synchronous** media: that is, they involve people communicating at the same time and often in the same (virtual) space. Writing, however—in the traditional sense, anyway—is different, because it's **asynchronous**. It also requires an important trade-off. Writing has worked well for a long time as a communication technology because it's relatively easy to distribute. Someone using writing to communicate doesn't have to move from place to place: she may simply write something down and send it. However, to use a metaphor from very current communication technologies, writing has low bandwidth compared to other media. If someone is speaking to you, you can infer meaning from words themselves but also from vocal inflections, facial expressions, hand gestures, posture, and even from how close the other person is to you. You can't do that when you write and read. So, writers and readers can send and receive on the cheap, but they carry a burden of making their words work extraordinarily hard.

This idea has a very clear implication for your own written arguments—an important enough implication that we'd say it pretty loudly if you were standing right in front of us. But, since this is writing, we'll use boldface: **just because an argument you're making is clear in your own head, that doesn't mean it's automatically clear to people who are reading the written version of your argument**. That's one of the reasons it's a good idea to circulate the writing you do to others before you turn it in for a grade or circulate it in high-stakes situations.

Fortunately, the to-do list for "flow" is relatively short. Throughout Englishlanguage writing, it turns out that there is a small number of strategies for achieving coherence. These strategies help writers follow a key principle for communicating with readers as effectively as possible on the assumption that they're not looking over their readers' shoulders pointing out what they *really* need to know. That principle is called **the given-new contract**. This contract implies that you as a writer will start your projected readers with something relatively familiar and then lead them to less familiar material. It's an idea that is simple to state, but it's powerful, and it works at different levels of a document. At the level of overall document design, consistent visual items on each page (page number location, headings, "white" space, fonts) help create a familiar visual field that works like a container for whatever new information is coming next. As you read earlier in this book, a lot of a writer's job in an introduction, after all, is orienting readers so that they're at least familiar with the broad topic before the writer gets specific—with an argument, for example. But the contract helps sentence-level coherence, as well. It's very helpful to readers if you create a cycle in which you try to put "given" information at the start of sentences and shift "new" information to the ends, and then recycle the "new" information as "given" information in sentences that come up. The principle of **end emphasis** helps here: readers tend to latch more onto how sentences end than onto how they begin. Skilled writers know this is often the case, so they'll reserve end-of-sentence slots for new or challenging information, since they know they often have a little more of their readers' attention at those spots anyway.

The given-new contract and the concept of end emphasis are a little tough to explain in abstract terms, so here's an example followed by some analysis. We've numbered the sentences to help make the analysis clear.

> 1 This textbook is freely circulable under the terms of a Creative Commons ("CC") license. 2 CC is a nonprofit organization that helps content creators, such as textbook authors, share their products in more diverse ways than traditional copyright allows. 3 While typical copyright restricts others from using an author's work unless they have the author's express consent, CC allows authors to pick and choose which restrictions to apply to their work by using one of several free licenses. 4 For example, this book is available via an "Attribution-NonCommercialShareAlike" agreement: adopters of the textbook may use it free of charge and may even modify it without permission, but they must agree not to try to sell it or share it with others under different licensing terms.

Each sentence in this passage shows our attempt to honor the given-new contract. Here's how:

1. The first sentence introduces the term "Creative Commons" near its end. We're assuming that you may not know (much) about CC, so we're trying to exploit end emphasis to introduce it here very early in the paragraph.
2. This sentence immediately recycles CC and defines the term more fully. The sentence ends with the important (and "new") idea that CC allows for a wider range of options than copyright.
3. Now, the passage explains in a little more detail the point it just made about copyright restrictions and goes on to clarify the contrast with CC, ending with the "new" information that CC allows authors to choose from several licenses.
4. Not surprisingly, the next sentence shows what the previous sentence introduced by giving an example of a relevant CC license.

In addition to using the principle of end emphasis, writers who honor the given-new contract frequently use several other strategies.

Stock transition words and phrases

Many writers first learn to make their writing flow by using explicit, specialpurpose transitional devices. You may hear these devices called "signposts," because they work much like highway and street signs. When steel boxes weighing 2 tons and more are rolling around at high speeds, it's important that their operators are repeatedly and clearly told exactly where and when to go with as little ambiguity as possible.

Here's a list of stock, generic, all-purpose transition words and phrases, organized by their basic functions. Keep in mind that there are differences among these that can make a difference and that determining what those differences is is beyond the scope of this book. It's a matter of experience.

To add or show sequence: again, also, and, and then, besides, equally important, finally, first, further, furthermore, in addition, in the first place, last, moreover, next, second, still, too

To compare: also, in the same way, likewise, similarly

To contrast: although, and yet, but, but at the same time, despite, even so, even though, for all that, however, in contrast, in spite of, nevertheless, notwithstanding, on the contrary, on the other hand, regardless, still, though, yet

To give examples or intensify: after all, an illustration of, even, for example, for instance, indeed, in fact, it is true, of course, specifically, that is, to illustrate, truly

To indicate place: above, adjacent to, below, elsewhere, farther on, here, near, nearby, on the other side, opposite to, there, to the east, to the left

To indicate time: after a while, afterward, as long as, as soon as, at last, at length, at that time, before, earlier, formerly, immediately, in the meantime, in the past, lately, later, meanwhile, now, presently, shortly, simultaneously, since, so far, soon, subsequently, then, thereafter, until, until now, when

To repeat, summarize, or conclude: all in all, altogether, in brief, in conclusion, in other words, in particular, in short, in simpler terms, in summary, on the whole, that is, to put it differently, to summarize

To show cause and effect: accordingly, as a result, because, consequently, for this purpose, hence, otherwise, since, then, therefore, thereupon, thus, to this end, with this object in mind

As we just told you, avoiding ambiguity in academic and professional writing is important. But it's not as important as avoiding it on highways, in factories, or around high-voltage equipment or explosives. In those contexts, lots of signposts with lots of redundancy are vital. In many writing situations, you can expect your readers to pick up other useful clues for coherence, so it's somewhat less important to use a lot of these "stock" or generic transition words. In fact, if you overuse them (for instance, in an essay in which your first paragraph starts with "first," your second paragraph starts with "second," and on and on), it can get annoying.

Pronouns

If you're old enough vaguely to remember the Schoolhouse Rock series, you might remember the episode about pronouns ("he," "she," "her," "him," "you," "we," "they," "it," "one," "this," "that," and some others) and how they can stand for nouns, even if the nouns have long names. The idea is that pronouns make speaking and writing more efficient. But you may not have learned that pronouns are at least as powerful as cohesive devices. Since pronouns work by referring back to nouns that have previously been mentioned, they can help writers carry the ideas their nouns represent across sentences and paragraphs.

You may have been told to limit your use of pronouns or even avoid them altogether. This is bad advice, but it's understandable: pronouns work very well when they clearly refer to their antecedents, but they can create significant comprehension problems, misdirection, and vagueness when they don't.

Repetition

Contrary to a lot of advice novice writers get, repetition is effective. For example, as you'll learn later in this book (or now if you want to read ahead, of course), many rhetorical strategies that are thousands of years old and that exist in several languages use repetition. It's a time-honored way to signal importance, create a sense of rhythm, and help audiences remember key ideas. But repetition gets a bad reputation because it can become redundant. (Yes, that sentence used repetition to get its point across. It's no accident that it had a lot of "r"s.)

Repetition can involve individual words, phrases, or grammatical structures. When you repeat similar structural elements but not necessarily the words themselves, you are using **parallelism**, a special variety of repetition that not only helps coherence but also helps you to communicate that similarly important ideas should be read together. When sentences are written using non-parallel parts, it's certainly possible for readers to understand them, but it creates work for the reader that usually isn't necessary. Compare these sentences:

Student writers should learn to start projects early, how to ask for advice from teachers and peers, and when to focus on correcting grammar.

Student writers should learn to start projects early, to ask for advice from teachers and peers, and to figure out when to focus on correcting their grammar.

See the difference? The first sentence is comprehensible: the commas, for example, let you know that you're reading a list. But the extra adverbs ("how" and "when") get in the way of the sentence's clarity. And that problem, in turn, means that it's hard to see clearly how each item in the list relates to the others. In the revised sentence, though, it's a lot clearer that each of the three items is something student writers should "learn to" do. That relationship is made clear by the repeating grammatical pattern:

Student writers should learn

- to start projects early
- to ask for advice
- to figure out when to focus on grammar

Example

Here's an example of some writing that uses a variety of coherence strategies. We know it well because one of us wrote it. It's a short essay, written for a broad academic audience in a U publication, about the current state of the English language. To clarify the analysis that follows, we've underlined a few of the transition devices.

Teaching (and Learning) Englishes

Jay Jordan

University Writing Program

I teach English-language writing, and I'm a native speaker of the English language. Being a native speaker might seem to be an excellent basic qualification for my job: at the very least, it should necessarily make me the model of English usage. However, it actually makes me very unusual.

According to The British Council, approximately 1.5 *billion* people around the world use English. Roughly 375 million of them are like me: they have learned English since birth, and most of them live in countries like the US, Canada, Great Britain, Australia, and New Zealand that are traditional English-language centers.

That still leaves over a billion English users. 375 million of *those* people live in countries that were British colonies until the middle of the last century, such as Ghana, India, Kenya, and Nigeria.

But the largest number of English speakers—50% of the global total—are in countries that were not British colonies and that don't have much of a history with English. Count China, Indonesia, Japan, Malaysia, and South Korea among them. So, most English speakers aren't where we might expect them to be. In addition, they're not using English in ways we might expect, either, which helps explain why I'm referring to them as "users" and not "writers" or "speakers." Most people who use English around the world do so in specific circumstances in order to get very specific things done. Many Indians, for instance, might use English in publications and to transact business over the phone, Hindi in a government office, Gujarati at the store, and maybe one of several other languages at home.

What does this mean for my teaching and research? People and information move around globally more so now than ever, and that movement makes diverse uses of English feed back into the US. As students at the U (and the U is not alone) become more culturally and linguistically diverse, I often have as much to learn from them as I have to teach them.

This short example uses each of the coherence strategies described above:

- Overall, the example attempts to honor the given-new contract. It starts on familiar territory—or at least, with an attempt to orient the reader very quickly to the writer's personal approach. And it also makes a statement about the writer that the reader likely intuitively agrees with: namely, he's a native speaker of English, which makes him well qualified to be an English teacher. But the first paragraph ends with a surprising claim: being a native English speaker means being unusual. Here, then, the writer starts with what's comfortable but then uses end emphasis to reinforce the "new" information at the end.
- The writer does use several stock transitions: in fact, one of them —"however"—helps introduce the surprising sentence at the end of the introduction by clearly signposting something different or unexpected. And, as another example, the fourth paragraph starts with "but," which signposts another transition to information that contradicts what comes before. (You may have been told never to start sentences with conjunctions like "but" or "and." It turns out that it's generally fine to do that. Just be aware of your readers' preferences.)
- Pronouns appear to be the most common cohesion device in the essay. At the start of the third paragraph, for example, "that" stands in for the statistic in the previous paragraph, which would be hard to write out all over again. But "that" also

carries forward the sense of the statistic into the next paragraph. And "those people" carries the statistic forward to the next sentence. (Really, "those" is actually an adjective that modifies "people," but it's enough like a pronoun that we're handling it like one here.)

- Repetition is also common in this essay. Words are repeated—or at least, put very close to other words that are very similar in meaning. "English" and "British colonies" clearly help tie together the third and fourth paragraphs. And sentences show parallelism. See, for instance, paragraph four: "So, most English speakers aren't where we would expect them to be. In addition, they're not using English in ways we might expect, either."

To Do

1. Identify at least three other specific cohesion devices used in the example essay. Be prepared to say what kind of device it is and what effect it has on your reading. Also be prepared to suggest what would happen if it weren't there.
2. Re-read the 750-1,000 words you wrote before you read this chapter, paying particular attention to coherence. Now, revise it to improve its flow.

Read: Developing Your Final Draft

LEARNING OBJECTIVES

1. Revise your paper to improve organization and cohesion.
2. Determine an appropriate style and tone for your paper.
3. Revise to ensure that your tone is consistent.
4. Edit your paper to ensure that language, citations, and formatting are correct.

Given all the time and effort you have put into your research project, you will want to make sure that your final draft represents your best work. This requires taking the time to revise and edit your paper carefully.

You may feel like you need a break from your paper before you revise and edit it. That is understandable—but leave yourself with enough time to complete this important stage of the writing process. In this section, you will learn the following specific strategies that are useful for revising and editing a research paper:

- How to evaluate and improve the overall organization and cohesion
- How to maintain an appropriate style and tone
- How to use checklists to identify and correct any errors in language, citations, and formatting

Revising Your Paper: Organization and Cohesion

When writing a research paper, it is easy to become overly focused on editorial details, such as the proper format for bibliographical entries. These details do matter. However, before you begin to address them, it is important to spend time reviewing and revising the content of the paper.

A good research paper is both organized and cohesive. Organization means that your argument flows logically from one point to the next. Cohesion means that the elements of your paper work together smoothly and naturally. In a cohesive research paper, information from research is seamlessly integrated with the writer's ideas.

Revise to Improve Organization

When you revise to improve organization, you look at the flow of ideas throughout the essay as a whole and within individual paragraphs. You check to see that your essay moves logically from the introduction to the body paragraphs to the conclusion, and that each section reinforces your thesis. Use Checklist 12.1 to help you.

Checklist 12.1

Revision: Organization

At the essay level

- Does my introduction proceed clearly from the opening to the thesis?
- Does each body paragraph have a clear main idea that relates to the thesis?

- Do the main ideas in the body paragraphs flow in a logical order? Is each paragraph connected to the one before it?
- Do I need to add or revise topic sentences or transitions to make the overall flow of ideas clearer?
- Does my conclusion summarize my main ideas and revisit my thesis?

At the paragraph level

- Does the topic sentence clearly state the main idea?
- Do the details in the paragraph relate to the main idea?
- Do I need to recast any sentences or add transitions to improve the flow of sentences?

Jorge reread his draft paragraph by paragraph. As he read, he highlighted the main idea of each paragraph so he could see whether his ideas proceeded in a logical order. For the most part, the flow of ideas was clear. However, he did notice that one paragraph did not have a clear main idea. It interrupted the flow of the writing. During revision, Jorge added a topic sentence that clearly connected the paragraph to the one that had preceded it. He also added transitions to improve the flow of ideas from sentence to sentence.

Read the following paragraphs twice, the first time without Jorge's changes, and the second time with them.

Picture this: You're standing in the aisle of your local grocery store when you see a chubby guy nearby staring at several brands of ketchup on display. After deliberating for a moment, he reaches for the bottle with the words "Low-Carb!" displayed prominently on the label. (You can't help but notice that the low-carb ketchup is higher priced.) Is he making a smart choice that will help him lose weight
Over the past decade, increasing numbers of Americans have jumped on the low-carbohydrate bandwagon.
and enjoy better health—or is he just buying into the latest diet fad? ^ some researchers estimate that approximately 40 million Americans, or about one-fifth of the population, have attempted to restrict their intake of foods high in carbohydrates (Sanders & Katz, 2004; Hirsch, 2004). Proponents of low-carb diets say
                    not only   but also
they are ^ ~~the~~ most effective way to lose weight. ~~They~~ ^ yield health benefits such as
                                              Meanwhile,
lower blood pressure and improved cholesterol levels. ^ some doctors claim that low-carbohydrate diets are overrated and caution that their long-term effects are unknown. Although following a low-carbohydrate diet can have many benefits—especially for people who are obese or diabetic—these diets are not necessarily the best option for everyone who wants to lose weight or improve their health.

Follow these steps to begin revising your paper's overall organization.

1. Print out a hard copy of your paper.
2. Read your paper paragraph by paragraph. Highlight your thesis and the topic sentence of each paragraph.
3. Using the thesis and topic sentences as starting points, outline the ideas you presented—just as you would do if you were outlining a chapter in a textbook. Do not look at the outline you created during prewriting. You may write in the margins of your draft or create a formal outline on a separate sheet of paper.
4. Next, reread your paper more slowly, looking for how ideas flow from sentence to sentence. Identify places where adding a transition or recasting a sentence would make the ideas flow more logically.
5. Review the topics on your outline. Is there a logical flow of ideas? Identify any places where you may need to reorganize ideas.
6. Begin to revise your paper to improve organization. Start with any major issues, such as needing to move an entire paragraph. Then proceed to minor revisions, such as adding a transitional phrase or tweaking a topic sentence so it connects ideas more clearly.

Collaboration

Please share your paper with a classmate. Repeat the six steps and take notes on a separate piece of paper. Share and compare notes.

TIP

Writers choose transitions carefully to show the relationships between ideas—for instance, to make a comparison or elaborate on a point with examples. Make sure your transitions suit your purpose and avoid overusing the same ones. For an extensive list of transitions, see Chapter 8 "The Writing Process: How Do I Begin?", Section 8.4 "Revising and Editing".

Revise to Improve Cohesion

When you revise to improve cohesion, you analyze how the parts of your paper work together. You look for anything that seems awkward or out of place. Revision may involve deleting unnecessary material or rewriting parts of the paper so that the out-of-place material fits in smoothly.

In a research paper, problems with cohesion usually occur when a writer has trouble integrating source material. If facts or quotations have been awkwardly dropped into a paragraph, they distract or confuse the reader instead of working to support the writer's point. Overusing paraphrased and quoted material has the same effect. Use Checklist 12.2 to review your essay for cohesion.

Checklist 12.2

Revision: Cohesion

- Does the opening of the paper clearly connect to the broader topic and thesis? Make sure entertaining quotes or anecdotes serve a purpose.
- Have I included support from research for each main point in the body of my paper?
- Have I included introductory material before any quotations? Quotations should never stand alone in a paragraph.
- Does paraphrased and quoted material clearly serve to develop my own points?
- Do I need to add to or revise parts of the paper to help the reader understand how certain information from a source is relevant?
- Are there any places where I have overused material from sources?
- Does my conclusion make sense based on the rest of the paper? Make sure any new questions or suggestions in the conclusion are clearly linked to earlier material.

As Jorge reread his draft, he looked to see how the different pieces fit together to prove his thesis. He realized that some of his supporting information needed to be integrated more carefully and decided to omit some details entirely. Read the following paragraph, first without Jorge's revisions and then with them.

One likely reason for these lackluster long-term results is that a low-carbohydrate diet—like any restrictive diet—is difficult to adhere to for any extended period. ~~Most people enjoy foods that are high in carbohydrates, and no one wants to be the person who always turns down that slice of pizza or birthday cake.~~ In commenting on the Gardner study, experts at the Harvard School of Public Health (2010) noted that women in all four diet groups had difficulty following the plan. Because it is hard for dieters to stick to a low-carbohydrate eating plan, the initial success of these diets is short-lived (Heinz, 2009). Medical professionals caution that low-carbohydrate diets are difficult for many people to follow consistently and that, to maintain a healthy weight, dieters should try to develop nutrition and exercise habits they can incorporate in their lives in the long term (Mayo Clinic, 2008). Registered dietician Dana Kwon (2010) comments, "For some people, [low-carbohydrate diets] are great, but for most, any sensible eating and exercise plan would work just as well" (Kwon, 2010).

(https://s3-us-west-2.amazonaws.com/courses-images/wp-content/uploads/sites/190/2016/05/31200224/onelikelyreason.jpg)

Jorge decided that his comment about pizza and birthday cake came across as subjective and was not necessary to make his point, so he deleted it. He also realized that the quotation at the end of the paragraph was awkward and ineffective. How would his readers know who Kwon was or why her opinion should be taken seriously? Adding an introductory phrase helped Jorge integrate this quotation smoothly and establish the credibility of his source.

EXERCISE 2

Follow these steps to begin revising your paper to improve cohesion.

1. Print out a hard copy of your paper, or work with your printout from Note 12.33 "Exercise 1".
2. Read the body paragraphs of your paper first. Each time you come to a place that cites information from sources, ask yourself what purpose this information serves. Check that it helps support a point and that it is clearly related to the other sentences in the paragraph.
3. Identify unnecessary information from sources that you can delete.
4. Identify places where you need to revise your writing so that readers understand the significance of the details cited from sources.
5. Skim the body paragraphs once more, looking for any paragraphs that seem packed with citations. Review these paragraphs carefully for cohesion.
6. Review your introduction and conclusion. Make sure the information presented works with ideas in the body of the paper.
7. Revise the places you identified in your paper to improve cohesion.

Collaboration

Please exchange papers with a classmate. Complete step four. On a separate piece of paper, note any areas that would benefit from clarification. Return and compare notes.

WRITING AT WORK

Understanding cohesion can also benefit you in the workplace, especially when you have to write and deliver a presentation. Speakers sometimes rely on cute graphics or funny quotations to hold their audience's attention. If you choose to use these elements, make sure they work well with the substantive content of your presentation. For example, if you are asked to give a financial presentation, and the financial report shows that the company lost money, funny illustrations would not be relevant or appropriate for the presentation.

Using a Consistent Style and Tone

Once you are certain that the content of your paper fulfills your purpose, you can begin revising to improve style and tone. Together, your style and tone create the voice of your paper, or how you come across to readers. Style refers to the way you use language as a writer—the sentence structures you use and the word choices you make. Tone is the attitude toward your subject and audience that you convey through your word choice.

Determining an Appropriate Style and Tone

Although accepted writing styles will vary within different disciplines, the underlying goal is the same—to come across to your readers as a knowledgeable, authoritative guide. Writing about research is like being a tour guide who walks readers through a topic. A stuffy, overly formal tour guide can make readers feel put off or intimidated. Too much informality or humor can make readers wonder whether the tour guide really knows what he or she is talking about. Extreme or emotionally charged language comes across as unbalanced.

To help prevent being overly formal or informal, determine an appropriate style and tone at the beginning of the research process. Consider your topic and audience because these can help dictate style and tone. For example, a paper on new breakthroughs in cancer research should be more formal than a paper on ways to get a good night's sleep.

A strong research paper comes across as straightforward, appropriately academic, and serious. It is generally best to avoid writing in the first person, as this can make your paper seem overly subjective and opinion based. Use Checklist 12.3 on style to review your paper for other issues that affect style and tone. You can check for consistency at the end of the writing process. Checking for consistency is discussed later in this section.

Checklist 12.3

Style

- My paper avoids excessive wordiness.
- My sentences are varied in length and structure.
- I have avoided using first-person pronouns such as *I* and *we*.
- I have used the active voice whenever possible.
- I have defined specialized terms that might be unfamiliar to readers.
- I have used clear, straightforward language whenever possible and avoided unnecessary jargon.
- My paper states my point of view using a balanced tone—neither too indecisive nor too forceful.

Word Choice

Note that word choice is an especially important aspect of style. In addition to checking the points noted on Checklist 12.3, review your paper to make sure your language is precise, conveys no unintended connotations, and is free of biases. Here are some of the points to check for:

- Vague or imprecise terms
- Slang
- Repetition of the same phrases ("Smith states..., Jones states...") to introduce quoted and paraphrased material (For a full list of strong verbs to use with in-text citations, see Chapter 13 "APA and MLA Documentation and Formatting".)
- Exclusive use of masculine pronouns or awkward use of *he* or *she*
- Use of language with negative connotations, such as *haughty* or *ridiculous*
- Use of outdated or offensive terms to refer to specific ethnic, racial, or religious groups

Using plural nouns and pronouns or recasting a sentence can help you keep your language gender neutral while avoiding awkwardness. Consider the following examples.

- **Gender-biased:** When a writer cites a source in the body of his paper, he must list it on his references page.
- **Awkward:** When a writer cites a source in the body of his or her paper, he or she must list it on his or her references page.
- **Improved:** Writers must list any sources cited in the body of a paper on the references page.

Keeping Your Style Consistent

As you revise your paper, make sure your style is consistent throughout. Look for instances where a word, phrase, or sentence just does not seem to fit with the rest of the writing. It is best to reread for style after you have completed the other revisions so that you are not distracted by any larger content issues. Revising strategies you can use include the following:

- **Read your paper aloud.** Sometimes your ears catch inconsistencies that your eyes miss.
- **Share your paper with another reader whom you trust to give you honest feedback.** It is often difficult to evaluate one's own style objectively—especially in the final phase of a challenging writing project. Another reader may be more likely to notice instances of wordiness, confusing language, or other issues that affect style and tone.
- **Line-edit your paper slowly, sentence by sentence.** You may even wish to use a sheet of paper to cover everything on the page except the paragraph you are editing—that forces you to read slowly and carefully. Mark any areas where you notice problems in style or tone, and then take time to rework those sections.

On reviewing his paper, Jorge found that he had generally used an appropriately academic style and tone. However, he noticed one glaring exception—his first paragraph. He realized there were places where his overly informal writing could come across as unserious or, worse, disparaging. Revising his word choice and omitting a humorous aside helped Jorge maintain a consistent tone. Read his revisions.

Beyond the Hype: Evaluating Low-Carb Diets

I. Introduction

Picture this: You're standing in the aisle of your local grocery store when you
~~an overweight man~~
see ^ ~~a chubby guy~~ nearby staring at several brands of ketchup on display. After
deliberating for a moment, he reaches for the bottle with the words "Low-Carb!"
displayed prominently on the label. ~~(You can't help but notice that the low-carb~~
~~ketchup is higher priced.)~~ Is he making a smart choice that will help him lose weight
and enjoy better health—or is he just buying into the latest diet fad?

EXERCISE 3

Using Checklist 12.3, line-edit your paper. You may use either of these techniques:

1. Print out a hard copy of your paper, or work with your printout from Note 12.33 "Exercise 1". Read it line by line. Check for the issues noted on Checklist 12.3, as well as any other aspects of your writing style you have previously identified as areas for improvement. Mark any areas where you notice problems in style or tone, and then take time to rework those sections.

2. If you prefer to work with an electronic document, use the menu options in your word-processing program to enlarge the text to 150 or 200 percent of the original size. Make sure the type is large enough that you can focus on only one paragraph at a time. Read the paper line by line as described in step 1. Highlight any areas where you notice problems in style or tone, and then take time to rework those sections.

Collaboration

Please exchange papers with a classmate. On a separate piece of paper, note places where the essay does not seem to flow or you have questions about what was written. Return the essay and compare notes.

Editing Your Paper

After revising your paper to address problems in content or style, you will complete one final editorial review. Perhaps you already have caught and corrected minor mistakes during previous revisions. Nevertheless, give your draft a final edit to make sure it is error-free. Your final edit should focus on two broad areas:

1. Errors in grammar, mechanics, usage, and spelling
2. Errors in citing and formatting sources

For in-depth information on these two topics, see Chapter 2 "Writing Basics: What Makes a Good Sentence?" and Chapter 13 "APA and MLA Documentation and Formatting".

Correcting Errors

Given how much work you have put into your research paper, you will want to check for any errors that could distract or confuse your readers. Using the spell-checking feature in your word-processing program can be helpful—but this should not replace a full, careful review of your document. Be sure to check for any errors that may have come up frequently for you in the past. Use Checklist 12.4 to help you as you edit:

Checklist 12.4

Grammar, Mechanics, Punctuation, Usage, and Spelling

- My paper is free of grammatical errors, such as errors in subject-verb agreement and sentence fragments. (For additional guidance on grammar, see Chapter 2 "Writing Basics: What Makes a Good Sentence?".)
- My paper is free of errors in punctuation and mechanics, such as misplaced commas or incorrectly formatted source titles. (For additional guidance on punctuation and mechanics, see Chapter 3 "Punctuation".)
- My paper is free of common usage errors, such as *alot* and *alright*. (For additional guidance on correct usage, see Chapter 4 "Working with Words: Which Word Is Right?".)
- My paper is free of spelling errors. I have proofread my paper for spelling in addition to using the spell-checking feature in my word-processing program.
- I have checked my paper for any editing errors that I know I tend to make frequently.

Checking Citations and Formatting

When editing a research paper, it is also important to check that you have cited sources properly and formatted your document according to the specified guidelines. There are two reasons for this. First and foremost, citing sources correctly ensures that you have given proper credit to other people for ideas and information that helped you in your work. Second, using correct formatting establishes your paper as one student's contribution to the work developed by and for a larger academic community. Increasingly, American Psychological Association (APA) style guidelines are the standard for many academic fields. Modern Language Association (MLA) is also a standard style in many fields. Use Checklist 12.5 to help you check citations and formatting.

Checklist 12.5

Citations and Formatting

- Within the body of my paper, each fact or idea taken from a source is credited to the correct source.
- Each in-text citation includes the source author's name (or, where applicable, the organization name or source title) and year of publication. I have used the correct format of in-text and parenthetical citations.
- Each source cited in the body of my paper has a corresponding entry in the references section of my paper.
- My references section includes a heading and double-spaced, alphabetized entries.
- Each entry in my references section is indented on the second line and all subsequent lines.
- Each entry in my references section includes all the necessary information for that source type, in the correct sequence and format.
- My paper includes a title page.
- My paper includes a running head.

- The margins of my paper are set at one inch. Text is double spaced and set in a standard 12-point font.

For detailed guidelines on APA and MLA citation and formatting, see Chapter 13 "APA and MLA Documentation and Formatting".

WRITING AT WORK

Following APA or MLA citation and formatting guidelines may require time and effort. However, it is good practice for learning how to follow accepted conventions in any professional field. Many large corporations create a style manual with guidelines for editing and formatting documents produced by that corporation. Employees follow the style manual when creating internal documents and documents for publication.

During the process of revising and editing, Jorge made changes in the content and style of his paper. He also gave the paper a final review to check for overall correctness and, particularly, correct APA or MLA citations and formatting. Read the final draft of his paper.

Beyond the Hype: Evaluating Low-Carb Diets

Jorge Ramirez

Anystate University

BEYOND THE HYPE: EVALUATING LOW-CARB DIETS

Picture this: You're standing in the aisle of your local grocery store when you see an overweight man nearby staring at several brands of ketchup on display. After deliberating for a moment, he reaches for the bottle with the words "Low-Carb!" displayed prominently on the label. Is he making a smart choice that will help him lose weight and enjoy better health—or is he just buying into the latest diet fad?

Over the past decade, increasing numbers of Americans have jumped on the low-carb bandwagon. As of 2004, researchers estimated that approximately 40 million Americans, or about one-fifth of the population, were attempting to restrict their intake of food high in carbohydrates (Sanders & Katz, 2004). Proponents of low-carb diets say they not only are the most effective way to lose weight but also yield health benefits such as lower blood pressure and improved cholesterol levels. Meanwhile, some doctors claim that low-carb diets are overrated and caution that their long-term effects are unknown. Although following a low-carbohydrate diet can benefit some people, these diets are not necessarily that best option for everyone who wants to lose weight or improve their health.

PURPORTED BENEFITS OF LOW-CARBOHYDRATE DIETS

To make sense of the popular enthusiasm for low-carbohydrate diets, it is important to understand proponents' claims about how they work. Any eating plan includes a balance of the three macronutrients—proteins, fats, and carbohydrates—each of which is essential for human health. Different foods provide these macronutrients in different proportions; a steak is primarily a source of protein, and a plate of pasta is primarily a source of carbohydrates. No one recommends eliminating any of these three macronutrient groups entirely.

However, experts disagree on what protein: fats: carbohydrate ratio is best for optimum health and for maintaining a healthy weight. Since the 1970s, the USDA has recommended that the greatest proportion of one's daily calories should come from carbohydrates—breads, pastas, and cereals—with moderate consumption of proteins and minimal consumption of fats. High-carbohydrate foods form the base of the "food pyramid" familiar to nutrition students.

Those who subscribe to the low-carb philosophy, however, argue that this approach is flawed. They argue that excess weight stems from disordered metabolism, which in turn can be traced to overconsumption of foods high in carbohydrates—especially refined carbohydrates like white flour and sugar (Atkins, 2002; Sears, 1995; Agatson, 2003). The body quickly absorbs sugars from these foods, increasing the level of glucose in the blood. This triggers the release of insulin, delivering energy-providing glucose to cells and storing some of the excess as glycogen. Unfortunately, the liver turns the rest of this excess glucose into fat. Thus, adherents of the low-carb approach often classify foods according to their glycemic index (GI)—a measurement of how quickly a given food raises blood glucose levels when consumed. Foods high in refined carbohydrates—sugar, potatoes, white breads, and pasta, for instance—have a high glycemic index.[1]

Dieters who focus solely on reducing fat intake may fail to realize that consuming refined carbohydrates contributes to weight problems. Atkins (2002) notes that low-fat diets recommended to many who wish to lose weight are, by definition, usually high in carbohydrates, and thus unlikely to succeed.

Even worse, consuming high-carbohydrate foods regularly can, over time, wreak havoc with the body's systems for regulating blood sugar levels and insulin production. In some individuals, frequent spikes in blood sugar and insulin levels cause the body to become insulin-resistant—less able to use glucose for energy and more likely to convert it to fat (Atkins, 2002). This in turn helps to explain the link between obesity and Type 2 diabetes. In contrast, reducing carbohydrate intake purportedly helps the body use food more efficiently for energy. Additional benefits associated with these diets include reduced risk of cardiovascular disease (Atkins, 2002), lowered blood pressure (Bell, 2006; Atkins, 2002), and reduced risk of developing certain cancers (Atkins, 2002).

Given the experts' conflicting recommendations, it is no wonder that patients are confused about how to eat for optimum health. Some may assume that even moderate carbohydrate consumption should be avoided (Harvard School of Public Health, 2010). Others may use the low-carb approach to justify consuming large amounts of foods high in saturated fats—eggs, steak, bacon, and so forth. Meanwhile, low-carb diet plans and products have become a multibillion-dollar industry (Hirsch, 2004). Does this approach live up to its adherents' promises?

RESEARCH ON LOW-CARBOHYDRATE DIETS AND WEIGHT LOSS

A number of clinical studies have found that low-carbohydrate diet plans are indeed highly effective for weight loss. Gardner et al. (2007) compared outcomes among overweight and obese women who followed one of four popular diet plans: Atkins, The Zone, LEARN, or Ornish. After 12 months, the group that had followed the low-carb Atkins plan had lost significantly more weight than those in the other three groups. McMillan-Price et al. (2006) compared results among overweight and obese young adults who followed one of four plans, all of which were low in fat but had varying proportions of proteins and carbohydrates. They found that, over a 12-week period, the most significantly body-fat loss occurred on plans that were high in protein and/or low in "high glycemic index" foods. More recently, the American Heart Association (2010) reported on an Israeli study that found that subjects who followed a low-carbohydrate, high-protein diet lost more weight than those who followed a low-fat plan or a Mediterranean plan based on vegetables, grains, and minimal consumption of meats and healthy fats.[2] Other researchers have also found that low-carbohydrates diets resulted in increased weight loss (Ebbeling, Leidig, Feldman, Lovesky, & Ludwig, 2007; Bell, 2006; HealthDay, 2010).

Although these results are promising, they may be short-lived. Dieters who succeed in losing weight often struggle to keep the weight off—and unfortunately, low-carb diets are no exception to the rule. HealthDay News (2010) cites a study recently published in the Annals of Internal Medicine that compared obese subjects who followed a low-carbohydrate diet and a low-fat diet. The former group lost more weight steadily—and both groups had difficulty keeping weight off. Similarly, Swiss researchers found taht, although low-carb dieters initially lost more weight than those who followed other plans, the differences tended to even out over time (Bell, 2006). This suggests that low-carb diets may be no more effective than other diets for maintaining a healthy weight in the long term.

One likely reason is that a low-carbohydrate diet—like any restrictive diet—is difficult to adhere to for any extended period. In commenting on the Gardner study, experts at the Harvard School of Public Health (2010) noted that women in all four diet groups had difficulty following the plan. Because it is hard for dieters to stick to a low-carbohydrate eating plan, the initial success of these diets is short-lived (Heinz, 2009). Medical professionals caution that low-carbohydrate diets are difficult for many people to follow consistently and that, to maintain a healthy weight, dieters should try to develop nutrition and exercise habits they can incorporate in their lives in the long term (Mayo Clinic, 2008). Registered dietician Dana Kwon (2010) comments, "For some people, [low-carbohydrate diets] are great, but for most, any sensible eating and exercise plan would work just as well" (Kwon, 2010).

OTHER LONG-TERM HEALTH OUTCOMES

Regardless of whether low-carb diets are most effective for weight loss, their potential benefits for weight loss must be weighed against other long-term health outcomes such as hypertension, the risk of heart disease, and cholesterol levels. Research findings in these areas are mixed. For this reason, people considering following a low-carbohydrate diet to lose weight should be advised of the potential risks in doing so.

Research on how low-carbohydrate diets affect cholesterol levels in inconclusive. Some researchers have found that low-carbohydrate diets raise levels of HDL, or "good" cholesterol (Ebbeling et al., 2007; Seppa, 2008). Unfortunately, they may also raise levels of LDL, or "bad" cholesterol, which is associated with heart disease (Ebbeling et al., 2007; Reuters, 2010). A particular concern is that as dieters on a low-carbohydrate plan increase their intake of meats and dairy products—foods that are high in protein and fat—they are also likely to consume Increased amounts of saturated fats, resulting in clogged arteries and again increasing the risk of heart disease. Studies of humans (Bradley et al., 2009) and mice (Foo et al., 2009) have identified possible risks to cardiovascular health associated with low-carb diets. The American Heart Association (2010) and the Harvard School of Public Health (2010) caution that doctors cannot yet assess how following a low-carbohydrate diet affects patients' health over a long-term period.

Some studies (Bell, 2006) have found that following a low-carb diet helped lower patients' blood pressure. Again, however, excessive consumption of foods high in saturated fats may, over time, lead to the development of clogged arteries and increase risk of hypertension. Choosing lean meats over those high in fat and supplementing the diet with high-fiber, low-glycemic-index carbohydrates, such as leafy green vegetables, is a healthier plan for dieters to follow.

Perhaps most surprisingly, low-carbohydrate diets are not necessarily advantageous for patients with Type 2 diabetes. Bradley et al. (2009) found that patients who followed a low-carb or a low-fat diet had comparable outcomes for both weight loss and insulin resistance. The National Diabetes Information Clearinghouse (2010) advises diabetics to monitor blood sugar levels carefully and to consult with their health care provider to develop a plan for healthy eating. Nevertheless, the nutritional guidelines it provides as a dietary starting point closely follow the USDA food pyramid.

CONCLUSION

Low-carb diets have garnered a great deal of positive attention, and it isn't entirely undeserved. These diets do lead to rapid weight loss, and they often result in greater weight loss over a period of months than other diet plans. Significantly overweight or obese people may find low-carb eating plans the most effective for losing weight and reducing the risks associated with carrying excess body fat. However, because these diets are difficult for some people to adhere to and because their potential long-term health effects are still being debated, they are not necessarily the ideal choice for anyone who wants to lose weight. A moderately overweight person who wants to lose only a few pounds is best advised to choose whatever plan will help him stay active and consume fewer calories consistently—whether or not it involves eating low-carb ketchup.

REFERENCES

Agatson, A. (2003). *The South Beach Diet*. New York, NY: St. Martin's Griffin.

The American Heart Association. (2010). American Heart Association comments on weight loss study comparing low carbohydrate/high protein, Mediterranean style and low fat diets. http://americanheart.mediaroom.com/index.php?s=43&item=473

Atkins, R. C. (2002). *Dr. Atkins' diet revolution*. New York, NY: M. Evans and Company.

Bell, J. R. (2006). Low-carb beats low-fat diet for early losses by not long term. *OBGYN News, 41*(12), 32. doi:10.1016/S0029-7437(06)71905-X

Bradley, U., Spence, M., Courtney, C. H., McKinley, M. C., Ennis, C. N., McCance, D. R....Hunter, S. J. (2009. Low-fat versus low-carbohydrate weight reduction diets: effects on weight loss, insulin resistance, and cardiovascular risk: A randomized control trial [Abstract]. *Diabetes, 58*(12), 2741–2748. http://diabetes.diabetesjournals.org/content/early/2009/08/23/db09-0098.abstract

Ebbeling, C. B., Leidig, M. M., Feldman, H. A., Lovesky, M. M., & Ludwig, D. S. (2007). Effects of a low-glycemic load vs low-fat diet in obese young adults: A randomized trial. *Journal of the American Medical Association, 297*(19), 2092–2102. http://jama.ama-assn.org/cgi/content/full/297/19/2092?maxtoshow=&hits=10&RESULTFORMAT=&fulltext=ebbeling&searchid=1&FIRSTINDEX=0&resourcetype=HWCIT

Foo, S. Y., Heller, E. R., Wykrzykowska, J., Sullivan, C. J., Manning-Tobin, J. J., Moore, K. J....Rosenzweigac, A. (2009). Vascular effects of a low-carbohydrate high-protein diet. *Proceedings of the National Academy of Sciences of America, 106*(36), 15418–15423. doi: 10.1073/pnas.0907995106

Gardner, C. D., Kiazand, A., Alhassan, S., Kim, S., Stafford, R. S., Balise, R. R....King, A. C. (2007). Comparison of the Atkins, Zone, Ornish, and LEARN Diets for change in weight and related risk factors among overweight premenopausal women. *Journal of the American Medical Association, 297*(9), 969–977. http://jama.ama-assn.org/cgi/content/full/297/9/969#AUTHINFO

Harvard School of Public Health (2010). The Nutrition Source. Carbohydrates: Good carbs guide the way. http://www.hsph.harvard.edu/nutritionsource/what-should-you-eat/carbohydrates-full-story/index.html#good-carbs-not-no-carbs

HealthDay. (2010). Low-fat diets beat low-carb regiment long term. http://www.nlm.nih.gov/medlineplus/news/fullstory_95861.html

Hirsch, J. (2004). The low-carb evolution: Be reactive with low-carb products but proactive with nutrition. *Nutraceuticals World*. http://www.nutraceuticalsworld.com/contents/view/13321

Mayo Foundation for Medical Education and Research (MFMER). (2010). Weight-loss options: 6 common diet plans. http://www.mayoclinic.com/print/weight-loss/NU00616/METHOD=print

McMillan-Price, J., Petocz, P., Atkinson, F., O'Neill, K., Samman, S., Steinbeck, K.....Brand-Miller, J. (2006, July). Comparison of 4 diets of varying glycemic load on weight loss and cardiovascular risk reduction in overweight and obese young adults: A randomized controlled trial. *Archives of Internal Medicine, 166*(14), 1466–1475. http://archinte.ama-assn.org/cgi/content/full/166/14/1466

National Institute of Diabetes and Digestive and Kidney Diseases. (2010). National Diabetes Information Clearinghouse: What I need to know about eating and diabetes. http://diabetes.niddk.nih.gov/dm/pubs/eating_ez/index.htm

Reuters Health. (2010). Low-carb diet can increase bad cholesterol levels. http://www.nlm.nih.gov/medlineplus/news/fullstory_95708.html

Seppa, N. (2008). Go against the grains, diet study suggests: Low-carb beats low-fat in weight loss, cholesterol. *Science News, 174*(4), 25. http://www.sciencenews.org/view/issue/id/34757

Key Takeaways

- Organization in a research paper means that the argument proceeds logically from the introduction to the body to the conclusion. It flows logically from one point to the next. When revising a research paper, evaluate the organization of the paper as a whole and the organization of individual paragraphs.
- In a cohesive research paper, the elements of the paper work together smoothly and naturally. When revising a research paper, evaluate its cohesion. In particular, check that information from research is smoothly integrated with your ideas.
- An effective research paper uses a style and tone that are appropriately academic and serious. When revising a research paper, check that the style and tone are consistent throughout.
- Editing a research paper involves checking for errors in grammar, mechanics, punctuation, usage, spelling, citations, and formatting.

About the Author

OER books are usually blends of different texts, so I cannot speak to the original Lumen authors' backgrounds.

Here is a little bit of background about myself, though (written in that third person that is always a warning sign for individuals, as *Seinfeld* episodes show us).

Josh Dickinson is an Associate Professor of English at Jefferson Community College in Watertown, NY. He teaches English and Education courses with a focus upon American Literature, Native American Literature, and non-Western Literature. Josh attended SUNY Jefferson, SUNY Potsdam, Syracuse University, and Colgate University.

Josh also supervises Jefferson's EDGE (concurrent enrollment) English offerings at over a dozen local high school and BOCES sites.

He enjoys participating in the National Novel Writing Month contest, having completed seven novels so far each November. Josh has officiated high school soccer matches for 25 years and supports pro teams Tottenham Hotspur, FC Barcelona, and Borussia Dortmund.

At the Canadian Museum of History, Ottawa: Go Habs, Go!

CC licensed content, Original